Lecture Notes in Computer Science

Commenced Publication in 1973
Founding and Former Series Editors:
Gerhard Goos, Juris Hartmanis, and Jan van Leeuwen

Rynson W.H. Lau   Qing Li
Ronnie Cheung   Wenyin Liu (Eds.)

Advances in Web-Based Learning – ICWL 2005

4th International Conference
Hong Kong, China, July 31 - August 3, 2005
Proceedings

 Springer

Volume Editors

Rynson W.H. Lau
Qing Li
Wenyin Liu
City University of Hong Kong
Dept. of Computer Science
Kowloon, Hong Kong
E-mail: {Rynson.Lau,itqli,csliuwy}@cityu.edu.hk

Ronnie Cheung
The Hong Kong Polytechnic University
Dept. of Computing
Kowloon, Hong Kong
E-mail: csronnie@comp.polyu.edu.hk

Library of Congress Control Number: 2005929198

CR Subject Classification (1998): H.4, H.3, I.2.6, H.5, K.3, D.2, I.2

ISSN   0302-9743
ISBN-10   3-540-27895-8 Springer Berlin Heidelberg New York
ISBN-13   978-3-540-27895-5 Springer Berlin Heidelberg New York

Springer is a part of Springer Science+Business Media

springeronline.com

© Springer-Verlag Berlin Heidelberg 2005
Printed in Germany

Typesetting: Camera-ready by author, data conversion by Scientific Publishing Services, Chennai, India
Printed on acid-free paper   SPIN: 11528043   06/3142   5 4 3 2 1 0

Preface

With the rapid development of Web-based learning, a new set of learning environments including virtual classrooms, virtual laboratories and virtual universities are being developed. These new learning environments, however, also introduce new problems that need to be addressed. On the technical side, there is a need for the deployment of effective technologies on Web-based education. On the learning side, the cyber mode of learning is very different from traditional classroom-based learning. On the management side, the establishment of a cyber university imposes very different requirements for the set up.

ICWL 2005, the 4th International Conference on Web-Based Learning, was held in Hong Kong, China from July 31 to August 3, 2005, as a continued attempt to address many of the above-mentioned issues. Following the great success of ICWL 2002 (Hong Kong, China), ICWL 2003 (Australia), and ICWL 2004 (China), ICWL 2005 aimed at presenting progress on the technical, pedagogical, as well as management issues of Web-based learning. The conference featured a comprehensive program, including a number of tutorials, two keynote talks, a main track containing regular as well as short paper presentations, and an application track. We received a total of 99 submissions from all over the world. The Program Committee selected 33 papers as regular papers for presentation in the main track, an acceptance rate of about 33%. Due to the high-quality submissions, the Committee decided to further accept 9 papers as short papers for presentation.

We would like to thank the International Program Committee for spending their valuable time and effort in the review process. We would also like to thank the Organizing Committee for their contributions to this conference in many different ways. In addition, we would like to thank Wan Zhang for her efforts in preparing the proceedings.

We would like to thank the two keynote speakers, Paul Vitanyi and Timothy Shih, for their insightful keynote speeches. Finally, we would like to thank our sponsors, The ACM Hong Kong Chapter, the City University of Hong Kong, The Hong Kong Polytechnic University, The K.C. Wong Education Foundation, and The Hong Kong Pei Hua Education Foundation.

July 2005

Kamal Karlapalem
Qing Li
Rynson W.H. Lau
Ronnie Cheung
Wenyin Liu
Ming Cheung

Organization

ICWL 2005 was jointly organized by The Hong Kong Polytechnic University and the City University of Hong Kong in conjunction with the Hong Kong Web Society.

Honorary Co-chairs

Keith Chan   The Hong Kong Polytechnic University
Frances Yao   City University of Hong Kong

Conference Co-chairs

Kamal Karlapalem   IIIT (India)
Qing Li   Hong Kong Web Society

Program Co-chairs

Rynson W.H. Lau   City University of Hong Kong
Ronnie Cheung   The Hong Kong Polytechnic University

Organization Co-chairs

Hong-Va Leong   The Hong Kong Polytechnic University
Marian Choy   City University of Hong Kong

Communications Coordinator

Taku Komura   City University of Hong Kong

Treasurer

Chong Wah Ngo   City University of Hong Kong

Publication Co-chairs

Wenyin Liu   City University of Hong Kong
Ming Cheung   City University of Hong Kong

Media Chair

Frederick Li   The Hong Kong Polytechnic University

Application Co-chairs

Joseph Fong   City University of Hong Kong
Reggie Kwan   The Open University of Hong Kong
Kenneth Lau   ICON Limited

Tutorial Chair

Howard Leung   City University of Hong Kong

Publicity Co-chairs

Lam Fok Kwok   City University of Hong Kong
Qun Jin   Waseda University, Japan

Local Arrangements

Edward Ho   The Hong Kong Polytechnic University

International Program Committee

Brian d'Auriol   University of Texas, USA
Howard Beck   University of Florida, USA
Stephane Bressan   National University of Singapore, Singapore
Wentong Cai   Nanyang Technological University, Singapore
Jiannong Cao   The Hong Kong Polytechnic University, China
Keith Chan   The Hong Kong Polytechnic University, China
Shi-Kuo Chang   University of Pittsburgh, USA
Arbee Chen   National Tsing Hua University, Taiwan
Marian Choy   City University of Hong Kong, China
Jo Coldwell   Deakin University, Australia
Tharam Dillon   Sydney University of Technology, Australia
Guozhu Dong   Wright State University, USA
Ling Feng   University of Twente, Netherlands
Joseph Fong   City University of Hong Kong, China
Andrzej Goscinski   Deakin University, Australia
Edward Ho   The Hong Kong Polytechnic University, China
Runhe Huang   Hosei University, Japan
Weijia Jia   City University of Hong Kong, China

Table of Contents

e-Learning Platforms and Tools

A Core Model Supporting Location-Aware Computing in Smart
Classroom
Hongliang Gu, Yuanchun Shi, Guangyou Xu, Yu Chen 1

Student Adoption Towards Web-Based Learning Platform
Heidi Fung, Allan Yuen 14

ALIAS: An Automated Lab Information Administration System
Hongen Lu, Sujan Pradhan 20

An Online Template-Based Authoring System for E-Learning
Simon Hui, James Liu 38

Design and Implementation of a J2EE-Based Platform for Network
Teaching
Qinming He, Ling Qiu, Zhen He 49

A Web-Based Classroom Environment for Enhanced Residential
College Education
Kai Cheng, Limin Xiang, Toyohiko Hirota, Ushijima Kazuo 56

Adaptive Internet Interactive Team Video
Dan Phung, Giuseppe Valetto, Gail Kaiser 66

A Prototype of the Web-Based Marine Training Environment
Xie Cui, Liu Xiuwen, Jin Yicheng 78

P2P Video Synchronization in a Collaborative Virtual Environment
Suhit Gupta, Gail Kaiser 86

Virtual Experiment Services
Li-ping Shen, Rui-min Shen, Ming-lu Li 99

Learning Resource Deployment, Organization and Management

Designing a Learning Objects Repository–The Views of Higher
Education Faculty
  Philippos Pouyioutas, Maria Poveda 111

A Novel Resource Recommendation System Based on Connecting to
Similar E-Learners
  Fan Yang, Peng Han, Ruimin Shen, Zuwei Hu 122

MECCA-Learn: A Community Based Collaborative Course
Management System for Media-Rich Curricula in the Film Studies
  Marc Spaniol, Ralf Klamma, Thomas Waitz 131

Building Learning Management Systems Using IMS Standards:
Architecture of a Manifest Driven Approach
  *José Luis Sierra, Pablo Moreno-Ger, Iván Martínez-Ortiz,
  Javier López-Moratalla, Baltasar Fernández-Manjón* 144

Constructing a SCORM-Compliant Intelligent Strategy Repository
  *Yi-Chun Chang, Ching-Pao Chang, Chiung-Hui Chiu, Yi-Chi Chen,
  Chih-Ping Chu* 157

Effortless Construction and Management of Program Animations on
the Web
  Jaime Urquiza-Fuentes, J. Ángel Velázquez-Iturbide 163

Practice and Experience Sharing

Student Centered Knowledge Level Analysis for eLearning for SQL
  Joseph Fong, Jickhary Lee, Anthony Fong 174

Web-Based Chinese Calligraphy Retrieval and Learning System
  Yueting Zhuang, Xiafen Zhang, Weiming Lu, Fei Wu 186

Computer-Assisted Item Generation for Listening Cloze Tests and
Dictation Practice in English
  Shang-Ming Huang, Chao-Lin Liu, Zhao-Ming Gao 197

The Gong System: Web-Based Learning for Multiple Languages, with
Special Support for the Yale Representation of Cantonese
David Rossiter, Gibson Lam, Vivying Cheng 209

A Novel Multi-agent Community Building Scheme Based on
Collaboration Filtering
Yu Sun, Peng Han, Qian Zhang, Xia Zhang 221

Semantic Caching for Web Based Learning Systems
Xiao-Wei Hao, Zhang Tao, Lei Li 226

An Approach to Acquire Semantic Relationships Between Words from
Web Document
Xia Sun, Qinghua Zheng, Haifeng Dang, Yunhua Hu, Huixian Bai ... 236

Grounding Collaborative Knowledge Building in Semantics-Based
Critiquing
Anders I. Mørch, William K. Cheung, Kelvin C. Wong, Jiming Liu,
Cynthia Lee, Mason H. Lam, Janti P. Tang 244

Real-Time Adaptive Human Motions for Web-Based Training
Frederick W.B. Li, Becky Siu, Rynson W.H. Lau, Taku Komura 256

Experiences in Using an Automated System for Improving Students'
Learning of Computer Programming
M. Choy, U. Nazir, C.K. Poon, Y.T. Yu 267

Automatic Leveling System for E-Learning Examination Pool Using
Entropy-Based Decision Tree
Shu-Chen Cheng, Yueh-Min Huang, Juei-Nan Chen, Yen-Ting Lin ... 273

A Web-Based Environment to Improve Teaching and Learning of
Computer Programming in Distance Education
S.C. Ng, S.O. Choy, R. Kwan, S.F. Chan 279

The Design and Implementation of Digital Signal Processing Virtual
Lab Based on Components
Jianxin Wang, Lijuan Liu, Weijia Jia 291

A Design for Generating Personalised Feedback in Knowledge
Construction
Jude Lubega, Lily Sun, Shirley Williams 302

Refining the Results of Automatic e-Textbook Construction by
Clustering
Jing Chen, Qing Li, Ling Feng 311

ANTS: Agent-Based Navigational Training System
  Yu-Lin Jeng, Yueh-Min Huang, Yen-Hung Kuo, Juei-Nan Chen,
  William C. Chu 320

An Educational Virtual Environment for Studying Physics Concept in
High Schools
  Ruwei Yun, Zhigeng Pan, Yi Li 326

Mobile e-Learning

Mobile Learning with Cellphones and PocketPCs
  Minjuan Wang, Ruimin Shen, Ren Tong, Fan Yang, Peng Han 332

A Novel Mobile Learning Assistant System
  Ren Tong, Zuwei Hu, Peng Han, Fan Yang 340

Context-Sensitive Content Representation for Mobile Learning
  William C. Chu, Hong-Xin Lin, Juei-Nan Chen, Xing-Yi Lin 349

Pedagogical Issues

Managing Student Expectations Online
  D.A. Newlands, J.M. Coldwell 355

Collaborative Virtual Learning Environment Using Synthetic Characters
  Zhigeng Pan, Jiejie Zhu, Mingming Zhang, Weihua Hu 364

Devising a Typology of LOs Based on Pedagogical Assumptions
  Emanuela Busetti, Giuliana Dettori, Paola Forcheri,
  Maria Grazia Ierardi 375

Using Web Based Answer Hunting System to Promote Collaborative
Learning
  Guanglin Huang, Wenyin Liu 387

The Impact of E-Learning on the Use of Campus Instructional Space
  Tatiana Bourlova, Mark Bullen 397

The Research of Mining Association Rules Between Personality and
Behavior of Learner Under Web-Based Learning Environment
  Jin Du, Qinghua Zheng, Haifei Li, Wenbin Yuan 406

Author Index 419

A Core Model Supporting Location-Aware Computing in Smart Classroom

Hongliang Gu, Yuanchun Shi, Guangyou Xu, and Yu Chen

Computer Science and Technology Department, Tsinghua University,
Beijing 100084, P.R. China
ghl02@mails.tsinghua.edu.cn, xgy-dcs@mail.tsinghua.edu.cn,
{shiyc@, yuchen@}tsinghua.edu.cn

Abstract. Location-aware application ns need not only rapid location-related query, but also proactive spatial event service, both of which the traditional database system does not excel at. Aiming at the deficiencies of database system, we present a light-weighted proactive spatial service model for Smart Classroom: ASMod. This model adopts such new technologies as combined spatial index, refreshing-up & suspension-notification service process method and smart active update policy. Consequently it can not only proactively provide spatial event service, but also offer more efficient location-related query service than database system. Besides, it is facilely integrated into a multi-agent system, which makes it convenient to be applied into Smart Classroom.

1 Introduction

Smart Classroom[3] is a Smart Space[1] on tele-education, which beyond the traditional classroom, works on pervasive/ubiquitous computing mode. As an indispensable characteristic of pervasive/ubiquitous computing, location-awareness is becoming a prevalent mode of service's providing and modules' interaction in Smart Classroom. How to support and implement location-aware computing becomes one of our research focuses on Smart Classroom.

As Fig. 1 shows, location-aware computing system has a layered structure consisting of three parts: location-aware applications, location server and position system. The position system, in the lowest layer, determines the objects' locations, which is represented by either geometric coordinates or symbolic notation [2]. The location server, in the middle layer, on the one hand, takes charge of storing and managing all objects' locations; on the other hand, provides all location-aware services to the applications in the highest layer. The position system of Smart Classroom is the Cricket V2.0[4, 5] system, in which, like GPS, each unit knows its own geometric coordinate location and then sends its location to the location server by a wireless network.

In location-aware computing, most located-objects[6] (including not only physical entities, such as users, devices, but also services or resources with location attributions) have their scopes. A scope is possibly a located-object's shape, or the service/interaction area of an application etc, only in which the interaction occurs or the service is offered. For example, as shown in Fig. 3, the scope of Smartboard (a large-

R.W.H. Lau et al. (Eds.): ICWL 2005, LNCS 3583, pp. 1–13, 2005.
© Springer-Verlag Berlin Heidelberg 2005

sized touch screen) is a sector-like shape before it in the 2-D space. From a viewpoint of the applications, the requirement of location-aware computing encompasses two categories: 1) one is location-related query, 2) and another is spatial event service.

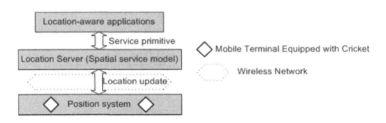

Fig. 1. Layered structure of location-aware computing system

- Location-related query means that the applications inquire the location server of the information with respect to their or indicated locations. This kind of location-aware service is like the SQL service provided by the spatial database system. For example:
- Q 1: Which student is/how many students are in Classroom526? (Here the spatial condition is relevant to an indicated location).
- Spatial event service means that the applications demand the location server can be automatically conscious of the varying of spatial relationship between the objects (which hereafter represents "located-object") to induce the corresponding interaction or service, and the service result is in the form of event notification. For example:
- Q 2: When a user enters the scope of Smartboard, notify me along with the relevant information (user's name, location, etc.)

In the first kind of service, the location server is just to respond to the applications' query request to provide service, and the provision mode is passive. On the contrary, in the second kind of service, the location server can spontaneously provide service according to the varying of spatial relationship, and the provision mode is active, self-conscious or proactive[7].

Besides providing two kinds of service, the location server encounters other problems yet. First, multi-agent middleware is Smart Space's popular software infrastructure[8]. Hence how to integrate the location server into a multi-agent system is also taken into consideration. Additionally, objects' location in Smart Classroom is more dynamic (or mobile) and more large-scale than the data of traditional spatial database, which also aggravates the location server's burden. The facts above all must be carefully treated in implementing the location server.

Spatial service model is the essential implementation method of location server. However, traditional spatial database system is not competent for the role of service model, due to various causes, such as the disability in offering spatial event service and the low efficiency on providing location-related query service etc. Aiming at the main drawbacks of traditional spatial database, we present a new spatial service model, which, with a light-weighted structure, but only proactively provides location-dependent service, but also offers more efficient spatial query service than traditional database system. Just due to the above features, it is called a light-weighted proactive model. Besides those advantages, it can be facilely integrated into a multi-agent system.

The remainder of this paper is organized as follows: Section 2 analyzes the corresponding drawbacks of the traditional spatial database. Section 3 introduces the key technologies of our spatial service model. Section 4 explains our model's service interface. Section 5 presents the performance analysis on the model. Last, in section 6 we draw our conclusion.

2 Drawbacks of Database Model on Location-Aware Computing

Location-aware applications demand the location server not only to provide a service for location-related query, but also to proactively offer spatial event service. However, the traditional service model, which is based on spatial database, e.g. GIS (geo graphic information systems)[9], is incompetent for both requirements.

First, database service is a query-respond mode. Database[1] can only select/filter out what meets with the conditions from its stored data according to applications' query requests. It can not self-consciously provide service, e.g. giving applications notifications, according to the varying of environment (namely the inter-object spatial relationship). This service mode is difficult in offering proactive spatial event service.

Second, the mode that the database obtains and updates its data is also passive and un-intelligent. Database refreshes its data only after receiving external explicit commands. It can not consciously obtain location data from the external (namely the position system) according to data's state. For example, if the service model recognizes a certain object to be a person, it will at a higher frequency obtain the object's location data from the position system (so that the location it stores is more 'fresh' and nearer to the person's actual location); on the contrary, if it recognizes another object to be a computer, it will at a lower frequency obtain the data[2], for a computer more seldom move than a person. That is, the fact that the managed objects are mobile calls for an active and conscious data update. However, the kind of update policy is difficult to achieve in the passive and mechanical data update mode of database.

Last but not least, database also does not excel at rapid responding to location-related query in an environment of high mobility and large scalability. In Smart Space, the most important aim of location-related query service is real-time and low-latency. However, for pursuing the synthetic performance, database is a tradeoff between responding latency, transaction integrity, concurrency control, consistency management, and data recovery etc. In Smart Space, the other database's functions are dispensable or at least minor than the responding speed. Therefore, in view of this special feature, our model is designed as a light-weighted mode, which emphasizes rapid-response while simplifies the other functions.

---

[1] Hereafter "database" represents "database system".
[2] Hereafter without the special explanation, "data" means "location data".

3   Key Technologies of Our Solution

Aiming at those drawbacks of database on accommodating location-aware computing, we present our spatial service model: ASMod, which but only supports both proactive spatial event service and location-related query service with low latency, but also has such advantages as active high-quality data update, facile integration into multi-agent system etc. At first, let's introduce its key technologies.

3.1   Combined Spatial Index

In 2-D space, each object has its spatial properties, such as scope and location, which can be described into a geometric entity with variable members such as sharp (polygon, circle etc), centroid coordinates, edge length etc. Therefore we use an entity[3] to represent an object. In 2-D space, the basic spatial relationship between two entities is containment, intersection or disjunction, which we call spatial θ operator. Further, the complicated spatial conditions can be expressed by the basic spatial relationship.

One kernel issue of spatial service model is to use what structure to organize entities, and implement basic spatial operation, which relates to a problem of spatial index. Spatial index is to dynamically organize (including insert and delete) spatial entities, and base on basic spatial operation to quickly filter out the result (which is also named search). According to the Smart Classroom's facts, we select a combined spatial index for ASMod, which combines the technologies of R-tree and Quad-tree.

3.1.1   R-Tree Structure

An R-tree[10],[11] is a dynamic self-maintaining and height-balanced tree, which has O (log n) insert, delete and search complexity. R-tree is suitable for organizing of multi-dimensional data, such as space data. In view of those advantages of R-tree, after comparing with other data structure, we choose R-tree as the main index structure. R-tree works on basis of point and rectangle, where each node is a non-zero-sized rectangle, superior nodes contain inferior nodes completely, and leaf nodes represent geometric entities. Like in B-tree, search in R-tree is a top-down spatial comparison. Likewise, insert and delete have corresponding algorithms similar to B-tree, such as node splitting, node merging and deleting etc. An example of located-objects' scopes and corresponding R-tree is illustrated in Fig. 2.

Due to on basis of point and rectangle, though R-tree has a notable efficiency in the space consisting of regular[4] geometric entities, it does not always work well in Smart Classroom, for all scopes of located-objects are not close to rectangles, where R-tree renders the performance's degradation. For avoiding this, we bring in a notion of quad-tree, which is used to corporate with R-tree.

3.1.2   Quad-Tree Structure

Quad-tree[12] is a four-forked tree, in which the children number of every node is always equal to four. Quad-tree fulfills recursive decompositions of space, where each

---

[3] Hereafter "entity" represents "geometric entity".
[4] "Regular" means the entity is itself a rectangle, or consists of rectangles.

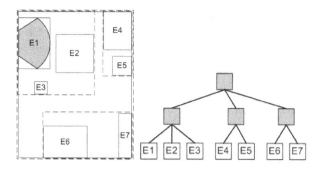

Fig. 2. Located-objects' scopes and R-tree

step of decomposition is to divide a space into 4 sub-spaces, each of which responds to a child of the divided space, and sub-space is also called *cell*. In Quad-tree, a geometric entity, especially irregular entity, can be represented by maximal cover, and then mapped into a node set (or cell set) of quad-tree. The maximal cover is the smallest set of quadtree cells covering the entity. Fig. 3 is an example about Smartboard's scope, the maximal cover and the quad-tree representation. In the quad-tree representation, the black leaf nodes mean the cells covered by the scope, and the white leaf nodes are the uncovered cells. In quad-tree, we can define the following operation theorems:

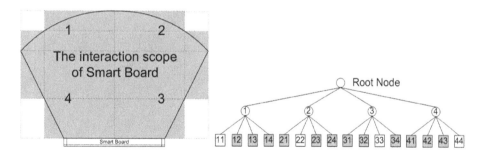

Fig. 3. An example of an object's scope and its Quad-tree representation

- Containment: An entity s is contained by an entity t iff, for each cell x in the maximal cover of s, there exists exactly one cell in the maximal cover of t that is an ancestor of x (i.e. it contains x) or is equal to x.
- Intersection: An entity s intersects with an entity t iff there exist two cells x and y in the maximal covers of s and t respectively such that x is equal to y, x is an ancestor of y, or y is an ancestor of x.

By means of quad-tree representation and operation theorems, we can rapidly judge the spatial relationship between two entities in a certain space: containment or intersection or disjunction (the remainder relationship which does not belong to containment or intersection). Though Quad-tree has those advantages above, it is not optimal to use Quad-tree solely in Smart Classroom, for in Smart Classroom there are some situations unsuitable to Quad-tree. For example, most scopes are regular in Smart Classroom; moreover, the entities are possibly distributed unevenly in the space, which brings about the index tree's imbalance along with the searching efficiency's degradation. In view of the characteristics of Smart Classroom, we adopt a combination method of R-tree and Quad-tree.

3.1.3 Combination Method of R-Tree and Quad-Tree

The combined spatial index of ASMod takes R-tree as its main index, and Quad-tree as its secondary index. The structure of the combined spatial index is interpreted as follows:

First, in ASMod, if an entity is regular, it is directly indexed by R-tree; otherwise, use a minimum bounding rectangle (MBR) to represent it, and add the MBR into R-tree. A MBR is the smallest rectangle aligned to coordinate system axes, which can completely contain an entity.

Then, if a node in R-tree is a MBR, it will be extended with a quad-tree corresponding to the entity. That is, this node has a field pointing at the root node of the entity's quad-tree representation. We call the combined index structure as RQ-tree. For example, since in Fig. 2, E1 is the MBR of an object, we extend it with its quad-tree representation. As a result, the corresponding RQ-tree representation is as Fig. 4 shows. Now we can define the operations of RQ-tree as follows:

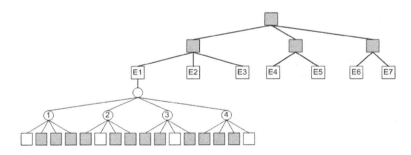

Fig. 4. An example of Smart Classroom's RQ-tree representation

- Search. This operation is to judge which entities in the RQ-tree contain or intersect an appointed entity. The latter entity is called reference entity. The search algorithm (here the spatial condition uses the containment operator) is described as follows:
1. If the reference entity ε is irregular, then construct its MBR ε'; otherwise $\varepsilon' = \varepsilon$.
2. In the R-tree, according to the R-tree's search algorithm, use ε' as the reference entity to search out the raw result entity set.
3. For each entity σ in the raw entity set, do the following steps:
4. If σ is not a root of quad-tree, then add σ into the result set and loop to step 3.

5. According to the quad-tree's relative coordinate and space-dividing standard, divide σ into the quad-tree representation. And then according to the quad-tree's operation theorems, judge whether ε contains σ. If containing, then add σ into the result set. Loop to step 3.
6. At last, return the result set.

The algorithm above just aims at the spatial condition on containment. Likewise, we can easily think out the condition on intersection or disjunction. Here we skip it.

– Insert. This operation is described as follows: 1) if the inserted entity is irregular, construct the MBR ε' and insert it to the R-tree; else insert the entity into the R-tree directly. 2) If the entity is regular, go to the end. 3) If the entity's quad-tree representation does not exist, generate it. 4) Let the inserted node point at the quad-tree's root.
– Delete. This operation is as follows: 1) if the entity points at a quad-tree, cut off the link between the entity and its quad-tree. 2) Delete the entity's node from R-tree.

3.2 Two Kinds of Service Process Mechanisms

A main function of ASMod is to provide both location-related query service and spatial event service for the application agents. How to use its index technology to implement the location-awareness service above is a field of service process mechanism. Aiming at the two kinds of service, ASMod has two distinct process mechanisms.

Location-related query service is a query-respond time sequence. In this mode, the service process is like a procedure call: once the request comes, the server immediately translates the request's spatial condition into RQ-tree's spatial operation and instantly executes the operation, which filters out the entity set meeting the conditions and returns it to applications. And once service is fulfilled, all data generated by the process will be removed. We name the process mode as query-driven instant mechanism.

For example, in Q 1, 1) on receiving the query request, according to the scope of Classroom526, ASMod first generates an entity. The entity is called search entity, for it corresponds to not an object but the search's spatial condition. 2) Then in the RQ-tree, ASMod searches which or how many entities are contained in this search entity, that is, takes the search entity as the reference entity to execute a search. 3) And then from the primary result set, ASMod filters out those entities which can not meet with other non-spatial conditions (here the condition is that its property must be a student), 4) Last ASMod returns the result to the application. After the process is fulfilled, the corresponding search entity is erased.

In ASMod, each entity corresponding to an object has a pointer pointing to the object. Therefore, in some sense, finding the entity means finding the objects. Thus, in the step 3 of the process above, system can quickly process other conditions filtering. If the entities of two objects are identical, the two objects compose into a chain and the entity points at the chain's head. The relationship and structure is as Fig. 5 illustrates.

However, spatial event service can not be directly realized as the mode like database systems, due to its own characteristics. Because what the applications need is not merely query result but event notification, when applications submit their request, the server doesn't know when to execute query process. Could we adopt a periodic query mode based on traditional database system? That is, the system automatically emit applications' querying request repetitively and execute the same query process again and again, and on finding the query result change, notify applications with query result. Unfortunately, the method is too low-efficient to be viable. For example, we can envisage such a policy in Q 2: every 2 minutes the system queries who is in Smartboard's scope, and once finding that the result is different from the previous, notifies the applications that someone leaves or enters the scope. In this example, most queries are meaningless and resource-consuming, for they get the same result because most object do not perhaps move at all during each query interval. Moreover, the average response time is proportional to the query interval, about 1 minute, which violates the system's real-time purpose. In general, this method is un-viable for its low efficiency and flagrant latency.

Aiming at the dilemma in implementing spatial event service, we present a new method: update-driven suspension-notification mechanism. The mechanism is as follows: When an application submits its request for a certain spatial event service, it must submit its agent handle together, and then switch to wait, namely being suspended. On receiving the request, according to the scope of spatial condition, ASMod immediately generates a search entity, which has a pointer pointing at the application (in fact, the application's agent handle), and inserts the entity into the RQ-tree. We define the update policy of the RQ-tree as follows:

1. Whenever an object's location changes (such as moves, logins and logouts), the entity corresponding to the object must be updated.
2. Updating encompasses two steps: delete the object's entity pe from previous location (except login), and insert the entity ne according to its new location (except logout).
3. During deleting, a search takes place to find out those search entities intersect, or contained the reference entity pe. Then ASMod adds the applications pointed at by those found out entities into the out-notification list. The out-notifications include semi-out-of-scope, out-of-scope etc, which respectively mean the object goes out of their scope partly (when intersecting) or entirely (when disjointing).
4. Likewise, during inserting, a search also takes place to find out those search entities intersect, or contained the reference entity ne. Then ASMod adds the applications into the in-notification list. The in-notifications include semi-enter-scope, enter-scope etc, which respectively mean the object enters their scope partly (when intersecting) or entirely (when contained).
5. Condense the notifications and activates the operation. If an application is both in the out-notification list and in the in-notification list, the application is erased from the lists. Meanwhile, merge the application emerging at several times in a list into one. For each application in the out-notification/in-notification list, ASMod respectively sends the out-notification or in-notification to it, and activates its corresponding operation.

According to the mechanism's explanation above, we can easily think out the detailed service process of Q 2. Here we skip it. In addition, in this mechanism, when an application submits a request, the corresponding search entity is inserted in RQ-tree, if the entity existed, the entity will not be inserted actually. What ASMod does is to compose the applications into a chain, and to make the entity point to the chain's head. Likewise, when an application abolishes its request, ASMod needs to delete the corresponding search entity, if the entity points to more than one application, ASMod does not delete the entity actually, but remove the current application's link from the application chain. The relationship between the index structure and applications (agents) is also as Fig. 5 illustrates. Due to the remarkable characteristics that the search occurs only after data's updating, and that the service's result is mainly a notification, this mechanism is entitled such a name.

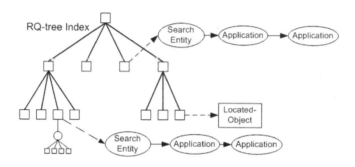

Fig. 5. Index structure in service process

3.3 Data Update Policy

An obligation of ASMod is to manage the 'fresh' location data (namely mobile located-objects' location) which includes obtaining location data from position system (as Fig. 1 shows), and updating the data. How to obtain and update location data relates to the model's data update policy, which acts as an interface between the spatial service model and the position system. On this field, there is a contradiction: on the one hand, the data's precision demands high updating frequency so that the location stored in the server is nearer to the mobile object's actual location; on the other hand, the too high updating frequency not only aggravates the server's burden, but also imposes a heavy load on the wireless network, so as to induce the longer latency of the system. On the issue, we present our method.

Being different from the passive update mode of database system, ASMod actively obtains objects' location without any external command, by means of polling the position system. Besides the feature above, ASMod adopts a smart active update frequency policy, which assigns update frequency according to object's mobility factor and its velocity. The general principle of the update policy is summarized as follows:

1. Define an object's velocity as follows:

$$\overline{velocity} = \sum Displacement \Big/ \sum Interval \tag{1}$$

Where, displacement is the scalar distance between two locations got from the adjacent polls; and interval is the time difference between two adjacent polls, and Σ means to calculate the sum during a period of time.

2. The update frequency is proportional to object's velocity and object's mobility factor:

$$Frequency = mf \times \overline{velocity} \tag{2}$$

Where, mf is the mobility factor of a certain kind of objects, which reflects the object's priority. For example, an important person has a higher value than a minor device.

The whole process of date update is summarized as follows: according to the update frequency policy, ASMod polls the position system, and then stores the location data into the corresponding place, and once finding the location differ from the previous, activates some possible update-driven suspension-notification mechanism mentioned above. Since the process begins from the bottom layer (position system), and last possibly effects top layer service, we call it the refreshing-up & suspension-notification process.

4 Service Interface

To provide the location-awareness service, ASMod offers several service primitives to applications, which can be easily integrated into multi-agent system. The main primitives are listed in Table 1.

Table 1. Main service primitives

Primitive	Main parameters	Return Value	Meaning
Notifica-tionCus-tomize	ScopeDescription; InScopeHandleRoutinePointer; OutScopeHandleRoutinePointer; Agent handle/ID; OtherCondition	Suc-cess/Fail	Submit a request for spatial event service.
Notifica-tionAbolish	ScopeDescription; Agent handle/ID	Suc-cess/Fail	Abolish the previous request for spatial event service.
QueryRe-quest	SpatialCondition; OtherQueryCondition	Query Result	Submit a request for location-related query, and wait for result.
Asynchro-nousQue-ryRequest	SpatialCondition; OtherQueryCondition; ResultHandleRoutinePointer	Suc-cess/Fail	Submit a request for location-related query, but immediately return.

Note: as far as the function is concerned, only one primitive, namely QueryRequest, can express location-related query service. The cause that we add in another primitive, AsynchronousQueryRequest, is to improve the whole system's flexibility and convenience. Especially when the query latency is long, applications need not wait for the result.

5   Performance Analysis

To evaluate the performance of ASMod, we take some theoretic reasons and comparisons with the existing systems. Though it is not easy to fulfill an all-around analysis on our model's performance in comparison with other counterparts, we can take the partly analysis on some sections of performances, based on the reasonable simplification. The partly analysis on the performance is focused on those aspects below:

One of the model's performances is the latency on responding location-related query. Some traditional spatial service system in location-aware projects, such as the Hybrid Location Model[13], are based on the Object-Relation Database Management System (ORDBMS), by means of adding the user-defined spatial data type, spatial operator, and spatial function (UDF) into the ORDBMS. Compared with our system, those systems do not adopt the similar spatial index to ASMod. The comparison on the time complexity between ASMod and the ORDBMS model is listed in Table 2. In the table, n is the total number of all entities in the Smart Space, and m is the maximal cell number of the entities' quad-tree representation. In fact, in the Smart Space, the totality of query is much larger than that of inserting and deleting; meanwhile, for the applications, the need of rapid response on the searching is thirstier than that of the other two operations. Hence, in comparison with the extra cost on inserting and deleting, the profit of search is more worthwhile.

Table 2. Time complexity of ASMod .vs. ORDBMS model

operation		ORDBMS model	ProSerMod
For regular entity	Search	$O(n)$	$O(\log n)$
	Insert	$O(1)$	$O(\log n)$
	Delete	$O(1)$	$O(\log n)$
For irregular entity	Search	$O(n+m)$	$O(\log n+\log m)$
	Insert	$O(1)$	$O(\log n)$
	Delete	$O(1)$	$O(\log n)$

Another criterion on the model is to evaluate the function and efficiency on supporting proactive spatial event service. To compare two kinds of model by a quantitative measurement, we bring forward a concept, Notification Quality of Service (NQoS), which is defined as the time difference between the time when actual objects' spatial relationship is met and the time when the application receive the notification. As mentioned above, since the database model does not directly offer proactive spatial event service, we have to take the periodic query mode on database as the comparative system with ASMod. Due to adapting the update-driven suspension-notification mechanism, ASMod can follow the location's updating immediately to notify applications. The only delay is the time taken to update the RQ-tree and search in it. Hence, as far as the NQoS is concerned, ASMod is nearly a zero-delayed system. On the contrary, even though despite of the latency brought by the numerous periodically-emitted null queries, the average delay of the periodic query mode on database is also about the half of query request's interval (providing the location varying occurs according to a uniform distribution between two requests). However too frequent query request (namely too short query interval) is unpractical, for it may overwhelm the system. Thus, on the NQoS of supporting proactive spatial event service, ASMod is bound to have the advantages of light system burden as well as nearly zero-delay responding over the periodic query mode base on database.

The last standard is to evaluate the efficiency of data update. The general principle of ASMod's policy is to take the totality update frequency as a scarce resource and assign the percentiles of the total update times in a unit interval according to object's historical velocity. The policy is based the theory of objects' inertia that an object's current and future moving is determined from its past locations. This policy conforms to the most cases in the Smart Space, so that it can keep both the total deviation of data and the total times of data update nearly minimal. Therefore, judged from the analysis above, in comparison with the passive mode of database model, ASMod's update policy is active as well as reasonable, which really embodies the active mode's advantages over the passive one.

6 Conclusion

In this paper, on the basis of anatomizing the drawbacks of the traditional database systems on supporting location-aware computing, we present our solution, ASMod, a proactive spatial event service model. Based on the performance analysis by the theoretic reasons and comparisons with the existing system, ASMod shows its advantages, such as supporting proactive spatial event service with nearly zero delay and low complexity, offering location-related query service with higher efficiency than the database system, and the facility in being integrated into the multi-agent system. A prototype as it is current, over a period of usage in our project, more experimental data will prove its potential.

References

1. http://www.nist.gov/smartspace/
2. Hightower, J.; Borriello, G.: Location Systems for Ubiquitous Computing. ACM Transactions on Information Systems, Vol 34, No 8, 2001, pp.57-66
3. Yuanchun Shi, Weikai Xie, Guangyou Xu, et al.: The smart classroom: merging technologies for seamless tele-education. IEEE Pervasive Computing, Vol 2, No 2, 2003, pp. 47-55
4. http://cricket.csail.mit.edu

5. Adam Smith, Hari Balakrishnan, Michel Goraczko, et al.: Tracking Moving Devices with the Cricket Location System. Proc Mobisys'04, 2004, pp.1-14
6. Schilit,B. Theimer,M.: Disseminating active map information to mobile hosts. IEEE Network, Vol 8, No 5, 1994, pp. 22-32
7. David Tennenhouse: proactive computing. Communications of The ACM, Vol 43, No 5, 2002, pp.43-50
8. Weikai Xie, Yuanchun Shi, Guanyou Xu, et al: Smart Platform - A Software Infrastructure for Smart Space (SISS). Proc 4th IEEE International Conference on Multimodal Interfaces, 2002, pp.429-434
9. C. D. Tomlin: Geographic Information Systems and Cartographic Modeling. Prentice Hall,1990
10. Norbert Beckmann, Hans-Peter Kriegel, Ralf Schneider, et al: The R*-tree: an efficient and robust access method for points and rectangles. Proc ACM SIGMOD1990, 1990, pp.322-331
11. Antonin Guttman: R-trees: a dynamic index structure for spatial searching. Readings in database systems(3rd ed), Morgan Kaufmann Publishers, 1998, pp.90-100
12. Rui Ding, Xiaofeng Meng: A Quadtree Based Dynamic Attribute Index Structure and Query Process. Proc the 2001 International Conference on Computer Networks and Mobile Computing, 2001, pp. 446-451
13. Changhao Jiang, Peter Steenkist: A Hybrid Location Model with a Computable Location Identifier for Ubiquitous Computing. Proc UbiComp 2002, 2002, pp.246-263

Student Adoption Towards Web-Based Learning Platform

Heidi Fung[1] and Allan Yuen[2]

[1] Hong Kong Shue Yan College
heidi_fung@hkbn.net
[2] Centre for Information Technology in Education,
The University of Hong Kong
hkyuen@hkucc.hku.hk

Abstract. Today, computers and Internet technology have an established presence in higher education. Most of the universities and tertiary institutions have enhanced their classroom courses with online learning systems. It takes time to familiarize people with any young technology and there is no exemption for the academic. This case study provides an in-depth understanding on the implementation of an e-learning platform in a post-secondary college for its first year adoption. Traditional systems are often slow to change and subject to various existing constraints. The study especially emphasizes on investigating the student adoption of this web-based learning system and seeks to find out the crucial factors influencing student adoption. It appeared that there was resistance to accept the new technology by the teaching staff and the students. Lecturers have been unable to find effective ways to use the system in their courses and students have encountered problems in using the system.

1 Introduction

1.1 Background of the Study

In this digital era, computers and Internet technology have an established presence in higher education. Most of the universities and tertiary institutions have enhanced their classroom courses with electronic learning (e-learning) systems. Naturally, not every lecturer or student finds the system to his or her liking. The potential benefits of World Wide Web as aids to teaching and learning may not be fully realized due to poor acceptance by users (Liaw, 2002). It is important to understand why certain individuals jump right onto this web-based learning platform while others hesitantly stand aside. With the technology ready for use is not enough. To gain a high acceptance of innovative educational technology, teachers and students at least have to possess the necessary skill in operating the system. More important, they need to have the understanding of the usefulness of the system and know how to deploy it in assisting the achievement of their objectives. Since the ultimate goal of using e-learning system is the enhancement of effective learning, the benefits of the system cannot be achieved if student adoption rate is low. Thus, it is necessary for education providers to

R.W.H. Lau et al. (Eds.): ICWL 2005, LNCS 3583, pp. 14–25, 2005.
© Springer-Verlag Berlin Heidelberg 2005

understand how students perceive the technology and their concerns in order to find out the crucial factors influencing student adoption. Based on the findings, attractive and effective strategies for applying technology in education can then be developed.

1.2   Research Motivation and Objectives

As a privately-funded tertiary institute without any financial support from the government or other organizations, the resources of ABC Higher Education College (AHEC) are very limited. The restricted capital does not allow the College keeping pace with the state-of-art educational technology. Together with a traditional culture inherited from the founders, the technology used in the College is relatively lagged behind. By noticing the benefits of e-learning system, AHEC has adopted Interactive Learning Network (ILN) in the academic year 2003/2004 to support the classroom teaching and learning. As more educational institutes and other organizations have the intention to utilize web technology in their training programmes, an understanding of the learner adoption is necessary to provide insight on successful implementation. The detailed study and the context in which it occurred may be useful to other institutions intent to adopt web-based learning system in their training programmes.

2   E-Learning and Technology Adoption

2.1   Web-Based Learning in Higher Education

Due to the significant benefits of web-based learning and the important demands that education be more accessible, many higher educational institutions have introduced e-learning system that serves as a complementary mechanism to enhance learning to their traditional face-to-face classroom courses. Nowadays, there are majority of classroom courses exploiting Internet technology to some extent. There is a growing number of college students expected a technology component in their classes (Sanders & Shetlar, 2001). Studies supported that the introduction of web-based learning system in higher education promote student learning (Laffey & Musser, 1998; Soner, 2000). The online platform provides a safe environment that encouraged students to express themselves more freely and provided them with the opportunity to discuss issues they were reluctant to introduce in the classroom (Gifford & Durlabhji, 1996; Hazari & Schnorr, 1999; Parkyn, 1999). Students often write more and learn from one another in the interactive virtual community. According to Frey, Yankelov and Faul (2003), web-enhanced strategies also provide an effective means for developing relationships between students and instructors, at least from students' perspectives.

2.2   Interactive Learning Network (ILN)

Interactive Learning Network (ILN) is a community-building environment designed to support virtual education communities of practice where teachers and students work as teams and engage in reflective, collegial pattern of work. It was developed by a local university to help students and lecturers in conducting teaching, sharing course materials and collaborating in different aspects. ILN establishes an online environment which aims at equipping teachers with the tools to provide scaffoldings for students to engage in collaborative and cooperative activities. Similar to other e-learning systems, ILN allows both synchronize and asynchronize communication among users. It has built-in features such as Announcement, Resources, Task, Forum, Calendar, Chart, Quiz, and Evaluation, allowing users to customize features on their own community. The features are easy to use without requiring knowledge of any programming language.

2.3   Information Technology Adoption

Information technology (IT) adoption has been studied in great detail in recent years. It can be examined at two levels: the organizational level and individual level (Dasgupta, Granger, & McGarry, 2002). The emphasis at the organizational level study is on the investment whereas the focus at the individual level study is on the acceptance of the technology. People always have a mistaken belief in the success of Internet technology that "Build it and they will come" (Patel & McCarthy, 2000). In fact, having the technology available and accessible is no guarantee that people will find it useful, find it easy to use, or even find it at all. A variety of factors have been found affecting technology acceptance and usage. According to Liaw (2002), individual computer and Internet experience, self-efficacy, and motivation are all key factors for individual use of the web. Individual student's demographics, learning styles, particular life characteristics, access to the necessary technical resources, past experience with the technology, and the need for interaction and Internet connectivity, all may play a role in the students' adoption of technology. The major factors are summarized as follows: Resistance to Change (Byrne, 2002), Perceived Usefulness and Perceived Ease of Use (Davis, 1989; Venkatesh & Morris, 2000), Computer Self-efficacy (Loyd & Loyd, 1985; Murphy, Coover, & Owen, 1989), Attitude (Rainer & Miller, 1996), Motivation (Davis, Bagozzi, and Warshaw, 1992), Prior Experience (Martinez & Mead, 1988; Moon, 1994; Price & Winiecki, 1995; Smith & Necessary, 1996), Lecturer's Involvement (Slatter, 1998; Sloan, 1997; Fullan, 1991; Jiang & Ting, 1998), Mandatory vs. Voluntary Use (Brown et al., 2002; Frey, et al., 2003; Venkatesh & Morris, 2000).

3   Methodology

The research is conducted in the form of a case study, which allows the coverage of the contextual condition on the implementation of web-based learning platform in AHEC. Case study is preferable "when 'how' or 'why' questions are being posted, when the relevant behaviors cannot be manipulated, and when the focus is on a contemporary phenomenon within some real-life context" (Yin, 2003). The current study aims to investigate the student adoption of an e-learning system in the College, which is "a contemporary phenomenon within a real-life context". A unique strength of case study is its ability to deal with a full variety of evidence. The flexibility in dealing with multiple sources of evidence allows the researcher to gather data from different sources within the College. Participant-observation, student reflection reports, and interviews were employed as fact-finding techniques. The use of multiple sources of evidence allows investigator to address a broader range of historical, attitudinal, and behavioral issues so as to derive an affluent description of the phenomenon and an in-depth exploration on the perception of ILN from the perspectives of both students and lecturers. The concept of triangulation can be applied which serves to clarify meaning by identifying different ways the phenomenon is being seen, help to reduce researcher bias and provide a better assessment of the findings and conclusion (Flick, 1992).

3.1   Participant-Observation

Being a teaching staff member of AHEC, the researcher has employed the participant-observation as one of the sources of evidence of the study. Participant-observation provides certain unusual opportunities for collecting case study data (Yin, 2003). The researcher is able to gain access to the students and staff in the College, and collect relevant documents in a convenient manner. As the contact person of the Champion, the researcher has the ability to manipulate some of the events related the ILN implementation. Realizing the potential biases, which may be produced in participant-observation, other sources of evidence are used to interpret the same phenomenon.

3.2   Student Reflection Reports

To capture students' perception of ILN, five groups of student have been invited to write reflection reports on ILN in the first semester of the year of study. Each of the groups consisted of five members, were selected from five sections of the Management Information Systems (MIS) course. Students were told to report their perception on the ILN, give comments on the ILN implementation in the College, and provide suggestions for improvement. The students have to submit the written reports by the end of the semester. Purposeful sampling was used to ensure the respondents have experienced using ILN in their learning. It was also expected that these students could provide feedback with their knowledge in MIS.

3.3   Interviews

Individual interviews were used to gather opinions of the staff members on ILN implementation. Six lecturers from five departments were invited to contribute to the study. The objectives of the interviews are to explore lecturers' perception of ILN and understand the student adoption from the instructor's perspective. These interviews, conducted at the end of second semester, provided valuable insights into the thoughts and perceptions of the lecturers from different departments about the ILN. An informal interview with the computer technician was held at the end of the second semester. It was expected to find out the technical supports requested by the teaching staff on operating ILN and to know, from the technician's perspective, the factors affecting the student adoption of ILN. With the aim of understanding the ILN implementation plan and expectation on the usage of ILN from the management, the Associate Academic

Vice President was invited as the informant of two interviews held in October 2003 and July 2004 respectively.

4   Findings and Analysis

In order to facilitate the ILN implementation, the College has set up a Champion team responsible to take all initiative to support the teaching staff in using ILN. The Champion originally consisted of six teaching staffs from different faculties. A workshop was organized to give a general introduction and an overview of the major features of ILN in early October 2003. Afterward, Champion members started organizing their departmental-based workshops to deal with the individual problems and issues relating to their specific subject area. All the activities were in voluntary basis and no reporting was required. There has been a significant increase in the subscription of ILN in the second semester. Table 1 shows the usage of ILN for the year of study. The number of subscription is not referring to the number of students using ILN since one student might have subscribed to more than one course. The community established in the second semester was less than that in the first semester not necessarily implying a drop in the usage rate since some of the courses are year courses which only needed to be set up once in the first semester.

Table 1. Number of community established and student subscription in ILN in 2003/04

Subject	Community		Subscription	
	Semester 1 (Sep03)	Semester 2 (Jan04)	Semester 1 (Sep03)	Semester 2 (Jan04)
Accounting	8	17	224	523
Business Administration	25	21	86	301
Chinese Language & Literature	12	0	201	0
Computing	7	9	299	262
Counseling & Psychology	24	4	434	257
Economics	18	5	271	227
Journalism & Communication	4	5	41	160
Law	0	2	0	0
Eng	2	8	0	0
Sociology	28	12	0	315
Social Work	19	17	228	542
Total	**147**	**100**	**1784**	**2587**

4.1   Students' Reflection

The students provided detail evaluation on the design, function and operation of the system in the reflection reports. They have indicated what they perceive the advantages and the deficiencies of the system. Based on their perceived shortages, they have provided a number of suggestions for improvement. In addition, they have specified the obstacles to implement ILN in the College and have made some recommendations on increasing the acceptance. Major categories are as follows: (1) the students hold a positive general attitude towards ILN, (2) some students perceived ILN is user-friendly, (3) students mainly used the 'Resources', 'Announcement', and 'Forum' of ILN since these were the features mostly used by their lecturers and they agreed the advantages of using ILN, (4) some students have difficulties in subscribing the course due to the procedures were not clear, and (5) students have addressed the deficiencies of ILN and provided suggestions accordingly, such as system features.

From the students' perspectives, the obstacles that affect ILN implementation in the College included: (1) lack of promotion and training, (2) no incentive to use, and (3) unpopular College's e-mail system. Students have made some recommendations to the College for raising the acceptance and usage of ILN: (1) provide training, (2) encourage lecturer usage, (3) offer incentives to student usage, (4) encourage using of College e-mail system, (5) allow auto-subscription, (6) improve IT infrastructure of the College, and (7) augment functions of ILN.

4.2 Lecturers' Opinion

Even though the lecturers have realized the deficiencies of the system, most of them held a positive attitude towards ILN. They reflected that the system could be user-friendlier and the design could be improved such as simplifying the subscription procedure and allowing instructors to personalize their communities. For identification, R1 to R6 are used to represent the six respondents respectively and their profile is shown in Table 2.

Table 2. Profile of the interviewees

	Department	Subject(s) taught	Computer competency	ILN user
R1	Accounting	Accounting	Low	Yes
R2	Accounting	Accounting	High	No
R3	Business Administration	Management, Accounting	Media	Yes
R4	Chinese Language & Literature	Chinese Language, Chinese Literature	High	Yes
R5	Economics	Economics, Computer	High	Yes
R6	English Language & Literature	English Language	Low	No

Among the respondents, four of them (R1, R3, R4, R5) have adopted ILN. They used ILN for part of their courses in a trail basis in the first semester and fully employed it to all their teaching courses in the second semester. For the two non-users, R2 claimed that he was too busy to afford the time to use the system though he believed that ILN might be useful to his teaching. While R6 explained that the English Language subject she has taught mainly focus on verbal and face-to-face interaction and feedback. Since the students have classes twice a week, the classroom time allowed her to do all the interaction with them in class. So she perceived ILN is not that applicable and important to her teaching subjects.

The most popular features used by the respondents were the 'Resources' and 'Announcement'. They were the only features used by R1 and R3. Though R1 believed this kind of platform encourages more interaction and discussion, she could think of very little opportunity to integrate other features with the accounting subjects that emphasize on computation. R3 explained that she did not know how to use other features. Among the four ILN users, R5 used the most of the features.

According to the respondents' knowledge, the students mainly used ILN to download learning materials like lecturer notes or exercise solutions. Some students just ignored it if they perceived the materials were not important to them. R4 added that because the students have realized the trend of using Internet technology in teaching and learning, they feel comfortable to use this technology to do their assignment. As a lecturer teaching Chinese subjects, R4 found that students who are not good at using computer or weak at typing Chinese are not willing to use the system. The respondents have indicated some crucial factors influencing student adoption towards ILN: lecturer use, usefulness, convenience, lecturers' involvement, ease of use, incentive, and group norm.

Some respondents suggested the College to hold regular workshops or seminars for both lecturers and students introducing the functions of ILN and teaching how to use the system. To have ILN widely used by the lecturers, the College might required all the faculty members and students using ILN in all courses. In terms of technical support, there are rooms for improvement, including machines as well as the arrangement of manpower. It is suggested to upgrade the IT infrastructure of the College because ILN run very slowly with the current facilities. As R5 pointed out that "if the system cannot allow speedy file uploading and provide large capacity, there won't be much content to attract the students to use it." If the performance of ILN can be enhanced, both lecturers and students will be more willing to use the system.

4.3   Technician's Perspective

According to the technician, lecturers who were not familiar with Internet environment have difficulty in understanding the structure of ILN. They did not know how to get into their sub-community, they were not sure how and why the students need to subscribe, and they were not clear about the functions of ILN. Lecturers who were familiar with Internet applications adapt to the system quickly. They did not need much support on using ILN. Sometimes they even reported to technicians the limitations or bugs of the system that might not be noticed by the technicians. The technician found the lecturers' opinions valuable for the improvement of ILN. The technician has specified three factors which might affect the student adoption: ease of use, lecturer's involvement, and peer group norm.

4.4   Response from Management

According to the College senior management there is neither solid planning for the ILN implementation nor expectation on the increasing rate for the ILN usage as it is hard to set the target. But she would like to see an improved take up rate for the coming year. The usage figure of the first year can be used as the referent for the future usage. The use of ILN by the teaching staff will be kept voluntary since the management feels staff has to move willingly and that generally any attempt at coercion is likely to fail. All the initiative to support ILN implementation would leave to the Champion. The College senior management suggested conducting regular workshops for teaching staff on operating the system and how to integrate ILN to their courses.

5   Discussion

The findings of the study reveal a number of crucial factors influencing the student adoption of ILN.

Usefulness.   Students like the feature more if they found it useful and ease their study. Negative attitudes might be resulted if the students cannot see the usefulness of the system. Having a useful system is the students' desire, so they suggested adding more features to the system. If the lecturers and the College can more fully utilize ILN to give value to the students, a higher adoption rate would be expected to follow.

Lecturers' Involvement.   Lecturers take an important role as a change agent in influencing the students' usage. If their lecturers require them to subscribe to the course, most of the students will probably do so. The lecturers, as well, determine the community content which affects the student's attitude towards the system and their perception of its usefulness. Delay feedback, lack of useful material, or inactive features discourage students' usage.

It appears that most of the lecturers are still at an early stage in their understanding of the appropriate use of ILN, or lack of the skill to use it. In order to raise the usage, lecturers need to know which features have value to students and be sensitive to the needs of students. The College has to grapple with how to provide lecturers and students with appropriate knowledge and skills in this changing environment (Fallshaw, 2000). The focus of professional development programs for teaching staff should shift from learning technology skills to how technology can be used as a tool to enhance teaching and learning (Newhouse, Trinidad, & Clarkson, 2002). The success of the system depends on the cooperation of both them. Lecturers may discuss and compromise with their students on the strategies used.

Ease of Use.   Users reluctant to use a system that is complicated and difficult to use. To assist individuals in accepting a system, it is necessary to facilitate them in developing a positive perception on the ease of use of the system (Yuen & Ma, 2002). If the students can attend training workshop and get some hands-on experience before actual usage, they may be more willing to use the system. On the other hand, the design and the presentation of the system also affect the student's perceived ease of use. As the students used to visit web sites with colorful animation, big icons, and frames, the text-based design of ILN would give them an impression of complicated and hard to understand.

Computer Self-Efficacy.   Although students need not be a computer expert, a minimal technical literacy is required since minor problems with technology might happen on occasion. If students cannot resolve the problems, they may find it frustrating. In using web-based learning platform, students need to possess ability and feel comfortable in computer operating, web surfing, and e-mail communication. A feeling of computer self-efficacy might be cultivated through computer training. As the younger students gain more computer experience and knowledge through increased computer exposure at lower form, the effect of computer self-efficacy might be diminished in the future years.

Students' Attitude.   Students with negative attitudes only spot the drawbacks of ILN. In order to foster positive attitudes toward a new system, the focus should be on expounding the benefits of use (Brown, et al., 2002). It is expected that when students learn more about the value of the system, say, through promotion by the College or the lecturer, their attitude would be changed. The design and the performance of the system would also affect the students' attitude towards the system. Apparently, in mandatory situation, student attitudes may not be a prime factor in adoption. As more secondary and primary schools using web-enhanced learning, improvement in student attitudes toward web-based instruction will be observed.

Access to the Required Technology.   Some students found it takes a long time to upload and download files and the system is not stable for some features. These may be due to the speed of the channel used or the performance of the machine. This type of experience will lead to a negative attitude towards the system and affect the adoption. According to Wilson and Weiser (2001) stable technology in use may be a critical component to the IT adoption. It is necessary for the College to upgrade the information and communication technology of the campus continually.

Incentive.   As the College students have been quite used to the classroom-learning mode since kindergarten, changes hardly happen without incentive and support. Providing grade motivation for facilitating online discussion or other activities would encourage students to use the system (Wilson & Weiser, 2001).

Group Norm.   The student adoption will also be affected by the peer group. When students find a majority of the class use the system, they are expected to follow suit since they do not want to be lagged behind. In order to make using ILN a usual practice, both the College and the lecturers can more fully utilize the system for various purposes.

Timing.   The resistance to use might be greater if the system is introduced at the middle of the term when everything has been settled. As ILN was not ready for use until mid-October, most of the lecturers would like to leave the system to next semester.

Thus it would be preferable to have the online community ready for use at the beginning of the semester so that students are more likely to perceive it a component of the course. It would be even better for the students start using ILN in their first year of study in the College since new students are more readily in adapting new things in a new environment.

6 Conclusion

Though it is believed that Internet would provide a constructivist and collaborative environment for learning, students' acceptance would be critical to the success of the e-learning. The ultimate success of web-based learning system depends on the adoption by both the teaching staff and the students. The College is believed to have considerable influence on or control over the adoption of a technology. Traditional systems are often slow to change. Cultivation and development of the necessary condition requires considerable time and resources, and are often subject to various existing constraints. If the College can operate in coordination in several ways, ILN can be used extensively and can help students achieving an excellent learning performance.

6.1 Limitations of the Study

While the study identifies a number of crucial factors influencing student adoption, the study is not without limitations. Owing to the differences in composition and mission of schools, results from this study may have only limited applicability to other institutions. The limited scales of study do not allow the research findings to be generalized and are confined to the conclusions within the context of this study. The use of participant-observation may produce biases as the researcher is an 'insider' of the case. The interpretation of data may be influenced by the integrity and sensitivity of the researcher. Since the researcher is the only instrument of data collection and analysis, everything filters through the perceptions of the researcher. The researcher may possess expectations and assumptions, which can color the interpretation of data and the selection of data.

6.2 Suggestions for Future Research

According to some studies, the determinants' effect on behavioral intention reduces over time (Venkatesh & Morris, 2000). As ILN has been used by AHEC for only a year, the influence of the variables might change over time as students gain more experience with the system. Future study on a longitudinal perspective is suggested to explore any changes in the effect of the crucial factors. More is not necessarily better. As one of the purposes for using ILN is to have effective learning but not solely high usage, future research might focus on the effect of system usage on individual performance. As Frey (2003) indicates that students' perception of e-learning might differ in different courses, future study in examining students' perception and attitude toward ILN in different courses is suggested. Since the current study suggests a significant effect of the lecturer usage to the student adoption, it is important to examine the adoption of the teaching staff. More complex design researches need to be developed in order to establish a clear relation between lecturer employment and student adoption.

References

1. Brown, S.A., Massey, A.P., Montoya-Weiss, M.M., & Burkman, J.R. (2002). Do I really have to? User acceptance of mandated technology. *European journal of Information Systems*, 11, 283-295.
2. Byrne, R. (2002). Web-based Learning Versus Traditional Management Development Methods. *Singapore Management Review*, 24(2), 59-68.
3. Dasgupta, S., Granger, M., & McGarry, N. (2002). User Acceptance of E-Collaboration Technology: An Extension of the Technology Acceptance Model. *Group Decision and Negotiation*, 11(2), 87-100.
4. Davis, F.D. (1989). Perceived Usefulness, Perceived Ease of Use, and User Acceptance of Information Technology. *MIS Quarterly*, September, 319-340.
5. Davis, F.D., Bagozzi, R.P., & Warshaw, P.R. (1992). Extrinsic and intrinsic motivation to sue computers in the workplace. *Journal of Applied Social Psychology*, 22(14), 1111-1132.
6. Fallshaw, E.M. (2000). IT Planning for Strategic Support: Aligning Technology and Vision. *Tertiary Education and Management*, 6(3), 193-207.
7. Flick, U. (1992). Triangulation revisited: Strategy of validation or alternative? *Journal for the Theory of Social Behaviour*, 22, 175-198.
8. Frey, A., Yankelov, P., & Faul, A. (2003). Student perceptions of Web-assisted teaching strategies. *Journal of Social Work Education*, 39(3), 443-457.
9. Fullan, M.G. (1991). *The new meaning of educational change*. (2nd ed.). London: Cassell.
10. Gifford, L.J.L., & Durlabhji, N.K. (1996). Preparing to teach a class by Internet. *College Teaching*, 44, 94-96.
11. Hazari, S., & Schnorr, D. (1999). Leveraging student feedback to improve teaching in Web-based courses. *T.H.E. Journal*, 26, 30-32.
12. Jiang, M., & Ting, E. (1998). Course design, instruction, and students' online behaviors: A study of instructional variables and student perceptions of online learning. *American Educational Research Association*, San Diego, CA.
13. Laffey, J., & Musser, D. (1998). Attitudes of preservice teachers about using technology in teaching. *Journal of Technology and Teacher Education*, 6, 223-241.
14. Liaw, S.S. (2002) Understanding user perceptions of World-wide web environments, *Journal of Computer Assisted Learning*, 18, 137-148.
15. Loyd, B.H., & Loyd, D.E. (1985). The reliability and validity of instruments for the assessment of computer attitudes. *Educational and Psychological Measurement*, 45, 903-908.
16. Martinez, M.E., & Mead, N.A. (1988). Computer competence: The first national assessment. Princeton, NJ: *National Assessment of Educational Progress*.
17. Moon, S. (1994). The relationships among gender, computer experience, and attitudes toward computers. *Mid-South Educational Research Association*, Nashville, TN.
18. Murphy, C.A., Coover, D., & Owen, S.V. (1989). Development and Validity of the Computer Self-Efficacy Scale. *Educational and Psychological Measurement*, 49, 893-899.
19. Newhouse, C.P., Trinidad, S., & Clarkson, B.D. (2002). Quality pedagogy and effective learning with information and communications technologies (ICT): a review of the literature. Western Australian Department of Education. Perth: Specialist Educational Services.
20. Parkyn, D.L. (1999). Learning in the company of others: Fostering a discourse community with a collaborative electronic journal. *College Teaching*, 47, 88-90.

21. Patel, K., & McCarthy, M.P. (2000). *Digital transformation: The essentials of e-business leadership*. New York: McGraw-Hill.
22. Price, R., & Winiecki, D. (1995). Attitudes and skill levels of college students entering a typical introductory college computing course. *Journal of Computing in Teacher Education*, 12(1), 20-25.
23. Rainer, R.K., & Miller, M.D. (1996). An Assessment of the Psychometric Properties of the Computer Attitude Scale. *Computers in Human Behavior*, 12(1), 93-105.
24. Sanders, D.W., & Shetlar, A.I. (2001). Student Attitudes toward Web-Enhanced Instruction in an Introductory Biology Course. *Journal of Research on Computing in Education*, 33(3), 251-262.
25. Slatter, J.M. (1998). Developing a Web-assisted class: An interview with Mark Mitchell. *Teaching of Psychology*, 25(2), 152-155.
26. Sloan, A. (1997). Learning with the Web: Experience of using the World Wide Web in a learning environment. *Computers & Education*, 28(4), 207-212.
27. Smith, B.N., & Necessary, J.R. (1996). The computer ability scale: Replication and extension involving college computer literacy student. *AERA Business Education and Information Systems Research Special Interest Groups proceedings*. Washington, DC: American Educational Research Association.
28. Soner, Y. (2000). Effects of an educational computing course on preservice and inservice teachers: A discussion and analysis and use. *Journal of Research on Computing in Education*, 32, 479-495.
29. Venkatesh, V., & Morris, M.G.. (2000). Why don't men ever stop to ask for directions? Gender, social influence, and their role in technology acceptance and usage behavior. *MIS Quarterly*, 24(1), 115-140.
30. Wilson, R.L., & Weiser, M. (2001). Adoption of Asynchronous Learning Tools by Traditional Full-Time Students: A Pilot Study. *Information Technology and Management*, 2(4), 363-375.
31. Yin, R.K. (2003). *Case Study Research: Design and Methods* (3rd ed.). London: Sage Publications.
32. Yuen, H.K., & Ma, W.K. (2002). Gender Differences in Teacher Computer Acceptance. *Journal of Technology and Teacher Education*, 10(3), 365-382.

ALIAS: An Automated Lab Information Administration System

Hongen Lu and Sujan Pradhan

Department of Computer Science and Computer Engineering,
La Trobe University, Bundoora, Melbourne, VIC 3086, Australia
{helu, sujan}@cs.latrobe.edu.au

Abstract. In the context of higher education, the current manual system of allocating labs to students is not only time consuming but is also inefficient and inconvenient. In this paper, we present a web-based lab administration system, ALIAS, which provides a flexible and comprehensive tool to assist e-learning. The tool solves most, if not all, problems related to the administration of lab allocation. It also provides functions that cannot be achieved manually, such as the multiple lab allocation strategies. These strategies make the system flexible and comprehensive. This innovative tool not only enriches student experience through interactive learning but also assists both the student and staff in making the process less time consuming; the end result is higher efficiency and more time for academic learning.

1 Introduction

Web-based learning, be it in higher education, corporate, government or health care sector, has been rapidly developing over the past several years. One of the prominent advantages of e-learning is the flexibility of delivery. Asynchronous learning, such as this, allows the learners not only to work at their own set pace but from virtually any location they choose. Of these, higher education has been the most notable in setting the trend. Existing buzz words, such as virtual classrooms or virtual universities, have been and still are used to describe this type of learning environment. Many other types of traditional learning are converted into a more coherent web-based e-learning environment as these buzz words keep growing. Although adaptation of e-learning curriculum has been well accepted by many web users, there still remain challenges in creating innovative e-learning environments within the higher education sector. The focus of this paper is in exploring one of these challenges. It assesses the needs and specifies the requirements of Department of Computer Science and Computer Engineering at La Trobe University in developing a university laboratory administrative system, and proposes a feasible technical solution to meet these needs and requirements.

The current manual system of allocating labs to students is not only time consuming for lecturers and head tutors but is also inefficient, inconvenient,

R.W.H. Lau et al. (Eds.): ICWL 2005, LNCS 3583, pp. 26–37, 2005.

causes lapse in communication, and increase in human resources. The whole process begins with a design of a lab signup sheet made up of preference features (i.e. lab day, lab time) by the staff. They are distributed during lecture where the students indicate which labs they would like to attend in order of preference, usually from 1-7. Once all of the sheets have been turned in these preferences are then manually sorted according to the student's preference(s) by the staff. The staff may opt to use a spreadsheet tool or sort them manually on paper. The final allocation is posted in a bulletin board visible to students.

Using a manual system such as the one above has drawbacks. The first notable point that comes to mind is the increase in error. For example, lab clashes may not be avoided if a chosen lab times are not checked for each of the student's subject during lab signups; this checking could save student time and hassle later. The other point is a waste of valuable time; the tasks become repetitive and administrative for the staff. Moreover, the students are obliged to fill out the proforonoo ohcoto if thcy wiah to be allocated, this causes unnecessary hassles if the student was absent on the day of the signups. Depending on the number of students enrolled in a subject the role of assigning labs can become quite challenging if there are conflicts such as those who are not able to attend certain labs due to unknown restrictions. These problematic reasons have given a rise to the creation of Automated Lab Information Administrative System (ALIAS), where a reduction or a complete elimination in administrative tasks is the key.

Many research works have been done in the field of web-based learning, such as [8] and [9], which apply agent technology in online collaborative learning. On the other hand, there is not any notable commercial software which solely target laboratory administration; however there are a few commercially available softwares which offer the capability of ALIAS. WebCT [12], for example, offers many integrated features in web-based learning. It targets the higher education sector in delivering e-learning by letting lecturers design a subject's structure online; this is where it is most similar to ALIAS. Its similarity also extends to the concept of innovative curriculum, which develops, integrates, and delivers e-learning contents.

Another example that is relevant to innovative curriculum in e-learning is MIT's (Massachusetts Institute of Technology) OpenCourseWare [11] project introduced in 1999. Its initiative to make e-learning a thing of the past has given a new meaning to education "knowledge and ideas are shared openly and freely for the benefit of all" [11]. Although this initiative has received a mass amount of funding its goal of sharing its faculty's core teaching materials openly to anyone, who has an internet connection, tops as one of the most innovative curriculum in web based learning.

2   Description of System Design

The web-based lab administrative system will be accessible to students and staff alike from anywhere with an internet connection. Students will be prompted to log in to ALIAS with the same username and password they use for other study hall accounts at La Trobe University. Once logged in, they will be shown their current registered classes; they will have an option to click on the classes to view lab availability for each class. They will also be given an option to view lab availability, which corresponds to classes they have not yet registered. Students will be allowed to sign up for labs even though they have not yet officially enrolled in a subject, as the staff is obliged to sign them up per Department policy. The lab administrative system will have four consecutive modes, each with time deadlines- preference, allocation adjustment, final, and post-mortem mode.

During preference mode, students are allowed to state their preferences for each subject they are enrolled in or will be enrolling in the near future. They will also be able to view, adjust, or delete their preferences during this mode. If students are not able to attend any of the given lab choices options will be provided to state the reasons for the time conflict. These students will be flagged as unallocated students. Since there is a great deal of autonomy within the head tutors, an option will be provided during the post-mortem mode for them to allocate these students manually to any given lab which may have spots remaining.

During allocation adjustment mode, students are allowed to view their allocated labs once the lab allocation has occurred. Currently, time will be used as a trigger to allocate students, however it should be noted that in the future certain students (i.e. high priority students, part time students) will be given preference to certain labs per Department policy. The time, in this case, refers to the expiry date for signups. Students may also be allowed to adjust their allocation provided that there are still spots remaining. If students who are not placed in labs for any reason (i.e. the labs become full, unavailability of labs) they will be automatically flagged as unallocated students.

During final mode, students are able to view the final student allocation. During this mode, lab adjustment by the students is not allowed. An algorithm heavily based on recursive formulation [2] is used for allocation (i.e. students with first preference are allocated until labs are full; remaining first preference students are allocated to second preference labs and so on until all the students have been allocated). The staff will be able to manually assign those students, who were unallocated during the allocation adjustment mode, to an appropriate lab if they choose to do so.

During post-mortem mode, any lab related issues, such as assigning of grades or recording lab attendance by head tutors can be configured per each need.

Staff will have access to view their corresponding labs either before or after the final allocation is complete. They should be able to view all the students per each lab allocation for their own subject. They can also adjust the final list as per their own requirement, as well as allocating those students who were flagged as unallocated. A facility will be provided to export the lab allocation list to a spreadsheet. Staff will also be able to send individual or group e-mails relating to any lab work to corresponding lab lists if desired.

It should be noted that before students are able to state their preferences during the preference mode above, either a lecturer or a head tutor will be able to set up labs. During the set up, they will be given options to define any parameters and constraints (i.e. define the minimum, maximum and optimum size for labs) for each lab. Please note that tutorials are treated in the same manner as labs in the context of this paper.

This web based learning tool is designed to automate the current manual gruelling task of assigning labs to students. It will streamline the whole process, from setting up of labs to final allocation, and conducting post-mortem if required. Furthermore, students will also have a great degree of convenience in selecting and viewing lab preferences as long as they have a connection to the Internet.

3 Functional Analysis

Functional analysis will be briefly analysed through the demonstration of use case analysis. An overview of all the functionalities is presented in Figure 1 below, which shows the relationships among the actors and use cases. Each of these actors will be identified and a few significant use cases explained.

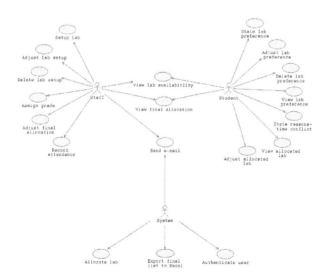

Fig. 1. Use Case Diagram - Overview

Actors Defined. Staff refers to either a lecturer or a head-tutor. They set the policies and guidelines- intricacies of lab existence, on how the labs are set up. They are responsible for making sure each student registered in their subject is allocated to a lab. Student refers to all current registered students at La Trobe University. They are the direct recipients or beneficiaries of the system since they are the ones who need to sign up for labs. They are responsible for filling out a lab signup form before a deadline for a given subject and making any necessary adjustments before a final allocation occurs. The system refers to the server system itself; it will perform various tasks including validating user input, authentication, allocating labs (i.e. business logic), and communication with external environments, such as exporting data to spreadsheet. The server will also act on a set of rules which will be preconfigured into the system. Examples of such rules include sending automatic e-mail messages to students to notify of any lab notices- lab quizzes, attendance, etc.

Selected Use Cases Defined. In the 'Set up lab by staff' use case the system will provide staff with lab names and attributes; the staff will choose the required number of labs and fill in the remaining attributes. In the 'State lab preference by student' use case a form with several lab options will be provided. Labs will contain information such as day, time and location; a preference will be selected by a student based on this information. Finally, in the 'Allocate labs by system' use case the system takes in the student's preferences as parameters and runs an algorithm to allocate labs to students. The algorithm partly takes their preferences and capacity level (optimal size for a number of students in a given lab, as defined by staff) into consideration.

4   Domain Analysis

The core of the high level domain class diagram, Figure 2, includes the following classes: Student, Lab, Preference and LabSignUp. These four classes represent the main thrust of the lab allocation process. The identified classes and their relationships are shown in at an analysis level (i.e. different from that of a design class diagram).

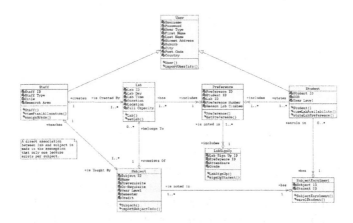

Fig. 2. Class Diagram

5   Data Analysis - Entity Relationship Diagram

ER diagrams are used to model relational databases, showing the relationships among various entities; an entity is equivalent to a database table. Figure 3 displays all of the entities within the system, as well as relationships amongst them.

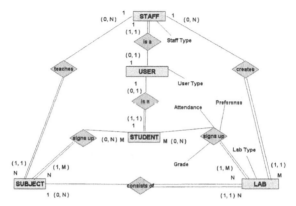

Fig. 3. ER Diagram

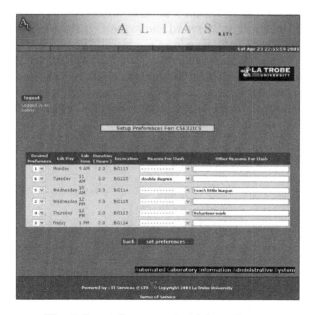

Fig. 4. Input Screen - select lab preferences

6   User Interface Analysis

The screenshot in Figure 4 is an example of a look and feel of the system; the example represents an input screen during selecting of lab preferences for a subject by students. They are able to select their preferences given all the attributes of a particular lab. The drop down box has a list of relevant reasons as to why a student may not be able to attend a particular lab.

7   System Architecture and Implementation

This section attempts to briefly explain the inner workings of ALIAS and how they are glued together.

7.1   System Architecture

The language level system architecture, Figure 5, reflects the types of programming languages/techniques used to accomplish a certain architectural goal- a close similarity to the J2EE design patterns in [1]. The middleware software components consist of the following: web server (Apache) and application server (Jakarta Tomcat), firewall software, RDBMS (Oracle 9i), and fault tolerant web server software all deployed under Linux Red Hat operating system. Tomcat will provide support for JSP and servlet, the main language used for this architecture.

A HTTP request is received by JSP/servlet container (Tomcat) via Apache web Server [5], which resides within a firewall. If the request is for a static web page however, Apache will not forward the request. If the request is for authenticating a user (password will be encrypted via HTTPS), a function call from a business tier Java class will be made via a plug-in to the university Lightweight Directory Access Protocol (LDAP) [3] system. If the request involves accessing a data store, a dynamic SQL or stored procedure will be performed to extract the data. The data will be sent in the form of a result set or in XML format by

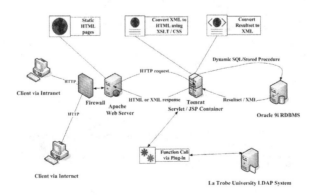

Fig. 5. System Architecture

the Oracle 9i RDBMS. If it is a result set data, it will be converted to XML and wrapped inside an object (this is done to support heterogeneous environment where XML [7] and [10] data can be easily rendered). Before forwarding the response on to the Apache web server, XML data is then converted to XHTML using XSLT [6] and CSS. It is assumed that all connections are made through HTTP, thus the reason for XHTML conversion. The following will be used for client side GUI- JavaScript, XHTML, CSS, XML and XSLT.

7.2   Lab Allocation Algorithm

The pseudo code of lab allocation algorithm is given in Figure 6.

7.3   Multiple Lab Allocating Strategies

To allocate students into appropriate labs is not a simple task as it seems. Different lecturers have different teaching styles, and the requirement of each subject is different; same goes for diverse background of students. Based on the previous lab allocation algorithm, we propose multiple strategies to suit the needs of

```
-System determines if an allocation date for a given subject has already passed
-If date has already passed
    -then START LOOP
    -get all the names of students who stated lab preference as 1st...Nth
      preference
    -check whether slots are still available in a pre-existing lab (the same 1st...Nth
      preference)
    -if there are more slots available
          -then insert students with no time conflicts into these available slots
    -else if no slots are available
          -then add these students to a table with their preference information
    -if the number of students in the table is greater than 0
          -then check whether spots are still available in pre-existing labs
            (student's 2nd...Nth preference)
    -if there are more slots available
          -then insert students with no time conflicts into these available slots
    -else if no slots are available
          -then add these students to a table with their preference information
    -if the number of students in the table is greater than 0
          -then check whether spots are still available in pre-existing labs
            (student's 3rd...Nth preference)
    -REPEAT until all of the student's preferences are depleted
    -if there were more students than labs available
          -then flag these students as unallocated students
    -check the allocations of students who stated time conflicts
    -if the students had preferences and were not allocated
          -then flag these students as unallocated students
    -END LOOP
```

Fig. 6. Algorithm Pseudo Code

both staff and students. They provide great flexibilities; moreover, some functions are unavailable in manual allocation process. Subject lecturer can decide which strategy to apply depending on the feature and situation of the subject. These strategies are innovative and unique in ALIAS- some of which can only be achieved in such an online lab management system.

First Sign First Allocate (FSFA). This strategy is designed to encourage students to sign in their labs as soon as possible, so the whole process could be finished in a short time frame. This is always required in most of the programming language subjects. Their labs begin from the second week of teaching and their lab performance throughout the semester is accounted for in the final result. FSFA strategy assigns labs according to the time students sign in and the availability of their choices. The earlier you sign in, the most likely you can get your first preferred lab.

Performance Allocation Strategy. Student performance is also of concern when allocating labs. A friendly and encouraging atmosphere is a key for a successful lab. Mixing strong students with some weak ones in a lab is a good practice to let them learn from each other. Relevant student subject results can be retrieved from the university LDAP system.

Background Allocation Strategy. For some courses, such as English language and international business, many staff would like to divide students into lab groups according to their background. It is shown that international students, as well as local students, can benefit a lot in these subjects if they have a chance to share their knowledge with classmates from different cultures. Similar to performance allocation strategy, relevant information is available from the university LDAP system.

Fairness Allocation Strategy. ALIAS provides a new way to manage student lab allocations. With this centralised administrative tool, it is easy to consider a single student's all lab allocations, which is impossible if lecturers do this manually. Most of the complaints from students with manual allocation are about the fairness. A student is very disappointed and frustrated if all of his/her first few preferences are not satisfied for several courses. To avoid such situations, we propose this strategy to ensure that across all courses students are fairly allocated. The idea is that a weight is assigned for each subject, such as W_{java}; and for student S_i in this subject, his/her final lab allocation is given a score $SCORE_{S_i}^{Java}$ according to which preference is satisfied; the fairness for S_i is:

$$F(S_i) = \frac{\sum_{j=1}^{N} W_j * SCORE_{S_i}^j}{N}$$

For all the students, this strategy ensure that $|maxF(S_i) - minF(S_i)| < \epsilon$, ε is a threshold. Fairness allocation strategy tries to allocate students into labs evenly, that is to minimise the special cases which often students would complain about their final allocations. This cannot be accomplished without ALIAS, a web based lab management system, which has the comprehensive information needed to consider the big picture.

8 Testing

Structural and functionality testing examines the extent to which ALIAS meets the expected functional requirements. They verify that the system performs all the desired functions and conforms to the requirement specifications. Before completion of the project a wide range of normal and erroneous input data would be used to validate each feature of all the behaviours of the system, to ensure that the applications perform efficiently, correctly, and most importantly, bug-free in a real world environment. Different types of testing- white box, black box and usability, were conducted to ensure that the software conforms to the highest of standards.

As a subset of unit testing, specific knowledge of programming codes were used to conduct white box testing. Many of these tests involved writing a small amount of code to test a portion of any given functionality. Unlike white box testing, black box testing is done from the end user's point of view. Many functionalities were tested by entering inputs and recording the outputs from the system.

Usability testing (UT) encompasses a range of methods that identifies how users interact with a prototype or a complete website. During development, the purpose of UT is to diagnose and be informed where changes need to be made so that the final product can be greatly improved. If there are any issues concerning alternative design it can be compared using UT to produce a better one; also, comparisons can be likely made with similar lab administration websites.

ALIAS will use UT for the following reasons- to ensure that the user interface design is intuitive and easy to use (this means that the use of menus and the navigation is easy to understand and have a natural feel to it), to confirm that all forms and other input screens have a natural flow of control, to make sure that error messages are informative and not intimidating in any way, and to ensure that server response times are reasonably acceptable.

A survey consisting of questionnaires for UT has been conducted; this survey is used to identify the level of acceptance from the users' point of view. Depending on the result of the survey modifications can be made to the system, if necessary, accordingly.

The two graphs in Figure 7 and Figure 8 are results of conducting UT by subjects and grade levels. A weighted average was taken from the answers provided by the students to determine the final percentage level. The same number of students can be classified in both of these: students enrolled in a subject or by their year level of study. However, it may be the case the same student who replied in the latter graph may not be enrolled in one of the subjects in the first graph. In analysing the survey ODE and 4th year students seems to have the highest level of satisfaction whereas OJA and 1st year students seems to have the least. Furthermore, it can be concluded from the survey that an overall satisfaction has been reached within the department.

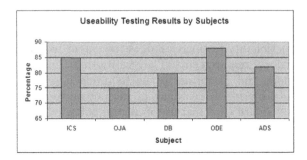

Fig. 7. Useability Testing Results by Subjects

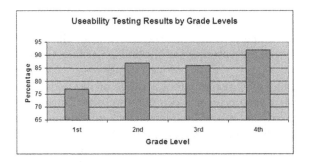

Fig. 8. Useability Testing Results by Grade Levels

9   Conclusion

This paper describes a tool for automating lab administration in a web-based learning environment. The current manual lab allocation system consists of too much overhead. It not only takes up extra human resources, but it also comprises of several inconveniences which make it difficult to focus on the primary goal of teaching. The redundancies and discrepancies caused by the lab system can spill over to a domino effect within the staff in the department. This amounts to avoidable human errors or loss of time due to menial administrative tasks. In meeting the demands of a viable solution to the problem at hand, a tool in web-based learning has been proposed. The tool, ALIAS, solves most, if not all, problems related to the administration of lab allocation. It also provides functions that cannot be achieved manually, such as the multiple lab allocation strategies. These strategies make the system flexible and comprehensive. This innovative tool not only enriches student experience through interactive learning similar to [4] but also assists both the student and staff in making the process less time consuming; the end result is higher efficiency and more time for academic learning.

A few possibilities for future work include the capability to export documents in various formats, not just spreadsheets. Several strategies to allocate labs will be explored to suit various demands. It is essential that the tool remains flexible and extensible so that customization does not become burdensome. With this possibility the tool can be released to other departments within this or other universities in the future. Rigorous testing, however, would be a priority before such event takes place.

References

1. Alur, D., Crupi, J., Malks, D.: Core J2EE Patterns: Best Practices and Design Strategies, Prentice Hall, 2nd Edition, 2003.
2. Bender, E.: Mathematical Methods in Artificial Intelligence, Wiley-IEEE Computer Society Press, 1st Edition, 1996.
3. Carter, G.: LDAP System Administration, O'Reilly Publishing, 1st Edition, 2003.
4. García, A., Rodríguez, S., Rosales, F., Pedraza, J.L.: Automatic Management of Laboratory Work in Mass Computer Engineering Courses, IEEE Transaction on Education, Vol. 48, No.1, February 2005.
5. Hall, M., Brown, L.: Core Servlets and JavaServer Pages, Prentice Hall Publishing, 2nd Edition, 2003.
6. Kay, M. H.: XSLT Programmer's Reference, Wrox Publishing, 2nd Edition, 2003.
7. Knobloch, M., Kopp, M.: Web Design with XML, John Wiley and Sons Publishing, 1st Edition, 2002.
8. Lu, H.: Mediator based Open Multi-Agent Architecture for Web based Learning, In Proceedings of the 2nd International Conference on Web-based Learning (ICWL 2003), Lecture Notes of Computer Science, Springer-Verlag, Melbourne, Australia, August 2003.
9. Lu, H.: Open Multi-Agent Systems for Collaborative Web based Learning, International Journal of Distance Education Technologies, A Publication of Idea Group Publishing, Information Science Publishing, USA, 2004.
10. Maruyama, H., Tamura, K., Uramoto, N,, Murata, M., Clark, A., Nakamura, Y., Neyama, R., Kosaka, K., Hada, S.: XML and Java, Addison Wesley Publishing , 2nd Edition, 2002
11. http://ocw.mit.edu/index.html
12. http://www.webct.com

An Online Template-Based Authoring System for E-Learning

Simon Hui and James Liu

Industrial Centre, The Hong Kong Polytechnic University, Hong Kong, China
{iccshui, icdjliu}@inet.polyu.edu.hk

Abstract. This paper presents an online authoring system that allows users to create interactive course content and course structure on the Internet in a fast and easy way without any programming knowledge. The underlying CMS (Content Management System) provides the flexibility of XML-based application interface to publish content for Flash courseware or other online learning systems such as WebCT. An extensive library of Flash Templates is provided for course presentation and interactivity. With the templates and the CMS, this online authoring system allows minimum course development efforts from tutors and delivers interesting learning experience to students. In this paper, a primary school courseware is developed to demonstrate the effectiveness of the system.

Keywords: publishing tool for e-learning, online authoring system, template-based courseware, content management system, Zope application.

1 Introduction

For non-programmer teaching professionals, there is a need for rapid content authoring without the need to program and to use sophisticated commercial authoring tools. Standard Web-authoring tools [1] such as FrontPage, Dreamweaver, Photoshop and Flash, each covers some of all the aspects of course development such as course presentation, course navigation, multimedia and interactivity. When interactivity is concern, JavaScript or Action Script [2] programming will be necessary.

As a result, a course developer has to grasp deep understanding of suitable tools that are expensive in terms of purchase cost as well as training time, and the production of consistent courseware is complex and difficult to control.

Course interface design also causes headaches. Web authoring tools have limited methods to separate presentation and content. A tutor without design experience or with limited time can only achieve non-appealing visual effects and unfriendly user interface.

In an effort to free a tutor from the above problems, we have developed a one-stop authoring system for e-learning with a built-in Flash template library that includes many quiz features such as Drag and Drop, Multiple Choice, Hot Spots, etc. The authoring system supports content editing as well as navigation. Online access and

R.W.H. Lau et al. (Eds.): ICWL 2005, LNCS 3583, pp. 38–48, 2005.

multi-author support makes it possible for tutors to work online any where, any time, without having to install any software in their PCs. All these features supported in an integrated system are attractive for general non-technical users.

2   System Architecture

In this section, we will describe the architecture overview, account management, course content management, course navigation and template-based user interface and XML support. The description will help to outline the design of the online system.

2.1   Architecture Overview

The system design (see Fig. 1) is based on client/server architecture to support multi-author online access. When a client's request is sent to the server, the server will query on the OODB (Object Oriented Database) based on the request and process the query result. Once the process is finished, the result is sent back to the client in the form of XML response. The client will then parse the XML response into Flash recognizable data and render the data with a designated Flash template. OODB is chosen as the server database due to its good support in creation and management of hierarchical objects over RDB (Relational Database). An ODBMS

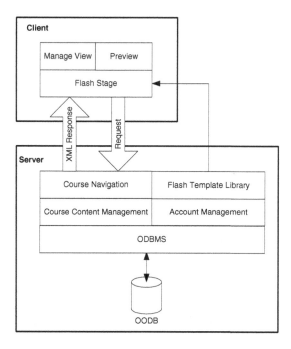

Fig. 1. Architecture Overview

(Object Database Management System) is then adopted to implement the CMS (Content Management System) on top of OODB. As the core of the online authoring system, the CMS supports a package of course management features such as course framework, navigation, account management and separation of presentation from content.

On the client side, a Flash Stage object (a swf file) is responsible for handling server response, parsing course content, and dressing the content with different Flash templates. On top of Flash Stage there are 2 types of user interfaces: Manage View and Preview.

2.2 Account Management

Account management provides 3 functions: User Registration, Authentication and Permission. When a user first logs in the system, he or she will be required to fill in the Registration form so that the system would be able to recognize him or her as a valid user according to provided information. Authentication is performed when a registered user log in, the system will validate his or her user information and authorize entry permission.

2.3 Course Content Management

Course content management deals with how the course content is developed and organized. While template-based interface brings simplicity in editing, it also brings limitations in structure. A two-level course structure can only fit in a two-level template. An alternative would be to have a n-level (for example n=5) course structure fixed for the system templates so that it can fit with m-level of course structure as long as m<=n (for example m=2, 3, 4, 5). Great effort will be needed to design templates in order to keep the style and navigation consistent in adjusting to different type of course structures and the number of templates will be limited as well.

2.4 Course Navigation

Two kinds of navigation are to be considered here: the courseware navigation for the students/readers and the management navigation for the course builder. Common look and feel courseware navigation is built in each template so that all course objects applied with a template can be navigated consistently. Linear navigation is adopted because users would not get 'lost' easily by only making simple decision when browsing such as next page or the previous.

Management navigation needs to provide a more flexible path because a course builder will need to perform a relatively complex operation in the management view. A course builder will usually need to quickly access back and forth the course objects located at different places for editing or referencing. Since the course content is organized in a tree structure, an expendable tree menu is provided for fast access to different levels of objects in a limited space.

2.5 Template-Based User Interface and XML Support

Template-based user interface provides simplicity, robustness, and flexibility. It also supports interactivity because all templates are Flash objects. A client-side component called Flash Stage is used for integrating the course content and the selected Flash template in client side before it is shown to the users. Course object (along with its attributes) is packaged in a form of XML Response message before it is sent to the client. XML is selected not only because Flash Stage component supports XML parsing, but also the course contents can be transformed to other system by way of XML. By parsing the XML Response message, the Flash Stage component transforms the course data into Flash values and gets the attached file name of the selected Flash template. The selected Flash template is then called from the server's Flash Template Library and sent to the Flash Stage for integration with the course values.

Flash Stage supports two kinds of Flash user interface depending on the applied Flash templates: Manage View for editing data and Preview for getting the real picture. Manage View is implemented in a WYSIWYG (What You See Is What You Got) manner. For example, multiple choices, fill-in blanks and selection boxes are different in layout and each has its own way for editing. After editing, the user can simply switch to the Preview interface for a peep of the final effect, where the static data becomes interactive and animated with fun. In Fig. 2 and Fig. 3, the Management View and the Preview View of multiple choices are shown.

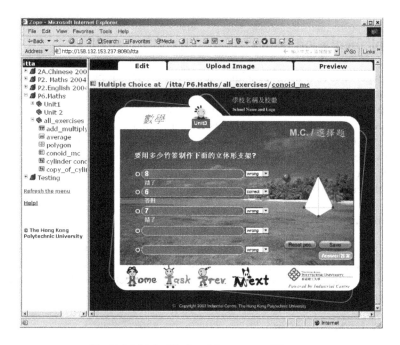

Fig. 2. Multiple Choices Management View

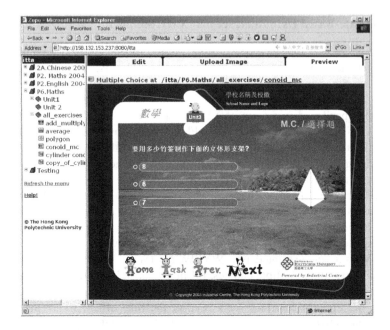

Fig. 3. Multiple Choices Preview View

3   Implementation Issues

In this paper, the following techniques are used: OODB design, extending Zope, Python, output xml, scalability of template, Flash Stage parsing and integration, navigation and embedded Flash interface. In order to implement a system based on the above techniques without too much cost, an open source application server, Zope is used as the underlying content management system. The following paragraphs will first introduce Zope 2.0, and then describe some challenges in extending Zope 2.0 to support course content management and Flash user interface. Some issues about exporting the course content will also be discussed.

3.1   Zope 2.0

Zope 2.0 [3] is an open source application server written in Python. Zope is a highly object-oriented Web development platform that provides clean separation of data, logic and presentation, an extensible set of built-in objects and a powerful integrated security model.

3.2   Account Management

The multi-author access to the authoring tool is easily implemented by the inheritance of a Zope account management object: 'User Folder', with the built-in methods that support user registration, authentication and permission setting. Each User object (see Fig. 4) in the User Folder represents a course builder account and contains the authentication information.

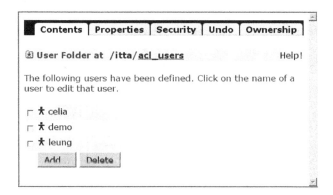

Fig. 4. Account Management

3.3 Course Framework

Zope 2.0 comes with an OODB (Object Oriented Database) which allows users to represent data as objects with attributes and organize the relations of objects in a way similar to the real world. Some built-in objects are provided with basic functions such as Folder and Simple Item. These objects are defined in classes written in Python language and can be extended to build advanced course objects such as 'Subject', 'Unit', 'Topic' with special attributes and functions.

In developing the template-based authoring system, 12 classes are built by extending a built-in class 'Folder', among which 10 aggregations and 12 inheritance relations are defined and compose a course framework that seems to match most aspects of a typical course structure. Following is a list of these classes with description:

- TBAT: Template-based Authoring Tools.
- Subject: Top course object that contains Units.
- Unit: Smaller course object that contains Topics.
- Topic: Base class of smallest course object.
- CourseA: Course object (type A).
- CourseB: Course object (type B).
- CourseC: Course object (type C).
- MC: Assessment object (Multiple Choice).
- TrueFalse: Assessment object (True & False).
- Fill: Assessment object (Fill in the blank).
- Drag: Assessment object (Drag & Drop).
- Spot: Assessment object (Spot the Error).

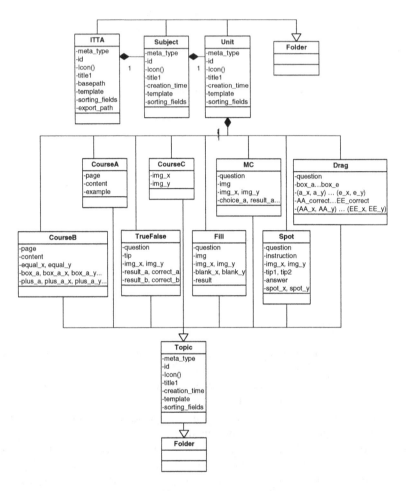

Fig. 5. Class Diagram

In Fig. 5, the UML Class Diagram [4] shows the inheritance and aggregation relations among the classes. For example, we can clearly see such an inheritance path:

ITTA ← Subject ← Unit ← MC

which means:

- An ITTA object contains and manages multiple Subject objects.
- A Subject object contains and manages multiple Unit objects.
- A Unit object contains and manages multiple MC objects.

We can also find such an aggregation path:

Folder ← Topic ←MC

which means:

- All MC objects inherit properties and methods from Topic.
- All Topic objects inherit properties and methods from Folder.
- All MC objects inherit properties and methods from Folder.

3.4   Course Content Management

The built-in content management interface of Zope 2.0 provides almost everything a developer need to build the course content management interface for the authoring system. A new feature is added to the course content management (Fig. 6) that allows the course builder to 'order' the objects. By 'ordering the objects', we mean that a course builder can change the presentation order of an object by *moving* the object.

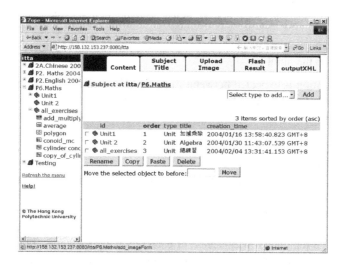

Fig. 6. Subject Management

3.5   Integrating Content and Style

By attaching a style page called ZPT page, Zope can dress its objects into any HTML style. To extend this ability and integrate course content with Flash Style – Flash Template, several issues should be considered:

- Where should the integration happen? Client side or server side?
- In which component?
- What is necessary information for the integration?
- How to integrate once we have this information?
- How to do it without changing much of the existed Zope publishing?
- Is it possible to make the integration transparent?
- How should Zope communicate with the Flash template?
- What information should Zope publish?
- When and how to assign a Flash template for the specific course object?

It is possible to make the integration transparent because the object-based structure of Zope allows an object to have its own methods in transforming the data. There is no limit in what the transformation result must be – it could be HTML, XML or Flash. The Zope object's properties also contain enough information necessary for the integration. For example here's a list of the properties and their description of a 'Drag & Drop' object:

–Preferred Flash template: a Flash file name.
–URL of previous, next, home page: for navigation.
–Current Subject: subject name.
–Current Unit: unit name.
–Drag & Drop question: sentence.
–ID of 5 box-items: items to be matched. Missing ID indicate a removed item.
–Correct destination of 5 drag-items: non null.
–Recorded position of each drag-item: remember where the user put them last time.
–Calculated position of each box-item: items are placed with equal interval according to the number.

Communication is expected between Zope and Flash in integrating content coming from Zope and style coming from Flash template. The choice of language is not much since only Python and ZPT are recognized by Zope and only Action Script is recognized by Flash. Fortunately both Flash and Zope support XML by providing XML parser and XML publisher, which make indirect transformation from Zope object to Flash Action Script values possible.

The Stage object – a Flash movie is the perfect environment for that kind of transformation not only because it can load course content by XML but also load course template in the form of a Flash sub-movie.

The Template Library – a Zope Folder object linked to server file system provides the storage of 8 templates. Web access of each template is supported by Zope object's URL. Synchronization between the Library and the server file system make it a simple matter for the course designer to edit each template without interfering the job of the course builders.

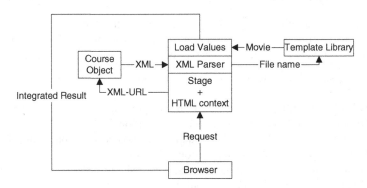

Fig. 7. Integration Process

As shown in Fig.7, after a user's request is directed to the Stage object, in order to fill the Stage with meaningful course content, the Stage object calls the XML publish method to get the XML representation of the object. It then uses a XML Parser to transform the result into Action Script values. From these values the preferred Flash template's file name is extracted and the movie is loaded from the template library into the Stage object. The final integration is done by loading the Action Script values into the Flash template movie.

3.6 Export Course to Local

Export function is provided in the template-based authoring tool similar to the save function of standard PC software. The exported files include the Stage object, the XML files that represent the course content with navigation information and the Flash template movies for style selection. Since the collection of files can work locally without server support, it can be published to a CD or another online platform such as WebCT.

3.7 Working with WebCT

WebCT is an online course management system with tools like course syllabus, multimedia, discussions, chat, assignments, quizzes and so on. Despite the various management and delivery functions it provides for the teaching professionals, WebCT has virtually no support for rich content and interaction. The course authors using WebCT have an option to learn to use advanced software such as Macromedia Flash and upload the resulted Flash Movie into WebCT. But this requires advanced programming experience and the resulted movies are usually isolated files without support for course structure and navigation.

On the other hand, the online template-based authoring system provides an easy way to build rich and interactive course content without advanced programming knowledge. The result of template-based authoring system can be easily exported and uploaded to WebCT. By integrating the template-based authoring system result and the WebCT, course authors are able to develop course contents with interactive templates and still enjoy the many benefits provided by the WebCT.

4 Primary School Courseware Development

In this paper, a primary school courseware is developed with the template-based authoring tool. The development took place in a primary school server installed with the authoring tool. A course builder then registers and logs in to his or her own 'course space' on the Internet, and starts to develop a rich media and interactive courseware (in office or home) in a few steps. The following is a fraction of operation sequence in developing the primary school courseware:

- Add a Subject 'chinese_terms' in Root folder.
- Enter Subject 'chinese_terms'and upload a background image for the Subject.
- Add 2 Units 'word' and 'sentence' in the Subject.

- Enter Unit 'word'.
- Add a 'Fill in the Blank' object: 'word1'.
- Enter 'word1' to input the answer and the correct answer, and position the input box in the Flash edit interface.
- Return back to Unit 'word'.
- Copy the 'word1' object and paste it in the same Unit and name the new object 'word2'.
- Enter 'word2' and change question, answer and their position.
- Use the tree menu to navigate to Subject level.
- Click Preview to see the final Flash result.
- Click Export to export the movie.

5 Conclusions

An online template-based authoring system is designed and developed to assist non-programmer course builders in rapid course development. Account and content management features from Zope 2.0 are extended and applied to the core of the system. A multi-authoring space and 3 classes of course object are built in supporting the 3-level course structure. A library of 8 Flash templates is produced for content integration and a linear or tree menu is provided in navigating the system.

The demonstration of the system in a primary school course development shows that a course builder can access the authoring system online any time, anywhere. The course builder can build a course easily and quickly in a few steps without much technical efforts. Because the system is based on Flash templates, a tutor is able to achieve professional-like visual design and interactivity. The tutor can also export the courseware in a CD or online.

References

1. Banks, B., McGrath, K.: E-Learning Content Advisory Paper. FD Learning (2003) 11-12
2. Heins, T., Himes, F.: Creating Learning Objects With Macromedia Flash MX (2002) 8-9
3. Spicklemire, S., Frienly, K., Spicklemire, J., Brand, K.: Zope Web Application Development and Content Management, New Riders (2002) 17-36
4. Jager, D.: Using UML for software process modeling. Software Engineering, ESEC/FSE'99, Proceedings, Springer (1999) 91-108

Design and Implementation of a J2EE-Based Platform for Network Teaching

Zhen He[1,2], Ling Qiu[3], and Qinming He[1]

[1] College of Computer Science,
Zhejiang University, Hangzhou, China 310027
hezhen_hz@sohu.com, hqm@cs.zju.edu.cn
[2] College of Information Science and Technology,
Zhejiang Shuren University, Hangzhou, China 310015
[3] School of Information Systems,
Singapore Management University, Singapore 259756
lqiu@smu.edu.sg

Abstract. Nowadays e-learning is playing an important role in remote education, group training and tertiary education. In this paper, we first address the importance and functionality of e-learning in modern education; we then present an e-learning tool—network teaching platform ETP, which is implemented by techniques of J2EE, analyze the system functionality, and give the details of system design. Our practice shows that the platform is functionally stable for practical usage.

1 Introduction

Nowadays e-learning is playing an important role in remote education, group training and tertiary education. Especially in tertiary education, e-learning is being highly valued due to several reasons such as the expansion of institutions, scattered campuses and the deployment of computerized teaching [1]. The advance of campus Internet has provided a good infrastructure for e-learning, and has also pushed the wide applications of e-learning tools and platforms [7].

Based on the teaching aspects and requirement of our university, we develop a J2EE-based platform (i.e., ETP) for network teaching. There are several motivations: (a) improving the methods by e-learning so as to motivate the initiatives of learners; (b) providing a humanized platform for learning interactively and in real time; and (c) allowing further extension of the learning platform.

We adopt techniques of J2EE for the development of our teaching platform. This is based on the following considerations. Firstly, with the advances of Java techniques, Java has been widely used in the developing of Web applications. Secondly, J2EE applies techniques of composition [5,4]. This allows the components reusable, and thus can shorten the period of programming. Thirdly, Java language is independent of the running environment, thus a Java-based system is compatible and transplantable among different running platforms.

As compared with some other existing e-learning platforms, our ETP has the following aspects. First, some basic functions of e-learning platforms are inte-

R.W.H. Lau et al. (Eds.): ICWL 2005, LNCS 3583, pp. 49–55, 2005.
© Springer-Verlag Berlin Heidelberg 2005

grated in the system. These functions include online assignment system, course-ware management, message management, and online communications. Second, the organization and management of assignments are tightly associated with knowledge points. The system also provides an efficient and convenient way for judging of assignments. Third, the system provides various kinds of assign-ments and allows submission of assignments in multimedia formats (e.g., images, source code of programs, and compressed packages). Fourth, users are classified into *five* groups, namely system administrators, teaching affair administrators, members of teaching instructional groups, lecturers, and students. This classifi-cation is based on the labor division in teaching practice. For example, normally the knowledge points and assignment database of certain course are determined by all lecturers who are lecturing this course, thus they are performed by the members of teaching instructional groups, instead of the lecturers. Some other teaching platforms may only distinguish administrators and end-users. Such clas-sification may not be close to the teaching reality, and may not be able to well satisfy the practical requirements. Our classification is more effective in terms of reflecting the teaching practice.

The remaining sections are organized as follows. In Section 2, we present the architecture of ETP and describe in detail the design of the functionality. In Section 3, we give the details for several technical points of the system imple-mentation. Finally in Section 4, we discuss several related issues and conclude the paper by pointing out research directions for future study.

2   Architecture of ETP

2.1   Functional Design of ETP

The ETP possesses the functions required by most teaching activities. Based on the different labor division in teaching activities, we provide respective functions for aforementioned *five* groups of users. The functions owned by all groups are logging in the forum, communicating with other users in the forum, and manag-ing the messages. Priorities are assigned to users in different groups when they distribute messages. Figure 1 shows an overview of functional design of ETP.

In practice, there exists mutual associations among different actions in teach-ing activities. This is the main concern in our functional design. In our ETP, those mutual associations are classified into *four* categories, namely, association of courses, association of assignments, association of users, and association of messages. The functional design of each association is presented as follows.

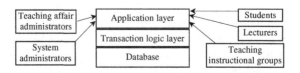

Fig. 1. Overview of functional design of ETP

(1) **Course Association.** In our ETP system, the entities associated with a course include the course itself, teaching tasks of this course, knowledge points of this course, a database of assignments for this course, etc. One course can be taught by several lecturers. A teaching task is the teaching loading for a lecturer taking a course for certain class. Each course owns a tree of knowledge points and a database of assignments. Once a course is created by the system, the entries of all associated entities are generated. The newly created course will appear in the list of candidate courses while generating teaching tasks. The system will not generate teaching tasks for a course that has not yet been created. Similarly, before deleting a course from the system, all teaching tasks of this course have to be deleted firstly. The root node of the knowledge tree and the database of knowledge points for the newly created course are also generated automatically by the system. Users can now add knowledge points as nodes or leaves into the tree, and further add records of the knowledge points in the database. In other words, each assignment is attached to certain node in the tree of knowledge points. The tree can be organized by the order of chapters and sections, or be organized in a hashing way.

(2) **Assignment Association.** There are two concepts related to assignment association, i.e., assignment task and assignment. The assignment task is the assignment created by a lecturer. This assignment task is supposedly to be distributed on certain distributing date to students who are taking this course for accomplishment. The assignment is a copy of the assignment task automatically created by the system for each student on the distributing date.

There are *three* states of an assignment task, namely editing, distributed, closed. Correspondingly, there are *six* states of an assignment, namely unstarted, started, finished, unfinished, submitted, deadlined. The transferring of states of an assignment task and the assignment is carried out by a thread running in background. When an assignment task is deleted by a lecturer, the related assignment for each student is also deleted automatically. However, students are allowed to backup their assignments before the deleting operation of the system.

(3) **User Association.** Lecturers and students are two kinds of users in ETP. The management of users is accomplished by the module of teaching affair management. In the system, we set up two separate databases for the forum and the main part of the system. Each of the databases maintains its own list of users. To keep the consistency of users in two lists, we provide an interface to synchronously update records in both databases when we are operating in one database, such as appending, updating, and deleting user records.

(4) **Message Association.** In the design of message module, we classify messages into *four* categories (i.e., system msg, teaching affair msg, course msg, and teaching msg) based on the range and receivers to which the messages are distributed in practice. There are some constraints of message sending and receiving. For example, system messages can be sent to individuals (students or lecturers) or all users; teaching affair messages can be sent to individuals, students taking certain assignment task, all students taking certain course, or all system users; course messages dedicated to certain course are normally distributed by

the teaching instructional group, and can be sent to individuals, students taking certain assignment task, and all students taking certain course, but cannot be sent to all users; teaching messages are distributed by certain lecturer dedicated to certain teaching task, and can be sent to some or all students taking this task.

2.2   Technical Framework of ETP

We adopt Struts [6] as the framework for the implementation of system workflow. This is based on the following considerations. First, Struts is an MVC framework [3] based on Sun J2EE platform, and is implemented by Servlet and JSP techniques. Secondly, Struts integrates Servlet, JSP, self-defined labels, and information resource into a unified framework [6], thus it saves a lot of time because developers need not to write codes to implement MVC schema. Based on Struts, we design the framework of ETP as shown in Figure 2. The system working flow is described as follows (also refer to Figure 2). The browsers at client side firstly send HTTP requests to the controller. Then controller receives a request as an event, and decides how to handle it based on the aspects of the request. If the request is a static page (e.g., a page with extension .jsp), then it is forwarded directly to the page. Otherwise, if the request is a dynamic page (e.g., a page with extension .do), then based on the mapping configured in struts_config.xml file, the controller decides to which transaction logic the request should be sent for handling. The transaction logic timely updates the status of the workflow.

Given the workflow, we divide the system into *three* modules, namely, logic processing module (Action class), data access module (Event class), and page module (JSP). Their functions are described as follows. The Action class firstly transfers the parameters in requests to Event class, then obtains data sent back from Event class, and lastly transfers the data to JSP in predefined formats. According to the parameters transferred from Action class, the Event class reads required data from the database (or updates the database) via Caster JDO as the bridge, and sends back the required data to Action class. The page module is responsible for displaying the refreshing of views triggered by Action class.

Moreover, we adopt Caster JDO technique (instead of JDBC) for the connection with database. This is because JDO technique can map the tables in a database into classes that are similar to JavaBean such that it provides more convenience for database access. We also adopt OQL (object-oriented query

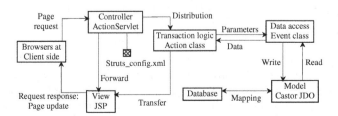

Fig. 2. Technical framework of ETP

language) as our database query language because it is more compatible with Caster JDO technique [2]. The grammar of OQL is similar to that of SQL, but it allows users to query object models instead of querying database directly.

3   Main Techniques

The ETP system is an integrated e-learning platform for network teaching. It is multi-functional, in which we adopt several remarkable techniques. Due to the limit of page space, we only introduce several important techniques in what follows. These techniques include component technique, Applet technique, Java thread technique, input/output stream technique, and forum technique.

(1) **Component Technique.** The component technique is applied in our system for implementing the uploading, downloading, or browsing of courseware, assignments in multimedia file formats, and teaching materials. Figure 3 shows the snapshot of interface for uploading, downloading, and browsing. Here we apply SmartFile component such that by writing a simple JSP file we can implement the above functions by specifying the saving directories for all documents. For example, if we create directory Data as the root for all uploading and downloading files and subdirectories course and edutask for different types of files, then the saving directory for certain teaching task can be implemented by the following statement: String path = " Data\edutask\edutaskId ", where edutaskId is the Id of the teaching task in the database.

(2) **Applet Technique.** Applet technique is used to implement the management of assignments (creating, editing, marking, submitting, etc.), trees of knowledge points, and databases of examination questions. There are advantages and disadvantages of using Applet technique. One of the disadvantages is that it requires very long time to download large amount of data because Applet caches all required data at one time in the beginning. The advantage of this aspect is that after downloading users can freely browse all data without delay. Some other techniques only cache currently visited data, and incur delay when users browse previous or next pages. Considering that in practice all operations of assignments are consecutive processes, we use Applet to eliminate the delay of paging up and paging down.

Fig. 3. Interface snapshot

In our system, the tree structure is used widely, such as tree of knowledge points and tree of examination question databases. The JTree class in Applet provides a convenient way to generate all these trees. Another reason of using Applet technique is that it can present a friendly user interface.

(3) Java Thread Technique. Java thread technique is used to implement the distribution and closing of assignment tasks. We use ThreadStart class (background running) to start the thread PubCompleteThread which is in charge of distributing and closing assignment tasks timely. The tasks of the thread include: checking the dates of distributing and closing for all non-distributed and non-closed assignment tasks in the database, checking whether there are assignment tasks to be distributed or closed, and updating the states of assignment tasks. This thread hibernates for a period of time after one time of running, and wakes up and runs again.

(4) Input/Output Stream Technique. The input/output stream technique is used to import and export large amount of data in batch. The teaching affair administrators need to input large amount of data to the system. These data include information of lecturers, students, and all courses. In our system, all these information can be imported from excel files in batch. We define the formats of data saved in excel files. Users can conveniently upload their well formatted excel files by clicking related buttons. Once the excel files are uploaded, the system will read the data line by line from the files, and extract the fields from the raw data and save them to the system databases.

(5) Forum Technique. The forum in ETP is a revised version based on Jdon forum (note: Jdon forum is an open-source forum implemented in Java). It is implemented by adding several interfaces between the forum and the other part of the system. The main tasks of the interfaces are to implement the consistency of user list in two databases (forum database and main body database) as mentioned in Subsection 2.1.

4 Conclusion

We have presented the design and implementation of a J2EE-based platform for network teaching. The platform has been used in teaching practice for two years. It has been proven that it has brought great convenience for teaching and learning crossing campuses in a university.

In future work, we plan to provide more functions that might be required in practice and plan to improve the performance by applying some new techniques.

References

1. Alonso, C. M. and D. J. Gallego. *La informática en la práctica docente (Vols. I and II)*. UNED, Madrid, 2000.
2. Cheng, W. and P. Poddar.   JDBC, CMP or JDO?, July 2003.   `http://www.ftponline.com/javapro/2003_07/online/wcheng_07_25_03/default.aspx`.

3. Davis, M. Struct, an open-source MVC implementation. `http://www-900.ibm.com/developerWorks/cn/java/j-struts/index_eng.shtml`.
4. Deitel, H. M., P. J. Deitel, and S. E. Santry. *Advanced Java 2 Platform: How to Program*. Prentice Hall, 2001.
5. Eckel, B. *Thinking in Java*. Prentice Hall, 2002.
6. Goodwill, J. *Mastering Jakarta Struts*. Wiley Publishers, August 2002.
7. Holzinger, A. *Multimedia Basics, Volume 2: Learning. Cognitive Basics of Multimedial Information Systems*. Laxmi-Publications, New Dehli, 2002.

A Web-Based Classroom Environment
for Enhanced Residential College Education

Kai Cheng, Limin Xiang, Toyohiko Hirota, and Ushijima Kazuo

Faculty of Information Science, Kyushu Sangyo University,
3-1 Matsukadai, 2-chome, Higashi-ku Fukuoka 813-8503, Japan
{chengk, xiang, hirota, ushijima}@is.kyusan-u.ac.jp

Abstract. In this paper, we describe a web based virtual classroom environment, called WTS (Web-based Teaching Support), to enhance classroom based residential teaching and learning. WTS implements an online view of physical classrooms with the "desks" and "seats". Teaching information associated with "classrooms" is managed by a database system. WTS also includes such capabilities as online attendance check, personalized notification for course participants, as well as a variety of tools to facilitate lecture preparation and post-lecture processing for teachers. We discuss the main design issues and the implementation details. We also evaluate its usefulness by analysis of real-world teaching data.

1 Introduction

College education is primarily conducted on the basis of classroom, a physical place where students and teachers get together and face-to-face interactions take place. Although online learning without face-to-face interactions is getting increasingly popular, residential college education will still be important and cannot be replaced in the foreseeable future. This is because the social aspects of college, e.g., learning in groups, informal faculty-student discussions, and so on, are too valuable and important [4]. Frequent faculty-student contact in and out of classes is the most important factor in student motivation and involvement. Faculty concern enhances students' intellectual commitment and encourages them to think about their own values and future plans [5].

One problem with the classroom-based education is the poor cost / performance record due to the lack of efficient way to manage detailed information for high quality in-class teaching. First, from the viewpoint of pedagogical psychology, it is important for teachers to bear in mind the names and faces for all students participating in their classes. However, this will be a heavy mental burden even for a middle-sized class with tens of students. Second, teachers usually want keep track of the changing attitude of students by observing how student attend a course. A possible way is to observe how a student takes seats in the classroom. This is much more cumbersome because it requires efficient way to gather and manage detailed information about the class participation for all students.

R.W.H. Lau et al. (Eds.): ICWL 2005, LNCS 3583, pp. 56–65, 2005.
© Springer-Verlag Berlin Heidelberg 2005

To cope with these problems, we have been developing a web-based teaching support system, called WTS (Web-based Teaching Support). Instead of focusing on putting teaching contents online, our system is aimed to efficiently manage teaching information by implementing an analogy to physical classrooms with desks and seats. Information associated with courses, participants, teachers are managed in a database system. Students take attendance by simply registering their seat numbers. After registration, they can view an image of their own appearing on the classroom layout.

In the following sections we will describe in detail about the design and implementation of the system. In section 2, we give a brief overview of the system, outline its main features. In section 3, we describe in detail the issues in design implementation of each feature. Section 4 includes the design of the underlying database that supports implementation of the features described so far. We report some evaluation results in section 5. Section 6 includes the concluding remarks.

2   Overview of the Web-Based Classroom Environment

In this section, we give a brief overview of the web-based classroom environment, WTS. Further details will be given in the following sections. WTS supports an online view of a physical classroom with desks and seats and allows online attendance taking by entering seat numbers. It enhances a "real" classroom by management of detailed information about the associated teaching and learning activities, e.g., lecture notes, lecture schedule, course participation and test results.

Fig. 1. The Web view of a classroom (left) and a physical classroom (right) where all students personally hold a rental PC

The system has the following features:

1. *Password Protected Access.* Users (students or faculty members) accessing to the system should provide a valid user id together with a password. The authenticated id is used to enforce access control. Students are only allowed to access their own study records, while teachers can view and modify records of all stu-

dents in his/her class. User id is also used to retrieve associated information for personalization.

2. *Online Attendance Check*. After logging, a student can take attendance online simply by entering his seat number. System records the provided seat number and the associated information about the courses, IP addresses from which this attendance check is made. Attendance check is open for the students who registered to the course and during the time when the course is given.

3. *Seating Layout View*. The system enables an online view of classroom layout. An identification image is displayed as a representation of the student who is taking the specific seat. This feature makes it very convenient for instructors to tell who are sitting on that seat by name and face.

4. *Personal Notification*. Students can check participation status and test grades of their own. They can also ask questions and report problems about the courses and the system as well.

5. *Scheduled Publication Area*. Lecture notes and other resources are put online in accordance with the teaching schedule. For example, sometimes, lecture notes have to be made available after the lecture finished, whereas test questions should be put online for the specific time period.

6. *Aggregate and Statistical Analysis*. The system supports quick summary report and a variety of statistical analysis. This feature cuts the tedious and error-prone statistics work for instructors.

Despite of the above mentioned features, WTS also supports course scheduling and preparation.

3   Enhanced Classrooms with Teaching Information Management

In this section, we describe in detail the design and implementation of three features of importance in WTS. As WTS is a database based application, the implementation involves database operations. We postpone the description of database design to the next section.

As the system is written in PHP script language, in the following description, we use the form of $var, $array[$i] to represent scalar and array variables respectively as in most script languages, such as PHP, Perl, etc.

3.1   Course Scheduling

A course consists of a series of lectures with respect to related sections of course content. Course content is described in detail in syllabus. Lectures have to be scheduled correctly for the specified day of the week (DOW) and period of a day. To automate the course scheduling, the following data or parameters should be provided.

1. N: number of lectures that constitute the course with an course id cid;
2. $day1, $day2: initial and final dates of the term when a course is taught;
3. $holidays: holidays and other specified days that no lecture is given; Holidays are stored in database, allowing insert, update, and delete.

4. $dow, $period: the day of the week and the period for the course to be taught. Both $dow and $period for the course can be retrieved from database.

With these data and/or parameters, system can automatically generate a schedule for the course:

(1) Initialization. set $i=1; repeat (2)~(6) until $i > $N
(2) gets a $day on the $dow from [$day1, $day2] in order;
(3) check if $day is in $holidays;
(4) if $day is a holiday, goto (2) and repeat;
(5) otherwise, insert <$cid, $i, $day> into the schedule list
(6) $i++, goto (2) and repeat;

3.2 Online Attendance Check

Once a student has logged in to the system, he can check the courses that he can attend. In a specific time period, a student is allowed to attend at most one course. Suppose current time is $time, which is in the class period $period. $period and student id $sid are used to retrieve the courses information. If there are some courses to attend, the participation check screen appears and the student is asked to enter his seat number, $seatno. The $sid, $seatno, $time and the associated session data are then recorded in database. Session data is used to validate the operation, e.g., an IP address out of the valid scope will cause rejection to the database.

Once the attendance check finished, students can view their attendance status for this course since its beginning. This is much more convenient than a paper-based attendance check, whose results will be given in a few days and the results may be error-prone.

3.3 Classroom Layout

We now describe the implementation of classroom view. The feature requires a variety of information to be retrieved. First, the layout of the specified classroom should be retrieved from database. The layout is a list of the coordinates and the associated seat number for all seats in that classroom. Second, a list of the occupied seats, i.e. the coordinates and the student id for the one who took the corresponding seat, should also be provided. Finally, the parameters about the classroom have to be described as follows:

1. $layout: list of all seats, in the form of (row, col, pos)=>seatno
2. $seated: list of occupied seats, in the form of (row, col, pos)=>sid
3. $maxrow, $maxcol, $desksize: classroom parameters

Provided these data, we can draw the layout of a classroom as follows.

```
drawLayout($layout,$seating,$maxrow,$maxcol,$desksize){
   for ($i=1; $i<=$maxrow; $i++){ //row by row drawing
      beginNewRow()
      for ($j=1; $j<=$maxcol; $j++){
         beginNewDesk();
```

```
    for ($k=1; $k<=$desksize;$k++){
       beginNewSeat()
         if (empty($layout[$i][$j][$k]) continue;
       else $seatno = $layout[$i][$j][$k];
       if (empty($seated[$i][$j][$k])
          drawSeat($seatno,null);
       else{
          $sid = $seated[$i][$j][$k];
          drawSeat($seatno,$sid);
       }
       endNewSeat();
    }
    endNewDesk();
  }
  endNewRow();
 }
)
```

drawSeat($seatno, $sid) is a function that draws a seat with number $seatno on the desk If student id $sid is null, it draws a black seat. Otherwise an image provided by the student will be attached on the seat. Student id and name will also be printed there.

4 Database Design

The features described so far depend heavily on the database system. In this section, we present the database design issues. We begin with the design of a conceptual mode using ER diagram. We them give the details on how to transform the ER model to relational database scheme.

The conceptual model of the system is depicted in Fig. 2. The ER diagram consists of 6 entity sets (including 2 weak entity sets), and 4 relationship sets. A course consists of a series of lecture. **Lecture** is called a *weak entity set* with *owner* **Course** due to the lack of a natural way to identify it. Similarly, **Seat** is a weak entity set with owner **Classroom** since a seat can not exist independent of a classroom.

Course, **Student**, **Teacher** and **Classroom** are obviously entity sets. However, it is not easy to tell whether **Timetable** should be an entity or relationship. We take Timetable as an entity instead of relationship is for two reasons. Firstly, actually there is a timetable independently designed by registration office staff. Secondly and most importantly, other relationships, say **Study** and **Schedule** depend on an entity that identifies a unique lecture. Such entity is neither **Course**, since a same course may be given by more than one instructor, nor **Teacher**, as one instructor may hold more than one course.

Relationship **Study** describes how student takes courses. The multiplicity constraint M:N, means that a student can take one or more courses and a course can be taken by one or more students. Since a course can simultaneously be given by different instructors at different time, in different classrooms, students have to decide which one to take. Relationship **Schedule** describes the arrangement of dates that a course will be given. The multiplicity constraint is M:N. That is, each course can be given in several times and each content part can be taught by different instructors at different times. Finally, relationship **StudyRecord** describes details about learning activities of students over time. Students take attendance by entering their seat numbers, which will be stored in this **StudyRecord**.

Let R(A1, A2,..., An) represent a relation scheme, where R is relation name, and Ai(i=1,2,...,n) are attributes. Key attribute is indicated by underlining the corresponding attribute. We can transform the conceptual model in Fig. 2 to the following relational database scheme.

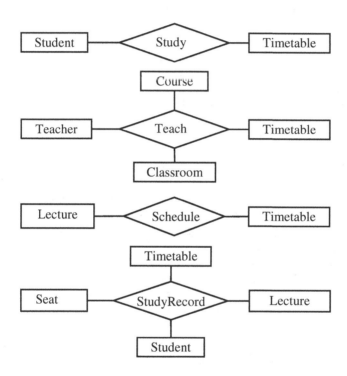

Fig. 2. Entity-Relationship (ER) Model

Course(<u>cid</u>, cname, credit, cyear, cterm)
Student(<u>sid</u>, sname, sex, dept, classid, sdate)
Teacher(<u>fid</u>, fname, sex, dept, office, tel)
Classroom(<u>roomid</u>, rname, capacity, maxrow, maxcol, desksize)
Seat(<u>roomid, seatno</u>, row, col, pos)
Lecture(<u>cid, seq</u>, title, detail)
Timetable(<u>tid</u>, fid, cid, classid, wday, period, roomid)
Study(<u>sid, tid</u>, sdate)
Schedule(<u>tid,seq</u>,sdate)
StudyRecord(<u>sid, tid, seq, srdate</u>, srtime, seatno, ipaddr, hostname, grade)

The detailed information for drawing the layout of a classroom is kept in relations **Classroom** and **Seat**. In **Classroom**, *maxrow* and *maxcol* define the rows and columns of desks in the classroom, while *desksize* indicates the number of seats in each desk, whose typical values are 1, 2, and 3. Seats in each classroom are listed in relation **Seat**. Each seat is associated with the coordinates <*row*, *col*, *pos*>, where *row* and *col* are coordinates of desk and *pos* is a number representing the position of a seat in the desk, e.g., 1 represents the first (leftmost) seat, 2 represents the second seat next to 1, and so on. Given the *roomid* and *seatno*, it is easy to locate seat in the classroom layout.

5 Evaluation Analysis

To evaluate the proposed system, we have analyzed data of the teaching activities accumulated in the past year. The goal is to (1) explore if there are any associations between the seating layout and the test grades. If any what the associations would like to be; (2) find the quantitative evidence to the system's effect. In this section, we present results about these preliminary analyses.

5.1 Deployment Environment

The system has been deployed in the faculty of information science. Our college was set up in 2002 and now there are about 600 enrolled students and 22 faculty members. As a newly-founded college, our faculty is enriched by leading educational infrastructure that can afford to support efficient education. The infrastructure includes:

1. *Personal hold rental PCs*. All students hold a rental notebook type PC once they enroll in the college.
2. *Network sockets for all seats*. Students can access to the Internet through network sockets on all seats of all classrooms.
3. *Lecture video recording*. All lectures given in our faculty are recorded on video. The video archives are online available and can be retrieved through web browsers.

The WTS system has supported two undergraduate courses, "database systems", and "data structures and algorithms" during the last year. The evaluation is based in data accumulated so far.

5.2 Associations Between Seating Layout and Test Grades

In general, students often taking a seat on front of the classroom seem to be those who are join the class aggressively. In contrast, students who often take seats on the rear half of a classroom tend to be inactive because they may be not quite interested in the course.

We analyze the accumulated study records, to see if this can be justified. To investigate the association between seating and test grades for course 'X' of class 'A', we issue the following SQL queries to the database server.

```
SELECT S.row, ROUND(AVG(R.grade),1)
FROM StudyRecord R, Timetable T,
     Classroom NATURAL JOIN Seat S
```

```
WHERE R.tid=T.tid AND S.roomid=T.roomid AND T.cid='X'
     AND S.seatno=R.seatno AND R.classid='A'
GROUP BY S.row
ORDER BY S.row
```

The results for class X of "database systems" and classes for Y, Z of "data structures and algorithms" are shown in Table 1. From the table, we can find that test results are partially associated with seating rows in that

Averagely, students on the first 1~2 rows are better than others. This is shown in Table 1 by bold typed numbers on the right-hand side of each column. Class X and Class Y have two rows with peculiar good grades while in Class Z, only first row with better grades. On the other hand, students seated behind seem not fall into the worst group. The worst groups (underlined in Table 1) are found on the front half near the central line. Table 1 seems to suggest that,

Table 1. Seating status and the grades

Class A		Class B		Class C	
Row	Avg. Grade	Row	Avg. Grade	Row	Avg. Grade
1	**77.5**	1	**83.0**	3	**78.0**
2	**77.0**	2	**85.5**	4	71.5
3	68.0	3	**77.5**	5	70.0
4	65.5	4	_61.5_	6	72.5
5	72.5	5	75.5	7	66.0
6	_64.0_	6	75.5	8	_61.0_
7	69.5	7	74.0	9	72.5
8	69.5	8	79.0	10	74.5
9	69.5	9	72.0	11	72.0
10	66.0	10	74.5	12	73.0
11	67.5	11	74.5	13	69.5

1. Students always taking seats on the first 1~2 rows are the most active learners and their test results are often much better than the rest. In this case, we can say that the association is obvious.
2. The worst group of students is most likely found on the first half of seats near the central row. This indicates that although they did their best and took part in the course quite actively, the results may still be not ideal.
3. Students seating on behind half of classroom form a group between the best and the worst.

5.2 The Quantitative Evidence to the Effects of WTS

Although we have obtained numerous informal feedbacks from both instructors and students during the deployment, without quantitative evidence to the effects of WTS, it is still not quite enough.

To deal with this problem, we have examined the change of absentees for two classes that began to use the system on the half way of the course "data structures and algorithms". As shown in Fig. 3, both class A and class B began to use the system from the lecture 6. The paper-based records for lecture 1 though lecture 5 were manually entered by the instructor after deployment of the system.

From Fig. 3, we can see that due to the deployment of WTS, the number of absentees actually drops down. There are an average 13 absentees in class A during lecture 1~5. However, after WTS is put in use, the average number of absentees' decreases to 9. Similar result can be found in class B: The average number of absentees for lecture 1~5 is 8, whereas the number for lecture 6~13 is down to 6. Therefore, we can conclude that *the deployment of the WTS has positive impact on the improvement of attendance rates.*

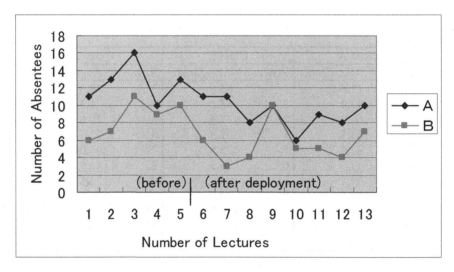

Fig. 3. Change of absentees before and after deployment of WTS: After WTS is put in use, the average number of absentee decreases in both class A and class B

6   Concluding Remarks

The Web provides a convenient platform for efficient content delivery at low cost while the database technology enables efficient management of large amount of data. Combination of the two gives a promising way to enhance traditional classroom based education. In this paper, we have described a web-based teaching support system, WTS. Instead of supporting learners for individual learning as in most E-learning systems, WTS was aimed to support teachers for efficient management of online teaching information. The online view of classroom layout was designed to facilitate teacher-student communications. By preliminary analyses, we have shown the usefulness and potential of the proposed system.

Our future work is to improve the flexibility and scalability of the current system for adoption in more courses. We are also going to investigate the possibility of combining features of E-learning features so as to support off-campus learning. A possible extension is to combine the legacy systems, e.g., lecture video recording system, with the proposed WTS system, so that students can take the "recorded" course if they missed the "live" one. Students can also use the system for review purpose.

References

1. Sheard, J., Lynch, J.: Challenges of web-based learning environments: Are we student-centred enuf? In: Second International Conference on Web-Based Learning (ICWL2003). (2003) 1–11
2. Madjarov, I., Boucelma, O., B´etari, A.: An agent- and service-oriented e-learning platform. In: Third International Conference on Web-Based Learning (ICWL2004). (2004) 27–34
3. Boschmann, E.: The Electronic Classroom: A Handbook for Education in the Electronic Environment. Information Today (1995)
4. Ullman, J.D.: Improving the efficiency of database-system teaching. In: SIGMOD Conference. (2003) 1–3
5. Chickering, A. W., & Gamson, Z. F. Seven Principles of Good Practice in Undergraduate Education. *AAHE Bulletin*, (1987) 39, 3-7.

Adaptive Internet Interactive Team Video

Dan Phung[1], Giuseppe Valetto[2], and Gail Kaiser[1]

[1] Columbia University, New York, USA
[2] Telecom Italia Lab, Turin, Italy

Abstract. The increasing popularity of online courses has highlighted
the lack of collaborative tools for student groups. In addition, the introduction of lecture videos into the online curriculum has drawn attention
to the disparity in the network resources used by students. We present an
e-Learning architecture and adaptation model called AI^2TV (Adaptive
Internet Interactive Team Video), which allows virtual students, possibly some or all disadvantaged in network resources, to collaboratively
view a video in synchrony. AI^2TV upholds the invariant that each student will view semantically equivalent content at all times. Video player
actions, like play, pause and stop, can be initiated by any student and
their results are seen by all the other students. These features allow group
members to review a lecture video in tandem, facilitating the learning
process. Experimental trials show that AI^2TV can successfully synchronize video for distributed students while, at the same time, optimizing
the video quality, given fluctuating bandwidth, by adaptively adjusting
the quality level for each student.

1 Introduction

Life-long and distance learning programs such as the Columbia Video Network
have evolved from fedexing lecture video tapes to their off-campus students to
streaming videos over the Web. The lectures might be delivered "live", but are
more frequently post-processed and packaged for students to watch (and re-
watch) at their convenience. This introduces the possibility of forming "study
groups" among students who can view the lecture videos together and pause,
rewind, or fast-forward the video to discussion points, thus approximating the
pedagogically valuable discussions that occur during on-campus lectures. To that
end, we provide an e-Learning architecture supporting virtual student groups.

Conventional Internet-video technology does not yet support *collaborative
video viewing* by multiple geographically dispersed users. It is particularly challenging to support WISIWYS (What I See Is What You See) when some of
the users are relatively disadvantaged with respect to bandwidth (e.g., dial-up
modems) and local computer resources (e.g., old graphics cards, small disks).
We have adopted technology for "semantically compressing" standard MPEG
videos into sequences of still JPEG images. This technology automatically selects the most semantically meaningful frames to show for each time epoch, and

R.W.H. Lau et al. (Eds.): ICWL 2005, LNCS 3583, pp. 66–77, 2005.

can generate different sequences of JPEG images for a range of different compression levels. It was designed with typical lecture videos in mind: for instance, it recognizes that it is more important to see the blackboard content after the instructor has finished writing, than showing the instructor's back as she writes it on the board.

The remaining technical challenges are *synchronizing* and *adapting* the downloading and display of the image sequences among the distributed students, including support for shared video player actions. We have developed an approach that achieves this using three mechanisms working in tandem. First, the software clocks of the video clients for each student are synchronized using NTP, hence they use the same time reference with respect to the image sequences, where each image is associated with its start and end times relative to the beginning of the sequence. Second, the video clients communicate with each other over a distributed publish-subscribe event bus, which propagates video actions taken by any user to all the group, as well as other events occurring on the video clients. Finally, since we are particularly concerned about disenfranchised user communities that have relatively low bandwidth, the third and main contribution of AI^{2}TV concerns optimizing the video quality according to the bandwidth constraints of each user, while enforcing group synchronization.

A distributed feedback control loop dynamically adapts each video client regarding group synchronization and video quality. The controller relies on sensors embedded in each client to periodically check information about the synchronization state, the buffering level and the bandwidth perceived at each client, and on actuators that in response tune local configuration parameters, such as the choice of both the next image to display and the next image to retrieve from the semantic compression levels available. A single controller is used for all clients in the same group, so it can detect and react to "skew" across the clients; it may reside on the video server or on another host on the Internet.

This paper presents the architecture and dynamic adaptation model of AI^{2}TV, describes how it tackles the challenges of quality optimization and synchronization in collaborating video viewing, and provides an evaluation of the effectiveness of our approach, with empirical results obtained with real lecture videos.

2   Motivation and Background

Correspondence courses have been available for over a century, e.g., the University of Wyoming[1] began offering extension courses in 1892, Correspondence courses have traditionally been designed for individual students with a self-motivated learning style, studying primarily from text materials.

An NSF Report [2] discusses how technology, from radio to television, to audio and video cassettes, to audio and video conferencing, has affected distance education. The report states that the recent use of Internet technologies, especially the Web, has "allowed both synchronous and asynchronous communication among students and between faculty and students" and has "stimulated renewed interest in distance education". It also mentions that "stimulating interaction among students" can help reduce dropout rates, which it says may be higher in distance education than in traditional courses. Finally, it cites some studies that "suggest the Web is superior to earlier distance education technologies because it allows teachers to build collaborative and team-oriented communities".

Even if some Internet–based tools, like instant messaging, application or desktop sharing, and co-browsing can be used to facilitate the communicative aspects of synchronous collaboration, dedicated support for synchronous collaboration in long–distance education over the Web remains a major concern in courses where group work is encouraged [3], since there are few educational tools that offer that kind of support to a group of online students [4]. However, it seems that Web-based video streaming should enable synchronous collaboration "situated" by collaborative lecture video viewing, approximating the experience of on-campus students physically attending the lecture and class discussion.

Our AI^2TV project contributes to synchronous collaboration support for lifelong and distance education, and specifically to the area of collaborative video viewing, to foster virtual classrooms and borderless education. Our design is intended for small classes or small study groups within a larger class, and reaches out to disenfranchised users with dial-up level bandwidths, who still constitute a significant portion of the Internet user community [5], to allow them to collaborate with other users that enjoy higher bandwidth resources.

Collaborative video viewing poses a twofold problem: on the one hand, all users **must** be kept synchronized with respect to the content they are supposed to see at any moment during play time; on the other hand, each individual user **should** be provided with a level of quality that is optimized with respect to her available resources, which may vary during the course of the video.

One way to address the problem of balancing the group synchronization requirement with the optimization of individual viewing experiences is to use videos with cumulative layering [6], also known as scalable coding [7]. In this approach, the client video player selects a quality level appropriate for that client's resources from a hierarchy of several different encodings for that video. Thus a client could receive an appropriate quality of video content while staying in sync with the other members of the group. a We use *semantic compression* to produce a video with cumulative layering. The semantic compression algorithm, developed by Liu and Kender [8], reduces a video to a set of semantically significant key frames. That tool operates on conventional MPEG videos and outputs sequences of JPEG frames. The semantic compression algorithm profiles video frames within a sliding time window and selects in that window key frames that have the most semantic information. By increasing the size of the window, a key frame will represent a larger time slice, which means that a larger window size will produce less key frames as compared to a smaller window size setting.

A conceptual diagram of a layered video produced from this semantic compression is shown in Fig. 1. Note that the semantic compression algorithm produces an effectively random distribution of key frames: when there are pockets of relatively high frequency semantic change, more key frames are produced.

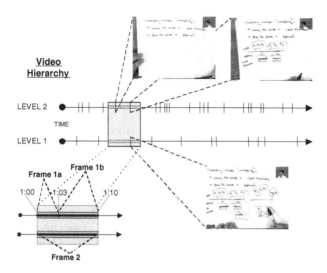

Fig. 1. Semantic Video Scenario

Therefore, the resulting video plays back at a *variable* frame rate, which adds substantial complexity to the bandwidth demands of the client.

The bottom-left in-set shows the juxtaposition of individual frames from two different quality levels. Each frame has a representative time interval [start:end]. For the higher level, Frame 1a represents the interval from 1:00 to 1:03, and Frame 1b represents the interval from 1:04 to 1:10. For the lower level, Frame 2 represents the entire interval from 1:00 to 1:10. In this diagram, Frame 2 is semantically equivalent to Frame 1a and 1b together. However, in real JPEG frame sequences produced from the same MPEG video for different quality levels, start and end times of frame sets rarely match up that precisely.

Through the use of the Liu/Kender video compression algorithm, we can potentially provide semantically equivalent content to a group of students with diverse resources, by adjusting the compression level assigned to each client while watching the video. Thus, for our purposes, synchronization of collaborative video boils down to showing semantically equivalent frames at all times.

To adjust the video clients in response to the changing environment, we use an "autonomic" controller, to maintain the synchronization of the group of video clients while simultaneously fine tuning the quality seen by each student. The controller remains conceptually separate from the controlled video system, and employs our decentralized workflow engine, named Workflakes [9]. Said workflow coordinates the behavior of software entities, as opposed to conventional human-oriented workflow systems; the use of workflow technology for the specification and enactment of the processes coordinating software entities was previously suggested by Wise at al. [10]. Workflakes has previously been used in a variety of more conventional "autonomic computing" domains, where it orchestrates the work of software actuators to achieve the fully automated dynamic adaptation of distributed applications [11, 12]. In AI^{2}TV, Workflakes monitors the video clients and consequently coordinates the dynamic adjustment of the compression (quality) level currently assigned to each client.

3   Architecture and Adaptation Model

3.1   System Architecture

AI^2TV involves the following components: a video server, video clients, an autonomic controller, and a common communications infrastructure, as shown in Fig. 2.

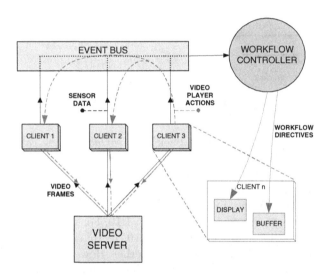

Fig. 2. AI^2TV Architecture

The video server provides the educational video content to the clients. Each lecture video is stored in the form of a hierarchy of versions, produced by running the semantic compression tool multiple times with different settings. Each run produces a sequence of JPEG frames with a corresponding frame index file. The task of the video server is simply to provide remote download access to the collection of index files and frames over HTTP. The task of each video client is to acquire video frames, display them at the correct times, and provide a set of basic video functions. Taking a functional design perspective, the client is composed of four major modules: a time controller, video display, video buffer that feeds the display, and a manager for fetching frames into the buffer.

The time controller's task is to ensure that a common video clock is maintained across clients. It relies on NTP to synchronize the system's software clocks, therefore ensuring a common time base from which each client can reference the video indices. Using this foundation, the task of each client is simplified to displaying the client's needed frame at the correct time. Since all the clients refer to the same time base, then all the clients are showing semantically equivalent frames from the same or different quality levels.

The video display renders the JPEG frames at the correct time into a window and provides a user interface for play, pause, goto and stop. When any participant initiates such an action, all other group members receive the same command, thus all the video actions are synchronized. Video actions are time stamped so that clients can respond to those commands in reference to the common time base. The video display uses the current video time and display quality level to index into the frame index for the frame to be displayed. Before trying to render the needed frame, it asks the video buffer manager if it is available. The video display also includes a control hook that enables the autonomic controller to adjust the current display quality level.

The video manager constitutes a downloading daemon that continuously downloads frames at a certain level into the video buffer. It keeps a hash of the available frames and a count of the current reserve frames (frames buffered) for each quality level. The buffer manager also includes a control hook that enables external entities to adjust the current downloading quality level.

The purpose of the autonomic controller is to ensure that, given the synchronization constraint, each client plays at its highest attainable quality level. The architecture provides an end-to-end closed control loop, in which sensors attached to a generic target system continuously collect and send streams of data to gauges. The gauges analyze the incoming data streams and recognize adverse conditions that need adaptation, relaying that information to controllers. The controllers coordinate the expression and orchestration of the workflow needed to carry out the adaptation. At the end of the loop, actuators attached to the target system effect the needed adjustments under the supervision of the controller. In the AI^2TV case, sensors at each client monitor for currently displayed frame, its quality level, the quality level currently being fetched by the manager, the time range covered by buffer reserve frames, and the current bandwidth. Gauges are embedded together with the controller for expediency in design and to minimize communication latency. They receive the sensor reports from individual clients, collect them in buckets, similar to the approach in [13], and pass the bucket data structure to the controller's coordination engine. A set of helper functions tailored specifically for this application operate on this data structure and produce triggers for the coordination engine. When a trigger is raised, it enacts a workflow plan, which is executed on the end hosts by taking advantage of hooks (i.e., the actuators) embedded in the clients.

Communication among the video clients, as well as between the sensors and actuators at the clients and the autonomic controller, is provided by an asynchronous event bus that channels video player actions, sensor reports, and adaptation directives.

3.2   Adaptation Model

The adaptation scheme consists of two levels: a higher level data flow, and a lower level adjustment heuristic. The former directs the flow of data through a

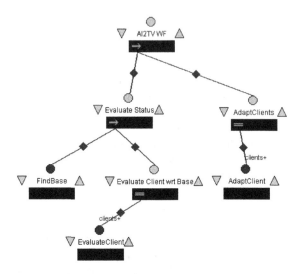

Fig. 3. AI^{2}TV Workflow diagram

logical sequence to provide a formal decision process, while the latter provides the criteria as to when to make certain adjustments.

The higher level logic is shown in Fig. 3. The diagram shows the task decomposition hierarchy according to which the adaptation workflow unfolds. Note that the evaluation of clients' state with respect to the group (`EvaluateClient`) and the issuing of adaptation directives (`AdaptClient`) is carried out as a set of parallel steps. Also note that the multiplicity of those parallel steps is dynamically determined via the number of entries in the `clients` variable.

The adaptation scheme at the lower level falls into two categories: directives that adjust the client in response to relatively low bandwidth situations, and those that take advantage of relatively high bandwidth situations. When a client has low bandwidth, it may not be able download the next frame at the current quality level by the time it needs to begin displaying that frame. Then both the client and buffer quality levels are adjusted downwards one level. If the client is already at the lowest level (among those available from the video server), the controller calculates the next possible frame that most likely can be successfully retrieved before its own start time while remaining synchronized with the rest of the group. The client is then directed to jump ahead to that frame. When a client has instead high bandwidth, the buffer manager starts to accumulate a reserve buffer. Once the buffer reaches a threshold value (e.g., 10 buffered frames), the controller directs the manager to start fetching frames at a higher quality level. Once sufficient reserve is accumulated also at that higher level, the client is then ordered to display frames at that quality level. If the bandwidth drops before the buffer manager can accumulate enough frames in the higher-level reserve, the buffer manager drops back down one quality level.

4   Evaluation

Our assessment considers the ability of AI^2TV to synchronize the clients and to optimally adjust their video quality. Our results were computed from client configurations simulating small study groups which consisted of 1, 2, 3, and 5 clients together running a semantically summarized video for 5 minutes, with sensors probing clients state every 5 seconds. The compression hierarchy we employed has 5 different quality levels.

We define a baseline client against which the performance of our approach is compared. The average bandwidth per level is computed, by summing the size in bytes of all frames produced at a certain compression level and dividing by the total video time. The baseline client's quality level is static for the duration of the video. We provide the baseline client with the corresponding bandwidth to the video server for its chosen level by using a bandwidth throttling tool shaperd. Note that using the average as the baseline does not account for the inherent variability in video frame rate and likely fluctuations in real-world network bandwidth, where adaptive control can make a difference. Each controller-assisted client is assigned an initial level in the compression hierarchy and the same bandwidth as the baseline client for that hierarchy level. For each experimental trial, we record any differences resulting from the controller's adaptation of the clients' behavior *versus* the behavior of the baseline client, with respect to synchrony and frame rate.

4.1   Evaluating Synchronization

The primary goal of our system is to provide synchronous viewing of lecture videos to small groups of geographically dispersed students, some possibly with relatively meager resources. Our initial experiments evaluate the level of synchronization for several small groups of clients involved in a video session. Each client is preset at a designated level of compression and given the average baseline bandwidth required to sustain that compression level. To measure the effectiveness of the synchronization, we probe the video clients at periodic time intervals and log the frame currently being displayed. This procedure effectively takes a series of system snapshots, which we can evaluate for synchronization correctness. We check whether the frame being displayed at a certain time corresponds to one of the valid frames for that time, on *any* quality level. We allow an arbitrary level here because the semantic compression algorithm ensures that all frames designated for a given time will contain semantically equivalent information. We obtain a score by summing the number of clients not showing an acceptable frame and normalizing over the total number of clients. A score of 0 indicates a fully synchronized system.

These experiments showed a total score of 0 for all trials, meaning that all of the clients were viewing appropriate frames when probed. Notwithstanding the variations in the frame rate and/or occasional fluctuations in the actual bandwidth of the clients, no frames were missed. This result demonstrates that the chosen baseline combinations of compression levels and throttled bandwidths do not push the clients beyond their bandwidth resource capacity.

Then we ran another set of experiments, in which the clients were assigned more casually selected levels of starting bandwidths. Said casual selection is representative of real-world situations, like receiving Internet audio or audio/video streams, where users must choose a desired frame rate for the transmission of the content. The user may have been informed that she is allocated a certain bandwidth level from her Internet service provider, but may actually be receiving a significantly lower rate. The clients were assigned bandwidths one level lower than the preset quality level. We ran this set of experiments first without the aid of the autonomic controller and then with it. In the former case, clients with insufficient bandwidth were stuck at the compression level originally selected, and thus missed an average of 63% of the needed frames. In the latter case, the same clients only missed 35% of the needed frames. Although both situations show a significant amount of missed frames, these results provide evidence of the benefits of the adaptive scheme implemented by the autonomic controller.

The data show how in typical real-world scenarios, in which network bandwidth fluctuations and the variable video frame rate do not permit an informed decision about the most appropriate quality level, the adaptive technology of our autonomic controller makes a significant positive difference.

4.2   Evaluating Quality of Service

The most interesting technical innovation of the AI^2TV system is our autonomic controller approach to optimizing video quality. Here we analogously use a scoring system relative to the baseline client's quality level. We give a weighted score for each level above or below the baseline quality level. The weighted score is calculated as the ratio of the frame rate of the two levels. For example, if a client is able to play at one level higher then the baseline, and the baseline plays at an average n frames per second (fps) while the level higher plays at 2*n fps, the score for playing at the higher level is 2. The weighted score is calculated between the computed average frame rates of the chosen quality levels. Theoretically, the baseline client should receive a score of 1. Note that we formulated this scoring system because other scoring systems (e.g., [14, 15, 16]) measure unrelated factors such as the synchronization between different streams (audio and video), image resolution, or human perceived quality, and are not constrained by the group synchronization requirement. This restriction mandates a scoring system sensitive to the relative differences between quality hierarchies.

Our experiments show that baseline clients scored a group score of 1 (as expected) while the controller-assisted clients scored a group score of 1.25. The one-tailed t-score of this difference is 3.01, which is significant for an α value of .005 (N=17). This result demonstrates that using the autonomic controller enabled our system to achieve a significant positive difference in the quality of service (QoS) aspect that relates to received frame rate. Note that the t-score does not measure the degree of the positive difference: To demonstrate the degree of benefit, we measure the proportion of additional frames that each client is able to enjoy. We found that, overall, those clients received 20.4% ($\pm$ 9.7, N=17) more frames than clients operating at a baseline rate.

Running the client at a level higher than the average bandwidth needed puts the client at risk for missing more frames, because the autonomic controller is trying to push the client to a better but more resource-demanding level. To evaluate that risk, we also count the number of missed frames during a video session, which is intended as a separate measure of QoS characteristic with respect to the measure of relative quality described above. In all of our experiments, there was one single instance in which a controller-assisted client missed some frames: in particular it missed two consecutive frames in a time region of the semantically compressed video that demanded a higher frame rate, while at the same time the fluctuating bandwidth available to that client was relatively low.

5   Related Work

Yin *et al.* [17] provide an adaptive multimedia distribution system based on streaming, multicast and compression technology. They show that they can improve the level of QoS, but do not discuss user-level action synchronization, and use quality degradation rather than semantic compression to adapt to client resource constraints. Cen *et al.* provide a distributed real-time MPEG player that uses a software feedback loop between a single server and a single client to adjust frame rates [18]. Their architecture incorporates feedback logic to each video player, which does not support group synchronization, while the work presented here explicitly supports the synchronization of semantically equivalent video frames across a small group of clients.

An earlier implementation of AI^{2}TV is described in [19]. In that version, a collaborative virtual environment (CVE) supported a variety of team interactions [20], with the optional lecture video display embedded in the wall of a CVE "room". Video synchronization data was piggybacked on top of the UDP peer-to-peer communication used primarily for CVE updates, which did not work very well due to the heavy-weight CVE burden on local resources.

Our approach to synchronization can be classified as a distributed adaptive scheme that employs a global clock and operates proactively. The main difference compared to other approaches, such as the Adaptive Synchronization Protocol [21], the work of Gonzalez and Adbel-Wahab [22], or that of Liu and El Zarki[23], is that our approach is not based on play-out delay. Instead, we take advantage of layered semantic compression coupled with buffering to "buy more time" for clients that might not otherwise be able to remain in sync, by putting them on a less demanding level of the compression hierarchy.

Liu *et al.* provide a comprehensive summary of the mechanisms used in video multicast for quality and fairness adaptation as well as network and coding requirements [24]. Our work can be framed in that context as a single-rate server adaptation scheme to each of the clients because the video quality we provide is tailored specifically to that client's network resources.

6   Conclusion

We present an e-Learning architecture and prototype system that allows small, geographically dispersed student groups to collaboratively view lecture videos in synchrony. To accommodate disenfranchised users with relatively low-bandwidth, AI^2TV employs an "autonomic" (feedback loop) controller to dynamically adapt the video quality according to each client's network resources. We rely on a semantic compression algorithm to guarantee that the semantic composition of the simultaneously viewed video frames is equivalent for all clients. Our system distributes appropriate quality levels of video to clients, and automatically adjusts them according to their current bandwidth resources. We have demonstrated the advantages of this approach through experimental trials using bandwidth throttling to show that our system can provide synchronization of video together with optimized video quality to distributed student groups.

Acknowledgments

We would like to thank John Kender, Tiecheng Liu and other members of the High-Level Vision Lab for their help with their semantic compression software. We would also like to thank other members of the Programming Systems Lab, particularly Matias Pelenur and Suhit Gupta. Little-JIL was developed by Lee Osterweil's LASER lab at the University of Massachusetts, Amherst. Cougaar was developed by a DARPA-funded consortium; our main Cougaar contact was Nathan Combs of BBN. Siena was developed by the University of Colorado, Boulder, in Alex Wolf's SERL lab. PSL is funded in part by National Science Foundation grants CNS-0426623, CCR-0203876, EIA-0202063, EIA-0071954, CCR-9970790 and in part by Microsoft Research.

References

1. Miller, J., Ditzler, C., Lamb, J.: Reviving a Print-based Correspondence Study Program In the Wake of Online Education. In: American Association for Collegiate Independent Study: Distance Learning: Pioneering the Future. (2003)
2. : The Application and Implications of Information Technologies in Postsecondary Distance Education: An Initial Bibliography. Technical Report NSF 03-305, National Science Foundation, Division of Science Resources Statistics (2002)
3. Wells, J.G.: Effects of an on-line computer-mediated communication course. Journal of Industrial Technology **37** (2000)
4. Burgess, L.A., Strong, S.D.: Trends in online education: Case study at southwest missouri state university. Journal of Industrial Teacher Education **19** (2003)
5. Richtel, M.: In a Fast-Moving Web World, Some Prefer the Dial-Up Lane. The New York Times (2004)
6. McCanne, S., Jacobson, V., Vetterli, M.: Receiver-driven layered multicast. In: ACM SIGCOMM. Volume 26,4., New York, ACM Press (1996) 117–130
7. Li, W.: Overview of the fine granularity scalability in mpeg-4 video standard. IEEE Transactions on Circuits and Systems for Video Technology **11** (2001) 301–317

8. Liu, T., Kender, J.R.: Time-constrained dynamic semantic compression for video indexing and interactive searching. In: IEEE Conference on Computer Vision and Pattern Recognition. Volume 2. (2001) 531–538
9. Valetto, G.: Orchestrating the Dynamic Adaptation of Distributed Software with Process Technology. PhD thesis, Columbia University (2004)
10. Lemer, B.S., McCall, E.K., Wise, A., Cass, A.G., Osterweil, L.J., Jr., S.M.S.: Using little-jil to coordinate agents in software engineering. In: Automated Software Engineering Conference. (2000)
11. Valetto, G., Kaiser, G.: Using Process Technology to Control and Coordinate Software Adaptation. In: International Conference on Software Engineering. (2003)
12. Parekh, J., Kaiser, G., Gross, P., Valetto, G.: Retrofitting Autonomic Capabilities onto Legacy Systems. In: Journal of Cluster Computing, Kluwer (in press)
13. Gautier, L., Diot, C.: Design and evaluation of mimaze, a multi-player game on the internet. In: International Conference on Multimedia Computing and Systems. (1998) 233–236
14. Baqai, S., Khan, M.F., Woo, M., Shinkai, S., Khokhar, A.A., Ghafoor, A.: Quality-based evaluation of multimedia synchronization protocols for distributed multimedia information systems. IEEE Journal of Selected Areas in Communications **14** (1996) 1388–1403
15. Corte, A.L., Lombardo, A., Palazzo, S., Schembra, G.: Control of perceived quality of service in multimedia retrieval services: Prediction-based mechanism vs. compensation buffers. Multimedia Systems **6** (1998) 102–112
16. Wang, Y., Ostermann, J., Zhang, Y.Q.: Video Processing and Communications. Prentice Hall (2002)
17. Yin, H., Lin, C., Zhuang, J.J., Ni, Q.: An adaptive distance learning system based on media streaming. In: International Conference on Web-Based Learning. (2004) 184–192
18. Walpole, J., Koster, R., Cen, S., Cowan, C., Maier, D., McNamee, D., Pu, C., Steere, D., Yu, L.: A Player for Adaptive MPEG Video Streaming Over The Internet. In: 26th Applied Imagery Pattern Recognition Workshop, SPIE (1997)
19. Gupta, S., Kaiser, G.: A Virtual Environment for Collaborative Distance Learning With Video Synchronization. In: 7th IASTED International Conference on Computers and Advanced Technology in Education. (2004)
20. Dossick, S.E., Kaiser, G.E.: CHIME: A Metadata-Based Distributed Software Development Environment. In: Joint 7th European Software Engineering Conference and 7th ACM SIGSOFT International Symposium on the Foundations of Software Engineering. (1999) 464–475
21. Rothermel, K., Helbig, T.: An Adaptive Protocol for Synchronizing Media Streams. Multimedia Systems **5** (1997) 324–336
22. Gonzalez, A.J., Adbel-Wahab, H.: Lightweight stream synchronization framework for multimedia collaborative applications. In: 5th IEEE Symposium on Computers and Communications. (2000)
23. Liu, H., Zarki, M.E.: A synchronization control scheme for real-time streaming multimedia applications. In: Packet Video 2003. (2003)
24. Liu, J., Li, B., Zhang, Y.Q.: Adaptive video multicast over the internet. IEEE Multimedia **10** (2003) 22–33

A Prototype of the Web-Based Marine Training Environment

Cui Xie, Xiuwen Liu, and Yicheng Jin

Nautical Science and Technology Institute,
Dalian Maritime University, Dalian, China
xiecuidlmu@sohu.com
{liuxw, jycdmu}@dlmu.edu.cn

Abstract. This paper demonstrates an attempt to implement a training platform for marine education and training on the web. A 3D Web virtual training environment for marine education and training is created by re-using high fidelity shiphandling simulation software from existing marine simulators, combining e-learning tools and distributed virtual environment technology. The paper focuses on the 3D modeling, the creation of 3D worlds, the interaction design and the user interface layout of this system. A real-time interactive VR marine environment is critical to this training system. However, 3D multi-user online training on the web is a real challenge for the low network bandwidth and high network latency, which will certainly affect the interactivity of training. Many approaches are employed to optimize the usage of network bandwidth and to minimize the effect of network latency, such as LOD and image-based impostor (billboard) modeling technique, dead reckoning algorithm, partition the VE into areas of interest (AOI) and 2D visibility culling. Finally, a prototype system is implemented based on VRML and Java cooperation.

1 Introduction

In its strictest sense, Web-Based Training is the communication of information over the World Wide Web (WWW or Web) with the objective of instructing or training the user. It is also called e-Learning or online learning [1]. Web-based training is an effective method for users to enhance their learning and skills, both concerning cost and time for training considerations. The major advantage to users is its easy access.

Although most web-based training system employs multimedia technology and other e-learning tools to be attractive and effective for users, users often tend to be restricted to a predetermined learning path through reading and observation or do some exercise. However, the most effective approach to training is to "learn by doing"[2]. So, we take the high fidelity shiphandling simulation into our web-based marine training (WBMT) environment, in which users actually perform a task and experience the results just as if they were really there. There is a qualitative leap that changes the way we react and learn and that stimulates a wide range of both physiological and psychological learning accelerators that are hard-wired within us [2]. Moreover, the integration of distributed virtual environments (DVEs) creates a more friendly and

R.W.H. Lau et al. (Eds.): ICWL 2005, LNCS 3583, pp. 78–85, 2005.

efficient way for training. Since the synthetic virtual environments allow a group of geographically separated users to interact in real time [3,4] and give a shared sense of space, presence and time [5]. Then we merge the web technology and e-learning tools together to create new opportunities for marine personnel to enhance their learning and skills in a web-based environment. With these technologies, marine personnel are able to pursue training from anywhere, and at any time, via a PC and Web browser. To facilitate a variety of functionality in such innovative systems, we employ and extend some technologies to fulfill the users' needs. A three-layer architecture of our system has been presented in my paper [6]. This paper will present the prototype of WBMT environment on three main issues: the creation of 3D worlds, the interaction design and the user interface layout.

2   Creating a Virtual Marine Training World

2.1   Geometric Modeling

As a VR-based Marine training tool, the visual display is an essential component. This is represented by a set of entities, mostly 3D objects, in the virtual environment. In the first prototype system, all objects are created by MultiGen Creator with LOD method, for example, a complex object can be represented by 3 levels: the 3D geometry with texture, the 3D geometry with color and only the texture-based or color-based representation. Most simple objects are represented by one level detail model. Combining with image-based impostor method [7] and polygon reduction rules [8], only crucial shape information are kept for reducing the geometry complexity of each object, the storage space needed and the time required to transfer the objects from the server to a client. Additionally, the visibility factors are considered in our modeling process: only the coastwise buildings and mountains unoccluded by other closer ones are modeled, since our viewpoint is confined to the fairway when we navigate a ship to the port. For VRML [9–11] has already been a standard for the exchange of 3D descriptions on the Internet, all the models are finally exported to the VRML formatted files to construct the 3D training environment. In this process, further revising and optimizing of the VRML files into a compact format was carried out to speed up the loading time from the Internet. Also, all surface textures used in our system is compressed as JPEG image, each size (byte) is small. Moreover, "PROTO, DEF, USE and Inline" nodes in VRML are used to improve the efficiency of modeling the scene. Figure 1 shows a container model at the highest level of details in our system, its file (container.wrl) size is only 31K(bytes).

Then, we construct the scene-graph with quad-tree scene-partitioning technology to accelerate the visibility determination of a certain viewpoint in the scene and support the progressive downloading of the 3D scene according to the current viewpoint. Parent nodes of the quad-tree hierarchy structure describe special-relations between different parts of scene; Leaf nodes are the concrete objects with one or more representations (i.e. a pre-computed collection of models at different levels of detail or a pre-computed image-based impostor). Also each node contains the bounding box information. Finally we got a hierarchy scene-graph with clear semantics and spatial structure.

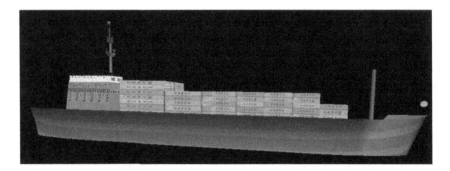

Fig. 1. A VRML model of container at highest level of detail

2.2   Creating a 3D Marine Training World

All the entities in the 3D world are divided into four types: static entity, animated entity, controllable entity and autonomic entity. Mountains, islands, cranes and buildings are all static entities. Animated entities change their state according to a function only of time and possibly a set of pre-defined behavior parameters, such as dynamic ocean waves. The controllable entity in our environment is a virtual ship reacting according to the laws of kinematics and the user's controlling actions. Autonomic entities respond to changes in their environment intelligently. A tugboat or a target ship like a computer generated force fall into this category. With this classification, three dynamic entities' behaviors can be implemented with different methods. Animated entities' behaviors are realized by various "interpolators" and "sensor" or by a "script" node with simple linear functions. Controllable ship's behaviors are realized with a "script" node to receive and react to various exterior events: receiving the helm command and engine command, sending the parameters to ship kinematics models to compute the next position, orientation, linear velocity and angle speed of the ship. Autonomic entity in our environment is ignored to reduce the amount of data to be transmitted over the network. With above work, all the entities in our virtual training environment are uniformly described, organized and managed.

The major technical difficulties encountered was the slowness of the downloading and launching times of the training, which makes the user waiting for more than a couple of seconds and destroys the interactivity. To reduce the bandwidth and computational demands of distributed simulation without introducing additional latency for information dissemination, we transmit less information about each entity and/or transmit entity updates less frequently. Aside from the raw geometry data, the shiphandling training requires the distribution of ongoing events and user actions (e.g. ship movements). For geometry data, we take the polygon simplification, levels of detail (LODs) and image-based impostors/texture mapping methods to reduce the amount of data requested over the network for faster response time. For ongoing events and user interactions, we take dead reckoning method to predict future behaviors of virtual ship by extrapolating behavioral information of the past [12], which works nicely for shiphandling simulation to reduce the amount of updates. 2D spatial culling is used to accelerate the visibility culling and make the DVE scalable. For that it is necessary to partition the VE into areas of interest (AOI)[13] and associate the areas with interest-groups. Combing above technology tactics, we create a 3D marine training scene (see figure 4).

3   Interaction Design

In our system, a virtual ship as an avatar embodies a training participant. There are two types interaction in the system: one is the interaction between the user and his (her) avatar, such as controlling avatar's position and pose by taking the helm or pulling the engine; the other is the interaction among users to keep the consistency of the virtual environment.

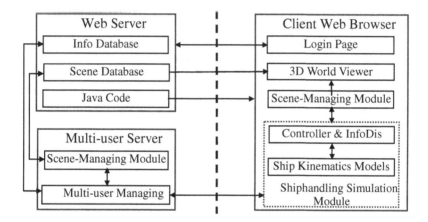

Fig. 2. System architecture in the shiphandling training process

The interaction between the user and his (her) avatar (ship) is implemented by combination of Java and VRML: VRML to provide the visual display and Java code to modify the VRML nodes, update or control the virtual world. The VRML External Authoring Interface provides the link between the two. The Java part is implemented as an applet. The applet provides interaction with user and communication with VRML scene. Java Applet also provides shiphandling simulation function with high fidelity found on the marine simulators [14]. Figure 2 shows the main function modules in our system. When a user gives a helm command or engines command from the controller component, this is transmitted to the ship kinematics model, which then computes the resulting new ship positions, orientations and speed. These are transmitted back to the Viewer and Controller components. The EAI for VRML makes it possible to modify VRML world during performing the shiphandling training.

Multi-user interaction is implemented by Java socket mechanism to administrate and track of each user's avatar (simulated ship) in virtual worlds. Each avatar's state update information is encapsulated into a data package for sending to the server, the server multicast or broadcast this package to all other clients in the same virtual world accordingly. Thus, each client can see the behavior and the state update of other clients, also can be aware of the changes in the scene. This mechanism maintains the consistency of the virtual environment and synchronization of all users□make the virtual worlds shared by multiple users.

The procedure of performing the shiphandling task is as follows. If the login and the training initialization are both successful, the user loads the static 3D scene data and the Java applet onto the local machine from the web server and connects to the multi-user server. The multi-user managing module will communicate with the applet on the client until the client logout. At the same time, it will add the new user's records and notify the scene-managing module of the new user login information. Then the scene-managing module will create the corresponding VRML node information about the new user. This node information is sent to all the online clients for creating the new user's avatar (ship) by the multi-user managing module. Furthermore, the multi-user managing module sends the current information of other avatars online to the new user for synchronization. Each user sends his (her) update information (ship positions, orientations and speed etc.) to the multi-user server every time unit with point-to-point communication mode, and the server multicasts or broadcasts this information to all online users immediately. In this way, an interactive environment with synchronous view is obtained. If the user logout, the scene-managing module will remove user's corresponding node information and inform all related users to remove his (her) avatar.

4   User Interface Design

The prototype of the WBMT environment offers many basic services: providing information, accessing to WBMT web-site, presentation of marine course material, tutorials, marine skill training, sharing knowledge/skills facility (chatting room), etc. In our case, the WBMT site interface layout is shown in Figure 3. Users' first login is necessary to enter the marine training page below. The next is to set the training environment information including the fog, wind, current, the daytime and ship type etc.

In order to achieve a friendly and appealing user interface, the interaction of the user with the virtual training world should resemble real situations. However, in order to meet the simulation training demands (e.g. reasonable response time, minimum hardware and software needs for the user), we must find an appropriate compromise between the desire to design a realistic 3D environment. Thus, we keep the main part of the high fidelity shiphandling simulation of the developed marine simulator and create a concise and plain interface to reduce the overhead associated with learning how to use the complex simulation.

Figure 4 shows the interface provided by a web browser, where the 3D VRML training world and the shiphandling interface created by one Java applet are embedded into a HTML page. The VRML world is a viewer showing the 3D vivid navigation environment. A controller performs most interactions between the user and the virtual ship for ease of use. Communication between the VRML world and the controller is achieved by the VRML External Authoring Interface (EAI)[15], which provides a set of methods that an external application can use to interact with, and dynamically update a 3D scene in real-time. Thus, the rudder or engine operations are mapped from the controller widgets to the virtual s ghip in the viewer through a Java Applet.

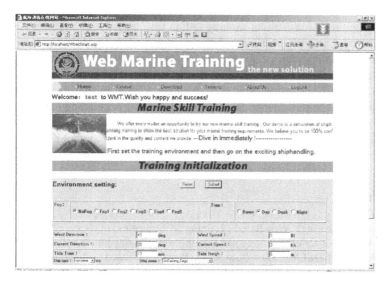

Fig. 3. The home page of the WBMT site

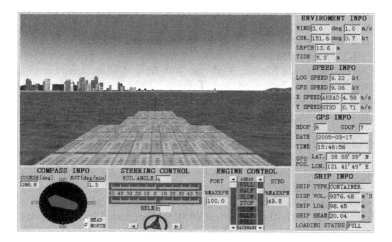

Fig. 4. The 3D shiphandling training environment.

5   Conclusions and Further Research

In this initial study, a web-based VR training system in the field of marine education and training, simulating the shiphandling procedure, has been introduced. A Web-base three-tier architecture has been employed in such a way that VRML and Java can be jointly used to provide both the simulation and presentation. The system creates an interactive and immersible virtual navigation world and allows many users to perform shiphandling and decision-making training online from anywhere, anytime. Although it's visual quality, immersion feeling is not as good as the large scale marine simulation system, this training paradigm can supplement the existing marine training system to improve marine education and training more efficiently.

This paper describes work in progress. There are a lot of further work needs to be done. We would like to reduce the initial waiting time for downloading the 3D scene by incorporate compression and progressive mesh techniques. Meanwhile, we would like to design an optimal and efficient scheduling policy for transmission object models and further effort is to improve the system scalability and it's functionality.

References

1. Ron KurtusAuthoring, Web-Based Training - Strategies to Succeed in eLearning http://www.school-for-champions.com/elearning/wbtauthoring.htm (revised 4 April 2004)
2. RANDALL KINDLEY, The Power of Simulation-based e-Learning (SIMBEL), http://www.flexiblelearning.net.au/leaders/ fl_leaders/fll02/papers/roleplay_fannon.pdf
3. N. D. Georganas et al. 1999. Distributed virtual environments. In Proceedings of IEEE Instrumentation and Measurement Technology Conference—IMTC/99. Venice Italy, May 24–26,1999.
4. Ch. Bouras & A. Philopoulos 1998. Distributed virtual reality environments over web for distance education. In Proceedings of EDEN Conference. Bologna, Italy, 24–26 June, 1998. pp. 481–484.
5. S. Singhal & M. Zyda 1999. Networked Virtual Environments: Design and Implementation. ISBN 0-201-32557-8, ACM Press.
6. Xie Cui , Jin Yicheng, Liu Xiuwen, YinYong. Web-Based Collaborative Learning System Design for Navigation Education and Training. Third International Conference on Web-based Learning –ICWL2004, pressed by Springer LNCS(Lecture Notes in Computer Science) 3143. Beijing, China, August 8-11, 2004. pp:271-276.
7. J. Shade, D. Lischinski, D. H. Salesin, T. DeRose, and J. Snyder. Hierarchical image caching for accelerated walkthroughs of complex environments.In Computer Graphics Proceedings, Annual Conference Series, pages 75–82, 1996.
8. D.Luebke, Developer's Survey of Polygonal Simplification Algorithms, IEEE Computer Graphics & Applications, 21(3), pp. 24-35, May 2001. http://www.cs.virginia.edu/~luebke/ publications/pdf/cg+a.2001.pdf
9. R. Carey & G. Bell 1997. The Annotated VRML97 Reference Manual. Addison-Wesley, 1997.
10. V. Honda, K. Matsuda, J. Rekimoto & R. Lea. Virtual Society: Extending the WWW to support a Multi-user Interactive Shared 3D Environment. Sony Computer Science Laboratory Inc.

11. Web 3D Consortium. The Virtual Reality Modeling Language (VRML)—Part 1: Functional specification and UTF-8 encoding". 1997,
http://www.web3d.org/technicalinfo/specifications/VRML97/index.htm
12. Aronson, J. 1997, 'Dead Reckoning: Latency Hiding for Networked Games', Gamasutra, URL: http://www.gamasutra.com/features/special/online_report/dead_reckoning.htm
13. Hagsand O., Lea R.,Stenius M., 'Using Spatial Techniques to Decrease Message Passing in a Distributed VE System'URL: ftp://ftp.sics.se/users/olof/VRML97/aura.ps.gz
14. Yin Yong, Ren Hong-xiang, Jin Yi-cheng, Sun Teng-da, "Graphic Technology of Distributed Marine Simulation System-V.Dragon 2000", JOURNAL OF SYSTEM SIMULATION, Vol.14 No.5,Beijing, 2002 , pp.617-619.
15. Web 3D Consortium. The Virtual Reality Modeling Language (VRML)—Part 2: External authoring interface. 1999 http://www.VRML.org/WorkingGroups/VRML-eai/Specification/

P2P Video Synchronization in a Collaborative Virtual Environment

Suhit Gupta and Gail Kaiser

Columbia University, 500 W. 120th Street,
New York, NY 10027, United States
{suhit, kaiser}@cs.columbia.edu

Abstract. We previously developed a collaborative virtual environment (CVE) for small-group virtual classrooms, intended for distance learning by geographically dispersed students. The CVE employs a P2P approach to the frequent real-time updates to the 3D virtual worlds required by avatar movements (fellow students in the same room). This paper focuses on our extensions to support group viewing of lecture videos, called VECTORS, for Video Enhanced Collaboration for Team Oriented Remote Synchronization. VECTORS supports *synchronized* viewing of lecture videos, so the students all see "the same thing at the same time", and can pause, rewind, etc. in synchrony while discussing the lecture via "chat". We are particularly concerned with the needs of the technologically disenfranchised, e.g., whose only Internet access if via dialup networking. Thus VECTORS employs semantically compressed videos with meager bandwidth requirements.

1 Introduction

Learning is essentially a social activity and is of paramount importance in engineering project-based courses, where a high degree of cooperation is required [8]. The Columbia Hypermedia IMmersion Environment (CHIME) system [5] [6], created by the Programming Systems Lab (PSL – http://www.psl.cs.columbia.edu) at Columbia University, was designed as a framework for distributed software development environments. CHIME's users would be software project team members who might be geographically dispersed, but could be *virtually* collocated within the same "room" or adjoining "rooms" of a MUD-like 3D virtual world. The layout and contents of this *groupspace* represent the software project artifacts and/or the on-going software process. This model is similar to the one at MIT iLabs [14].

CHIME has more recently evolved into a general collaborative and information management infrastructure. One example of the utilization of CHIME's framework architecture is the visualizing of segments of videos that are pre-taped lectures of classes held here in the Computer Science Department at Columbia University. Distance learning programs such as the Columbia Video Network and the Stanford Center for Professional Development have evolved from mailing (via Fedex and the like) lecture video tapes to their off-campus students to streaming the videos over the

R.W.H. Lau et al. (Eds.): ICWL 2005, LNCS 3583, pp. 86–98, 2005.
© Springer-Verlag Berlin Heidelberg 2005

Internet. The lectures might be delivered "live", but are frequently post-processed and packaged for students to watch (and re-watch) at their convenience. This introduces the possibility of forming "study groups" among off-campus students who view the lecture videos together, and pause the video for discussion when desired, thus approximating the pedagogically valuable discussions of on-campus students. Although the instructor is probably not available for these discussions, this may be an advantage, since on-campus students are rarely afforded the opportunity to pause, rewind and fast-forward their instructors' lectures.

However, collaborative video viewing by multiple geographically dispersed users is not yet supported by conventional Internet-video technology. It is particularly challenging to support WISIWYS (what I see is what you see) when some of the users are relatively disadvantaged with respect to bandwidth (e.g., dial-up modems) and local computer resources (e.g., archaic graphics cards, small disks). The VECTORS (Video Enhanced Collaboration for Team Oriented Remote Synchronization) plug-in was added to CHIME to allow users to synchronize on video based data. This was done by combining techniques that extract key frames from a video stream to create a semantically rich version of the video [13] and fast peer-to-peer UDP packet based synchronization [7], we allow groups of users to watch videos in synchrony, regardless of their bandwidth limitations. We have adopted technology (developed by others, Liu and Kender [13]) for "semantically compressing" standard MPEG videos into sequences of still JPEG images and utilized P2P techniques for synchronizing the semantic content across various clients.

2 Related Work

There has been a rich amount of work done in the field of Collaborative Virtual Environments (CVE) over the years. The key feature of research in CVE has been the social engineering aspect and the attempt to improve the user interface over which users communicate seamlessly with others [8] [15]. Prasolova-Forland discusses the mechanisms employed to improve social awareness in education [8][9] and has found that the traditional technical tools are not enough, and the mechanisms offered by CVEs provide a more promising supplement to the mechanisms in use already.

The advantage the 3D CVEs, with a MUD like interface, gives over traditional web-based collaborative environments is the ability for users to see what his/her peers are doing. We discuss CVEs further in our paper further describing CHIME. [28] In addition to the work that has gone into virtual environments that are geared towards educational purposes, stream synchronization is a widely studied topic in multimedia.

Most intra-stream synchronization schemes are based on data buffering at the sink(s) and on the introduction of a delay before the play-out of buffered data packets (i.e., frames). Those synchronization schemes can be rigid or adaptive [26]. In rigid schemes, such as [22], the play-out delay is chosen a priori in such a way that it accounts for the maximum network transfer delay that can likely occur across the sinks. Rigid schemes work under a worst-case scenario assumption and accept the introduction of delays that may be longer than necessary, in order to maximize the synchronization guarantees they can over even in demanding situations.

Contrary to a rigid approach, adaptive schemes [17] [23] [24] re-compute the delay parameter continuously while streaming: they try to "guess" the minimum delay that can be introduced, which still ensuring synchronization under actual operating conditions. In order to enhance quality of service in terms of minimized play-out delay, those schemes must accept some temporary synchronization inconsistencies and/or some data loss, in case the computed delay results are at times insufficient (due, to variations in network conditions) and may need to be corrected on the fly.

Our approach to synchronization can be classified as a centralized adaptive scheme that employs a local clock and operates in a reactive way. The most significant difference compared to other approaches, such as the Adaptive Synchronization Protocol [17], the work of Gonzalez et al. [21], or that of Liu et al. [20] (which can all be used equally for inter- and intra-stream applications), is that our approach is not based on the idea of play-out delay. Instead, we take advantage of layered semantic compression coupled with buffering to "buy more time" for clients that might not otherwise be able to remain in sync, by putting them on a less demanding level of the compression hierarchy.

Liu et al. provide a comprehensive summary of the mechanisms used in video multicast for quality and fairness adaptation as well as network and coding requirements [19]. To frame our work in that context, our current design and implementation models a single-rate server adaptation scheme to each of the clients because the video quality we provide is tailored specifically to that client's network resources. The focus in our work is directed towards the client-side end-user perceived quality and synchrony, so we did not utilize the most efficient server model. The authors believe that it would be trivial to substitute in a simulcast server adaptation model [26]. Our design also fits into the category of layered adaptation. Such an adaptation model defines a base quality level that users must achieve. Once users have acquired that level, the algorithm attempts to incrementally acquire more frames to present a higher quality video. In the work presented here, the definition of quality translates to a higher frame rate.

With respect to the software architecture, our approach most resembles the Lancaster Orchestration Service [26], since it is based on a central controller that coordinates the behavior of remote controlled units placed within the clients via appropriate directives (i.e., the VECTORS video buffer and manager). The Lancaster approach employs the adaptive delay-based scheme described above; hence the playback of video focuses on adapting to the lowest bandwidth client. That approach would degrade the playback experience of the other participants to accommodate the lowest bandwidth client. Our approach seems preferable, since it enables each client to receive video quality commensurate with its bandwidth resources.

Cen et al. provide a distributed real-time MPEG player that uses a software feedback loop between a single server and a single client to adjust frame rates [4]. Their architecture incorporates feedback logic within each video player and does not support synchronization across a group of players, while the work presented here explicitly supports the synchronization of semantically equivalent video frames across a small group of clients.

3 Our Solution

The goal was two-fold – to create a robust and dynamic collaborative virtual environment that would be a good enough framework for future plug-ins like video synchronization; and to create a near real-time video synchronization plug-in that would allow for students to participate in group based projects despite not being co-located.

3.1 CHIME

Our solution employs multiple extensible techniques that incorporate the advantages of the previous work on collaborative virtual environments. CHIME [5] [6] [28] is a metadata based information management and visualization environment, created to serve as a homogenous environment for heterogeneous applications and data for internet and intranet-based distributed software development. User movement however was the most interesting aspect with respect to the VECTORS plugin as it employed a P2P model. Since user position synchronization is a high frequency process, the publish/subscribe event system did not make for a good vehicle for this job, especially since the event system would add a large parsing overhead to each event that was as simple as coordinates in 3-space. We therefore do user synchronization using UDP packets on a peer-to-peer basis.

3.2 VECTORS

One of our goals for CHIME was to integrate video synchronization for users. Columbia University offers taped courses over the internet as part of their Columbia Video Network (CVN) department. These courses work well when the class is simply lecture based geared towards individuals with assignments that do not require group work. However, for courses like Software Engineering and Operating Systems, where team based software development is one of the critical pedagogical requirements, CVN is unable to deliver a full experience, especially since the students registered for these courses are geographically dispersed. Teams of students may need to watch multiple class lectures together and collaborate on them as they are in progress.

Students are not required by CVN to have the same resources in terms of bandwidth. In order to facilitate synchronized video feeds to diverse users, we had to deliver pre-canned and pre-processed semantically structured videos over heterogeneous Internet links to heterogeneous platforms in an efficient and adaptive manner. Video thus becomes an additional legitimate resource for mutual exploration in a distributed team's workflow.

Liu et al. [12] describe a similar project, however they are simply concerned with the QoS of the video and therefore their approach involves compression techniques

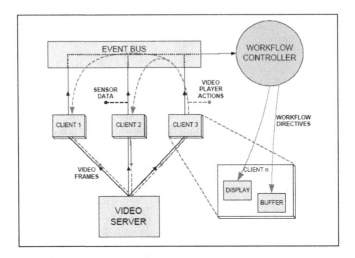

Fig. 1. The VECTORS Workflow

working with Mpeg-7 video. Moreover, they do not have the added requirement of embedding their video stream in a CVE. Our approach involves semantic structuring of the video, using technology previously developed by Liu and Kender [13]. Given this rich video stream consisting of the most representative frames, in terms of content, of the video, our goal was to try and give each user the best possible set of frames in order to enhance the video watching experience as much as possible while staying synchronized. However, instead of following approaches like those employed in commercial multimedia applications like Real Player (http://www.real.com/) or QuickTime (http://www.quicktime.com/) that drop every n^{th} frame upon encountering network lag, which may have the negative side-effect of dropping important segments of the video, we procure separate levels of key frame density, each targeted at different bandwidth levels.

We still, however, have to give each client the correct video feed. In order to do this, our approach was four fold

1. Pre-fetch as many of the key frames as possible at the highest possible quality to the client before a pre-determined meeting time for the group. Meeting times can be ascertained by probing the user's schedule or by simply getting this information from the student directly. Though, it turns out that most videos are watched impromptu without any prior notice.
2. Probe the clients' bandwidth and number of cached frames and report results to the system periodically.
3. React to bandwidth changes in real time by lowering/raising the client to a lower or higher quality feed.
4. Allow pause, rewind, etc. in synchrony while discussing the lecture material via "chat".

All the video streams are made available by the video server. Probing is done by using software probes [10] [11], and reports of any changes are sent to the respective clients. Each client receives data and based on how much video it has in cache, its current position in the video and its bandwidth, the client determines what the highest quality frame it can download next successfully before it has to view it; and downloads it. This will continue until the end of the video.

3.2.1 The Server

VECTORS was proposed to analyze automatic methods for deriving semantic video structure, by finding large-scale temporal and spatial patterns, by detecting redundancies and semantic cross-correlations over long disjoint time intervals, and by compressing, indexing, and highlighting video segments based on semantically tagged visual sequences. We further explored user interaction in distributed environments in both a three-dimensional virtual world as well as a local two-dimensional client. We also analyzed various server cluster configurations, wire protocols, proxies, local client caches, and video management schemes.

The pre-canned and pre-tagged semantically structured video (Figure 2), was placed on the video server. Since the server simply provided the frames to each of the clients, the decision-making responsibility regarding synchronization fell upon the clients themselves; thus leading to a non-centralized decision-making system. The ultimate goal of the server was to analyze classes of particular server cluster configurations, wire protocols, proxies, local client caches, and video management schemes; however, in experiments, we simply treated the server as a black-box that would provide frames over an HTTP stream upon demand from a client. Example of a video frame hierarchy is shown in Figure 2, where we see two example levels of the same video stream. Level 1 has a sparse set of frames while Level 2 is denser, even

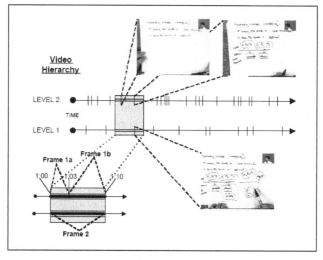

Fig. 2. Video Frame Hierarchy

though they semantically and pedagogically contain the same content. We would like to reiterate that audio was not semantically compressed and was therefore available as a separate and single file for the clients to download and play synchronously with the video stream.

Ultimately, the server consisted of two components, the semantically structured videos provided by Liu and Kender, and the scalable, proxy based video server. Since our goals lay in measuring the effectiveness the video synchronization in the 3D virtual client, we set up a simple web-server that contained the structured video content and simply served it to the clients.

3.2.2 The Client

The VECTORS Client Application, at the initial stage of development, focused on implementing, or at least making significant efforts to implement several functionalities which serve as the core of the VECTORS client side technology. The client that we chose for video synchronization was the CHIME client as it provided the perfect pluggable framework that allows users to see each other in a collaborative world where they can interact with one another and objects that represent heterogeneous back end data sources. The CHIME client is an authoring tool and perfect for pedagogical environments.

Since CHIME had the ability to visualize heterogeneous data sources and was built as a framework, VECTORS was built as a plug-in that visualized video with the added component that synchronized the video. Some of the basic components added to the VECTORS plug-in are –

GroupWare Synchronization – It provides a group-wide viewing session of a given video, each client remaining in sync with an overall video timeline. This is accomplished even if the various clients are at different network speeds (And thus are downloading a variety of different frames from the structured hierarchy that exists on the server).

Video Player in CHIME's 3D Environment – The player is designed to work inside the existing 3D environment offered by CHIME. CHIME utilizes a Crystal Space graphics engine, and all aspects of the video player must comply with constraints set forth by Crystal Space to ensure error free, 3D video display.

Downloadable Video Over HTTP – The video components after being processed and placed on the server, consists of an audio stream (typically a highly compressed, low quality sampled MP3 file, though it could be WAV or other popular audio formats), and a set of JPEG images which correspond to frames of the video at different points in time. These components are retrieved from the Web either before the video is run (in which case they will be cached for use at runtime), or during runtime, at which point they are cached for later use. Therefore, the server, upon processing the video stream into these subcomponents, must publish them to a web server, along with some meta data (such as the number of "compression levels" and start/end times for each frame at each level)

Adjustable Based on Bandwidth- The client adjust its downloading strategy based on the available bandwidth, to switch to different compression levels offered by the server. A compression level is defined as a set of key video frames, a subset of the overall sequential list of JPEG images from a broken-down MPEG video, where each member of this subset is declared to persist over a specific time range.

Cache – Videos, or portions thereof, that were previously downloaded should be stored locally for later use, in an effort to eliminate duplicate downloading. The cache should ideally store all levels of compression for a given video, and provide the best available compression level in response to any frame request. At the same time, the cache should abstract all methods of storage from the player, and simply provide the player with the location on disk of the JPEG frame file to play.

Cache Controller – The client intelligence that allows the users to stay synchronized.

3.3 Implementation Details

In order to get the system to work, we created a small UI within CHIME (see section 4 for figures) that activated a hook that we added into the 3D client. When activated, it would deploy a screen/portal on wall of the room that the client's avatar was in so as to display the downloaded frames within it. Each client was also gives a small cache where they could store pre-fetched video, several probes to monitor the various variables that would control synchronization as well as a cache controller.

The probes included a cache monitor, a bandwidth monitor and a monitor that stated the exact location of the video a client was watching. These are software probes [10] that gather simple metrics and send them back to the cache controller for evaluation, over the publish-subscribe event notification system. As pointed out before, each client sends position updates via a UDP stream to all fellow clients in neighboring rooms so that fellow clients could render avatars in their respective accurate positions. The CHIME servers as well as the Video server note all the clients that start up any given video and assume that they are part of the same student group that wishes to watch the video. Updates about time index of the video that a client is watching is sent to all the other clients in the group.

Before the video even starts, the client tries to ascertain whether the user wishes to watch a particular video by looking up the workgroup calendar and starts to pre-fetch the highest density of frames from the video server so as to provide the best possible video experience. The pre-fetching module is the same component activated when a client pauses a video allowing the client to buffer the next few frames in the idle time.

The cache controller gets information about the contents of the cache, i.e. about the availability of extra frames in the timeline, as well as the position in the video and the current bandwidth (calculated by a simple ping to the server). The cache controller, since having already parsed the hierarchy of frames available in every compression level (gotten by downloading a pre-determined structured document about the frames), makes a decision about which frame to download next in the available time between current time and the time when that frame will be displayed based on available download. The cache controller also knows the duration for which each from will be displayed on the client's screen and uses this information to try and optimize on the level and density of frames to be downloaded. Any pauses by the client are simply utilized to download the highest quality and density of frames possible before the client restarts the video again.

CHIME clients synchronize with one another (peer-to-peer) by sending a time index in the UDP stream at least once every 0.33 seconds. Therefore, our aim was to keep the client always synchronized within 0.33 seconds of one another. If any client got out of sync with the others, the cache controller for that client would either instruct the client to lower or raise the level of frames that were being downloaded.

All VCR functions like play/stop and pause events were sent on the event bus since they were more major events that required action rather than just adjusting. They were also events that needed guaranteed action, something that a UDP packet cannot guarantee. All the clients play, stop or pause depending on the event sent out.

A workflow engine [18] is typically centralized and our workflow engine here had to keep the client in synchrony. Since that was the cache controller's job, the cache controller served as the workflow engine for this project. We found that even though the cache controller was decentralized, it provided us with good results because the logic control for each cache controller was the same. Results of our tests are in Section 4.

4   Testing and Results

We used a test bed of up to 10 clients ranging from 400MHz laptops on a 56Kbit modem up to a 3GHz machine on a 100Mbit network. The resulting experiment kept the videos synchronized between all 10 clients within an error of approximately 4.38 seconds (for the first 7 minutes of the video), i.e. at no point was any client more than 4.38 seconds apart from any other. However, at this point, the system started showing more of a disparity especially on the laptops that do not have native 3D hardware support built in and therefore have to render the virtual environment in Software mode, thus slowing them down further. Figure 3 shows the extremely small variance between the various clients through the entire video while Figure 4 shows that even when we had a test bed of ten clients, they were essentially synchronized through the entire video content.

Some points to note during our test –

1. We started all the client's videos together. We did not attempt to have a client start significantly after the others to that it could "catch up" with the rest.
2. Our tests did not include any handheld devices. However, as long as a CHIME client would run on a handheld device and the PDA has internet connectivity, the synchronization should work in the same way.
3. We noticed that there was tremendous network congestion during the test. After investigation we found that the previously sparse traffic on account of the UDP streams had gone up tremendously. We found that since the position update events were relatively rare, when we used UDP streams for synchronization, the $O(n^2)$ streams (where n is the number of clients) with updates sent every 0.33 seconds from each client to every other client caused a substantial amount of traffic on the network.
4. We found the 3D client of CHIME to be an extremely heavy weight system that took up a lot of system resources on even the fastest machines used in our test.

Therefore each system found it hard to cope with simple task like parsing of synchronization data.

5. Related to the above point, we found that the system stopped working after 7 minutes of run time on account of running out of system resources.

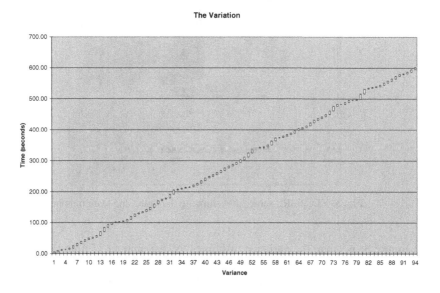

Fig. 3. Average variance of frames over time between clients

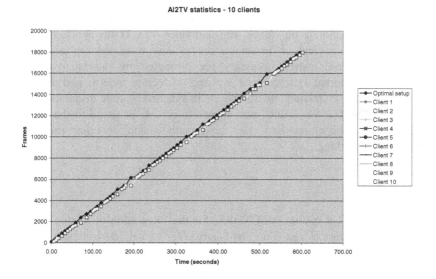

Fig. 4. Performance of 10 clients

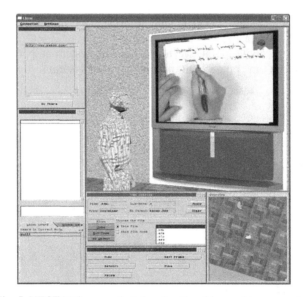

Fig. 5. VECTORS screenshot showing the video and team member

In Figure 3, we map the variance in frames vs. the amount of time taken to show them across the various clients and notice that the variance between two clients did not go over 4.5 seconds. Therefore, at no time were two clients more than 4.5 seconds apart.

Overall, our results show that with the video synchronization works as well as the collaborative tools available. VECTORS was extremely dependent on the stability of CHIME. However, stability issues aside, the system made for an excellent environment for enriching the educational experience. In small lab tests, simulated groups could collaborate on videos well and since VECTORS operated on a highly configurable pedagogical environment, the groups were able to access relevant educational materials when necessary (or prompted by the video). VECTORS successfully supported *synchronized* viewing of lecture videos, and allowed VCR functions like pause, rewind, etc. to operate in synchrony while discussing the lecture material via "chat". VECTORS was successfully able to attend to the needs of the technologically disenfranchised, i.e. those with dialup or other relatively low-bandwidth networking.

5 Conclusion

We had presented a system, VECTORS, for the integration of lecture videos, with video synchronization, into a low-bandwidth virtual environment specifically designed for virtual classrooms for distance learning students.

This system has been designed as a plug-in to the previously developed collaborative virtual environment (CVE), CHIME, for small-group virtual classrooms.

VECTORS uses a peer-to-peer synchronization approach to support group viewing of lecture videos. By utilizing this approach, we have found that groups of co-located or non-co-located students can work together on group based assignments. In order to cater to group members with low bandwidths, instead of going with traditional approaches that involve skipping every n^{th} frame of a video, VECTORS employs semantically compressed and pre-canned videos and adjusts the clients among various compression levels so that they stay semantically synchronized. The videos are displayed as a sequence of JPEGs on the walls of a 3D virtual room, requiring fewer local multimedia resources than full motion MPEGs. As the results demonstrate, we have achieved a high degree of synchrony and have thus created a robust and useful pedagogical environment.

Acknowledgements

The Programming Systems Laboratory is funded in part by National Science Foundation grants CNS-0426623, CCR-0203876, EIA-0202063, EIA-0071954 and CCR-9970790, and in part by Microsoft Research.

References

[1] C. Bouras, A. Philopoulos, Th. Tsiatsos, "e-Learning through Distributed Virtual Environments", J. of Network and Computer Applications, July 2001.

[2] Christos Bouras, Dimitrios Psaltoulis, C. Psaroudis, T. Tsiatsos "An Educational Community Using Collaborative Virtual Environments". ICWL 2002: 180-191

[3] Dan Phung, G Valetto, Gail Kaiser, "Autonomic Control for Quality Collaborative Video Viewing", Computer Science Dept., Columbia University TR# cucs-053-04

[4] J. Walpole, R. Koster, S. Cen, C. Cowan, D. Maier, D. McNamee, C. Pu, D. Steere, and L. Yu. A Player for Adaptive MPEG Video Streaming Over The Internet. In 26th Applied Imagery Pattern Recognition Workshop. SPIE, October 1997

[5] Stephen E. Dossic, Gail E. Kaiser, "CHIME: A Metadata-Based Distributed Software Development Environment", Joint 7th ESEC Conference and 7th International Symposium on the Foundations of Software Engineering, Sept. 1999

[6] S. Dossick, "Groupspace Services for Information Management and Collaboration", PhD Thesis, Columbia University, November 2000

[7] Stefan Fiedler, Michael Wallner, Michael Weber, "A Communication Architecture for Massive Multiplayer Games" Postion Paper, NetGames 2002

[8] Ekaterina Prasolova-Forland, "Supporting Social Awareness in Education in Collaborative Virtual Environments", Int. Conf. on Engineering Education, 2002

[9] Ekaterina Prasolova-Forland, "Supporting Awareness in Education: Overview and Mechanisms", In proceedings of ICEE, 2002

[10] Philip N. Gross, Suhit Gupta, Gail E. Kaiser, Gaurav S. Kc and Janak J. Parekh, "An Active Events Model for Systems Monitoring", Working Conference on Complex and Dynamic Systems Architecture, December 2001

[11] Gail Kaiser, Giuseppe Valetto, "Ravages of Time: Synchronized Multimedia for Internet-Wide Process-Centered Software Engineering Environments", 3rd ICSE Workshop on Software Engineering over the Internet, June 2000

[12] J. Liu, B. Li, and Y.-Q. Zhang, "Adaptive Video Multicast over the Internet", IEEE Multimedia, Vol. 10, No. 1, pp. 22-31, January/February 2003

[13] T. Liu, J. Kender, "A Hidden Markov Model Approach to the Structure of Documentaries", Content-Based Access of Image and Video Libraries, 2000

[14] http://i-lab.mit.edu

[15] S. Benford, D. Snowdon, C. Greenhalgh, "VR-VIBE: A Virtual Environment for Co-operative Information Retrieval", Computer Graphics Forum, 1995

[16] Thanasis Daradoumis, Fatos Xhafa, Joan Manuel Marquès, "Evaluating Collaborative Learning Practices in a Virtual Groupware Environment", CATE 2003

[17] K. Rothermel, T. Helbig, "An Adaptive Protocol for Synchronizing Media Streams", Multimedia Systems, Volume 5, pages 324-336, 1997

[18] Jason Nieh, Monica S. Lam, "A SMART Scheduler for Multimedia Applications", ACM Transactions on Computer Systems (TOCS), 21(2), May 2003

[19] J. Liu, B. Li, Y.Q. Zhang, "Adaptive video multicast over the internet" IEEE Multimedia, 10(1):22-33, January/March 2003

[20] H. Liu, M. E. Zarki, "A synchronization control scheme for real-time streaming multimedia applications", In Packet Video, April 2003

[21] A. J. Gonzalez, H. Adbel-Wahab, "Lightweight stream synchronization framework for multimedia collaborative apps", Comp. and Communications 2000

[22] D. Ferrari, "Design and application of a delay jitter control scheme for packet-switching internet works", In 2nd International Conference on Network and Operating System Support for Digital Audio and Video, pages 72-83, 1991

[23] J. Escobar, C. Partridge, and D. Deutsch, "Flow synchronization protocol", IEEE Transactions on Networking, 1994

[24] A. Campell, G. Coulson, F. Garcia, and D. Hutchison, "A continuous media transport and orchestration service", In SIGCOMM92: Communications Architectures and Protocols, pages 99-110, 1992

[25] http://unreal.epicgames.com

[26] Suhit Gupta, Gail Kaiser, "A Virtual Environment for Collaborative Distance Learning With Video Synchronization", CATE, March 2004

Virtual Experiment Services

Li-Ping Shen, Rui-Min Shen, and Ming-Lu Li

Department of Computer Science & Engineering, Shanghai Jiaotong Univ.,
HuaShan Rd. 1954#, Shanghai, 200030, China
{lpshen, rmshen, mlli}@mail.sjtu.edu.cn

Abstract. There is increasing recognition of the need for laboratory experience that is through these experiences that students could deepen their understanding of the conceptual material, especially for the science and engineering courses. Virtual Experiment has advantages over physical laboratory at many aspects. Nowadays virtual experiments are mostly stand-alone applications without standard interface, which are difficult to reuse. Moreover it is a challenging for compute and data intensive virtual instruments to be reasonably responsive. In this paper, we propose a virtual experiment model based on novel grid service technology. In this model we employ two-layered virtual experiment services to provide cheap and efficient distributed virtual experiment solution. This model could reuse not only virtual instruments but also compositive virtual experiments. In order to reuse successfully-deployed virtual experiment, we advance a uniform schema to describe a virtual experiment plan and process.

1 Introduction

As modern society steps into the information age, e-Learning has taken on increased importance in many facets of life. Universities give more and more courses through web-based courseware, and more and more employees begin to enrich their knowledge through courses provided by company intranet or education institutes. The present web-based courses are always composed of video, audio, figures, exercises and text, with little interactive and personal experience. There is increasing recognition of the need for laboratory experience. It is through these experiences that students could deepen their understanding of the conceptual material, especially for the science and engineering courses. Virtual Experiment (VE) could supply such a gap.

VE is powerful application software system which simulate physical lab environment. With the up-to-date computer and multimedia technology, VE could provide students highly immersion and rich experience. It is a high-valued teaching and learning tool, not only for e-Learning courses but also for traditional courses. It has many advantages over physical laboratory.

- A cost effective way to leverage expensive equipments and maintain physical laboratory by lab attendants. In the face of rapid technology advances, maintaining an up-to-date laboratory presents a significant challenge to universities [14].

R.W.H. Lau et al. (Eds.): ICWL 2005, LNCS 3583, pp. 99–110, 2005.

- Provide concurrent on-line instruction, visualization, repeated practice and feedback; break the geographical, lab space and time constraints.
- Provide experiments that can't really be done in the physical lab, e.g. an experimental study of Newton's second law, simulation of a nuclear power plant.
- Flexibility and adaptability. You can adapt a virtual instrument to your particular needs without having to replace the entire devices; however, the users generally cannot extend or customize physical instruments.
- Enabling convenient and economic access to expensive and specialized instruments reuse through remote control, enabling cooperative experiment and research.

Early players of VE include Virtual Physics Laboratory [16] in University of Oregon, Control the Nuclear Power Plant [17] in Swedish Linkopings University, The Interactive Frog Dissection [18] in University of Virginia, Visual Systems Laboratory [19] in University of Central Florida and Oorange for Experimental Mathematics [20] in Technique University Berlin. The common points of these VE are:

- Implemented as stand-alone applications using Java Applet and Virtual Reality techniques.
- Extensive effort have been put into these virtual experiments
- The main components of VE, virtual instruments (VI), are difficult to reuse.
- Technology used is typically beyond an average educator.

It is energy and capital consuming to design and develop a VE/VI to perform the functions of a traditional experiment/instrument. It is a waste of time and energy if we couldn't reuse these VEs/VIs. Not only the simulation VI needs to be reused, but also the expensive physical instruments do. Thanks to the advanced network technologies, scientists now could access remote instruments efficiently [15]. Though the core function is provided by a physical instrument, the interface to the user is the soft panel on the client PC and data are communicated between soft panel and the instrument driver through network which is transparent to the user, so the remote-control enabled instrument is also a VI. It is the trend to provide reusable and efficient VIs for the quick and cheap VE deployment. Albert Ip and Ric Canale introduces a conceptual model of reusable "virtual apparatus" for designing virtual experiments with emphasis on minimizing the technical burden on the teacher by using generic programmable objects in [2]. In their model, Virtual apparatus are software components that can be dynamically combined together to create a virtual experiment. Virtual apparatus could either run on a remote server, or download to the local client, according to the requirement of communication and computation.

In order to make VIs reusable and interoperable, VXIbus Consortium[7] has take great efforts to establish standards to ensure instrument hardware interoperability, while VXI plug&play Systems Alliance[8] addresses the software level interoperability of VIs. For example the VXI-11.1[9] defines TCP/IP-VXIbus Interface Specification and the VPP-4.1 specification [10] provides a standard Virtual Instrument Software Architecture (VISA). But VXI and VXIplug&play standards don't address the implementation of a VE as a whole, i.e. how to organize the instruments into a VE.

They only provide attributes access without functional and taxonomic description of a VI. It is an urgent requirement for us to devise a standard interface of VI and an intelligent mechanism for teachers to design a VE without much unnecessary effort.

It is also a challenge for compute and data intensive VI to be reasonably responsive. The XPort project [15] exploits a combination of advanced Grid services and remote instrument technologies to achieve interactive "better-than-being-there" capabilities for remote experiment planning, operation, data acquisition and analysis with several X-Ray crystallography facilities.

The outline of this paper is as follows. Section 2 describes the design requirements of VE. Section 3 set forth the layered structure of VE Services, which base on the grid services and Globus Toolkit 3. The model of the VE grid employing VE services is introduced at section 4 and section 5 concludes this paper.

2 Design Envisioning of Virtual Experiment

There is no doubt that VE is a complex system, it is an integral running environment which provide the container for involved VIs. On the basis of top-down analysis,VE consists of three parts: programming by programmers, designing by teachers and experimenting by students. A successful VE system must ensure that programmers could develop VE software according to standard architecture and interface for the sake of interoperability and easy maintenance, teachers with no other expertise but their own instructional field could design VE easily, and the students could enjoy and immerse VE anytime and anywhere with graphics interface. So different people may have different responsibilities here in the VE, a teacher need not be a programmer at the same time.

The VE model is based on the component model in software engineering. VE software components can be dynamically combined together to create a VE. There are three major components in the model [2]:

- Virtual Instruments
- Virtual Experiment work bench and
- Virtual Experiment constraints computing

VI is the main component that could be manipulated easily, interoperable, could be assembled together to form new experiment and could reflect behaviors of the real world. The VE work bench is the components container, managing and linking the VIs together. Work bench is the VI communication broker, only through which VIs could interact. The VE constraints computing component denotes the experiment principles, the expressions holding in the VI together. For example, when two moving objects collide on a smooth land (the friction coefficient is zero), then the applicable constraints are the momentum and energy conversation laws as equation 1. When the students interact with the VE by clicking, dragging and so on, these interactions fire up events of the VIs. The events are parsed and processed by the work bench, invoking constraints computing when necessary, altering the parameters of the VI, and creating response to the learner accordingly. In order to be reusable and interoperable, VI must have standard description and interface, and VE must have standard description of the constraints and rules.

m1v1(t1)+m2v2(t1)=m1v1(t2)+m2v2(t2)   and

1/2*m1(v1(t1))2+1/2*m2(v2(t1))2=1/2*m1(v1(t2))2+1/2*m2(v2(t2))2

let: (1)

mi : the mass of the ith object, i=1,2

vi(tj) : the velocity of the ith object at time tj , i=1,2, j=1,2

A VE isn't limited or confined to a stand-alone PC. In fact, with recent developments in network technologies and the Internet, it is more common for experiments to use the power of the connectivity for the purpose of task sharing. Typical examples include distributed instruments and monitoring, device remote access, as well as data analysis or result visualization from multiple locations. Most importantly, a successful VE should be reasonably responsive.

3   Virtual Experiment Services

Upon the analysis above, VE firstly is made up of distributed multi-vendor components, which reside in heterogeneous machine within different control domains, and which must provide standard interfaces and descriptions in order for reusability. Secondly, a VE, which must hold all its components together to produce high efficiency, should use open and standard protocols and interfaces. And finally VE demand high QOS and performance to construct a real-time and interactive environment. According to the three point checklist for the gird [5], it is reasonable that we use the novel Grid technology to construct a VE Grid to provide dependable, consistent, pervasive and inexpensive access to VEs.

Our proposed VE architecture is based on the widely acknowledged middleware product, the newly released version of Globus (GT3), which includes an Open Grid Services Architecture [1] implementation to provide an interoperable, industry-usable platform. There are three lays in GT3 architecture [6], from bottom up including: the GT3 core which implements all OGSI specified interfaces and the Grid Security Infrastructure, the GT3 base services which implement both existing Globus Toolkit capabilities(for example The Monitoring and Discovery Service (MDS), Globus Resource Allocation Manager (GRAM), GridFTP, Reliable File Transfer (RFT), Replica Location Service (RLS)) and new capabilities such as reservation and monitoring, and higher-level services.

Fig.1 describes the layered architecture of VE Services. The VE Services are organized in two hierarchical levels: the core VE Services layer and the high-level VE Services layer. The core VE Services layer offers basic services for VE resource lookup and location, and data management. These services include VE directory services, resource allocation services and data management services, which are implemented directly on top of generic grid services. The high-level VE services layer provides services for users to organize and access resources. It consists of VI access services, tool access services and result presentation services.

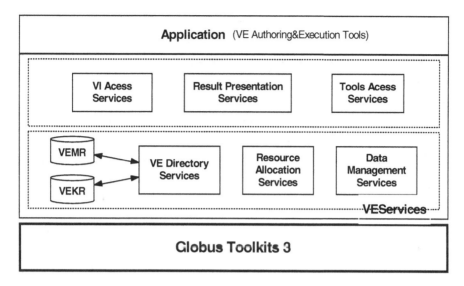

Fig. 1. Layered Architecture of VE Services

3.1 Core VE Services Layer

This layer employs basic grid services to provide data management and resource management. For the VE Services, data are the input/output data for the VI, analysis tools and constraint computing, while resources include VI, analysis & visualization tools and constraints computing tools besides the generic grid resources such as CPU, memory and database. The Core VE Services layer comprises three main services.

VE Directory Service (VEDS)
VEDS extends the basic Globus MDS service and it is responsible for maintaining a description of all resources used in the VE grid and responding to queries of available resources. The resources may be VI Services, tools and algorithms to analyze and visualize data, data source and data sinks, stored VE processes etc. Each metadata instance includes the following information: factory that allows a client to retrieve a reference to the service, category, keywords, the input/output parameters, typical execution time, constraints such as platform and human-readable description. The metadata information is presented by XML documents and is stored in a VE Metadata Repository (VEMR).

Another important repository is the VE Knowledge Repository (VEKR). VEKR stores and provides access to VE process performed within the VE Grid. It warehouses the VE's process information (past experience) and allows this knowledge to be reused. Once users have constructed successful VE processes they wish to be re-used, they can publish them as new services. In order to enable this function, firstly we need uniform description of a VE. The information needed here include the organization of the resources, the resources metadata description, the steps of the process and the experiment principles (constraints).

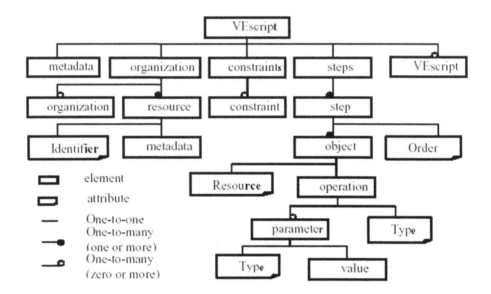

Fig. 2. VE Description Schema

Fig. 2 is our proposed model of the VE description. Vescript is the root element, consisting of four sub-elements: metadata, organization, constraints and steps. Vescript element can have zero or more nested sub-vescripts. Metadata element describes the VE process, including the same information as VEMR metadata. Organization element describes all the resources used during the whole VE process. It includes one or more resource sub-element and zero or more nested sub-organization. The metadata of resource element is extracted from the VEMR. Resource element has an attribute identifier which is unique within the vescript. The constraints element may have zero or more constraint sub-element which is expressed in MathML[21]. The steps element has an order attribute to indicate the operation sequence and one or more object sub-elements. The resource attribute of object references one of the resource identifiers defined in the resource element. The operation sub-element of object has type attribute to denote whether the operation is create, destroy, initialize, input, change or output. If the operation is initialize, input, change or output, one or more parameter elements are required to record the values.

The VE script is stored in VEKR as XML format, so we can transform the VE process data into human-readable reports on demand. The metadata of the VE process needs to be registered and stored into the VEMR. Once registered, this new process can be used as a service in its own right or as a part of a more complex VE process.

Resource Allocation Service (RAS)
This service is used to find the best mapping between a VE design and available resources, with the goal of satisfying the application requirements (network bandwidth, latency, computing power and storage) and grid constraints. RAS is

directly based on the Globus GRAM services. The selection process is based on the Condor matchmaking algorithm [12], and the resources requests are communicated via a synchronous, query-response protocol based on the ClassAds syntax defined within the Condor project [13]. A ClassAd is a set of expressions that must all evaluate to true in order for a match to succeed.

The location where each service of a VE is executed may have a strong impact on the overall performance of the VE. When dealing with very large data, it is more efficient to keep as much of the computation as near to the data as possible [4]. So the service location is always decided based on the location of preceding services. Another consideration is the compromise between communication and computation [3]. In general, when the computation power is provided by a server, the demand on communications will be high. For example, one virtual experiment uses powerful server to process the requests from the clients and returns the images. This approach generates a lot of traffic on the network and the response time is usually unpredictable. This approach is suitable in situations where the main processing cannot be provided by the client's machine. When sufficient computational power is provided by a local client machine, there will be less demand on communications. To create a reasonably responsive virtual experiment, a compromise has to be made to balance the requirements of communication and computation. A simple allocation algorithm leveraging the above considerations is used to determine the "best" resources as follows.

1. [
2. CompuTime=Typical Execution Time stored in VEMR;
3. CommuTime=inLatency + inData/inBandwidth+ outLatency +
    outData/inBandwidth;
4. Coex=1.2;
5. ExecTime= CompuTime + CommuTime*coex
6. Rank= 1/ExecTime;
7.]

Line 2 gives the computation time which is estimated as the Typical Execution Time stored in VEMR. Line 3 computes the time needed to transfer the input/output data, where inLatency/outLatency is the network latency of the input/output channel, inData/outData is the amount of the input/output data measured by bit and inBandwidth/outBandwidth is the bandwidth of the input/output channel. Line 4 and 5 gives the value of ExecTime where we give more power to CommuTime because communication time is prone to gain by reason of congestion. Finally rank is the reciprocal of ExecTime, which is the basis for selection.

Data Management Services (DMS)
The DMS is responsible for the search, collection, extraction, transformation and delivery of the data required or produced by the VI, analysis & visualization tools, and constraints computing tools. Data produced by a remote service may be either stored at the same host of the service executed or collected at a central database, or transferred to next service directly. This information is managed by DMS. DMS service is based on the Globus GridFTP, RFT and RLS services. The goal of DMS is

to realize individual warehouse, a single, large, virtual warehouse of a VE data. It deploys a data grid for a VE.

High-Level VE Services Layer

This layer includes services used to search, select and access resources of the VE grid. Moreover, this layer offers services of result visualization. It is the programming interfaces for VE work bench and VEAES developers. Main services are as follows.

VI Access Services (VIAS)

This service is responsible for the search, selection, and deployment of distributed VIs, employing the services provided by VEDS and RAS. The VIs may be simulation software, or remote control physical instruments. The VIs may be implemented as java applet which could be downloaded to the client side, or a web service which will be run at server side or a grid service which will be executed in a Virtual Organization [1]. No matter which kind it is, VI should have standard soft front panel. We don't recommend java applet VIs, because they are difficult to communicate.

Tool Access Services (TAS)

This service is responsible for the search, selection, and deployment of distributed VE tools, employing the services provided by VEDS and RAS. The tools may provide services for data analysis and management, VE constraint computing, and data visualization.

Result Presentation Services (RPS)

Result visualization is a significant step in the VE process that can help students in the VE result interpretation. This service specifies how to generate, present and visualize the data produced by VI and analysis tools. The result could be recorded and stored either as XML format or visualization format.

4   Model of Virtual Experiment Grid

After the general description of the VE Services, here we describe how they are exploited to model the VE grid. Fig.3 shows the different components of the VE grid. In this model teachers and students at the client side could access the resources at the back-end through VE services transparently.

4.1   Clients

The clients are environments for authoring, executing VE and accessing VE Services. A VE Authoring & Executing Tool (VEAET) is offered at client side. VEAET provides services for teachers to design VE plans easily, and for students to execute VE plans. A VE plan is represented by a graph describing resource composition. A node in the plan graph denotes access to one of the distributed resources including VI, tools etc, and a line between nodes describes the interaction and data flows between the services and tools. With this visual tool, a teacher can directly design the VE plan

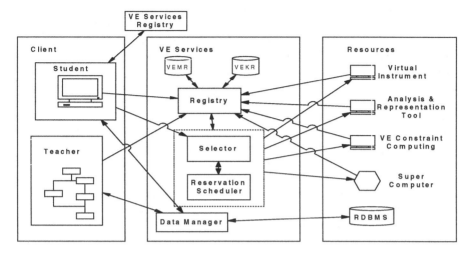

Fig. 3. Model of the Grid Service Based VE

by selecting and dragging. A VE plan could be recorded and stored as XML format locally or published remotely, with the schema figured in Fig.2.

A VE plan could be loaded and executed with VEAET by students anytime and anywhere. Every resource in the VE plan could be mapped and accessed through VI access services, tool access services and result presentation services. When a VE plan is loaded and set to startup, it will firstly get initialized by VEAET. VEAET, acting on the user's behalf, contacts a VE registry that a relevant Virtual Organization maintains to identify VE service providers. The request specifies requirements such as cost, location or performance. The registry returns handles identifying a VE Services that meet user requirements—or perhaps a set of handles representing candidate services. In either case, the user identifies appropriate services. Then VEAET issues requests to the VE services factory specifying details such as the VE operation to be performed, and initial lifetimes for the new VE service instance. Assuming that this negotiation proceeds satisfactorily, a new VE service instance is created with appropriate initial state, resources, and lifetime. The VE service, afterwards, initiates queries against appropriate remote VIs, tools and constraints computing, acting as a client on the user's behalf. Appropriate factories of the relevant resources are selected and then returned from the VE services to the client VEAET. The VEAET is responsible for activating execution on the selected resource as per the scheduler's instruction and then binds the new service instances to the VE plan.

A successful outcome of this process is that a VE plan is transformed into an executable VE. During the execution course, VEAET periodically updates the status of VE execution and records the VE process with the schema in Fig.2 as XML format. Teachers and students could publish a successfully executed VE process through VEDS for further reuse.

4.2 VE Services

The VE services comprise four modules. The registry, with two databases of VE Metadata Repository and VE Knowledge Repository, acts as a VEDS maintaining the registry information of the service providers. The selector uses Grid Resource Information Service to enquire about the dynamic status of resources and uses RAS to select best resources. The reservation scheduler is used to carry out resource reservation. And the data manager is responsible for index, storage and delivery of all the input/output data during the whole VE process.

When the selector receives a request in the form of a ClassAd, it invokes the matchmaking algorithm against the registry representing the available resources, and returns the match list, where the order is determined by the computed ranks, i.e. the "best" match is the first element of the list. The reservation scheduler then makes reservation decisions on behalf of the user. Considering that multiple instances of a resource may be created on a same host, and some resources (such as remote control device) couldn't be accessed by different applications simultaneously, reservation is very important for high-performance VE. The scheduler is based on very simple request-response syntax. A reservation request consists of the computing resources needed such as minimum memory, starting time, the time period and lock information, it returns SUCCESS if the reservation is made, else returns FAILURE and reply with a list of its available resources, available service time etc. If it fails and the user is yet satisfied with the returned parameters, a second time of reservation request will be issued to the same resource with renewed parameters, else a new request will be sent to the next "best" match.

When the "best" match is selected and reserved, the VE plan is ready to run at scheduled time. During the whole run time, the data manager is always at service to index, collect and transfer the input/output data of the VE.

4.3 Resources

The resources of the VE grid include the VI, analysis & visualization tools and VE constraint computing tools, in addition to the ordinary resources such as CPU, memory, and database. These resources may also be implemented upon grid services. For example, considering a VI where a range of sensors produces large volumes of data about the activity of genes in cancerous cells, these data record how each gene responds to the introduction of a possible drug. The analysis to identify potential drugs is both a compute and data intensive task. In order to provide cheap and efficient solutions, grid technology has been used to implement such VI services [11].

5 Conclusion and Future Work

The Grid Services infrastructure is growing up very quickly and is going to be more and more complete and complex both in the number of tools and in the variety of supported applications. In this paper, we propose a virtual experiment model based on novel grid service technology. This model puts forward two-layered virtual experiment services to provide cheap and efficient distributed virtual experiment solution. This model could reuse not only virtual instruments but also compositive virtual experiments. In order to reuse successfully-deployed virtual experiment, we advance a uniform schema to describe a virtual experiment plan and process. Moreover, we provide a visualized virtual experiment authoring tool for teacher to design an experiment with little effort.

In order for the comprehensive communication between the virtual experiment work bench and other components, future work will focus on further standardization on the virtual instrument interfaces and open VE Services. We will also pay much attention to the improvement of the responsiveness and to the cooperation virtual experiment. Finally we will realize and improve an efficient virtual experiment work bench and hope to see that a rich virtual instrument and tools library gradually come into being.

References

1. Foster et al., The physiology of the grid: An open grid services architecture for distributed systems integration, tech. report, Open Grid Service Infrastructure WG, Global Grid Forum, June 2002.
2. Albert Ip and Ric Canale, A Model for Authoring Virtual Experiments in Web-based Courses, presented at Australasian Society for Computers in Learning in Tertiary Education Conference, 1996.
3. Chuang Liu, Lingyun Yang, Ian Foster and Dave Angulo, Design and Evaluation of a Resource Selection Framework for Grid Applications, Proceedings of the 11th IEEE Symposium on High-Performance Distributed Computing, 2002.
4. Vasa Curcin and Moustafa Ghanem et al., Discovery Net: Towards a Grid of Knowledge Discovery, Knowledge Discovery and Data Mining Conference 2002, ACM 1-58113-567-X/02/0007
5. Foster, What is Grid? A Three Point Checklist, tech. report, http://www.gridtoday.com/02/0722/100136.htm
6. Thomas Sandholm and Jarek Gawor, Globus Toolkit 3 Core- A Grid Service Container Framework, tech. report, Globus project, www-unix.globus.org/ogsa/docs/alpha/gt3_alpha_core.pdf
7. VXI Consortium, http://www.vxibus.org/
8. VPP-2: System Frameworks Specification, VXI plug&play Systems Alliance, http://www-.vxidatacenter.com/news/vxispecs.html,2000.
9. VXI-11.1:TCP/IP-VXIbus Interface Specification, http://www.vxidatacenter.com/news/vxispecs.html,2000
10. VPP-4.1: Virtual Instrument Software Architecture, VXI plug&play Systems Alliance, http://-www.vxidatacenter.com/news/vxispecs.html,2000.
11. Rajkumar Buyya and Kim Branson et al., The Virtual Laboratory: A Toolset for Utilising the World-Wide Grid to Design Drugs, Proceedings of the 2nd IEEE/ACM International Symposium on Cluster Computing and the Grid, 2002.
12. M. Livny R. Raman and M. Solomon. Matchmaking: Distributed resource management for high throughput computing. In Proceedings of the Seventh IEEE International Symposium on High Performance Distributed Computing, Chicago, IL, July 1998.
13. M. J. Litzkow, M. Livny, and M. W. Mutka. Condor—A Hunter of Idle Workstations. In *Proc. of the 8th Int'l Conf.on Distributed Computing Systems*, pages 104–111, 1988.
14. Carnegie Mellon's Virtual Lab, http://www-.ece.cmu.edu/~stancil/virtual-lab/application.html

15. Donald McMullen and Randall Bramley et al., The Xport Collaboratory for High-Brilliance X-ray Crystallography, tech. report, http://www.cs.indiana.edu/ngi/sc2000.
16. Virtual Physics Laboratory, http://jersey.uoregon.edu/vlab/
17. Control The Nuclear Power Plant, http://www.ida.liu.se/~her/npp/demo.html
18. The Interactive Frog Dissection ,http://curry.edschool.virginia.edu/go/frog/
19. Visual Systems Laboratory, http://www.vsl.ist.ucf.edu/
20. Oorange for Experimental Mathematics, http://www-sfb288.math.tu-berlin.de/~konrad/articles/oorange/
21. Mathematical Markup Language (MathML) Version 2.0, http://www.w3.org/TR/MathML2/, 2001

Designing a Learning Objects Repository–The Views of Higher Education Faculty

Philippos Pouyioutas[1] and Maria Poveda[2]

[1] Department of Computer Science, Intercollege,
46 Makedonitissas Avenue, Nicosia 1700, Cyprus
pouyioutas.p@intercollege.ac.cy
[2] Department of Computer Science, University of Cyprus,
75 Kallipoleos Street, Nicosia 1678, Cyprus
mpoveda@ucy.ac.cy

Abstract. This paper presents the initial stages of the design of a National Learning Objects Repository for Cyprus (NLORC). It examines the views of the faculty members of Intrecollege, a College of Higher Education in Cyprus, with regards to the need of such a repository. These views were collected through a questionnaire. The NLORC will provide a web-based application allowing indexing, uploading and downloading of e-learning resources in Cyprus and the creation, modification and querying of Learning Objects (LOs). This paper presents a simple model that will underpin the development of the NLORC. After careful consideration and studying of the existing Learning Objects Metadata Standards, it has been decided that the NLORC application should be developed using a database system supporting object-orientation and temporal database features. As a result of this, the model presented herein suggests an object-oriented database structure to form a basis for the application and to cater for the storage of the LOs, keeping a record of the relations between them and allowing their retrieval and manipulation.

1 Introduction

A huge number of learning resources is available either on stand-alone machines, or on local networks or on the Internet. Some are restricted to particulars users and some are available without any restriction to anyone interested in using them. Learning Objects Repositories (LORs) are web-based applications allowing the sharing of learning resources over the web. These learning resources are better known as Learning Objects (LOs). A Learning Object (LO) is basically any digital asset which can be used to enable teaching and learning [10]. Learning Object Repositories (LORs) [1, 7, 9, 12, 14] allow the storage and manipulation of LOs. A comparison analysis of the various LORs models can be found in [31], where various models [2, 3, 6, 8, 13, 32] are explained and analysed. LORs are underpinned by database applications that provide the data structure representation of LOs. The properties (metadata) of the data structure representing the LO entity have been standardised across different countries and regions through Learning Objects Metadata Standards (LOMS) [5 7, 30] which provide a data dictionary for LOs.

R.W.H. Lau et al. (Eds.): ICWL 2005, LNCS 3583, pp. 111–121, 2005.

This paper presents the initial stages of the design of a National Learning Objects Repository for Cyprus (NLORC). Currently, there is no strategy for e-learning in Cyprus. A recent attempt towards defining such strategy was made in [4]. Our current research work involves the collection and centralisation of information regarding e-learning in our country. This will help us later to identify the main participants of the e-learning National network which will be supported by the NLORC. Herein, we present a simple model that will underpin the development of the NLORC. The model is an extension of the model proposed in [29] and was presented in [21]. After careful consideration and studying of the existing Learning Objects Metadata Standards, it has been decided that the NLORC application should be developed using a database system supporting object-orientation and temporal database features. Thus, we propose herein an object-oriented structure to form a basis for the database application. The database structure caters for the *relation* property of LOs (defined in most of the Learning Objects Metadata Standards). The structure can also be extended to support other properties that need complex representations that can only be supported by object-oriented database structures (such as temporal data). One such property is the one which specifies the duration of the availability of a LO.

The work presented herein is part of a project [11], which recently (December 2004) attracted a grant of 80000 Euros from the Cyprus Research Promotion Foundation (CRPF) and is in line within the e-learning applied research work carried out at Intercollege [15, 16, 17, 18, 19, 20, 21, 22, 23, 24, 25, 26, 27, 28]. The CRPF funded project is divided in two parts: (a) a comparison evaluation of e-learning services in Cyprus and (b) the creation of a National Learning Objects Repository. The main stages of part (b) are given below:

1. Literature Survey and Research on Learning Objects Repositories.
2. Investigation of the current status of distance-learning education in Cyprus.
3. Survey to analyze the attitude of academicians in Cyprus (University of Cyprus and Colleges of Higher Education) towards a National Learning Objects Repository. Statistical analysis of results according to University/College institutions, age, gender, academic rank, specialization of degree.
4. Design of an initial Data Dictionary for the Learning Objects data structure based on the research of (1) and the results of (3).
5. Survey to get feedback on (4) from the same user groups as the ones in (3).
6. Finalization of the Data Dictionary based on 5.
7. Design of the database application based on 6; the application will utilize object-oriented and temporal database features.
8. Development of the web-based database application and recording of data. Development of the Learning Network between the institutions taking part in the network. Development of the LOR.
9. Development of graphical interface for the LOR.
10. Post implementation evaluation. Users Feedback.

In the rest of this paper, in Section 2 we present an implementation model for the creation of LOs. In Section 3, we propose the object-oriented database structure, which provides the underlying structure for the development of the database application, which will underpin the development of the NLORC. The structure focuses on the *relation* property of LOs. We also give the running example of the paper. In Section 4, we present the results of a faculty questionnaire and the views of faculty members with regards to the NLORC and address the impact on the design of the Data Dictionary and hence the database application. Finally, we conclude by discussing our current and future work.

2   An Implementation Model

In this Section we explain how the proposed implementation model caters for the creation of LOs. The proposed model is an extension of the simple model proposed in [29] and was presented in [21]. In [29] a LO is defined as being either an atomic LO or a composite LO (consisting of other parts). All parts of a composite object are computed by (recursively) taking the union of all parts of the LO. In our model, LOs are built from scratch or by using existing LOs or by modifying existing LOs or by a combination of all the aforementioned ways. More specifically, a LO can be created in one of the following ways (a,b,c,d):

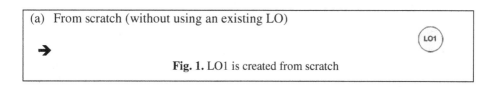

(a) From scratch (without using an existing LO)

Fig. 1. LO1 is created from scratch

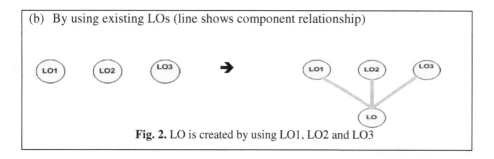

(b) By using existing LOs (line shows component relationship)

Fig. 2. LO is created by using LO1, LO2 and LO3

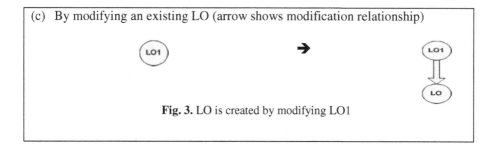

(c) By modifying an existing LO (arrow shows modification relationship)

Fig. 3. LO is created by modifying LO1

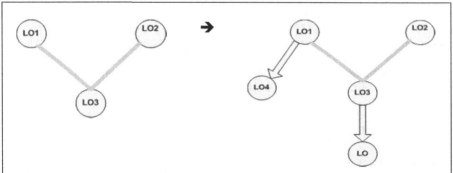

Fig. 4. LO is created by modifying LO3 by modifying LO1 (LO2 has been deleted – not shown)

(d) By a combination of (b) and (c) above

When a LO is modified through a modification of another LO to which it belongs to (as a direct or indirect component), all the LOs to which it (directly or indirectly) belongs, are also modified. As a result of this, a new LO is created for each LO modified. This is better explained through the given example. Given the LOs shown in the left part of Figure 5, we consider a user wanting to create a new LO as a version of LO7 with LO2 and LO1 modified and LO4 deleted. We also consider a user wanting to create a version of LO5 with LO2 and LO3 modified and LO1 deleted. The result of these changes is the creation of 4 new LOs, namely LO8, LO9, LO10 and LO11 for the first user and 3 new LOs namely LO12, LO13 and LO14 for the second user, as shown in the right part of Figure 5.

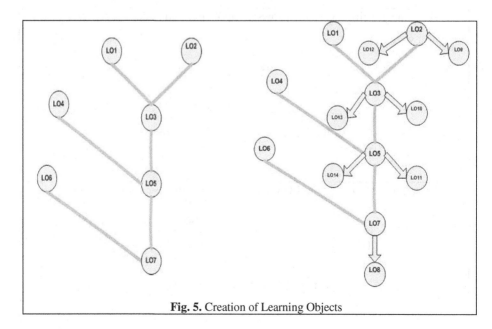

Fig. 5. Creation of Learning Objects

3   An Object-Oriented Database Structure for the NLORC

In this Section we present the object-oriented database structure that we propose for the database application for the NLORC. We do not herein concentrate on all the properties of LOs that need to be stored in such a model; a description of all these properties can be found in most Learning Objects Metadata Standards [5, 7, 30]. Furthermore, the identification of these properties is the subject of our current research work as explained in Section 4 of the paper. We therefore include only some basic properties and focus on the ones needed for the identification of the *relation* property, which keeps a record of which objects have used which objects as components (LOComponents, LOCKind) or as modified versions (LOModified, LOMKind). The object-oriented database structure is given below, using abstract object-oriented notation:

Learning-Object	
LOURI.	string
LOTitle:	string
LOCreator:	Creator
LOType:	string
LOModified:	Learning-Object
LOMKind:	string
LOComponents:	set of [LOC: Learning-Object, LOCKind: String]
LOALLComponents:	method

Using the Learning-Object object-oriented database structure we can build the database application for the NLORC. In order to show how the LOs could be stored and hence manipulated using this structure we give, in Table 1, the LOs of Figure 5, stored as class instances of the Learning-Object structure. When LOs are created as modifications of existing LOs or using/referencing other LOs, the LOMKind and LOCKind values are generated by the system based on the kind of modification/use.

The LOALLComponents is a method which returns **all** the components of a Learning Object (not only the LOModified LO and the other LOs which are stored in LOComponents) and is described by:

Given a Learning Object LOX LOX.LOALLComponnets = {LOX.LOModified} **Union** 　　　　　　LOX.LOComponents.LOC **Union** 　　　　　　(LOXI.LOALLComponents and 　　　　　　LOXI ∈ LOX.LOComponents.LOC)

The above method basically implements the *relation* property of LOs as it returns all the LOs used in the construction of a LO. The method can be made more generic by introducing a variable to specify the depth up to which we want to calculate the components of a LO. We can also extend the method to return only the components which are associated with particular type(s) of modification (LOMKind) and/or particular type(s) of components (LOCKind).

Table 1. The Learning Objects of the Right Part of Figure 5

LOURI	LOTitle	LOCreator	LOType	LOModified	LOMKind	LOComponents
LO1	Data Manipulation	C1	Text			
LO2	Data Model	C1	Text			
LO3	RDBMS Theory	C1	Interactive Resource			
LO4	Intro to RDBMS	C2	Interactive Resource			
LO5	RDBMS	C3	Interactive Resource			
LO6	OODBS	C4	Interactive Resource			
LO7	Databases	C5	Interactive Resource			
LO8	Intro to Databases	C6	Interactive Resource	LO7	isversionof	[LO6, ispartof], [LO11, ispartof]
LO9	Data Model Basics	C6	Text	LO2	isformatof	
LO10	Database Theory	C6	Interactive Resource	LO3	isversionof	[LO1, ispartof], [LO9, ispartof]
LO11	RDBMS Basics	C6	Interactive Resource	LO5	isversionof	[LO10, ispartof]
LO12	Data Modelling	C7	Text	LO2	isformatof	
LO13	RDBMS Theory	C7	Interactive Resource	LO3	isversionof	[LO12, ispartof]
LO14	RDBMS Basics	C7	Interactive Resource	LO5	isversionof	[LO4, ispartof], [LO13, ispartof]

4   Intercollege Faculty Views for the NLORC

In this section we present the results of a questionnaire that was distributed to Intercollege (the largest of the Colleges in Cyprus) faculty. The questionnaire aimed at finding out the beliefs of faculty in terms of the need of a NLOR and their attitude towards using (read/write access) other people's LOs and letting other people use their own LOs (read/write access). The results of this part of the questionnaire are presented in Table 2.

Table 2. Intercollege Faculty Views With Regards to a NLOR

	YES	N0	MAYBE
Q1. Do we need a LOR in Cyprus ?	77%	6%	17%
Q2. Would you use a LOR?	74%	6%	20%
Q3. Would you use (without modifying) other lecturers' LOs assuming you had the technical support and training?	40%	23%	37%
Q4. Would you use/modify other lecturers' LOs to create your own LOs if you were allowed to do so and you had technical support and training?	73%	12%	15%
Q5. Would you allow other lecturers to use (without modifying) your LOs?	76%	12%	12%
Q6. Would you allow other lecturers to use/modify your LOs to create their own ones, assuming they clearly refer/acknowledge your work?	89%	6%	6%

Table 2 clearly shows that that most of the Intercollege faculty members believe that there is a need for a NLOR. Most of them would use the NLOR and they have no problem allowing other people to use/modify their own LOs and vice versa. It is interesting to compare the results of Q5 with those of Q3 and the results of Q6 with those of Q4. The (YES+MAYBE) percentage of Q5 and the (YES+MAYBE) percentage of Q6 are higher than the corresponding ones of Q3 and Q4 respectively. Firstly, we have to note that the said percentages are all high and show the positive attitude of faculty members towards sharing LOs. Secondly, this comparison reveals that faculty members feel more willing to let other faculty members use their own LOs rather than using the LOs of other faculty members. This maybe explained due to the   fact   that   academicians   (and   researchers)   like   sharing   their   own findings/educational material but they are more sceptical in using other than their own material in teaching (especially if they cannot modify the teaching material and customize it to their needs).

Summarising the above results it is obvious that faculty members of Intercollege support our initiative and would make use of our proposed system. It is also interesting to note that the main reason specified by some faculty members not supporting our proposal is that by sharing our LOs with other faculty from other private Colleges we will loose a competitive advantage. We have to clarify here that

Intercollege is a private college and faces severe competition by other educational institutions in Cyprus.

Furthermore, the questionnaire aimed at identifying the main characteristics of LOs needed to implement the LO data structure. It presented to the faculty some core characteristics (title, description, creator, creation date, language, subject, keywords, duration, access (read/write)) asking to identify them as essential or not. Finally, the questionnaire asked faculty members to add any other characteristics they thought are essential to describe a LO. The results of this part of the questionnaire are presented in Table 3 and Table 4 below.

Table 3. Intercollege Faculty Views With Regards to LO Characteristics

Characteristic	Essential
Title	100%
Description	100%
Creator	82%
Creation Date	91%
Type	97%
Language	100%
Subject	97%
Keywords	97%
Duration	67%
Audience	85%
Access (Read/Write)	91%

Table 4. Suggested Characteristics for LOs

Suggested Characteristic
Date of Last Modification
Time Needed for Downloading
Aims, Objectives and Expected Learning Outcomes

Table 3 and Table 4 will help us design the Learning Object data structure presented in Section 3 and will thus provide us with the Data Dictionary and the Database Structures that will be used for the design of the database application of the NLOR. It is obvious from Table 3 that all of the above characteristics are considered essential and that most of them are considered absolutely essential. Furthermore, we agree that the suggested characteristics are also important and we will therefore consider them as well in our design. We will therefore incorporate all of them into our data structure.

Summarising, this questionnaire has helped us to:

1. verify our belief that there is a real need for a NLOR in Cyprus
2. identify some more characteristics that will be incorporated in the LO data structure.

5 Conclusions

This paper has presented an object-oriented database structure which can be used in a database application to implement a National Learning Objects Repository for Cyprus (NLORC). The NLORC will provide a centralised repository for a national network of e-learning service providers. The proposed structure focuses only on the *relation* property of Learning Objects. In order to design and develop fully the proposed structure, there is need for the development of a National Learning Objects Metadata Standard (NLOMS). For developing the NLOMS, our current work involves literature research and national research to identify the beliefs and needs of academicians in Cyprus. In order to achieve the latter, we have developed a faculty questionnaire that we distributed to Intercollege faculty. We are currently in the process of obtaining feedback from all the other institutions of higher education in Cyprus, which will provide us with a more complete picture of the views of the academicians in Cyprus. However, we believe that the overall results will not differ from the ones presented herein and which clearly indicate the support of the faculty members to our proposed system. Once the design of the NLOMS is completed, we will proceed with the development of the underlying database model which will underpin the development of the NLORC. Finally, after developing the NLORC, we will develop a graphical interface which will enable ease of access to end users.

References

1. ARIADNE: The ARIADNE Knowledge Pool System: a Distributed Library for Education, CACM, Vol. 44, No. 5, (2001) 73-78
2. Barrit, C., Lewis, D & Wiesler: CISCO Systems Reusable Information Object Strategy Version 3.0, http://www.cisco.com (1999)
3. Brown, J.: Academic ADL Co_lab, http://www.adlnet.org (2002)
4. CeE: Cyprus in eEurope, Benchmarking Cyprus in IT, a Readiness Assessment for Cyprus, http://www.kepa.gov.cy/eLearning (2004)
5. DCMS: Dublin Core Metadata Standard, http://au.dublincore.org (2005)
6. Dodds, P.: Advanced Distributed Learning Sharable Content Object Reference Model Version 1.2. The SCORM Content Aggregation Mode, http://www.addlnet.org (2001)
7. EdNA: Educational Network Australia, http://www.edna.edu.au (2005)
8. Elliot, S.: A Content Model for Reusability, http://www.cm-strategies.com/pdfs/elliot.pdf (2005)
9. GEM: Gateway to Educational Materials, http://www.geminfo.org (2005)
10. IEEE: Learning Technology Standards Committee http://ltsc.ieee.org (2005)

11. Kokkinaki, A & Pouyioutas, P.: A Comparative Evaluation of E-Learning Services in Cyprus and the Creation of a National Learning Objects Repository, Technical Report, Cyprus Research Promotion Foundation, (2004)

12. Law E. et al.: EducaNext: A Service for knowledge sharing. 3rd Annual Conference Leuven, 2003, http://www.educanext.org (2003)

13. L' Allier, J.J.: A Frame of Reference: NETg's Map to its Products, Their Structures and Core Beliefs, http://www.netg.com/research/whitepapers/index.asp (1997)

14. McGreal et. al.: EduSource: Canada's Learning Object Repository Network Metadata Standard, http://www.itdl.org/Journal/Mar_04/article01.htm (2004)

15. Pouyioutas, P, Poveda, M & Apraxin, D.: The Impact of Web-Based Educational Software: Off-the-Shelf vs. In-House Developed Software, Intl Journal of Information Technology Impact, Vol. 3, No. 3, (2004) 121-130.

16. Pouyioutas, P, Apraxin, D, Ktoridou, D, Poveda, M.: The InterLearning Web-Based Educational Software, IASTED Intl Conference on Web-Based Education, Austria, (2004) 595-600.

17. Pouyioutas, P, Poveda, M, Apraxin, D & Kalogerou, V.: InterLearning – A Comparison Analysis of Students' Perspectives, Intl Conference on Applied Computing, Vol. 2, Portugal, (2004) 70-74.

18. Pouyioutas, P, Poveda, M & Apraxin, D.: Students' Evaluation of the InterLearning Software, 16th World Conference on Educational Multimedia, Hypermedia and Telecommunications, Switzerland, (2004) 2264-2269.

19. Pouyioutas, P, Poveda, M & Apraxin, D.: Design, Development and Evaluation of Web-Based Educational Software, Intl Conference e-Society, Spain, (2004) 267-275.

20. Pouyioutas, P, Poveda, M, Soleas, G, Kalogerou, V, Apraksin, D & Kouroufexis, A.: The Intercollege Student Intranet, International Conference on WWW/Internet, Spain, (2004) 21-27

21. Pouyioutas, P & Poveda, M.: A Model for a National Learning Objects Repository for Cyprus, IASTED International Conference on Databases and Applications, Austria, February, (2005) 111-115

22. Pouyioutas, P, Poveda, M, Kalogerou, V & Apraksin, D.: The InterTest Multiple-Choice Web-Based Software, International Conference on Web-Based Education, Switzerland, February, (2005) 436-441

23. Pouyioutas, P, Kalogerou, V & Christou, C.: Using the InterTest Multiple-Choice Web-Based Software to Automate the Intercollege English Placement Test, International Conference on Learning Technologies, Italy, March, (2005) 369-375, also in WIT Transactions on Information and Communication Technologies, Vol 34, WIT Press.

24. Pouyioutas, P, Poveda, M &, Kalogerou, V.: The Intercollege Intranet and its Impact on Students and Faculty, submitted, Intl Journal of Information Technology Impact, (2005)

25. Pouyioutas, P, Poveda, M &, Kalogerou, V.: The Intercollege Faculty Intranet, accepted, International Conference on E-Society, Malta, June, (2005)

26. Pouyioutas, P, Poveda, M &, Kalogerou, A Student Evaluation of the NEPTON, accepted, International Conference on E-Society, Malta, June, (2005)

27. Pouyioutas, P & Kalogerou, V.: The InterTest Multiple-Choice Web-Based Software – Design and Evaluation of English Placement Tests, submitted, International Conference on Web-Based Learning, Hong Kong, July, (2005)

28. Pouyioutas, P & Kalogerou, V.: The Intercollege Web-Based Educational Environment (IWBEE), submitted, International Conference on Web-Based Learning, Hong Kong, July, (2005)

29. Rigaux, P & Spyratos, N.: Generation and Syndication of Learning Object Metadata, SeLeNe Self E-Learning Networks, IST-2001-39045, http://www.dcs.bbk.ac.uk/selene/ (2003)
30. SeLeNe: Self E-Learning Networks Metadata Standard, http://www.dcs.bbk.ac.uk/selene/ (2005)
31. Verbet, K. & Duval, E.: Towards a Global Component Architecture for Learning Objects: A Comparative Analysis of Learning Object Content Models. ED-MEDIA 2004, Switzerland. (2004)
32. Wagner, E. D.: Steps to Creating a Content Strategy for your Organization. The e-Learning Developer's Journal (2002).

An Novel Resource Recommendation System Based on Connecting to Similar E-Learners*

Fan Yang, Peng Han, Ruimin Shen, and Zuwei Hu

Department of Computer Science and Engineering, Shanghai JiaoTong University,
Shanghai, 200030, China

{fyang, phan, rmshen, huzw}@mail.sjtu.edu.cn

Abstract. E-learners always finds it is difficult to make a decision about which of learning materials best meet their situation and need to read, whilst instructors are finding it is almost impossible to reorganize different materials corresponding to individuals. Based on the investigation on real learners in the Network Education College of Shanghai Jiaotong University, we found that many learners share common need of learning resources if they have similar learning preferences and status during learning process. This paper proposes a novel E-Learning resource recommendation system based on connecting to similar E-Learners, which can find and reorganize the learners share similar learning status into smaller communities. Furthermore a recommendation platform is developed to enable the learner to share filtered resources.

Keywords: E-Learning, Resource Filtering, Recommendation System, learning communities.

1 Introduction

E-learning settings such as on-line courses offered in China often involve large numbers of students who have diverse professional background, learning preferences, and various learning needs. As a result, learners are finding it is difficult to make a decision about which of learning materials best meet their situation and need to read, whilst instructors are finding it is almost impossible to reorganize different materials corresponding to each learner separately. Thus it would be very useful an E-Learning system could automatically guide the learner's activities and intelligently generate and recommend learning materials that would improve the learning [1, 2].

Personalized recommendation approaches are first proposed and applied in E-commerce area for product purchase [3-5], which help customers find products they would like to purchase by producing a list of recommended products for each given customer [6, 7]. Literature review shows there are also many researchers have attempted to adopt recommender systems to e-learning sites. Research [8] described a mechanism focused on how to organize the learning materials based on domain ontology which can guide the learning resources recommendation according to

---

* Supported by National Natural Science Foundation of China under Grant No.60372078.

learning status. A multi-attribute evaluation method is proposed in [2] to justify a student's need and developed a fuzzy matching method to find suitable learning materials to best meet each student need. Research [9] presented a method to organize components and courseware using the hierarchy and association rules of the concepts, which can recommend the relative contents to students and also can help them to control the learning schedule. However, most of these methods missing one important issue in E-Learning Recommender System, that is, the natural learning behavior is not lonely but interactive which relying on friends, classmates, lecturers, and other sources to make the choices for learning. For example, during the learning process, a learner read a useful material, summarized what he/she has learned or got the answer of a typical question, some learners with similar learning status are likely need these resources. We did an investigation on real learners in the Network Education College of Shanghai Jiaotong University and found that many learners share common need of learning resources if they have similar learning preferences and status. If an effective method can be presented to help the similar learners to share useful learning resources, it will promisingly enhance the learning effect.

This paper proposes a novel E-Learning recourse recommendation system based on connecting to similar E-Learners, which can find and reorganize the learners share similar learning status into smaller communities. This system starts from the learning log data gathering and profile generation of each learner. The approach first creates Learner Agent for each learner, which can help to generate learner profile and monitor the learning behavior. During the learning process, each Learner Agent must register with a Group Agent and report its learning status dynamically. Based on the changeable behavior, the Learner Community Structure Exploiting Engine will run the community organization algorithm and reorganize the learners share similar learning status and preference into the same community. Furthermore, taking advantage of the organized learner communities, a Learning Resource Recommendation Platform is developed to visualize the details of learner community and recommended resources which finally enable learners can mutually meet the need of others in the same community. Experimental results show that this method can not only effectively reorganize learners share similar learning status into communities, but also enhance the recommendation accuracy.

2 System Description

This system is designed to have three main components 'Learner Information Monitoring and Profile Maintenance', 'Learner Community Structure Exploiting' and 'Learning Resource Recommendation Platform', shown in Figure 1.

Each component is connected to the E-Learning Interface, Learning Log Database and Learning Resource Database, which is supported by a domain conceptual map. We will discuss the details of each component as the following sections.

2.1 Learner Information Monitoring and Profile Maintenance

The implementation of technologies for developing recommender systems is strongly dependent on the type of information that is being used [10]. During the learning

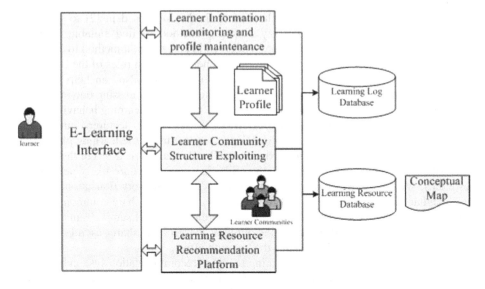

Fig. 1. Framework of the E-Learning Resource Recommendation System

process, learners will browse online courses, submit questions or assignments and perform exercises through the E-Learning Interface. All of these actions represent the learning status and need of learners. This component aims getting learning information for each learner that has registered in our E-Learning platform. It performs the task based on two basic strategies. One is to get learning status based on their individual learning history log data. The other is to create and maintain learner profile based on the analysis of learning status.

Since it is impossible for learners themselves to perform these tasks, we create LA (Learner Agent) acting on behalf of a real learner, which is in charge of two tasks:

1) Monitoring Learning behavior

LA will monitor the learning behavior of its learner, such as the materials learning path, access frequency, question submitted and resource query. All history learning behaviors are analyzed to construct a learning log database from multiple data source, such as web servers, courseware learning platform, question–and-answering system, online assignment system, discussion groups and so on. Whilst, all dynamic learning behaviors are monitored by the LA which can stimulate the system to find the similar learners and recommend interesting resources to other learners.

2) Profile Generation and Maintenance

In this system, a learner's profile consists of two parts. One is the Learned Resource List which is stored the learned learning materials, summarized learning experience or solution of a problem that a learner prefers to publish. The other is the learning status evaluation vector. Let $C = \{c_1,...,c_i,...,c_n\}$ be the set of Learning Concepts corresponding to specified learning domain. The learning status evaluation vector of learner a can be defined as $SV_a = \{(c_1,s_1),(c_i,s_i),(c_n,s_n)\}$, where $c_i \in C$ is a learning concept and s_i is a learning status on c_i of learner a. The Learning status evaluation can be obtained in two ways: explicit and implicit expressed. The explicit evaluation data discussed here could be learner's vote on a learning resource, score of a test etc., whilst the implicit evaluation data could be general evaluation considering complex learning behavior, such as access frequency, learning duration, etc. As well known, E-learning log data contains a wealth of detail compared to off-line learning data, which provides information essential to understanding learning behavior of students, such as what materials they see and what materials they may interest. This component analyzes both of the explicit and implicit learning data which can make a more accurate overall analysis of learning status than does the analyzing of access records only.

2.2 E-Learner Community Structure Exploiting

The "E-Learner Community" here is defined as a group of learners who share common learning status and mutually recommend relative learning resources meet the learning need.

This component creates another kind of agent, called Group Agent (GA), to serve as the manager of a smaller community of LAs. A GA is responsible for matching similar learners, managing the association of learners to communities and delivering resource recommendations. GA can interact with both the local LAs in its management domains and the other GAs.

This *multi-agent structure* can be modeled by associating LAs and GAs through the mapping $m: L \rightarrow G$, where $m(l)=g$ denotes the fact that learner l is a *member of the group* managed by g. All *LAs managed by g* are then defined by the set:

$$A_g = \{l \in L \mid m(l) = g\}$$ (1)

In the initialization step, each LA a will choose a GA g randomly and report its current SV_a. GA g thus constructs its member sets A_g and the Group Learning Status Evaluation Matrix SM_g based on SV of each member. During the learning process, LA a will send a message (a, c_i^a, s_i^a, SV_a) to GA g if the monitored learner has learned a concept, where a is the identification of LA, (c_i^a, s_i^a) is the 'concept-status' tuple and SV_a is the updated learning status evaluation vector.

The GA g received this enquire will send this message to its members and randomly forward to several other GA g', the match width is a number defined as *topSearch*. For each LA l received this message, l will check if it has learned this concept and the status difference between l and a is lower than a threshold α, defined as $S_i^l \neq NIL$ and $|S_i^a - S_i^l| < \alpha$, then it will calculate the similarity between SV_a and SV_l based Pearson Correlation Coefficient:

$$sim_{a,l} = \frac{\sum_i (s_i^a - \overline{s^a})(s_i^l - \overline{s^l})}{\sqrt{\sum_i (s_i^a - \overline{s^a})^2 \sum_j (s_i^l - \overline{s^l})^2}} \quad x \qquad (2)$$

If the similarity value is higher than a threshold β, that means LA a and l has similar learning status, then LA l will feedback $(l, Sim_{a,l})$ to g. Also if this message received by l is forwarded by GA g', l will feedback to g' and g' will return this message to g.

After a waiting time T, g will ascending sort the feedback results on the similarity value and choose the matched learner l with highest value. Then g will check if learner agent a and l are managed by the same group agent. If the answer is inverse, the GAs g and g' will calculate the inter-similarity of each learner agent using the method similar to equation (2) and move the learner agent from the group with smaller inter-similarity to another group. The primary algorithms are discussed as the following:

Algorithm 1. Community Organization Algorithm

Comment: find learners share similar learning status reorganize them into smaller learning community which can enhance the recommendation accuracy in the future.
Require: Learning resource
1. create the user agents;
2. create group agents;
3. for each user agent a do   // initialized Registration
4.   Choose a group agent g randomly (maybe the nearest)
5.   publish the private learning status vector SV_a

6. $A_g = A_g \cup a$ //add a into the member list of g

7. $SM_g = SM_g \cup SV_a$ //update learning status matrix of g

a) end for
8. for all users do (in random order)
9.   If a learner finished a unit learning then

10.   send a message to g and call: g.ReceiveEnquire (a, c_i^a, s_i^a, SV_a)

          // g finally returns the matched learners with similar learning status
11.   Ascending sort to the feedback results on the similarity value
12.   choose the matched learner l with highest similarity value

13.   if $a \in A_g$, $l \in A_{g'}$ and $g \neq g'$ then ExchangeLA(a, g, l, g')

          //If not in the same group, then move LA from the group with smaller
          //inter-similarity to another one
14. end for

2.3 Learning Resource Recommendation Platform

Based on the self-organized learning community, the Learning Resource Recommendation Platform is developed to enable personalized recommendation as shown in Figure 2.

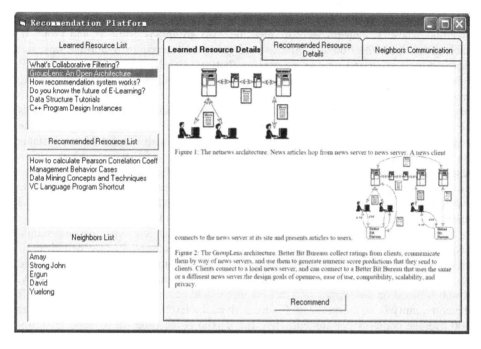

Fig. 2. Recommendation Platform

This platform has three main panels 'Learned Resource List', 'Recommended Resource List' and 'Neighbors List' in the left column. Click each object in the panel will activate the corresponding panel respectively shown as the right column. The 'Learned Resource List' visualizes the learned resources and enables the learner to recommend them. For example, if a learner chose the resource 'GroupLens: An Open Architecture', the associated panel 'Learned Resource Details' in the right column will activated and show the details of the content. If the learner think this resource is useful and pushed the button 'Recommend', the LA monitoring this learner will submit this request to manager GA. Thus the GA will deliver this resource to other distributed neighbor learners in the same group. The recommendation process is transparent to all students. The 'Recommended Resource List' illustrates the resources recommended by other neighbor learners. Also it can stimulate relative panel to show the details of the recommended content and enable the learner to vote on it. In particularly, 'Neighbors List' gives the learner community member list and the current learner can choose to communicate with one or several of them. All of the actions generated in this platform can be recorded and analyzed, which can be used to maintain the community structure.

3   Experimental Results

We chose 200 volunteers which are students of Network Education College of Shanghai Jiaotong University and choose the course 'Graduate English' as the test subject. We designed a sequence of tests which must be done before a required deadline. These volunteers were divided into two groups as group A and group B, each group has 100 students. Students of group A learned in a normal way and finished the tests based on our E-Learning Platform, whilst the students of group B were required to use the online recommendation system. That is to say, during the learning process, the system generated a LA for each student and several GAs to manage learner communities. Each LA monitored the performance of test which is considered as the learning status of relative concept. Thus the GAs ran the community-organization algorithm and group students with similar learning status into the same community. As the same time, the students of B were guided to learn test-relative materials, write down reading note and collect salutation for specified problem. They also were encouraged to recommend the learning resource through the recommendation platform along with the tests. Each student also can receive, read and evaluate the recommendation materials from other students.

Based on the scenario of this experiment, we consider 'concept, learning-status' enquire is occurred after a student finished a test. For each enquire, we will check if an exchange happened after the ReceiveEnquire algorithm and calculate the average exchange frequency per enquire/learner as the community organizing efficiency, which is based on the supposition that enquire would be matched in the same group if the community is well organized. Figure 3 gives the Exchange Frequency curve after 100 average enquires per student. Here the x-axial is the times of average learning-status enquires and y-axial is the community organizing efficiency. Portrayed as Figure 6, in the initial situation, we can see that when students are not well organized, the exchange frequency is high. This is because Group Agents often can not find matched students in its group and need to forward enquire to other GAs. After almost average 23 enquires is initiated, the system's ability to group students with similar learning status is obviously improved. Furthermore, it is settled to a stable state with students who share similar learning status are all grouped into the same community.

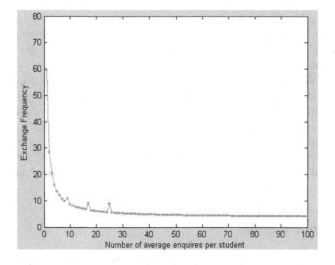

Fig. 3. Community Organizing Efficiency

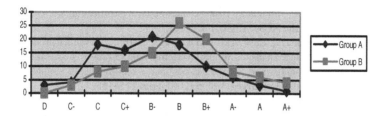

Fig. 4. Achievement Comparison between two volunteer groups

In order to qualify the efficiency of this system, we give a final exam after the students all finished the tests whose motivation is to certify if the usage of this system really help students to enhance learning effect. The detailed achievement comparison between these two volunteer groups can be seen in Figure 4.

Based on the analysis of the data from figure 5, we can see that the score distributed in [B, A+] is higher than group A, while the score distributed in [D, B-] is just inverse situation.

We also did an investigation among the 100 volunteers in group B. 54% students think this system is helpful and efficient, 29% students think that some recommended resources can not meet their need, 11% students think the matched neighbors is not really all similar with them, while 6% students think this system is not helpful for their study. We made an investigation on the 29% students which were not satisfied with some recommended resources. Most of them think these resources did have interesting titles but not the contents.

4   Conclusion and Outlook of Future Work

A novel E-Learning Recourse Filtering system is proposed in this paper, which takes the advantage of self-organized learner communities based on the learning status match method. The friendly-interface Recommendation Platform is also developed to help learners to share useful learning resource and communicate with similar neighbor learners. This mechanism can not only enhance the learning resource recommendation accuracy, but also greatly reduce the isolation of distributed learners and increase their learning motivation. In the future, we would introduce the Vector Space Model into our method to describe the features of resource content more precisely which would be helpful to enhance the recommendation accuracy.

References

1. Zaiane O.R., Web usage mining for better web-based learning environment. In Prof. of Conference on Advanced Technology for Education, pp 60-64, Banff, AB, June 2001.
2. Jie Lu, A Personalized e-Learning Material Recommender System, Proceedings of the 2nd International Conference on Information Technology for Application (ICITA 2004).
3. Lee L. and Lu TC., Intelligent agent-based systems for personalized recommendations in Internet commerce, Expert Systems with Applications Vol. 22, pp. 275-284, 2002.
4. Resnick P. and Varian H.R., Recommender systems, Communications of the ACM Vol. 40, pp. 56-58, 1997.

5. M. Balabanovic, Y. Shoham, Fab: Content-based, collaborative recommendation, Communications of the ACM, 40 (3), pp. 66-72, 1997.
6. Cheung K.W., Kwok J.T., Law M.H. and Tsui K.C., Mining customer product ratings for personalized marketing, Decision Support Systems Vol. 35 (2003), pp. 231-243.
7. Schafer J.B., Konstan J.A and Riedl J., E-commerce recommendation applications, Data Mining and Knowledge Discovery, Vol. 5 (2001), pp. 115–153.
8. Shen L.P. and Shen R.M., Learning Content Recommendation Service Based-on Simple Sequencing Specification, In Proceedings of Advanced in Web-based Learning (ICWL 2004), LNCS 3143, pp.363-370, 2004.
9. Luo S., Sha S., Shen D. and Jia W.J., Conceptual Network Based Courseware Navigation and Web Presentation Mechanisms, In Proceedings of Advanced in Web-Based Learning (ICWL 2002), LNCS 2436, pp.81-91, 2002.
10. Yang J.D. and Lee D.G., Incorporating concept-based match into fuzzy production rules, Information Sciences Vol. 104, pp. 213-239, 1998.

MECCA-Learn: A Community Based Collaborative Course Management System for Media-Rich Curricula in the Film Studies

Marc Spaniol[1,3], Ralf Klamma[1,3], and Thomas Waitz[2,3]

[1] RWTH Aachen University, Informatik V, Ahornstr. 55, D-52056 Aachen, Germany
{mspaniol, klamma}@cs.rwth-aachen.de
[2] Institute for Media Studies, Ruhr-Universität Bochum, Germany
thomas.waitz@ruhr-uni-bochum.de
[3] Forschungskolleg "Medien und kulturelle Kommunikation", Universität zu Köln,
Bernhard-Feilchenfeld-Str. 11, D-50969, Germany

Abstract. Even with a large number of course management systems at the market and already established in some universities, impact of these systems on the curricula design in the humanities and the cultural sciences is still marginal. Instead of complaining about the reluctance against technology in the non-technical disciplines we try to contribute to establishing an e-learning culture in these faculties. First we introduce on the one hand existing theories on knowledge creation and social learning in information systems research and on the other hand media-specific theories developed in the humanities. By combining these both approaches we achieve a deeper understanding of the underlying scientific methodologies and information systems' needs. Then we analyze the existing course management systems in the humanities and the cultural sciences with respect to these requirements. Our study indicates that no course management system covers all of these needs. Thus, we introduce MECCA-learn on top of the Movie E-learning Combination and Categorization Application (MECCA) as a basic course management system. It is deployed for a web based community of learners in a media-rich curriculum that allows a tight interaction between multimedia artifacts, their situational context and discourses on them.

1 Introduction

Course management systems like Blackboard and WebCT have been introduced into universities in recent years and reshaped university teaching and learning in many aspects. These systems help to build up reusable repositories of learning materials with support tools for teachers (e.g. curriculum design, course delivery, administration) and students (e.g. productivity, communication, involvement) with predictable institutional and infrastructural costs. Although these systems are in general able to support curricula in the humanities and the cultural sciences, most of the administrated courses in universities at the moment are originated from natural sciences, engineering, economics, and not

R.W.H. Lau et al. (Eds.): ICWL 2005, LNCS 3583, pp. 131–143, 2005.

surprisingly educational psychology. Universities, which use the current course management systems report a lack of acceptance in user communities of the humanities [5, 33]. The authors identify at least two reasons. First, there seems to be a general reluctance to use computer based systems. This might be true for some of the researchers and teachers in the humanities, but our experience shows that the majority are fascinated by possibilities of new technology as long as they match their research and teaching needs. Second, existing systems might be designed too narrowly. Thus, a simple transfer of information system (IS) metaphors [9] (e.g. workflow management [26], knowledge management [22], organizational memory [30]) successful in other domains might not be successful in general. Especially the humanities require a particularly sensitive design of information systems [7] that fits into their scientific methodology. For that reason, we have developed several information systems in tight cooperation with our colleagues from the cultural sciences and the humanities [15, 29, 16] within the collaborative research center on "Media and Cultural Communication".

In this paper we present MECCA-learn as a hypermedia course management system for media-rich curricula in the humanities and cultural sciences. Next, we introduce a framework for media-centric community learning in these disciplines. Then we compare some of the existing course management systems with respect to their suitability for the needs of learner communities in the humanities and the cultural sciences. Afterwards, we present MECCA-learn and a case study conducted in a community of practice in the film studies. The paper finishes with conclusions and an outlook on further research.

2   Media-Centric Learning Communities in the Humanities and the Cultural Sciences

Learner communities in the humanities and the cultural studies are coined by the discoursive nature of functioning within the humanities in general. This attitude of collaborating, thinking, working and thus learning is different from the common attitude in engineering or the natural sciences. Consequently, the needs of learner communities vary with respect to the support they need from course management systems. According to Snow [28], the type of knowledge creation and exchange in learning can be divided into to two styles. First, the 'linear type' of learning that is goal-oriented and transmission-centered. This means, old knowledge is replaced by new one as soon as it appears. Second, there is a 'non-linear type' of learning. Here, old knowledge isn't replaced but kept in the repository for a potential later usage. This style is **(multi-) media-centric** and resembles the functioning in the humanities. The rich media used in the discourse heavily depend on the situational context or are part of the discourse itself. Studies in organizational theory, linguistics, and experimental psychology [6, 10] generated similar results showing that the underlying knowledge generating systems (e.g. the human brain, the organization, the discourse) are not media independent. Thus, **hypermedia** metaphors are ideal to link the media to the knowledge system, and to express dependencies between them. Here, it is possi-

Table 1. Theoretical framing of activities in learning communities

Activities in learning communities	Knowledge conversions by Nonaka & Takeuchi [22]	Media specific operations	Operation type
Task creation Hypermedia document editing	implicit → explicit Externalization	*Transcription*	Human
Multimedia management Metadata management	explicit → explicit Combination	*Transcription*	(Semi-) Automatic
Task assignment Media centric presentation	explicit → implicit Internalization	*Addressing*	(Semi-) Automatic
Discourses Collaboration	implicit → implicit Socialization	*Localization*	Human

ble to capture the **discourses** about media by simultaneously providing a high degree of **collaboration possibilities**. Therefore, a joint (intellectual property protecting) **multimedia repository** is needed to share and exchange content. Thus, the question is: How can we integrate these functional requirements into a media-rich course management system (CMS) suitable for university-wide or even cross-university e-learning? The key point is simple: We have to provide an option for learners to hold media-centric discourses within courseware management systems. Consequently, the gap between a strictly sequential course organization and informal discourses will be bridged.

In our research center an operational media-theory has been developed that helps to understand the discursive nature of knowledge creation in the humanities. In order to transfer this theory on appropriate information system metaphors we have combined this theory with well known theories in information systems on knowledge creation (Nonaka and Takeuchi [22], Polanyi [23]) and social learning processes (Wenger [32]). This combination helped us to identify relevant activities performed by humans and machines in the information system. Based on the following three media operations [14, 10] the importance of the media in the discourses becomes visible:

- *Transcription* is a media dependent operation - either (semi-)automatic by the IS or manual by a human - that makes media collections more readable.
- The term of *(re-) addressing* describes an operation that intends to stabilize and optimize the presentation of content.
- *Localization* means an adaptation of global media into local practices.

Table 1 synthesizes knowledge conversions and media specific operations as a framework for media centric community learning process in the humanities. It comprises four distinct steps in a knowledge creation process and indicates whether the operation is performed by an individual (human) or by a machine (automatic). These successive steps may be repeated infinitely often, creating an often described continuous knowledge creation spiral. It oscillates between individuals and bigger social entities on the one axis and between implicit and explicit knowledge on the other axis. This knowledge creation process is called a learning process accordingly. The first step which implements **collaboration possibilities** is **assigning task** within learning community. It can be done by a tutor or a learner and is a *transcription* process. Therefore, a topic related to a certain media set of the **multimedia repository** is specified. In parallel, a new **hypermedia document** is created. Then, the task is processed automatically by the machine and descriptions compliant to the **MPEG-7 multimedia metadata standard** [13] are generated. Next, a **media-centric** *addressing* takes place when either multimedia artifacts are explored or hypermedia documents are presented. The cycle is closed, when **discourses** about **hypermedia documents** take place or the documents themselves initiate a new task. Thus, content of the information system has been adopted within the learning community by *localization* and the process may start anew. In the next section, we will give an overview on CMS in use and discuss whether these systems comply with the aforementioned needs of learning communities in the humanities.

3   Analysis of Existing Course Management Systems

There are many tools dealing with courseware management and e-learning in general. They vary from simple web based training tools to high level all-in-one systems combining workspaces, forums and learning materials. We now present related work in detail but confine the overview to those systems that are specially designed for use in academic education.

MIT OpenCourseWare (OCW) [19] is a free and open educational resource *addressing* faculty, students, and self-learners around the world. It is used for publication of MIT course materials and doesn't require any registration. Thus, MIT OCW offers courseware such as syllabi, readings, and sample solutions. Although it contains many MIT courses of various curricula, it isn't degree- or certificate-granting and doesn't provide access to MIT faculty. Its strength is its public accessibility and the wide range of materials available. However, it doesn't offer any specific means for *transcription* and *localization* among learners.

WebCT is probably the most widespread commercial CMS [25]. It offers a broad bandwidth of teaching and learning tools for development, delivery, and management of courses. The system is login based and offers students a possibility of learning at different levels. *Addressing* of e-learning content takes place via a shared workspace, but tasks can be assigned by tutors only. In addition, multimedia exploration is not central, but only a side effect. Collaboration and discourses are supported by forums, chat, or email. Access rights to these *localization* facilities depend on the user's rights. *Transcription* is based on SCORM [1], but there is no support to create designated hypermedia documents.

AIMS is a knowledge-based learning-content management system designed at Eindhoven University in the Netherlands to support both instructors and students [2]. Its intention is to provide an easy-to-use system that can either complement existing course delivery systems or can be used as a standalone learning content management tool. Thus, for *addressing* of e-learning content it enables tutors to author adaptive course sequencing driven by SCORM. *Tran-*

Table 2. Comparison of course management systems with respect to their support in *transcription, localization,* and *(re-) addressing* operations

		MIT OCW	WebCT	AIMS	CLIX	Moodle	Blackboard	Wiki	BSCW	MECCA-learn
	Access	Public	Via Login	Via Login	Via Login	Via Login	Via Login	Open or via Login	Via Login	Via Login
	Product type	Educational	Commercial	Educational	Commercial	Educational	Commercial	Open source	Educational or Commercial	Educational
Transcription	(Multimedia) Metadata Standard	No	SCORM	SCORM, LOM	SCORM	No	No	No	No	MPEG-7
	Hypermedia documents	No	No	No	No	No	No	Yes	No	Yes
(Re-) Addressing	Flexible task assignment	No	Only for tutors	Only for tutors	Only for tutors	Only for tutors	Workflows available	No	Workflows available	Yes
	Multimedia repository / centering	Only for download	Yes, but multimedia exploration isn't central	No	Only for download or via email	Upload only for assignments or via email	Yes, but multimedia exploration isn't central	Yes, but multimedia exploration isn't central	Yes, but multimedia exploration isn't central	Yes
Localization	Discourse support	No	Forum, Chat, Email	???	Forum, Chat, Email	Forum, Chat, Email	Forum, Chat, Email	Yes	Notes, Email	About any item
	Collaboration possibilities	No	Based on user groups	???	Based on user groups	Based on user groups	Based on user groups	Unlimited	Based on user groups	Based on user groups

scription is supported by LOM compliant management of teaching resources. However, support of *localization* among learners is not mentioned.

CLIX is a login based commercial course management system [12]. It fulfils the requirements of SCORM *transcription*. For *addressing* issues it contains several e-learning and course management tools that have most of their functionality restricted to tutors. E-learning content comprises web based tests, assessment tests, skill and competency management, and a virtual classroom for content presentation via browser. CLIX also includes communication tools for *localization*, such as forum, chat, or email.

Moodle stands for Modular Object-Oriented Dynamic Learning Environment [20]. It's considered to be the most prominent open source courseware system. Moodle is login based and offers tutors task assignment tools for *addressing*. For that purpose, Moodle offers three different categories of assignments: Weekly, topics, and social. Students are not allowed create assignments themselves but may upload their completed assignments or share materials via email. Based on the group rights *localization* is fostered via forums, chat, or email conversations. However, Moodle doesn't support *transcription* elements yet.

The mentioned systems so far mostly emphasize strict course organization, but don't facilitate in general the community wide *addressing* of multimedia artifacts. In addition, *localization* by means of collaboration among learners and discourses is mostly shifted to proprietary tools such as emails, etc. Thus, discourses and media are "separated", which leads to problems in media-centric studies. This deficit is tackled by the systems we will discuss next.

Blackboard Academic Suite^{TM} is a commercial login based e-learning environment to support widely diverse constituencies and education missions [4]. For *addressing* it offers a repository to share content of various file types without centering the media used. Additionally, it contains workflow facilities. Blackboard also comprises communication tools for *localization*, such as forum, chat, or email. Even though it offers almost all features to support learning processes in the humanities, its main drawbacks are that it doesn't support *transcription* elements up to now and that it lacks media centering in *addressing*.

Wikis are in Ward Cunningham's description "the simplest online database that could possibly work". A Wiki is an open source web based collaborative content management system that is also suitable for e-learning [31]. The strength of a Wiki is its openness in *localization*. Collaboration is almost unlimited and discourses may take place about any item. *Transcription* benefits from this concept,too. Hypermedia documents can be created by linking discourses with the underlying media, but metadata standards are not yet supported. In terms of *addressing* Wikis are suitable to manage multimedia content, but multimedia exploration is not central. Moreover, dedicated task management isn't supported.

BSCW (Basic Support for Collaborative Work) serves as a collaborative community content management system on the web [17]. It is a commercial tool also providing free of charge usage for educational institutions. Its *localization* features are very advanced for media-centric discourses and collaboration. Moreover, for *addressing* it offers support for versatile media formats to be shared as well as tasks to be defined within workflows. Nevertheless, multimedia exploration is not central, but only a side effect. *Transcription* is not supported, since collaboratively created documents are not suited to contain hypermedia.

Apart from the systems mentioned before, there are specific networking tools for course presentation and streaming of lectures. These are e.g. **Edutella** [21], **Prolearn TV** [27], or **Isabel** [24]. Since they focus on either presentation or management of e-learning content they haven't been discussed in detail. Table 2 condenses the previously mentioned CMS with respect to operations needed in media-centric curricula. For the sake of comparability, the features of MECCA-learn, which will be introduced in the following chapter, are included as well.

4   MECCA-Learn

In order to make e-learning successful among the communities of learners in the cultural sciences we provide them with a specially designed multimedia screening and classification application called MECCA (Movie E-learning Combination and Categorization Application) [16]. It is based on the Virtual Entrepreneurship Lab (VEL), which has been successfully applied in online entrepreneurship training, integrating ideas from "Berliner sehen" [8]. MECCA targets a multidisciplinary research community in a project of the film studies. The community is spatially distributed between the universities of Bochum and Bonn as well as the research center in Cologne. Its members have diverse backgrounds of education, e.g. film studies, history of art, graphical design and are on diverse levels of professionalism, i.e. full professors, research assistants, and students. Together, they share a joint enterprise within a research project on facial expressions in movies. MECCA allows the analysis of multimedia artefacts, the creation of tem-

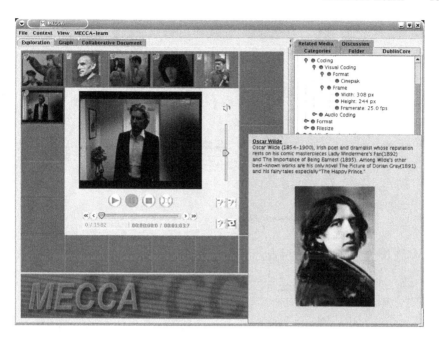

Fig. 1. MECCA user interface

poral decompositions and to (re-) classify artefacts according to the user's needs. Thus, it supports e-learning on the research level only. That means, MECCA (figure 1) is most suitable for researchers to collaborate in a distributed setting, but it does not focus on academic teaching. Therefore, the existing research oriented MECCA system has been further developed to suit the needs of media-rich curricula in the film studies. Dedicated features for course management and support of hypermedia documents have been added. With these features, it is now possible to represent discoursive acts within the CMS as in real on campus. By example of a task editing, we now present the key features of MECCA-learn.

The learning process starts with a human *transcription* by creating a task. In this aspect, MECCA-learn allows a loose structuring of courses and their decomposition into subtasks by a **flexible task arrangement** system. Due to the system's **collaboration possibilities** a task might be created by anyone and it is left to the user, to contribute to it or not. Because of the **media-centering** in the film studies the next step is the attribution of rich media to a task. This is accomplished by a reference to the respective medium within the metadata file of the task. For the sake of usability, a consecutive (semi-) automatic *transcription* step takes place. Here, information is captured by a concatenation of the basic element set of Dublin Core [3] and audio visual descriptors of MPEG-7. Since Dublin Core is popular in the humanities, but most suitable for print media, we have selected an excerpt of the extensive **MPEG-7 multimedia metadata standard** that allows a detailed metadata annotation of media as well as their temporal decompositions. MPEG-7 metadata about technical aspects of

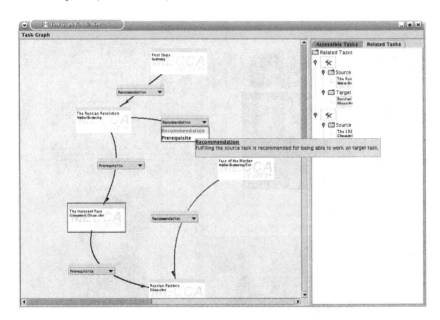

Fig. 2. Tasks assigned to a community member visualized as a graph

the medium such as visual encoding, frame rate, color space, etc. are extracted automatically by MECCA-learn. Additional information about the medium such as title, creator, etc. can be added manually by the users. In addition, there is an affiliated FTP-server serving as a collaborative **multimedia repository**. After completion, the resulting task and its affiliated media set are stored on the server. Then the task can be seen by all the users that have been assigned to it.

The e-learning process continues in an *addressing* of the **assigned tasks** and their **media-centric** presentation. Figure 2 shows the tasks assigned to a user. For the sake of usability, a graph representation can be selected in order to get an overview on the task dependencies. Since we allow the decomposition of tasks into subtasks, dependency types of tasks can be specified and visualized. When passing over the task, a tool-tip highlights additional information about the task, its creator and the date of creation. Since tasks might be assigned to an individual or a group, students have the option to collaborate and edit the related **hypermedia documents**.

The final step in the e-learning process takes place by *localization*. This is reflected in the **collaborative hypermedia documents** as well as the **discourses** about them. Figure 3 shows a **collaborative hypermedia document** that has been created for a particular task. The document is split into two sections. On the left hand side, the document iself is displayed. It consists of "containers" that might be filled with text, media, categorization elements, and media dependency graphs. All this information is stored as a MPEG-7 compliant graph description. Since the graph description is kept flexible, the references can be of different type and can be freely rearranged at any point in time.

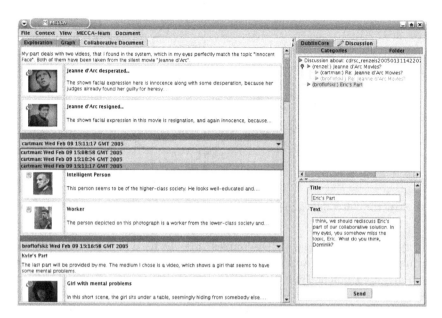

Fig. 3. A collaboratively created hypermedia document

Additionally, the document history can be traced back. For that reason, every "container" is tagged upon creation, edition, or deletion. Hence, documents can easily be restored by selecting the appropriate version of a particular container. The right hand side of the interface contains metadata about the collaborative document and its embedded rich media. The pane displays ongoing **discourses** as well as information about the media themselves. Finally, the **hypermedia document** or the **task** might be refined or newly created. Thus, closing the e-learning process and creating a continuous knowledge creation cycle.

From the technical side, MECCA-learn has been implemented as a Java application. Thus, it is platform independent which is of great importance, since our learning community in the humanities uses both MS Windows and Apple computers. On the server side, we have set up an eXist XML database [18] for the storage of the MPEG-7 metadata. All the content of MECCA-learn is stored compliant to MPEG-7. For the sake of manageability the documents of MECCA-learn are decomposed into several fragments (cf. figure 4). The core document is a so called MECCA-learn "task", interrelated with metadata files about "media". In order to express dependencies between "tasks" in case they exist they are referenced by MECCA-learn "task relationships" files. The MECCA-learn "task" element itself refers to potentially many MECCA-learn "media" and MECCA-learn "hypermedia" files. While the "media" files are used to link the "tasks" with the contained media set, the "hypermedia" file(s) contains the "task's" composition. Since the composition of the "hypermedia" file is a media centric process, it may also contain media itself. Consequently, the "hypermedia" file may also contain references to "media" files. Finally, there is the "discourse" doc-

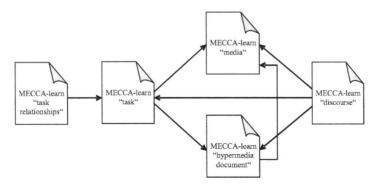

Fig. 4. Structural decomposition of tasks and their interdependencies in MECCA-learn

ument type in MECCA-learn. "Discourses" may be used to link them with tasks, hypermedia documents, and media. They are a central element used for discussion about any element type in MECCA-learn. Summarizing, MECCA-learn is an open and collaborative CMS that ranges from simple course organization up to discourse and complex collaboration support via hypermedia documents between students and instructors in media-rich curricula.

5   Conclusions and Outlook

Open CMS for university-wide or even cross-university e-learning in the humanities are still in infancy. Yet, web hosting of learner communities on basis of multimedia repository technologies is promising. Additionally, interleaving of media and their compositions by means of hypermedia is an important step facilitating media-rich curricula. We compared different selected course management systems already established in university teaching or propagated by research initiatives in e-learning. The results led to the development of a course management system called MECCA-learn. In our case study we demonstrated the usefulness of MPEG-7 as a metadata language for e-learning in media-rich curricula. Hence, the interrelation of collaborative hypermedia artifacts and media centric tasks make course management in the humanities more authentic, transparent, and flexible. In making such environments compatible to MPEG-7, the maturity of digital media management increases.

In the scope of the graduate course "pathos & passion" (english translation) at Ruhr-Universität Bochum, MECCA-learn is currently being evaluated. About twenty students use MECCA learn frequently as part of their curriculum. In the scope of their studies, they use MECCA-learn to take video screenings, share media collections, analyze media dependencies and create hypermedia documents out of them. Since the course has just begun and will last until the end of summer term 2005, the evaluation has not yet been completed. However, first feedback of students is very promising, in particular, related with the openness of MECCA-learn. Moreover, they enjoy using the system not in a subordinated learner's role but as an equal community member. On the data management level, the usage of MPEG-7 as framework for the description of e-learning content in media-rich studies is very promising. Due to the course's focus on media dependencies, MECCA-learn is able to capture all "low-level" technical information about media and combine them with "high-level" semantics. Although, main parts of the LOM [11] standard are already encapsulated within the MPEG-7 documents of MECCA-learn, compliance to LOM doesn't exist yet but is aspired in future versions. Thence, we research on a (semi-) automatic converter of e-learning content from LOM to MPEG-7. This will allow a seamlessly integration of learning materials already described by LOM into MECCA-learn.

Currently, we also do research on two other topics. The first issue aims at the analysis of intercultural aspects on learning. Here, the detection of disturbance patterns is of particular interest. Our aim is to extract constellations that are most likely subject to disturbances in the learning process. The second aspect focuses on a more artistic area of application. In cooperation with Nalin Sharda (Victoria University, Melbourne) we develop an application for Multimedia Inspired Story Telling (MIST). MIST concentrates on the creation of non-linear multimedia stories. Our task is to investigate the stories reception process and the factors leading to success or failure. Hence, we intend to use graph analysis tools to detect disturbance patterns in multimedia stories.

Acknowledgements

This work was supported by the German National Science Foundation (DFG) within the collaborative research centers SFB/FK 427 "Media and Cultural Communication", the SFB 476 "IMPROVE", and by the 6th Framework IST programme of the EC through the NoE on Professional Learning (PROLEARN) IST-2003-507310. We'd like to thank our colleagues for the many discussions. In particular, we thank our student workers Dominik Renzel and Monika Pienkos for the implementation of MECCA-learn.

References

1. ADL Technical Team. SCORM conformance requirements version 1.2. http://www.adlnet.org/screens/shares/dsp_displayfile.cfm?fileid=1059, 2004.
2. AIMS Project. AIMS: Adaptive Information System for Management of Learning Content. http://www.win.tue.nl/ laroyo/AIMS/index.htm, October 9 2003.
3. ANSI/NISO Z39.85-2001: The Dublin Core Metadata Element Set. http://www.niso.org/standards/resources/Z39-85.pdf, September 10 2001.
4. Blackboard Inc. Blackboard Academic Suite™. http://www.blackboard.com/docs/AS/Bb_Academic_Suite_Brochure.pdf, 2004.
5. S. E. Carson. MIT OCW Program Evaluation Findings Report. http://ocw.mit.edu/NR/rdonlyres/3DFAB417-0966-4CC-8025-94F1991302F6/0/Program_Eval_March_2004.pdf, 2004.
6. R. Daft and R. Lengel. Organizational informations requirements, media richness and structural design. *Management Science*, 32(5):554 – 571, 1986.

7. G. De Michelis, E. Dubois, M. Jarke, F. Matthes, J. Mylopoulos, K. Pohl, J. Schmidt, C. Woo, and E. Yu. Cooperative information systems: A manifesto. Technical report, Aachener Informatik-Bericht 96-21, RWTH Aachen, 1996.
8. K. Fendt. Contextualizing content. In M. Knecht and K. von Hammerstein, editors, *Languages across the Curriculum*, pages 201 – 223. National East Asian Languages Resource Center / Ohio State University, Columbus, 2000.
9. F. Flores, M. Graves, B. Hartfield, and T. Winograd. Computer systems and the design of organizational interaction. *ACM Transactions on Office Information Systems*, 6(2):153 – 172, 1988.
10. J. Fohrmann and E. Schüttpelz. *Die Kommunikation der Medien*. Niemeyer, Tübingen, 2004 (in German).
11. IEEE Learning Technology Standards Committee WG 12. Learning Object Metadata. http://ltsc.ieee.org/wg12/, 2004.
12. imc. Advanced Learning Solutions. http://www.im-c.de/, 2005.
13. ISO. Information technology – Multimedia content description interface – Part 8: Extraction and use of MPEG-7 descriptions. Technical Report ISO/IEC TR 15938-8:2002(E), International Organization for Standardization, 2002.
14. L. Jäger and G. Stanitzek, editors. *Transkribieren - Medien/Lektüre*. Wilhelm Fink Verlag, Munich, 2002.
15. R. Klamma, M. Jarke, E. Hollender, and D. Börner-Klein. Enabling communities by constructed media: The case of a web-based study environment for a talmudic tractate. In J. Fong et al. *Advances in Web-Based Learning, Proceedings of the First International Conference, ICWL 2002, Hong Kong, China, August 17-19, 2002*, volume 2436 of *LNCS*, pp. 275-285, Berlin Heidelberg, 2002. Springer-Verlag.
16. R. Klamma, M. Spaniol, and M. Jarke. MECCA: Hypermedia Capturing of Collaborative Scientific Discourses about Movies. *informing science. The International Journal of an Emerging Discipline, N. Sharda (Ed.): Special Series on Issues in Informing Clients using Multimedia Communications*, 8:3 – 38, 2005.
17. K. Klöckner. Bscw - educational servers and services on the WWW. In *Proc. of the International C4-ICDE Conf. on Distance Education and Open Learning "Competition, Collaboration, Continuity, Change"*, Adelaide, September 9-14, 2000.
18. W. Meier. eXist: An Open Source Native XML Database. In A. B. Chaudhri, M. Jeckle, E. Rahm, and R. Unland, editors, *Web, Web-Services, and Database Systems, NODe 2002 Web and Database-Related Workshops, Erfurt, Germany, October 7-10, 2002, Revised Papers*, volume 2593 of *LNCS*, pp. 169-183, Berlin Heidelberg, 2003. Springer-Verlag.
19. MIT. OpenCourseWare. http://ocw.mit.edu/index.html, 2005.
20. Modular Object-Oriented Dynamic Learning Environment (moodle). http://moodle.org/doc/, 2005.
21. W. Nejdl, B. Wolf, C. Qu, S. M. Decker, S., A. Naeve, M. Nilsson, M. Palmér, and T. Risch. EDUTELLA: A P2P networking infrastructure based on RDF. In *Proceedings of the 12th WWW Conference, Honululu, May 2002*, pp. 604-615, 2002.
22. I. Nonaka and H. Takeuchi. *The Knowledge-Creating Company*. Oxford University Press, Oxford, 1995.
23. M. Polanyi. *The tacit dimension*. Anchor Books, Doubleday&Co., New York, 1966.
24. J. Quemada, G. Huecas, T. de Miguel, J. Salvachua, B. Rodriguez, B. Simon, K. Maillet, and E. Law. EducaNext: A Framework for Sharing Live Educational Resources with Isabel. In *Proceedings of the 13th WWW Conference, Education Track, New York, May 2004*, pages 11 – 18, 2004.
25. G. Ronald. Introduction to WebCTs Features (CE v4). http://www.webct.com/service/ViewContent?contentID=18710281, 2005.

26. T. Schäl. *Workflow Management Systems for Process Organizations*, volume 1096 of *LNCS*. Springer, Berlin and Heidelberg, 1996.

27. P. J. Scott and K. Quick. Heroic failures in disseminating novel e-learning technologies to corporate clients: A case study of interactive webcasting. In *Proceedings of the 4th International Symposium on Information and Communication Technologies, Cape Town, South Africa, Jan 3-6, ACM Press*, 2004.

28. C. P. Snow. *The Two Cultures*. Cambridge University Press, Cambridge, 1959.

29. M. Spaniol, R. Klamma, L. Springer, and M. Jarke. Aphasics' communities learning on the web. In W. Liu, Y. Shi, and Q. Li, editors, *Advances in Web-Based Learning, Proceedings of ICWL 2004, Beijing, China, August 8-11*, volume 3143 of *LNCS*, pages 277–285, Berlin Heidelberg, 2004. Springer-Verlag.

30. E. W. Stein and V. Zwass. Actualizing organizational memory with information technology. *Information Systems Research*, 6(2):85 – 117, 1995.

31. J. Wagstaff. Wikipedia: It's Wicked. *The Wall Street Journal Online, Loose Wire*, 2004. http://www.theproduct.com/6m105/readings/spring04/encyclopedia.pdf.

32. E. Wenger. *Communities of Practice: Learning, Meaning, and Identity*. Cambridge University Press, Cambridge, UK, 1998.

33. V. Zafrin. Teaching in the Digital Age and philosophical differences. http://www.brown.edu/Departments/Italian_Studies/vhl/archives/2005/01/21/teaching-in-the-digital-age-and-philosophical-differences/, January 21 2005.

Building Learning Management Systems Using IMS Standards: Architecture of a Manifest Driven Approach*

José Luis Sierra[1], Pablo Moreno-Ger[2], Iván Martínez-Ortiz[2],
Javier López-Moratalla[2], and Baltasar Fernández-Manjón[1]

[1] Dpto. Sistemas Informáticos y Programación, Fac. Informática,
Universidad Complutense, 28040, Madrid, Spain
{jlsierra, balta}@sip.ucm.es
[2] Centro de Estudios Superiores Felipe II. Aranjuez. Spain
{pmoreno, imartinez, jlmoratalla}@cesfelipesegundo.com

Abstract. Among the existing web-based *Learning Management Systems* (LMSs), there is an exponentially increasing need of content interoperability. This has caused the apparition of different standardization initiatives. In this paper we describe our approach to the design of <e-Aula>, a new LMS which adheres closely to IMS standards in an attempt to evaluate the practical viability of those standards. The architecture of our system, focused on the IMS *manifest*, has yielded a powerful and modular system that goes beyond the initial intention of evaluating the proposed standard and can be used as a robust production system in a real environment. We describe our IMS driven approach, as well as an architecture based on this approach that has been implemented using well-known and robust Java based web technologies.

1 Introduction

The IMS proposals [10] are a comprehensive collection of specifications covering the needs of e-learning systems that allow a high durability, reusability and portability of the educational contents. For the last two years, the efforts of our group have been centered on the experimentation with these standardization proposals suggested by the IMS Global Consortium. In this way, we have implemented <e-Aula> [1,7,15], an IMS compliant *Learning Management System* (LMS) supporting several e-learning specifications: IMS CP (for packaging contents), LOM (for expressing metadata) [8], IMS QTI (for tests and assessments) and IMS LIP (for storing information about the learners). In <e-Aula> we use what we have called a *manifest driven approach* to the construction of an IMS based LMS, which is described in this paper.

The structure of the paper is as follows. Section 2 describes the details relative to IMS needed to understand the rest of the paper. Section 3 describes the manifest based approach itself. Section 4 describes the software architecture of <e-Aula>, which is

---

* The Spanish Committee of Science and Technology (projects TIC2001-1462, TIC2002-04067-C03-02 and TIN2004-08367-C02-02) has partially supported this work.

R.W.H. Lau et al. (Eds.): ICWL 2005, LNCS 3583, pp. 144–156, 2005.

based on this approach. Section 5 compares our approach with other related works. Finally, section 6 gives some conclusions and outlines some lines of future work.

2   The IMS Content Packaging and the Concept of Manifest

The IMS Content Packaging specification (IMS CP) defines how to aggregate the educational contents into *packages* in order to let different heterogeneous systems interchange these contents. This specification is available in the IMS web site together with the rest of IMS specifications [10]. The structure of these packages is depicted in Fig. 1a. According to this, a package is formed by a set of physical archives with the contents and a *manifest*. This manifest is a XML document that reflects global information about the package, the structure of the contents, their types and their possible organizations. More precisely, the manifest contains:

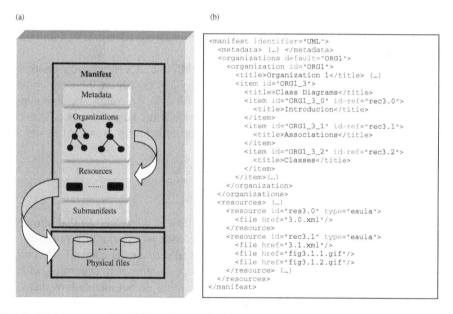

Fig. 1. (a) Structure of an IMS package, (b) fragment of an IMS manifest extracted from a course deployed on <e-Aula>. It has been simplified for presentational purposes and for the sake of clarity

- A section of *metadata* summarizing global (meta)information about the package. This metainformation follows the *Learning Object Metadata* (LOM) specification defined by the IEEE LTSC. LOM is also used to convey the metadata associated with the other elements in the manifest (resources, organizations, and submanifests).
- The description of the package's *resources*. In its simplest form a resource is associated with a physical archive with learning content. It is also possible to describe resources associated with a main file and a set of secondary files. This

makes it possible to bundle content sets like a main HTML file and the images related with this. Also, the resource can include metadata about itself and, most importantly, it defines the type of the content within it. Finally, each resource must have a unique identifier.

- The *organizations* of the resources. Each organization represents a tree structure whose nodes can refer to resources. The nodes in this tree are called *items* and they contain a reference to their corresponding resources using the unique identifiers of the resources. Therefore, an organization provides a tree based structuration of the resources of the package (and thus, of its physical files). It is also to be noted that a manifest can include several organizations, each one providing an alternative way to organize the contents, and therefore a different view of the package.

- The *submanifests*. A manifest can contain other simpler manifests that in turn exhibit the same structure outlined here.

In Fig. 1b a manifest taken from a course deployed on <e-Aula> is depicted. This example shows a tree based organization linked to different resources by means of the usual XML *id-idref* mechanism. In their turn, the resources contain URLs pointing at the actual files.

As a final remark, it is important to note that IMS does not impose any restrictions on the format or type of the content files. Usually LMSs support the most common formats for contents such as HTML and PDF files. In <e-Aula> we also support directly XML files created according to descriptive markup languages specific to each project. This adds all the benefits of the content structuring power of descriptive markup [5].

3   The Manifest Driven Approach

The previous section has presented the IMS manifest as a mechanism that allows the structuration of the contents in an IMS package with interoperability purposes. An IMS compliant LMS can *import* IMS packages and recover the educational contents using this manifest and it can *export* contents by packaging them according with the IMS CP specification. Nevertheless, IMS specifications do not dictate how this LMS must behave out of the scope of the aforementioned interoperability processes. As it has already been mentioned, in <e-Aula> we propose what we have called a *manifest driven approach*. In this approach *the manifest is used as the key element for driving the design and architecture of the entire LMS beyond interoperability processes*.

The manifest driven approach encourages that the LMS maintains continuously a representation of the manifest for each course. In this way, the manifest is used to structure contents not only when interoperating with other systems but also when these contents are managed inside the LMS. This way, for every operation executed on a course there will be a corresponding operation executed on its manifest. Consequently, for each course within the system, its manifest will be the fundamental reference for performing the different tasks related to the course: *presentation*, *edition*, *importation* and *exportation*. Next subsections analyze how the manifest driven approach facilitates these tasks.

3.1 Course Presentation

Course presentation can be naturally addressed by providing suitable browsing and presentation semantics to the organizational information included in its manifest. Indeed:

Fig 2. Presentation generated in <e-Aula> following the manifest driven approach on the manifest sketched in Fig. 1b. When the user clicks on an item, the associated resource is loaded

- When the learner needs to access the contents of a course, a tree structure displaying the *active* organization can be presented. Since this information is directly encoded in the manifest file, it will not be necessary to explore the content in order to work out its structure. The term *active* is remarked above because the concept of different organizations in a manifest lets the learner choose the organization that fits her better.
- When the learner selects in the tree each item she wants to read, its associated resource and the content type of this resource can be consulted in the manifest. For each supported resource type there is a specific module capable of processing the resource that will take care of the tasks needed to visualize it.

In Fig 2 the presentation of the course whose manifest is outlined in Fig. 1b is depicted.

3.2 Course Edition

Course edition can be seen conceptually as a similar process to course visualization. Being the manifest the core of the system, edition actions will be directly reflected in the manifest. More precisely:

- The instructor will be allowed to add new resources to a specific course as well as to remove and modify them. This includes stating the content type of the resource. Such operations will be automatically reflected on the manifest (Fig. 3a).
- For managing the organizations (i.e. for structuring the resources) the instructor is offered with a tree very similar to that seen by learners when visiting a course.

The instructor can then add or remove nodes in that tree. Those actions are directly reflected in the manifest by the addition/removal of items within the active organization. During this process, the instructor can assign to each node/item a resource from the previously gathered resource pool, which is also indexed in the manifest (Fig. 3b).

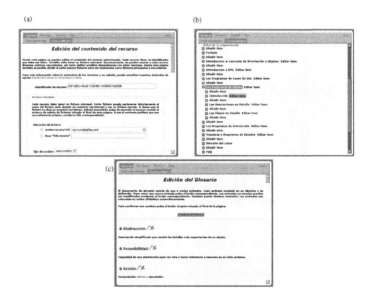

Fig. 3. Edition operations: (a) Inclusion of a new resource, (b) edition of the tree of an organization, (c) edition of an <e-Aula> *Glossary* resource

- For creation and modification of actual contents associated with the resources it is possible to adopt a similar strategy to the one that was used to display the selected resources upon learner petition. For every content type there is an associated edition module. When the instructor selects in the tree a resource to be modified, its edition module is launched thus allowing her to modify it using the web interface (Fig. 3c).

In <e-Aula> we have considered that course structure management (i.e. addition, removal and organization of resources) is more important for our evaluation purposes than content edition itself. Thus, <e-Aula> currently only includes edition modules for the content types specific of this system (e.g. <e-Aula> content pages, course presentations, glossary and F.A.Q.). Other common resource types, although supported for visualization, are not currently supported for edition (e.g. PDF, HTML, etc.). Those resources can be uploaded to the system but once there they cannot be directly edited. Typically, if instructors want to modify such files they will edit them with their usual edition tool and will upload them into the system. Nevertheless, due to the modularity of the manifest driven approach, the incorporation of new editors to <e-Aula> will be straightforward.

3.3 Course Importation

The importation facility allows the incorporation of packages produced in other LMSs. Importation is always a problematic functionality. Even though the IMS CP aims at facilitating this kind of processes, it is very broad. In effect:

- Several content types are permitted and there are no specific restrictions regarding the formats. Therefore it will be usual to find incoming packages including resources of types unknown or unsupported by the system.
- The importation facility must also manage situations that are more difficult. Effectively, the standards are not mature enough and they are subjected to evolution. Moreover, IMS incorporates an extension mechanism allowing vendors to add their own extensions to the standards. Consequently, an imported package can follow an unsupported IMS CP version or include unsupported vendor specific extensions.

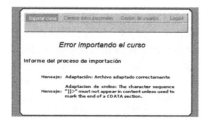

Fig. 4. A snapshot of the <e-Aula> importation system. Help of the user is required to adapt an incoming package with invalid syntax

The challenge of a sophisticated importation system, such as the included in <e-Aula>, is to try to understand and adapt the incoming packages. Due to the aforementioned factors this adaptation can require the help of a human user (Fig. 4). The manifest driven approach simplifies this complex process because mostly all the work can be done over the manifest. The manifest is indeed a clean and powerful element in which to centralize the efforts when designing an importation system. Any modification to the standards, any kind of strange resource type and even the version of the standard are always reflected in the manifest. That means that the steps required to import a package can be deduced from a deep examination of its manifest. In addition, many of the changes in the package produced by the execution of these steps can be limited to modifications of the manifest file. For example, when there is no possibility of adapting an alien resource and it must be removed, the action actually performed is to erase from the manifest the references to this resource. The content is still in the package but it does not cause any problems because the resources are always accessed using the manifest. The old manifest can be backed up so that the offending content can be revived when needed (and supported).

Upon completion of all the adaptation procedures during importation, the resulting manifest file is valid from both the standard's and the system's points of view. It can thus be safely displayed and/or edited.

3.4 Course Exportation

On many systems, the process of exporting content following the proposed standards can be a complex task, because it might imply scanning the course's internal representations in order to recover the IMS structures. However, with the manifest driven approach exportation is extremely simple, because the courses are internally represented by their manifests. Therefore the courses maintain full compatibility with IMS CP during their whole life in the LMS, being unnecessary to perform any kind of adaptation or additional processing beyond zipping the content together with the manifest file and storing it all in the file system

4 An LMS Architecture Based on the Manifest Driven Approach

During the inception phase of <e-Aula>, some important requirements were identified. Keeping in mind that IMS specifications were still young and thus prone to be changed (perhaps even disregarded by the community) the system should be as flexible as possible. It should not be a fixed application that once developed goes into production, but a lively, ever changing environment. For a few years following its construction, the system should evolve, adapting to the evolution of the standards and the irruption of new concepts. This means that internally complex monolithic systems should be avoided promoting instead modular systems in order to assure maintainability.

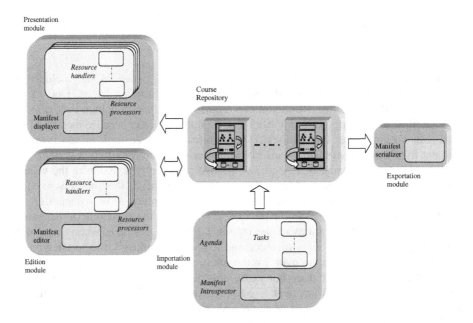

Fig. 5. Architecture of a manifest driven LMS

The manifest driven approach described in the previous section can be implemented by means of a modular and powerful architecture meeting the aforementioned requirements. This architecture has been implemented in the <e-Aula> system and tested in the development of several courses at *Complutense* University of Madrid (Spain). The next subsections describe this architecture. Subsection 4.1 gives an overview of the architecture. Subsections 4.2, 4.3 and 4.4 detail its different aspects. Finally, subsection 4.5 summarizes how this architecture is implemented in <e-Aula> using well-known web development standards.

4.1 Overview of the Architecture

In Fig. 5 the architecture for an LMS based on the manifest driven approach is depicted. The architecture must support the four main tasks described in section 2. Therefore a distinct module is included for each one of these tasks.

The architecture is organized around a *storage* module where the different courses are stored. This module maintains an explicit representation of the IMS manifest for each course. According to the manifest driven approach, all the operations performed on the courses are reflected on these representations.

The architecture of the presentation and the edition modules are similar and based on a delivery policy with *resource processors* able to select the most suitable *resource handlers* for each type of resource. They are detailed in subsection 4.2 and subsection 4.3. On its turn, the importation module exhibits an *agenda based architecture* [2], which is suitable to cope in a modular way with the complexities of this operation (see subsection 4.4). Finally, as mentioned before the structure of the exportation module is straightforward due to the explicit representation of the manifests in the storage module.

4.2 The Presentation Module

The previous section has already outlined the difficulties faced when building a LMS supporting the broad range of content types that an IMS based course can contain. Indeed, a mechanism that can react to the different content types and process them accordingly is required. In the LMS vocabulary, such a mechanism is called a *delivery system*. Following the underlying concepts of the manifest driven approach a three-step process is suggested which is parallel to the three layers defining the content type of a resource:

- The first step begins when a course is loaded. The action taken is to consult the required *application profile* in the manifest. The concept of *Application Profile* (AP) is the IMS term to designate a customization of a standard to meet the needs of particular communities of implementers with common application requirements. For each supported AP there is a different *resource processor*. From the perspective of the implementation, the presentation module will be equipped with a table listing the relations between the different APs and their corresponding resource processor objects. When the course is loaded, the corresponding resource processor is invoked. That processor will be responsible of handling all the requests related with the resources until a new course is loaded. After this step is completed, the system examines the manifest, loads the default organization and displays a tree reflecting the structure of the items. This is made by a component called *manifest displayer*.

- The second step is triggered whenever the learner clicks a node of the tree (which represents an item). The system queries the manifest about whether that item has an associated resource. If it does, the content type of the resource is consulted in the manifest. That information is transmitted to the active resource processor. Just like in the previous step, the resource processor contains a table relating each content type to an appropriate *resource handler*, which is a module capable of processing that content type.
- In the third step, the resource handler gets control and performs all the operations required by the content type. Such operations could include, among other things, formatting the content, adapting it to the learner's profile, adapting the content to the client's device or storing statistical data about the learner's visit to the item before and after the visit itself.

Notice that this organization allows the incorporation of new resource processors and new resource handlers in a modular and transparent way without interfering with the behavior of the presentation module.

4.3 The Edition Module

The edition module must handle two different problems: the edition of the structure of the course (edition of the manifest) and the edition of the course content (edition of the associated resources):

- For the edition of the resources it is possible to adopt the same delivery strategy followed in the edition module. Therefore, the content edition environment can be architected in a similar way, reusing the ideas used in the presentation module to trigger the appropriate resource handler.
- The edition of the structure of the course is carried out by a *manifest editor* component. This component reuses the ideas employed to visualize the navigation tree in the presentation module, adding the functionality to add/edit/delete nodes and link them to the resources edited.

As with the presentation module, the architecture of the edition module allows the incorporation of new edition facilities in a straightforward manner.

4.4 The Importation Module

The architecture of the importation module must be flexible enough to cope with the complexities of the importation process. This must implement a flexible behavior capable of reacting when confronted with different problems, even with the possibility of querying the user when more information is needed to perform the importation. Because of this, we propose an implementation based on an *agenda* similar to the proposed in [2] to simulate discrete systems.

According to the agenda based organization, when a package is imported the system parses the manifest, adding new tasks to the agenda to resolve the troubles encountered during the scan. These tasks (especially those that involve a query to the user) can create other tasks and add them to the agenda if it is needed for their resolution. In this manner, a complex process that requires a heterogeneous set of actions is dynamically split into simple tasks. More precisely:

- The importation begins with a deep scan of the manifest. This is carried out using a component called the *manifest introspector*. This generates a report that profiles, among other things, whether the manifest is a well-formed XML document, which version of the standard it follows, which other schemas (if any) are needed to understand it and under what AP it has been developed. This report is presented to the user, who decides how to continue.
- Depending on the user's response, the system generates a list of initial tasks for the agenda and starts working on them. Such tasks may include the modification of the manifest file, modification of the AP, adaptation of some resources or physical installation of the package.

This agenda based implementation makes it possible to add new types of adaptation tasks during importation in a transparent way (e.g. to adapt a new content type). Such an organization dramatically enhances the modularity and maintainability of this complex subsystem.

4.5 Implementing the Architecture

This architecture has been implemented in <e-Aula> using Java technologies in order to maximize maintainability, extensibility and robustness of the resulting implementation. More precisely, we have based our implementation on the Sun Microsystems' J2EE platform [11] complemented with the Apache Foundation's Struts framework [3]. From J2EE we adopt the multi-tier organization according to which applications are layered in different tiers (*client*, *web*, *business* and *persistence*). From Struts we adopt the organization in terms of the classical *Model-View-Controller* (MVC) design pattern. With this, each one of the presentation, edition, importation and exportation modules has its own view and a controller, which interact with a common model represented by the course repository and the manifests within it, as suggested by Struts. In addition they are disposed on a layered organization, as suggested by J2EE.

5 Related Work

LMSs have been widely adopted by institutions and instructional designers in order to fulfil certain needs and requirements in a field of ever increasing demands for effective education and training [4]. In many of these systems considerations like adherence to standards or content exchange are often secondary goals because, although being desirable, there are not usually a key point for customer satisfaction (be it a learner or an institution interested in buying the system to deploy their own content). On the contrary, we follow a more scholarly approach. Therefore, we focus on the evaluation of standards and the research in modular architectures, being aspects like user friendliness or the support for a wide spectrum of high quality content formats a secondary objective.

Many initiatives have adopted IMS as a basic interoperability mechanism. They range from commercial product like WebCT [18], which can be purchased by companies in order to deploy their own content, to initiatives like ADL-SCORM [16], which provides complementary specifications for obtaining high-quality content and systems in a variety of fields. While these initiatives pay only attention to IMS standards when it comes to interoperability issues (e.g. content exportation/importation), our manifest driven proposal goes a step forward. Indeed, we defend the use of the specifications (in particular, the IMS manifest) as central mechanisms to conceive, architect, design and implement the system.

There are alternative approaches to architect an LMS. One of the most relevant is proposed by the SAKAI project [14]. SAKAI's goal is to join different open source course management systems and related tools in a single open source architecture. To achieve this goal the SAKAI software is based in the MIT Open Knowledge Initiative (OKI) [13], which is a service-oriented framework to develop a Course Managment System. This approach focuses on the general architecture of a LMS, allowing the addition of the existing tools. The choice of specific standards is delegated on the different tools that implements local services. Our manifest driven approach, being more oriented to the development of such local services, can be complementary to this kind of proposals.

More similar to the <e-Aula> LMS are the large amount of e-learning tools based on scripting technologies (e.g. systems like ILIAS [9], Moodle [12] or Dokeos [6] are written in PHP, while WebCT Campus Edition [18] is written in Perl). While these products prove that it is possible to build large scale LMSs based on the mentioned technologies, in our opinion it requires a large amount of effort by developers when it comes to adding new functionalities and it affects their maintainability. Indeed, new developments, in particular large scale LMSs such as WebCT Vista [18], are being developed using Java technologies. On its turn, Java technologies are more robust and they meet better complementary requirements like modularity and maintainability. These have led us to adopt these technologies in <e-Aula>.

6   Conclusions and Future Work

In this paper we have described our manifest driven approach to architect IMS based LMSs. This approach is the result of our efforts in the development of <e-Aula>, a system aimed to evaluate different e-learning standards and e-learning modular architectures.

The manifest driven approach facilitates the main tasks contemplated in the LMS: course presentation, edition, importation, and exportation. In addition, this approach leads to a modular architecture that facilitates extensibility. Adding support for a new content type is just a matter of writing the code needed to prepare and display content in that format. This is also true when adding a new content editor to the system, or a new task for the agenda. The high degree of modularity of the architecture also enhances maintainability. It is easy to find the points in the source code where any changes could be needed, and these changes can be done will little impact on the rest of the system. While the complexity of the architecture is high (in terms of number of classes and files in the resulting implementation), this is the price to pay for achieving a very high degree of modularity, and therefore a better extensibility and an easier maintenance.

Our Java based implementation preserves the benefits of the architecture and also adds a high degree of robustness. Nevertheless we should point out as a drawback the need of more computing power on the server when compared with lighter applications based on scripting solutions (like PHP). While the choice between a large and robust system and a lightweight application will depend on the exact needs of each learning environment, the J2EE / Struts based solution is well suited for our purposes because it allows a continuous evolution of the system to accommodate our evaluation and research needs.

Currently the architecture based on the manifest driven approach is fully implemented in the <e-Aula> system. This LMS is fully functional and adheres strictly to the IMS CP standard. There is also partial support of the IMS QTI standard, which is also functioning as a stand-alone application, and some built-in adaptability features for different client platforms and user levels. As future work we are planning to incorporate advanced user modeling capabilities. The IMS LIP (Learner Information Profile) standard may be a supporting aid in this task. In addition, we are planning to apply further the *document oriented* approach promoted in [17] for both the incremental definition of new types of resources and the incremental construction of their associated handlers. Finally, we are planning to involve to field experts in the development of high-quality content that fully exploits the functionalities of our system. The advanced importation features incorporated in <e-Aula> should facilitate this task.

References

1. <e-Aula>. eaula.sip.ucm.es
2. Abelson, H.; Sussman, J.; Sussman, J. Structure and Interpretation of Computer Programs - Second Edition. MIT Press. 1996
3. Apache Struts. struts.apache.org
4. Avgeriou, P.; Papasalouros, A.; Retalis, S.; Skordalakis, M. Towards a Pattern Language for Learning Management Systems. Educational Technology & Society, 6(2), pp. 11-24. 2003
5. Coombs, J. H.; Renear, A. H.; DeRose, S. J. Markup Systems and the Future of Scholarly Text Processing. Communications of the ACM, 30 (11), pp. 933-947. 1987
6. Dokeos. www.dokeos.com
7. Fernández-Manjón,B.; Sancho, P. Creating cost-effective adaptive educational hypermedia based on markup technologies and e-learning standards. Interactive Educational Multimedia 4. 2002
8. IEEE Standard for Learning Object Metadata. IEEE Standard 1484.12.1-2002. 2002

9. ILIAS. www.ilias.uni-koeln.de/ios/index-e.html
10. Instructional Management System Global Consortium. www.imsglobal.org
11. Java 2 Enterprise Edition. java.sun.com/j2ee/
12. Moodle. moodle.org
13. OKI Project. www.okiproject.org
14. SAKAI Project. www.sakai.org
15. Sancho, P.; Manero, B.; Fernández-Manjón, B. Learning Objects Definition and Use in <e-Aula>: Towards a Personalized Learning Experience. Edutech:Computer-Aided Design Meets Computer Aided Learning, pp177-186. Kluwer Academic Publishers. 2004
16. Shareable Content Object Reference Model SCORM. www.adlnet.org
17. Sierra, J.L.; Fernández-Valmayor, A.; Fernández-Manjón, B.; Navarro, A.. ADDS: A Document-Oriented Approach for Application Development. Journal of Universal Computer Science, 10(9), pp 1302-1324. 2004
18. WebCT. www.webct.com

Constructing a SCORM-Compliant Intelligent Strategy Repository

Yi-Chun Chang[1], Ching-Pao Chang[1], Chiung-Hui Chiu[2],
Yi-Chi Chen[1], and Chih-Ping Chu[1]

[1] Department of Computer Science and Information Engineering,
National Cheng-Kung University, Tainan, Taiwan
{changyj, chucp}@csie.ncku.edu.tw
[2] Department of Computer Science and Information Education,
National Tainan University, Tainan, Taiwan

Abstract. Developing a pedagogical learning content that can be delivered among different Learning Management Systems (LMSs) is a critical task for most instructors. Although the Sharable Content Object Reference Model (SCORM) has proposed a mechanism allowing the exchange of learning contents between LMSs, to embed learning strategies to SCORM-compliant learning content is still an open issue. This paper proposes a mechanism to construct a SCORM-compliant strategy repository which contains learning strategies. The strategy repository can be adapted to satisfy the requirement of instructor for designing learning content with strategies embedded. The strategy repository presented in this paper is with the following advantages: (a) the strategies stored are domain independent; (b) the strategies offered are adaptable; (c) the strategies saved can be continuously evolved; (d) the strategies stored can be reusable.

1 Introduction

In classroom teaching and learning, the instruction model for the class usually can not satisfy all the learners. The major problem of the traditional learning environment is that one instructor must take care of more than one learner. To solve this problem, an adaptive learning must be considered in the learning process. The adaptive learning, which delivers different learning content to the learner according to the corresponding learning strategy, is the major advantage of LMS comparing to the traditional learning environment [1]. The learning strategy is an instruction sequence, which can be arranged by instructors to guide the learner through the learning process in an efficient and effective way. To achieve an efficient and effective learning process is the major goal for most instructors.

To reduce the effort of content development, SCORM provides the mechanisms to facilitate the accessing of reusable and sharable learning contents in the web. Although the standardization provided by the SCORM has solved the problem of compatibility of learning contents between LMSs, the structure and aggregation of learning contents supported by SCORM can not always fit the need of contents design based on the

R.W.H. Lau et al. (Eds.): ICWL 2005, LNCS 3583, pp. 157–162, 2005.

learning strategy. The sequencing in SCORM only provides the functionality of arrangement of presentation sequence of learning contents. To alter the presentation sequence of learning contents according to a strategy, the instructor needs to rewrite the sequence structure of the learning contents, resulting extra load in teaching. This paper proposes an approach of constructing a strategy repository which supports strategic learning in SCORM-compliant LMS.

The proposed SCORM-compliant strategy repository has the following features: (1) Domain independent: The learning strategies in the repository can be applied to various domains; (2) Adaptability: The learning strategies in the repository can be adapted according to learner's learning style; (3) Continuous evolution: Learning strategies can be verified and improved continuously; (4) Reusability: New learning strategies can be created by overlaying or combining existed strategies.

The rest of this paper is organized as follows. In the next section, we will briefly review related work; in Section 3, we shall illustrate our proposed strategy repository in detail. Finally, in the last section, we shall draw a conclusion.

2 Related Work

The technologies of SCORM v1.3 which defines a set of standard of learning content and system, includes content aggregation model (CAM), sequencing and navigation (SN), and run-time environment (RTE). The CAM describes how to build and organize the learning contents [3]. The sequencing reorganizes the presentation sequence of learning contents and provides the information of delivering learning contents according to the learning status of learner [4]. The RTE defines the integration and interaction between LMS and learner [5].

In addition, there are many learning contents authoring tools with the feature to edit SCORM-compliant learning contents. These tools can be found at 3rd Party Tool in the ADL web. For example, MINE and VOSSAT can generate automatically the manifest file, and then package with the learning contents into the SCORM-compliant zip file [7]. However, these authoring tools do not provide the functionalities of integrating learning strategy to existing learning contents. If the instructor wants to edit the existing learning contents with the learning strategy for a course, she/he needs to rewrite the presentation sequence of learning contents. The experience of the instructor controls the quality of the edited course, resulting in the quality of the edited course is unstable.

Besides, the Learning Systems Architecture Lab at Carnegies Mellon publishes SCORM Simple Sequencing Templates and Models [6]. The Simple Sequencing Templates contain the information of behaviors and relationships between learning contents according to learning strategy that it presented. In order to satisfy the requirements of instructors, the existing template can be overlaid on or combined with another strategic template to create a new strategic template. However, the Simple Sequencing Templates are not created by referring pedagogical theory.

The learning strategy should base on pedagogical theory to adapt different domains. The learning strategy may be affected by the representation of knowledge [2]. The knowledge can be classified into two types: declarative knowledge and procedural knowledge [8]. In this paper, we will demonstrate Teaching With Analogies Model (TWA), which is a learning strategy for declarative knowledge, to be an example of the learning strategy based on pedagogical theory.

The goal of TWA is a transferring concept from a familiar analog to an unfamiliar target. The analog and the target should have some similar features. To map the similar features, mapping is the process for comparing these features between the analog and the target [9]. The TWA model has six steps described as follows [10]:

Step1. Introduce concept of the target
Step2. Review concept of the analog
Step3. Identify similar features of the target and the analog
Step4. Map similarities
Step5. Draw conclusions about concept of the target
Step6. Indicate where analogy breaks down

3 Strategy Repository

Fig.1 is an example of the learning strategy, which is referenced from the TWA. In Fig.1, the Root Aggregation is a learning activity. The Aggregation-1 to Aggregation-6 are the steps of the TWA in order. The instructor can determine the organization of SCOs for each Aggregation. Furthermore, each learning strategy as in Fig.1 can be overlaid or combined to obtain another new learning strategy.

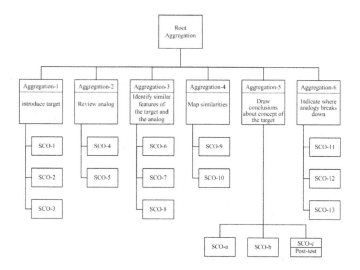

Fig. 1. TWA learning strategy

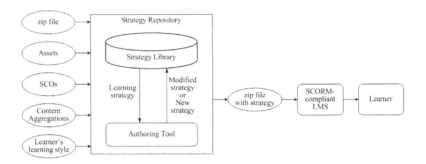

Fig. 2. The workflow of strategy repository

The strategy repository shown in Fig.2 contains two subsystems, the strategy library and the authoring tool. The strategy library stores the learning strategies for the authoring tool to access. The authoring tool has three main functions:

(1) Edit learning strategies: The tool can adapt the learning strategies according to learner's learning style, and then passes the adapted strategies to the Handler that we will illustrate its function later. This functionality enhances the strategy repository with the abilities of adaptability and continuous evolution.

(2) Edit the strategy metadata in relation with the strategy: Each learning strategy is with a strategy metadata which describes the information in relation with the learning strategy. The instructor can modify and/or add the strategy metadata, and then the strategy with modified and/or added strategy metadata is stored into the strategy library. This functionality enhances the strategy repository with the abilities of reusability.

(3) Binding learning strategy and the existing learning contents: This functionality allows the instructor to bind the existing learning contents and the learning strategy, and output as a SCORM-compliant package. The package with zip file presents a course that can be run in SCORM-compliant LMS.

Fig.3 presents the architecture of LMS, which includes the application of the strategy repository. In Fig.3, the architecture of LMS is composed of (i) the Strategy Repository, (ii) the Remote Content Repository, (iii) the Learning Profiles Repository, (iv) the Handler, (v) the SCORM-compliant LMS, and (vi) API instance. The interaction of a learner and the last two components conforms to the standard of the SCORM. Here, we present other parts of Fig.3 as follows:

(i) Strategy Library: It provides learning strategies.

(ii) Remote Content Repository: It composes of learning contents, including asset, SCO, and content aggregation.

(iii) Learner Profiles Repository: It stores learner profiles. The learner profiles are composed of the learning style preferences that may include the preference to text learning, image learning, and animation learning, and so on.

(iv) Handler: It consists of a strategy cache, a content cache, and an integrator. The strategy cache temporarily saves the learning strategies that are used recently, while the content cache temporarily stores the learning contents which are used

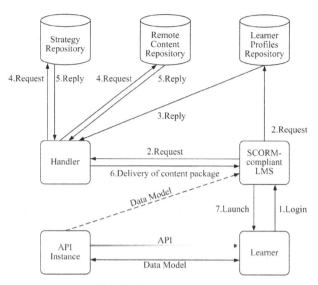

Fig. 3. The application of the strategy repository

recently. Both of the caches are for relieving the requirement bandwidth for delivering the replicated learning strategies and/or learning contents. The integrator is responsible for finding the best learning strategy and integrating the learning strategy and learning contents.

As shown in Fig.3, when a learner enters to the LMS and learns a course, the learning process in relation with the LMS will be as follows:

Step1. Login: When the learner enters the LMS, two possible responses will occur. If it is the first time for the learner to enter the LMS, a pre-test to know the learner's learning style will be provided. If it is not the first time for the learner to enter the LMS, the pre-test is not provided since the LMS has known learner's learning style.

Step2. Request: The LMS respectively sends the request to the Learner Profiles Repository and Handler, whether the pre-test is provided or not.

Step3. Reply: Upon the Learner Profiles Repository and Handler receive respectively the request, they match themselves with respective information according to the learner's learning style and the chosen course. The Learner Profiles Repository matches the learner's learning style and the learner profile first before sending the learner profile to the Handler. Meanwhile, the Handler searches whether the required learning strategies and learning contents are in the strategy cache and the content cache or not, respectively. If the result is negative, the *Step4* and *Step5* will be omitted.

Step4. Request: The handler sends the request to the Strategy Repository and Remote content Repository, respectively.

Step5. Reply: The Strategy Library searches the conformable learning strategies after the strategy metadata is matched with chosen course and the learner's learning style, and then sends the learning strategies to the Handler. Meanwhile, the Remote Content

Repository looks for appropriate learning contents in accordance with the chosen course, and then the appropriate learning contents are sent to the Handler for integration with the learning strategy.

Step6. Delivery of content package: The integrator in the Handler needs to find the best learning strategy according to the learner profile and to integrate the learning strategy and the learning contents, then the content package is delivered to the LMS.

Step7. Launch: Finally, the LMS delivers the package of learning contents to the learner.

4 Conclusions

In order to integrate learning strategy into existing learning content, this paper proposes a SCORM-Compliant strategy repository. The proposed SCORM-compliant strategy repository has the following features: (1) Domain independent; (2) Adaptability; (3) Continuous evolution; (4) Reusability. Meanwhile, we also present an application of the strategy repository to illustrate its utilization.

Reference

1. Tyler, R., W.: Basic principles of curriculum and instruction. Chicago: The University of Chicago Press (1949)
2. Murray, T.: Authoring Knowledge based tutors: Tools for content, instructional strategy, student model, and interface design. Journal of the Learning Sciences, Vol.7, No. 1. (1998) 5-64
3. Advanced Distributed Learning: SCORM Content Aggregation Model. (2003)
4. Advanced Distributed Learning: SCORM Sequencing and Navigation. (2003)
5. Advanced Distributed Learning: SCORM Run-Time Environment. (2003)
6. Learning Systems Architecture Laboratory, Carnegie Mellon University: SCORM Simple Sequencing Templates and Models. (2003)
7. Jin-Tan Yang, Chiung-Hui Chiu, Chun-Yen Tsai, Tsung-Hsien Wu.: Visualized Online Simple Sequencing Authoring Tool for SCORM-Compliant Content Package. IEEE International Conference on Advanced Learning Technologies (ICALT'04) August 30 - September 01 (2004) 609-613
8. Foshay, W. R., Silber, K. H., & Stelnicki, M.: Writing training materials that work. Jossey-Bass/Pfeiffer (2003)
9. Venville, G. J., & Treagust, D. F.: Analogies in biology education: A contentious issue," The American Biology Teacher, Vol.59, No.5. (1997) 282-287
10. Glynn, S, M., Explaining science concepts: A teaching with analogies model. In S. M. Glynn, R. H. Yeany, & B. K. Britton, (Eds.), The psychology of learning science. Hillsdale, NJ: Lawrence Erlbaum Associates (1991) 219-239

Effortless Construction and Management of Program Animations on the Web

Jaime Urquiza-Fuentes and J. Ángel Velázquez-Iturbide

Departamento de Informática, Estadística y Telemática, Universidad Rey Juan Carlos,
C/ Tulipán s/n, 28933 Móstoles, Madrid, Spain
{jaime.urquiza, angel.velazquez}@urjc.es

Abstract. We describe an extension of a programming environment to generate web-based program animations. Emphasis is put on requiring little effort from the instructor that handles the system. User interaction is reduced to a minimum, mostly for customizing the animations. Both construction and maintenance are considered in order to guarantee low effort in an actual educational scenario. We describe several aspects of a program animation: the different kinds of information that compose it, its construction process, alternative graphical designs for web publishing, and its implementation as a package. In general, the instructor will wish to use the system to construct and handle a collection of animations for one or several courses. Therefore, we also consider the creation and management of collections of animations in a effortless way. Finally, we describe our experience as well as related work.

1 Introduction

Software animations are used in computer science education since the early eighties [1]. They can be used in different scenarios [2]: passive or interactive lectures, laboratories, self-study, etc. In spite of their educational potential, they have not been incorporated into the mainstream of computer science education. The report of a working group organized at the ITiCSE 2002 conference contains information about three surveys made on educational use of visualizations [3]. The "preconference survey" contains detailed information about the factors that make the respondent or respondent's colleagues reluctant or unable to use animations. The options can be grouped into factors related to time necessary to prepare infrastructure (e.g. to install the software), time necessary to develop animations, and quality and adequacy of the tools to the course (e.g. to adapt animations to the teaching approach of a course).

Another working group [4] focused on how to reduce the effort to use animations in education. It identifies sources of workload for the instructor as well as advices to facilitate the adoption of animation systems. In particular, the authors argue for platform independence and give much importance to their dissemination among the education community. Both factors are typically enhanced through the Web.

We have developed an effortless approach to building and maintaining program animations [5], [6]. In summary, the integrated development environment (IDE) WinHIPE was extended to automatically generate static visualizations that the user

R.W.H. Lau et al. (Eds.): ICWL 2005, LNCS 3583, pp. 163–173, 2005.

can later customize to automatically constitute an animation. Animations are discrete, i.e. they are composed of a sequence of static visualizations or snapshots.

In this paper, we extend our framework to deal with Web-based animations. We are mainly concerned with providing the instructor an effortless tool. Within this framework, two different issues are addressed. Firstly, we deal with the problem of generating, using and maintaining individual animations. Secondly, we deal with the handing of collections of animation, i.e. their organization and web publishing. Afterwards, we describe our experience and discuss related work.

2 Web Animations

In this section we deal with the contents, construction process and graphical design of Web animations. Publishing algorithm animations on the Web is a topic that other authors addressed in the past [2]. Some web-based animation systems are applets designed ad-hoc to visualize particular algorithms [7], [8], [9], [10]. Other systems are more flexible, allowing the user to generate his/her own animations [11], [12], [13], [14], [15], [16], [17], [18]. In this paper we refer to the latter category.

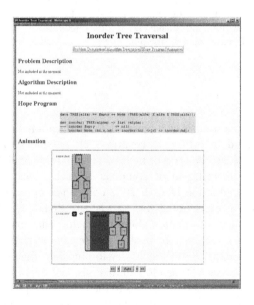

Fig. 1. A web animation as generated in a previous version of our system

In a preliminary work, we addressed the automatic generation of Web-based animations within the WinHIPE IDE [15]. The outcome was a dynamic web page with the structure of a lesson on a particular algorithm. It consisted in four sections (see Fig. 1). The two first sections described the problem statement and an algorithm solving the problem. These sections were generated with a dummy comment and the user had the responsibility of editing them afterwards to fully explain them. The third and fourth sections contained the source code of the program to animate and the animation itself, respectively.

Text contents and the graphical design of the web page could be changed with a web editor. However, any change in the animation had to be made from scratch. It does not require much effort but the user is not assisted in mundane tasks: looking for the program and expression files used as well as keeping the same customization information (expressions selected and graphical design of visualizations).

Our main concern is providing the instructor with a tool that allows him/her constructing web animations in an effortless way. Consequently, we have redesigned and reimplemented our tool. The contents of web pages and the internal construction process of web animations were modified. Finally, we also enriched the graphical design of web animations to improve their usability and flexibility.

2.1 Contents of Web Animations

Contents of web-based animations have been modified to provide a more friendly modification process. In effect, a web animation now contains all the information necessary to change it, either with respect to its look, or the contents of the textual sections or even the animation itself. Look information describes the style and layout of the web page that contains the animation. Textual contents include information about the problem statement and the algorithm used to solve it. Animation contents contain information to play and rebuild the animation: source code, evaluated expression, list of snapshots that form the animation, and configuration information describing the typographic features of visualizations.

In general, contents information can be classified into two classes. On the one hand, visible information can be processed and displayed by any web browser: HTML

Table 1. Different classes of contents and of information

Info. \ Cont.	Textual contents	Animation contents	Look contents
Maintenance information	XML elements describing the title and the problem and solution sections	XML elements describing source and expression code, the list of snapshots, and typography of visualizations	XML elements describing web page style
Visible information	HTML elements describing the problem and solution sections	HTML elements for source and expression code, the list of snapshots, and typography of visualizations	CSS style sheet

code, CSS information and images. On the other hand, maintenance information is necessary to modify or handle animations, and it is structured by means of XML. Given the lack of space, we do not describe here its DTD.

We want to remark that web animations are two-fold reusable. On the one hand, they are reusable by the user because a web animation now contains all the information necessary to modify it. On the other hand, they are reusable in different applications or platforms because their implementation is based on XML. Consequently, not only can they be used by the WinHIPE IDE but also by any application supporting XML.

To sum up, the contents of new web animations reduce the user effort to modify and maintain them because he/she no longer has to remember any kind of configuration or contents information. They also provide user and application reuse.

2.2 Construction and Maintenance Process

The construction and maintenance of web animations are divided into two phases: generation of the program animation and generation of the web animation (see Fig. 2).

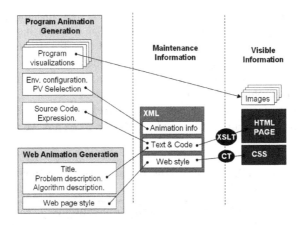

Fig. 2. Construction/maintenance process of web animations

In broad terms, the phase of program animation generation consists in the following steps: edition and compilation of the program, edition and evaluation of the expression and selection of the snapshots that will form the animation. The interested reader in a more detailed explanation of these steps can refer elsewhere [5], [6]. Maintenance information corresponding to animation contents is created here.

The web animation is also generated through the user interface provided by the WinHIPE IDE. Now, the user must provide maintenance information corresponding to textual and look contents.

Notice that user interaction is limited to building the program animation, explaining the problem and its solution, and specifying the web look of the animation. Any additional processing is automatic.

A final, automatic step generates all the visible information other than snapshots. By means of an XSL transformation (XSLT), HTML code is built (distributed in one or several HTML documents, as explained in the next subsection) corresponding to visible information of textual contents and the animation. The tags of this code are represented using a style sheet CSS that is built by means of a custom transformation (CT) of the maintenance information corresponding to the look contents.

2.3 Graphic Design of Web Pages

In our previous work [15], web-based animations consisted in an HTML page navigable by means of a local index and the scroll bar, where the textual contents and the animation were shown (see Fig. 1).

We have developed three new graphical designs. Two of them are inspired by general principles of web pages usability [19] (we call them Framed1 and Framed2), and the third one is intended to enhance flexibility of user interaction (we call it Star). The user may choose one of the four graphical designs by means of a navigation bar placed in the upper left corner (see Fig. 3a). The navigation bar also provides access to XML contents of the web animation.

The main usability requirements considered were: minimizing the amount of hidden information on the screen, adjusting navigation possibilities to a maximum of 20% of screen space, working the predictable response times (given that they depend on the number and size of snapshots), use of linked CSS and inline frames.

We show here a sample of the Framed1 graphical design (see Fig. 3a) as well as a schematic version for the other designs (see Fig. 3b). It uses an inline frame, and

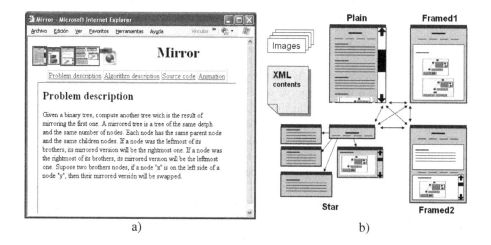

Fig. 3. a) A web animation of type Framed1. b) Elements of a Web animation package

allows the user accessing each section of the web animation with one single mouse click, leaving the use of the scroll bar (hidden information) just for those cases with contents of the section larger than space available on the screen. The title and links to the sections always are visible in the screen.

2.4 A Web Animation Package

A package of a web animation consists of all the maintenance information coded as an XML document, the snapshots that form the animation, and the web pages corresponding to the four possible presentation styles of the web animation. A package is stored in a directory. Fig. 4b illustrates this implementation decision.

3 Collections of Web Animations

Typically, an instructor will construct more than one or two animations. Given the effort required to find an animation system, installing it, learning its usage, building animations and performing other minor, mundane tasks, the instructor will wish to use the animation system for more than one topic [4]. Consequently, he/she will build and maintain a collection of animations, including their organization. It is also common to make changes in one or several animations, either with respect to their contents, their presentation style or their classification. In this section we describe support to handle collections of animations.

A collection is formed by a set of web animations about a common theme: a course, a class of problems, etc. The user may generate as many independent collections as he/she wishes. A given collection is internally organized hierarchically. The hierarchy may have an arbitrary depth. Each level of the hierarchy may have an arbitrary number of categories.

The hierarchical structure of collections as well as the nature of their contents drove us to use again XML as the supporting technology.

3.1 Construction and Management of a Web Collection

Constructing a collection typically starts by creating an empty collection. At least, this collection must have one category, which must be given a name. Another typical situation occurs when a new collection is created from one or several already existing categories which have grown as much as to deserve to be a collection by themselves.

Management of a collection consists in managing its hierarchical structure, managing web animations, and managing their look.

Management of the hierarchical structure comprises inserting, removing or modifying categories. When a category is inserted, it is given a name, a short description and its placement within the hierarchy. When a no-empty category is removed, the user is asked what to do with its contents: either deleting or moving them to a different category. Finally, a category may be modified by changing its name, its description or its placement. In all of these operations, name conflicts with the siblings of the category are checked.

The management of a collection also allows inserting a new animation, removing it (in this case, it can be physically deleted or it can be moved to another category), or even modifying a single animation (as explained in section 2.2).

Each category may have associated a given look, giving greater homogeneity to the collection. This association can be applied to all the animations of a category and also to its descendants. We also allow giving a particular look to an animation, independently from the look of its corresponding category. Finally, changes in the structure of a collection prompt the user to choose between the source look and the look of the target category, if it exits.

These operations are performed with a simple and intuitive user interface. It is similar to the directory interface of Windows Explorer (see Fig. 4). The left panel shows the hierarchical structure of the collection. There are also two panels at the right, where the upper panel shows the contents of the category selected at the left (sublevels and animations) and the lower panel allows showing and modifying the animation selected in the upper right panel.

3.2 Web Publishing of a Web Collection

Web publishing of a collection consists in transforming the internal, hierarchical XML structure into a web site by means of XSL transformations. A root page is created with a description of the collection and links to all the categories at the first level. One page is created for each category, containing the category title, its description and links to its associated animations and daughter categories. A map of the collection allows accessing directly to any category in the collection. Navigation within the collection is further facilitated by making available to all the pages in a category links to its father category, root page and to the collection map.

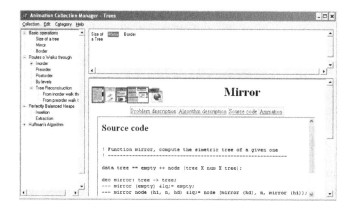

Fig. 4. User interface of the collection manager

4   Experience

We have just concluded the development within the WinHIPE IDE of the new tool for web-based animations. Therefore, we have limited experience with its usage in the classroom. Currently, we have only been able to use some animations during the first semester of the current academic year in a course on algorithms. In particular, we have displayed four animations on integers and sorting. For the next academic year, we plan to make a more extensive use of web animations. More importantly, we will be able to use the collection facilities to create a collection for such a course, develop web-based animations, and structure them into a hierarchy of categories.

We also plan to use and evaluate web animations and collections in the second semester of the present year in a programming languages course with a strong bias to functional programming [20]. We evaluated WinHIPE animations [6], but not their web version, with respect to "effortlessness" during a laboratory session. The results obtained were that students consider construction, use and maintenance of animations easy to learn and effortless tasks. Thus, they used them extensively for debugging.

We plan to evaluate web-based animations in different ways, depending on the education actor. With respect to teachers, we will track their success building and managing both web animations and the collection that contains them. With respect to students, we plan to evaluate their activity as follows. A number of animations, covering most of the topics in the course, will be available during the course and their usage will be monitored. During the last laboratory session, students will have to accomplish two tasks. First, they will answer a questionnaire about the animations available during the course. Afterwards, they will be asked to build several web animations and they will answer a questionnaire about the building process.

5   Related Work

As far as we know, the term "effortless" was used for the first time to describe the anonymous, non-web system by LaFollette et al. [21]. Effortless creation of animations (or simply "effortlessness") is a fuzzy term. Therefore it is too subjective to become an accurate measure. Korhonen et al. [22] tried to deepen into the understanding of effortlessness by estimating it for several animation systems and relating their results to several categories. They identified generality and presentation style as the categories (extracted from the taxonomy by Price et al. [23]) most relevant to effortlessness. However, more research is required to understand "effortlessness". A promising direction consists in identifying the approaches most widely used in effortless systems and studying how they manage to reduce workload to the user.

There is not much work on collections of web-based algorithm animations. There are repositories of teaching materials for computer science courses where we often find animations. These repositories are not structured or they are simply structured in several topics. An example of these repositories is SIGCSE Education Links [24]. It contains over eighty resources, that can be searched by keywords or browsed by several independent keys (all, by course, resource type, author, recent submissions, and most popular). Visualizations are one resource type containing 13 contributions.

The Computer Science Teaching Center [25] is another repository of CS laboratories. They should be high-quality laboratory materials to be shared by the community of CS educators. It contains 105 resources that can be browsed by category and review status. The category of visualization contains 35 resources.

Other repositories are specialized to algorithm visualizations and animations. The Complete Collection of Algorithm Animations [26] is probably the most popular, although other authors have also developed their own. They typically have a very simple structuring based on several topics (e.g. tree or sorting algorithms).

A final category of repositories related to web-based animations are repositories of exercises. They may be highly structured and therefore based on data bases or mark-up languages. However, they only contain static visualizations of exercises, so their utility is very limited in our context. Examples of these systems are eXercita [27] and SAIL [28], both of them based on LaTeX.

The emphasis in any of these categories is very different from ours. General repositories seek making available educational resources to instructors. They are typically supported by organizations or institutions. Algorithm repositories have the same aim but focused on animations. They are web sites developed by individuals. In both cases, the emphasis is on giving a simple structuring to facilitate searching and browsing, but they cannot be used freely by instructors. Repositories of exercises are typically developed by teams, and structuring is given much more importance. Exercises can be handled in more flexible ways, such as generating different instances of a given exercise or customizing an exercise for publication. They are research tools where individuals may make a big effort to yield polished exercises.

6 Conclusions

We have described an extension of a programming environment to generate web-based program animations. The emphasis is put on requiring little effort to the instructor that handles the system. Thus, user interaction is reduced to a minimum, and both construction and maintenance are considered. Not only single animations were considered but also the creation and management of collections of animations.

This work focuses on the effort required to the instructor. However, it is just one of the different issues that refrain educators and learners from using animations more widely. We expect to see improvements in different directions that will foster more wide usage of animations for computer science education.

Acknowledgments

This work is supported by the research project TIN2004-07568 of the Spanish Ministry of Education and Science.

References

1. Baecker, R., Price, B.: The early history of software visualization. In: Stasko, J.T., Domingue, J., Brown, M.H., Price, B.A. (eds.): Software Visualization. MIT Press, Cambridge MA (1998) 29-34
2. Pareja-Flores, C., Velázquez-Iturbide, J. Á.: Program execution and visualization on the Web. In: A. Aggarwal (ed.), Web-Based Learning and Teaching Technologies: Opportunities and Challenges. Idea-Group Publishing, Hershey, PA (2002) 236-259
3. Naps, T., et al: Exploring the role of visualization and engagement in computer science education. SIGCSE Bulletin 35(2) (2003) 131-152
4. Naps, T., et al: Evaluating the educational impact of visualization. SIGCSE Bulletin 35(4) (2003) 124-136
5. Naharro-Berrocal, F., Pareja-Flores, C., Velázquez-Iturbide, J.Á.: Automatic generation of algorithm animations in a programming environment. Proc. 30th ASEE/IEEE Frontiers in Education Conf. Stiples Publishing (2000) S2C 6-12
6. Velázquez-Iturbide, J.Á., Pareja-Flores, C., Urquiza-Fuentes, J.: An approach to effortless construction of program animations. Under review
7. Dershem, H.L., McFall, R.L., Uti, N.: Animation of Java linked lists. Proc. 33rd SIGCSE Technical Symp. Computer Science Education. ACM Press, New York (2002) 53–57
8. Hadlock, F., et al.: An Internet based algorithm visualization system. Journal of Computing Sciences in Colleges 20(2) (2004) 304 - 310
9. Najork, M.: Web-based algorithm animation. Proc. 38th Conf. Design Automation (2001) 506-511
10. Stern, L., Søndergaard, H., Naish, L.: A strategy for managing content complexity in algorithm animation. Proc. 4th Annual SIGCSE/SIGCUE Conf. Innovation and Technology in Computer Science Education. ACM Press (1999) 127-130
11. Akingbade, A., Finley, T., Jackson, D., Patel, P., Rodger, S.H.: JAWAA: Easy web-based animation from CS0 to advanced CS courses. Proc. 34th SIGCSE Technical Symp. Computer Science Education. ACM Press (2003) 162-166
12. Ross, R.J., Grinder, M.T.: Hypertextbooks: Animated, active learning, comprehensive teaching and learning resources for the Web. In: Diehl, S. (ed.): Software Visualization. LNCS, Vol. 2269. Springer-Verlag, Berlin Heidelberg (2001) 269-283
13. Esponda Argüero, M., Rojas, R.: Learning algorithms with an electronic chalkboard over the Web. Advances in Web-Based Learning – ICWL 2004. LNCS, Vol. 3143. Springer-Verlag, Berlin Heidelberg (2004) 1-10
14. Korhonen, A., Malmi, L.: Algorithm simulation with automatic assessment. Proc. 5th Annual SIGCSE/SIGCUE Conf. Innovation and Technology in Computer Science Education. ACM Press (2000) 160-163
15. Naharro-Berrocal, F., et al.: Automatic Web publishing of algorithm animations. Upgrade II(2) (2001) 41-45
16. Naps, T., Eagan, J., Norton, L.: JHAVÉ: An environment to actively engage students in Web-based algorithm visualizations. Proc. 31st SIGCSE Technical Symp. Computer Science Education. ACM Press (2000) 109–113
17. Rossling, G., Freisleben, B.: Program visualization using AnimalScript. Proc. First International Program Visualization Workshop. University of Joensuu Press (2001) 41-52
18. Sutinen, E., Tarhio, J., Teräsvirta, T.: Easy algorithm animation on the Web. Multimedia Tools and Applications, 19(2) (2003) 179-194
19. Nielsen, J.: Designing Web Usability. New Riders Publishing, Indianapolis IN USA, 1999

20. Velázquez-Iturbide, J.Á.: A programming languages course for freshmen. Proc. the 10th Annual SIGCSE/SIGCUE Conf. Innovation and Technology in Computer Science Education. ACM Press (2005) in press
21. LaFollette, P., Korsh, J., Sangwan, R.: A visual interface for effortless animation of C/C++ programs. Journal of Visual Languages and Systems 11 (2000) 27-48
22. Karavirta, V., et al.: Effortless creation of algorithm visualization. Proceedings of the Second Annual Finish/Baltic Conf. Computer Science Education (2002) 52-56
23. Price, B., Baecker, R., Small, I.: A principled taxonomy of software visualization. Journal of Visual Languages and Systems 4, 3 (1993) 211-271
24. ACM SIGCSE:SIGCSE Education Links. www.sigcse.org/topics/ (updated December 2004)
25. The Computer Science Teaching Center. www.cstc.org/ (updated 2003)
26. Brummund, P., Uti, N.V.: The Complete Collection of Algorithm Animations. cs.hope.edu/~alganim/ccaa (updated June 2001)
27. Gregorio-Rodríguez, et al: eXercita: A system for archiving and publishing programming exercises. In: Ortega, M., Bravo, J. (eds.). Computers and Education: Towards an Interconnected Society. Kluwer Academic Press (2001) 187-197
28. Kovourov, S. et al. SAIL: A system for generating, archiving and retrieving specialized assignments using LaTeX. Proc. 31st SIGCSE Technical Symp. Computer Science Education. ACM Press (2000) 300-304

Student Centered Knowledge Level Analysis for eLearning for SQL

Joseph Fong[1], Jickhary Lee, and Anthony Fong[2]

[1] Department of Computer Science, City University of Hong Kong, Hong Kong
csjfong@cityu.edu.hk
[2] Department of Electronic Engineering, City University of Hong Kong

Abstract. There are many different designs for eLearning on the Internet. The static webpage design can only provide fixed learning materials. The dynamic webpage design can change the page data depending on the students' input. The intelligent webpage design records students 'learning results for their knowledge level analysis and provides sequence and format to test the students for practicing and training accordingly. A student centered model enables the system to provide customized course contents and study guidance to individual student. The web-based application helps students of all levels with different educational background to achieve their learning goals effectively. This paper provides an eLearning system with intelligent dynamic web pages customized to each student's effective learning style in SQL (Structural Query Language) as a practical relational database language in the syllabus of an undergraduate Database Systems course.

1 Introduction

The eLearning mode has an increasing impact on learning and teaching in recent years, and it is clear that the role of eLearning in all walks of education will continue to grow[1]. The Internet is a worldwide collection of computer networks, cooperating with each other to exchange data using a common software standard[2]. Putting information on the Web is quite inexpensive compared with traditional publishing of putting information before a potential audience of millions[3]. Internet-based eLearning system has become part of the mainstream education. It supplements the traditional way of paper-based education. The architecture of the student centered model is divided into three levels: beginner, advance and expert learners. The system applies graduated questions to analyze students and to identify the student's knowledge level to provide suitable learning course contents for them. The system presents video and audio learning material for the students who adopt to eLearning.

SQL allows users to pose complex questions of a database. It provides a means of creating databases[4]. The SQL standard has been developed by workgroup[5] WG3 of TC97/SC21 of the ISO. The SQL itself is a non-procedural language which can be easily issued by an end user without a procedure to implement the command. A relational database stores data in tables (relations), whereas a database is a collection of

R.W.H. Lau et al. (Eds.): ICWL 2005, LNCS 3583, pp. 174–185, 2005.

tables. A table consists of records and each record has a fixed number of "fields" of a given data type.

The main objective is to build a resource that helps students who will use a relational database by SQL to find the resources and learning materials that they are looking for. Figure 1 is the architecture of the eLearning system which is student centered with intelligence web pages design to record students' learning ability and behaviors. The ODBC (Open Database Connectivity) interface allows applications to access data by use of SQL. It requests a connection with a data source, sends SQL to data source, and reports users back to a user. The application consists of a variety of features external to ODBC interface, including email, spreadsheet capabilities, online transaction processing and report generation. This webpage has membership system to keep the records of the students learning result[6].

How does one make the eLearning with good quality? The important criteria for evaluating quality in eLearning are in order of priority:

- It functions technically without problems across all users
- It has clearly explicit pedagogical design principles appropriate to students type, needs and context
- It has a high level of interactivity

For each of these criteria, only a minority of respondents of a survey on eLearning system response in their experience that the quality had been "excellent" or "very good"[7].

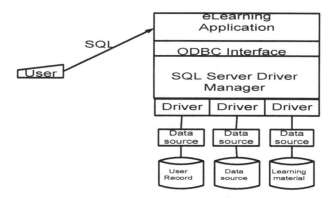

Fig. 1. Architecture of Student center intelligent eLearning system for SQL

2 Related Work

ChL.com[8]provides the Internet based eLearning tool for students study the SQL language. The system comes with text presentation and graphical interface which is a simple graphical tool for controlling the pages. FluffyCat.com[9] provides the Internet based eLearning tool for students to look for SQL language reference and examples. SQLzoo.net[10] provides the web based learning tool for students to study the SQL language. It gives live SQL worksheet for students to practice SQL commands in different platforms. Course2.com[11] provides the Internet based eLearning tool for students to study the SQL language. The graphic interface and pages linkage functions facilitate the students searching for SQL statements. wbi.cityu.edu.hk/webct[12] provides Internet based eLearning tool for students to download the learning materials and makes online quiz. Oracle 9i: SQL [13] provides the learning question and formal answer for students to practice the Oracle 9i SQL examination.

When compared with others, our eLearning system includes text, video and audio presentation, example demonstration, live database practice, test and quiz material, different level learning, Feedback to staff, subject partitioning, bookmarks, reports, student membership registration and frequent answer question. The webpage is intelligent to meet students' need.

3   Intelligent Web Pages Design for eLearning of SQL

The eLearning system in this project can be divided into four modules including Knowledge Level Analysis module, Beginner Learning module, Advance Learning module and Expert Learning module. The system will analyze the knowledge level of the students according to their academic qualification and professional experience, and then divide them into three knowledge levels of Beginner Learner, Advance Learner and Expert Learner. For beginners, the student does not have any post secondary school qualifications nor any professional experience. For advance learner, the student has either university qualification or professional experience. For expert learner, the student has both university qualification and professional experience. The functional specifications of the eLearning system can be shown in Figure 2.

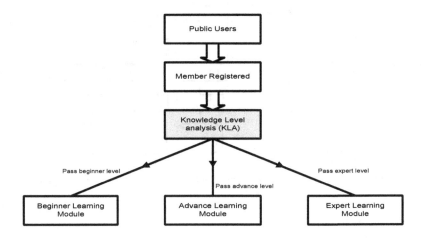

Fig. 2. New members registration for eLearning

Knowledge Level Analysis Module. An aptitude analysis test is given to the students for testing their knowledge level in using SQL. The test includes three levels of questions, Beginner, Advance and Expert. Each Question Module has randomly loaded the question from three question pools.

The system requests the students to answer the entire question in the test which takes about 30 questions. All tests are multiple choices

- Beginner Question Module (Total: 10 questions).The question pools are covered
  - SQL Standard / History basic concept (3 – 4 questions)
  - Data Manipulation Language (DML) Level 1 (3 – 4 questions)
  - Data Definition Language (DDL) Level 1 (3 – 4 questions)
- Advance Question Module (Total: 10 questions). The question pools are covered
  - SQL Common Element basic concept (3 – 4 questions)
  - Data Manipulation Language (DML) Level 2 (3 – 4 questions)
  - Data Definition Language (DDL) Level 2 (3 – 4 questions)
- Expert Question Module (Total: 10 questions). The question pools are covered
  - SQL Module Language basic concept (3 – 4 questions)
  - Data Manipulation Language (DML) Level 3 (3 – 4 questions)
  - Data Definition Language (DDL) Level 3 (3 – 4 questions)

The student needs to pass the minimum requirement in score of KLA test:

- In Beginner level module, the student's correct rate score must be greater than 80%
- In Advance level module, the student's correct rate score must be greater than 70%
- In Expert level module, the student's correct rate score must be greater than 60%

If the student fulfills the Beginner Level minimum requirement, the student will be assigned the Advance level learning module. The registered student must have answered all questions in Knowledge Level Analysis(KLA) system. The system will display total number of points in this test and assign the level of learning module to the student.

Beginner Level Module. The student learns to understand the basic concept of SQL statement and how to apply the statement into the database. The materials include the followings:

- The structure of the database
- The basic concept of SQL and database schema
- The contents of the tables
- The data type, literal, name and predicate in Table
- Query expression
- Table Expression
- Value Expression
- The definition of DDL, DML and Module statement
- The definition of independent DML statements
- How to use the "SELECT" statement in Database
- How to use the "SELECT FROM" statement in Database
- How to use the "SELECT BETWEEN" statement in Database
- How to use the "SELECT GROUP BY" statement in Database
- How to use the "SELECT IN/NOT IN" statement in Database
- How to use the "SELECT JOINS" statement in Database

- How to use the "SELECT LIKE" statement in Database
- How to use the "SELECT ORDER BY" statement in Database

Advance Learner Module. The students learn how to use the "Create" command to create table and other advance feature in SQL, and also the special statement to make the mathematic calculation. The materials include the following:

- How to use the "CREATE SCHEMA" statement
- How to use the "CREATE TABLE" statement
- How to use the "CREATE VIEW" statement
- How to use the "DECLARE" statement
- How to use the "OPEN" statement
- How to use the "FETCH" statement
- How to use the "CLOSE" statement
- How to use the "INSERT" statement
- How to use the "UPDATE" statement
- How to use the "DELETE" statement
- How to use the function statement in Database
- How to use the "AVG( )" statement in Database
- How to use the "COUNT( )" statement in Database
- How to use the "MAX( )" statement in Database
- How to use the "MIN( )" statement in Database
- How to use the "SUM( )" statement in Database

Expert Level Module. The student learns all the features and special functions in SQL. The materials include the followings:

- How to use the "GRANT" statement
- How to use the "DELETE" statement
- How to use the "UPDATE" statement
- How to use the "COMMIT" statement
- How to use the "ROLLBACK" statement
- How to use the "MODULE" statement
- How to use the "PROCEDURE" statement

4   Prototype of the Application Oriented eLearning System

The system in this project is implemented with a three tier client-server architecture. The client has the presentation interfaces that are implemented as HTML page on the student's computer side, which is embedded with the java script and run in the Internet Explorer web browser. The ASP application programs for performing the screen layer is for the users to login the system. The student model can update and adaptation resides in the middle layer server. The server-side application components communicate directly with the backend database storing information of learning materials and student model.

- **Client Tier (Student Side – Entity Class).** The client tier is a web browser running in the student computer. The browser functions as the user interface of the tutoring module and are responsible for handling adaptive presentation of course materials and providing adaptive navigation support. The user interface in ASP application program generates the HTML frame that is divided into three parts. The main page is dynamically page, which is changed by the student login. If the student login, the main page will be shown of the member functions and student information.
- **Middle Tier (Server Side – Control Class).** The middle tier resides in server side used to handle the student model initialization. It is responsible for receiving the student request and data. The middle tier consists of the S ASP (Active Service Page) Dynamic server page language.
- **Database Tier (Database Management System Side – Control Class).** The database management system stores the student personal information, lecture material, question for testing, student testing result, student knowledge level, administrators and teaching staffs records. It also resides on the server side and is composed of a back-end database server. By using the Microsoft ODBC Driver and program with ASP languages and SQL statements. Internet based eLearning for SQL is partitioned into 4 main modules, including the Interface Module, Database Control Module. This section describes the design to be used in detail of the design in the problem solving in this project as shown in Figure 3.

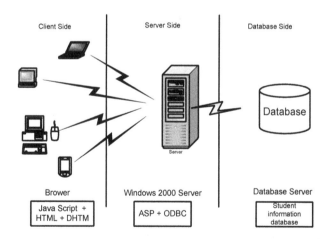

Fig. 3. The three tier architecture of the Internet Based eLearning for SQL

This section describes the detail functions of this project provided by the Internet webpage application. The whole project is divided to three main sections: Non-Member Section, Member Section and Administrator Section.

The Non-member section is provided with the Information Searching, Email to Web Master, Introduction of eLearning system, main topic catalog and hot topic preview section. By default, the learning material is divided to three sections, SELECT, FUNCTIONS and ADD/REMOVE which have high frequencies usage.

The Administrator or teaching staffs can modify the default topic and add the new topic into the eLearning System database. Moreover, the knowledge level definition is setup by the administrator or teaching staffs. In the lecture section user interface for retrieving SQL statement is the same as the SQL2.com. The students may click on the required topics on the categories displayed on the right hand side frame page. The contents within the categories windows supports are highlighted.

Non Member Student Without Registration Section. This module is interacted with the non member students to understand the learning material and provides a best environment and layout for student. It accepts the students to input the SQL statement to run and output the real world output result on the screen for student's reference. The system interfaces are generated by an ASP application program. All lecture note and testing questions are loaded from database. This provides the upload area for teaching staffs to update the lecture notes into the Webpage as shown in Figure 4.

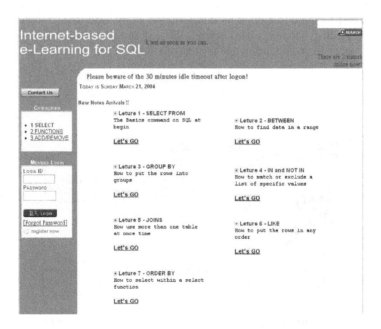

Fig. 4. The Index webpage of non-member student eLearning for SQL system

The Main Page of the non member student eLearning System is divided to four parts: login section, and course topic section, searching engine and lecture notes section.

The login section is used for students and teaching staffs to specify user ID and password. Moreover, the non-register students can show the introduction information of the course without login to member section. The Search section is used for all users to search any information from the database. The students can input the topic of the course and course description. This section displays the number of visitors online in this system.

The course topic section is used for user (non-registered student) to select what topic is interesting to preview. The students can view the brief and full description of the course topics. On the preview section, the students can click into detail description. On the top of the section, the "Contact us" button, the students may click on this button to send the email to the teaching staff to get more information about this system.

The lecture section is in the right hand side frames of a main frame. In order to provide a preview the brief description on the lecture, the system provides the current Topic (SELECT). The users interface for users to select what lecture to view the detail description. The students may click on the "Let's GO" and the detail information of this lecture will be displayed on the screen.

Member Student with Registration Section. This section is for who want to register the membership in the system. In the Member area, it is provided with six functions on the left hand frame.

- **Lecture** – It provides the formal lecture notes, example, video/audio and SQL trial test box. It is used to give some example of the SQL statement for students self study. The students also may click the play video button to view more detail voice lecture in the video. Otherwise, the students should put the SQL statement in the Test Box to find out the corresponding output result.
- **Self-Testing** – It provides the self-testing for students who want to practice at the testing environment. This section does not have time limit, deadline date for submision and testing result recording. Therefore the students can redo the testing many times after each login. Furthermore, the students will know the correct answers after the self-testing is completed.
- **Quiz / Quiz Result** - It provides the quiz for teaching staff to know the quality of the students learning. It is only assigned by the teaching staffs. The students are not allowed to execute the quiz function. For example, the quiz will be provided at the end of each month and the deadline date is one week lead time. The correct answer doesn't feedback after the finished quiz. The students may click the "Quiz Result" to view the quiz result and correct answers after the deadline date.
- **Update Info** - It provides the section for students to update the personal information.
- **Withdraw** – It provides the function for students to withdraw the membership from the system. After the students confirm the membership withdraws, all records of these students will be removed from the database.
- **Logout** – It provides the action for students to logout from the system. Moreover, the system will logout the students if there is no action after 30 minutes.

Fig. 5. Lecture material (SQL examples) for registered student

The system provides the Lecture notes for students self study. The lecture notes are divided into 3 levels, beginner, advance, and expert student, which are assigned by system depending on the students first knowledge level analysis testing. If the students finish the Knowledge Level Analysis testing, the system will display what level students have and assign the suitable lecture material for this student. Normally, the lecture notes include four parts, detail descriptions, detail example, video/audio demonstration and real time SQL statement test box. in Figure 5.

The video/audio demo plays the video of teaching staffs explain the lecture notes with voice and pointer point similar to the lecture in the classroom. It also provides different cases example for students to try testing on the test box in Figure 6.

Here the user interface allows the students to input the MS SQL format SQL statement in test box. After students input the SQL statement and click the "See the Result" button, the result will be displayed on the screen. Therefore the students can try the different cases which are not included in the current example.

The quiz section's questions and answers are designed by administrators or teaching staff that is hard coded in the database. The quiz section has the deadline date. The students must finish quiz before the deadline date. After the deadline date, the system will be posted with the correct answers and the mark of the quiz. Furthermore, the screen is displayed of how many questions are finished. It reminds the students to complete all question in every login. Therefore the students do not need to finish all questions in one time as shown in Figure 8.

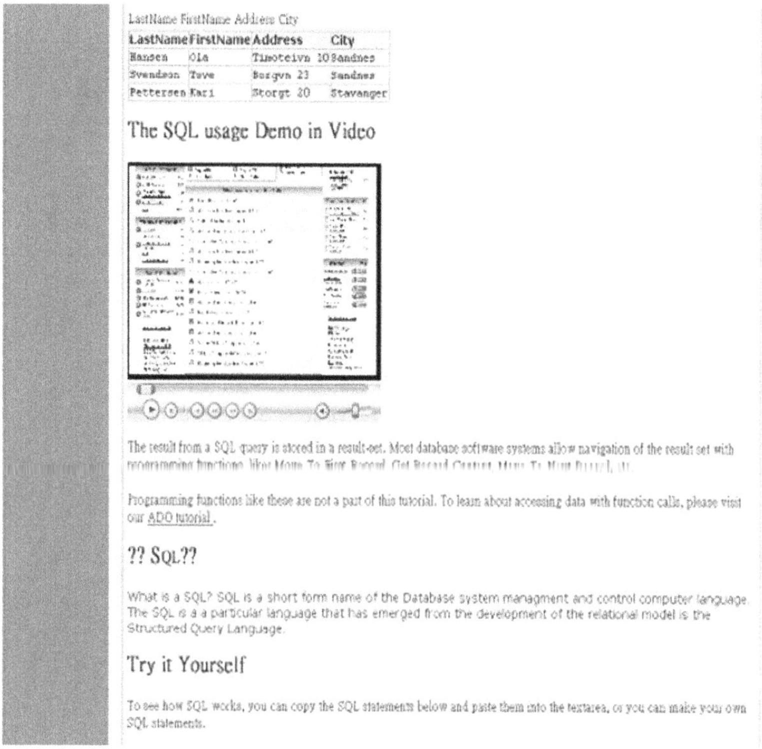

Fig. 6. Lecture material (video demo) for registered student

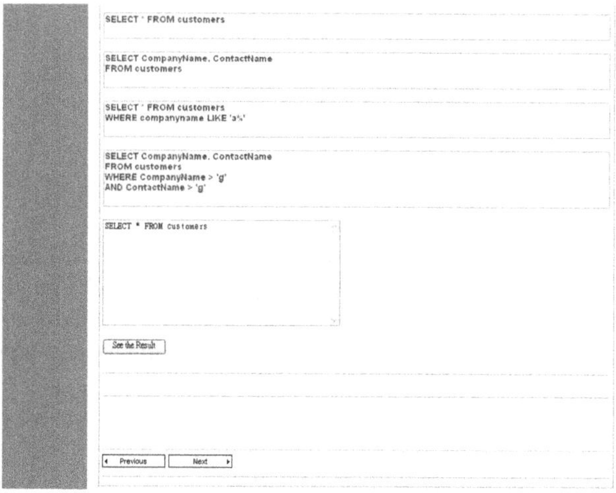

Fig. 7. Lecture material (SQL executable box) for registered student)

Please beware of the 30 minutes idle timeout after logon!
Today is Sunday March 21, 2004
Member : 1   We are very happy to see you again.

Are you Ready to start ? Please click here 0:10   [Start]

Testing Question for SELECT

[Next   ▶] 1

Table 1

Question 1
LastName FirstName Address City

Sno	Fname	Lname	Address	Tel_No	Position	Sex	Dob	Salary	Nin	Bno
SL21	John	White	19 Taylor St, Cranford, London	0171-884-5112	Manager	M	1-Oct-45	30000.00	WK442011B	B5
SG37	Ann	Beech	81 George St, Glasgow PA1 2JR	0141-848-3345	Snr Asst	F	10-Nov-60	12000.00	WK432514C	B3
SG14	David	Ford	63 Ashby St, Partick, Glasgow GII	0141-339-2177	Deputy	M	24-Mar-58	18000.00	WL220658D	B3
SA9	Mary	Howe	2 Elm Pl, Aberdeen AB2 3SU		Assistant	F	19-Feb-70	9000.00	WM532187D	B7
SG5	Susan	Brand	5 Gt Western Rd, Glasgow G12	0141-334-2001	Manager	F	3-Jun-40	24000.00	WK588932E	B3
SL41	Julie	Lee	28 Malvern St, London NW2	0181-554-3541	Assistant	F	13-Jun-65	9000.00	WA290573K	B5

○ List all staff with a salary greater than $10,000?

Please select the correct answer

○ SELECT sno, fname, lname, position, salary FROM staff WHERE salary > 10000

○ SELECT sno, fname, lname, position, salary FROM staff FROM salary > 10000

○ SELECT sno, fname, lname, position, salary FROM staff WHERE salary LARGER 10000

○ SELECT sno, fname, lname, position, salary FROM staff FROM salary LARGER 10000

[Submit]

[Next   ▶]

You have [   ]
seconds left

Question	Answered
1	●
2	●
3	●
4	●
5	●

● Not Finish yet

● Finihed !

Fig. 8. Self-testing user interface

5   Conclusion

The contribution of this paper is to propose using intelligent web pages approach to design an eLearning system to evaluate and record students' knowledge level and provide interactive learning material to students according to their abilities to learn. The approach has been proved to be feasible and interesting to most students.

References

1. Montgomery, S.M., Groat, L.N.,"Student learning styles and their implications for teaching", 2000.
2. Jay Cross, information architect of Internet Time Group, "eLearning", Training & Development, November 1999.

3. Murray, T., Shen, T., Piemonte, J., and Condit, C., "Adaptivity in the metalinks Hyperbook authoring framwork.", 2000.
4. Mitovic, A., "Porting SQL-Tutor to the web". In: Proceedings of International Workshop on Adaptive and Intelligent Web-based Educational Systems, Held in Conjunction with ITS 2000 19th June, 2000 Montreal, Canada.
5. The SQL standard, A complete reference, Rick F. van der Lans
6. Khan, B. H. (ed.), "Web Based Instruction". Englewood Cliffs, New Jersey: Educational Technology Publications, 1997.
7. Jane Massy, "Quality and eLearning Summary report, European eLearning Consultant and Analyst in April 2002.
8. SQL tutorial CHL, CHL - Information System and Information Technology courses center http://www.cs.unibo.it/~ciaccia/COURSES/RESOURCES/SQLTutorial/sqlcont.htm
9. Fluffy Cat.com - SQL Reference and Example Site. Larry Truett and www.FluffyCat.com, Larry Truett, http://www.fluffycat.com/sql/
10. A Gentle Introduction to SQL. By Andrew Cumming of the School of Computing of Napier University, Edinburgh, UK, http://sqlzoo.net/
11. SQL Course 2.com Advanced Online SQL Training, http://sqlcourse2.com/sql_interpreter.html
12. ELearning tools in City University of Hong Kong, http://wbi.cityu.edu.hk/webct/homearea/homearea
13. Oracle 9i: SQL with an Introduction to PL / SQL, Lannes L. Morris-Mu.

Web-Based Chinese Calligraphy Retrieval and Learning System

Yueting Zhuang, Xiafen Zhang, Weiming Lu, and Fei Wu

The Institute of Artificial Intelligence, Zhejiang University,
Hangzhou, 310027, P.R.China
{yzhuang, cadal, wufei}@cs.zju.edu.cn

Abstract. Chinese calligraphy is a valuable civilization legacy and there are some web sites trying to help people enjoy and learn calligraphy. However, besides metadata-base searching, it is very difficult to find advanced services such as content-based retrieval or vivid writing process simulating for Chinese calligraphy. In this paper, a novel Chinese calligraphy retrieval and learning system is proposed: First, the scanned calligraphy pages were segmented into individual calligraphy characters using minimum-bounding box. Second, individual character's feature information was extracted and kept. Then, corresponding database was built to serve as a map between the feature data and the original data of individual character image. Finally, a retrieval engine was constructed and dynamic writing process was simulated to help learners get the calligraphy character they are interested in and watch how it was written.

1 Introduction

When computer and Internet become more and more popular to the general public, less and less people have chances to write with a pen, and to enjoy the beauty of writing. Calligraphy is a kind of writing, and a popular communication tool in ancient China. It is not only delight to the eye and an inspiration to the spirit, but also a creative art. Yet you don't have to be an "artist" to learn calligraphy, you can learn the skills and write them every time you want. According to thousands years of learning experience, Chinese calligraphy learning process can be divided into three main consecutive steps: reading, understanding and simulating.

In terms of web-based learning and from the view of reading and understanding, key issues in such process are: how to manage all the data to display the beauty of the different calligraphy styles of the same character to learners, and how to help learners find the context of an interested character. From the simulating point, the key issue is how to set good writing example for learners to follow since it's impossible to trace the entire history to get a video to show how a particular calligraphy character was written. Correspondingly, our system consists of a large database managing all the scanned original data and its feature data, a retrieval engine helping learners find the same calligraphy character

R.W.H. Lau et al. (Eds.): ICWL 2005, LNCS 3583, pp. 186–196, 2005.

written in different styles by different people in different dynasties, and a simulator helping learners get a vivid idea about how a calligraphy character was written.

The remainder of this paper is organized as follows. Section 2 discusses the related works. Section 3 presents the system architecture. Section 4 gives the data structure. In section 5, main functions of web-based calligraphy learning system were described in detail. In section 6, the implementation and evaluation were done. And in the final part, conclusion and future works are given.

2   Related Works

Numerous researches have been done on exploring techniques for web-based learning such as [1] and [2]. But, these techniques don't fit web-based Chinese calligraphy learning well. Some web sites have been developed trying to fit learners' needs to enjoy and learn Chinese calligraphy, such as [3] and [4]. They do provide some basic information and many useful learning materials. However, they provide no advanced dynamic services such as content-based search to find calligraphy character that interestes the learner, and they do not tell the vivid writing process of an individual character to set a good example and let learners follow.

If it is a text query, "Google" is the biggest and fastest search engine. "Google" also provides image-searching function based on the name of the image. Yet, you can't submit a text query and retrieve character images similar to it. Lots of previous content-based image retrieval works used low-level features such as colors, textures and regions. However, such features cannot represent shape properties of a character, hence irrelevant images are frequently retrieved. Recently, there has been works to handle shape features effectively such as [5] and [6]). Still, they don't work well for calligraphy character image retrieval. Our previous work (see [7]) has proposed a new approach to retrieve calligraphy characters.

3   System Architecture

Fig.1 gives out an overview of our system architecture of web-based Chinese calligraphy learning. Its infrastructure mainly includes data collection, segmentation and feature extraction, which serve for advanced web-based learning purpose.

3.1   Data Collection

The original books, mostly ancient, were scanned at 600 dpi (dots per inch) and kept in DjVu format by researchers of our China-US million book digital library project (see [8]). These digitalized resources, together with their corresponding metadata are saved and packaged. The metadata standard (Edocument Metadata,Version 2.0) we used is released by the Zhejiang University Library. It combines two kinds of metadata: DC and MARC.

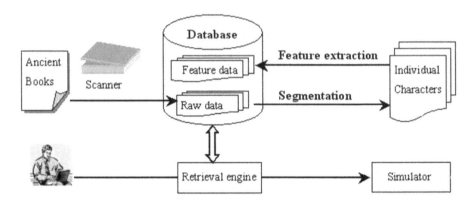

Fig. 1. Architecture of web-based Chinese calligraphy learning system

3.2   Segmentation

When digitized page images obtained, segmentation is needed in order to get feature information of individual calligraphy characters. Many researches have been done on segmentation of printed pages such as [9] and [10]. Yet no published paper has been done successfully on Chinese calligraphy page segmentation. It is mainly because calligraphy characters have more connection, and the background has more noise such as man-made seals. Our proposed segmentation approach first adjusts color luminance to get rid of red seals and smooth them to remove some noises. Then binarization was done, which is followed by projecting. After that, pages were cut into columns according to the projecting histogram, and columns continued to be cut into individual characters using minimum-bounding box as used in [10]. Fig.2 gives an example of our experiment, showing how a calligraphy page was cut into individual calligraphy characters.

Compared with [10], our segmentation approach made special constraint parameters to fit the characteristics of Chinese calligraphy. Let $x_{i,s}$ and $x_{i,e}$ denote the start and the end position of the ith cutting block. According to our long term segmentation experiences it subjects to the following constrains:

$$x_{i,e} - x_{i,s} \geq 5, i = 0, 1, 2 \cdots \cdots, n \tag{1}$$

$$2.5 \times \frac{1}{n} \times \sum_{i=1}^{n}(x_{i,e} - x_{i,s}) \geq 0.35 \times \frac{1}{n} \times \sum_{i=1}^{n}(x_{i,e} - x_{i,s}) \tag{2}$$

This is because according to thousands years of calligraphy writing experience, the width of individual character images in the same page tend to be similar. That is to say they have a minimum and maximum threshold for width, as described in formula 2. Let $wide_i$ and $height_i$ be the width and height of ith cutting block, then

$$0.6 \leq \frac{height_i}{wide_i} \leq 1.2 \tag{3}$$

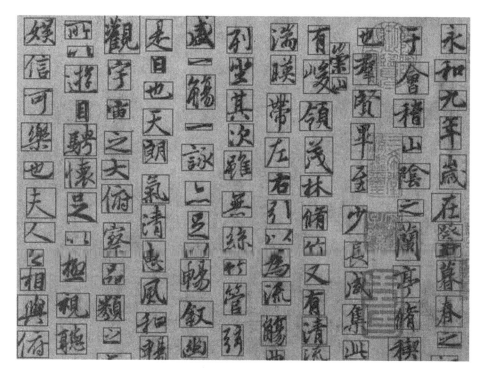

Fig. 2. An example of segmenting a page into individual characters using minimum-bounding box

Formula 3 tells the story that Chinese characters are always in square as introduced in [11].

With the above idea, most of the characters can be segmented automatically and correctly. But still, there are few man-made connections that can't be correctly segmented automatically such as in Fig.2, the fourth column from the right. In this case, we draw the minimum-bounding box to separate them. The minimum-bounding box which is in blue can be drag and drop manually.

3.3   Feature Extraction

After the segmentation was done, the next step is to extract features of individual calligraphy characters. In our approach, a calligraphy character is represented by its contour points instead of its skeleton as described in [6]. This is because skeleton representation is very sensitive to noise. As a result, it produces distorted strokes and proper shape of the character can't be detected.

According to the minimum-bounding box, we first normalize the individual character to 32×32 in pixels. Then, canny edge detector as introduced in [12] was employed to get its contour point's positions in Cartesian coordinates. Finally the values that denote the position of contour points were serialized to a string and kept in the database.

For learning purpose, a learner may want to know where an individual calligraphy character comes from and who wrote it. Therefore, the original location information of individual calligraphy characters, that is to say the location information of the minimum-bounding box should be kept too.

4   Data Structure

The scanned original image data is large and in disorder, needs further management. We build a special data structure to map the extracted feature data into the original raw data. The map consists of four tables: **book**, **works**, **character** and **author**, as shown in Fig.3. Many individual calligraphy characters compose a calligraphy works created by a calligraphist, namely an author. And many calligraphy works buildup a calligraphy book. The arrows show how these four tables are related by particular elements. In table of **character**, *co_points* is a string produced by the feature data of an individual calligraphy character.

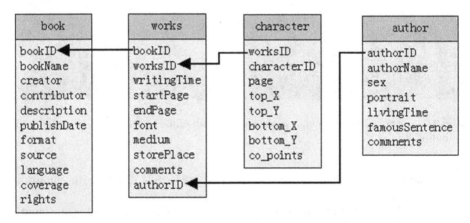

Fig. 3. Data structure for mapping feature data to raw data

With this map, it is easy to tell in which works and in which page an individual calligraphy character located by checking the table of **character** to find the *worksID*, the *page* and the *minimum-bounding box* (represented by *top_X*, *top_Y*, *bottom_X* and *bottom_Y*). It can also tells in which book this particular character can be found by searching the table of **works** using the key of *bookID*, and also who wrote this calligraphy character by checking the table of **author** using the key of *authorID*.

5   Key Calligraphy Learning Services

5.1   Learning Object Retrieval

For personalized learning purpose, different learners may be interested in different styles of the same calligraphy character. In our system, we use our new

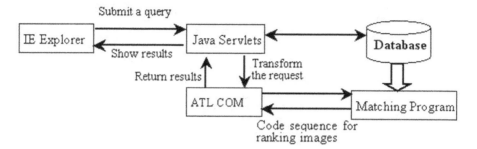

Fig. 4. Diagram flow of retrieval

content-based calligraphy character image retrieval approach (see detailed description in [7]). In that, we use inexact shape context matching. However, in terms of web-based learning its response time is beyond endurance: For a single query,the average retrieval time is about 3.6 minutes when the database consists of 336 isolated characters. In this paper, we develop a new architecture fit for web-base calligraphy character learning, shown in Fig.4.

Three ways are proposed to speed up the retrieval, one is preprocessing, another is classification, and the third is dimensionality reduction to reduce computing time. In preprocessing, shape features of every individual calligraphy character were extracted in advance, then serialized to a string and stored in the database, together with their corresponding metadata. Thus only the features of the query image need to be extracted dynamically.

For classification, complexity index was used besides the metadata. Let $f(x, y)$ be the gray value of a pixel. If a pixel belongs to the background, then let $f(x, y) = 0$, else $f(x, y) = 1$. Thus moment of the character image can be defined as:

$$m_{i,j} = \iint x^i y^j dxdy \qquad (4)$$

And the root of second-order central moment in X and Y direction are defined as follows:

$$\sigma_x = \sqrt{(m_{20} - m_{10}^2/m_{00})/m_{00}} \qquad (5)$$

$$\sigma_x = \sqrt{(m_{02} - m_{01}^2/m_{00})/m_{00}} \qquad (6)$$

Then complexity index C can be computed as

$$C = (L_x + L_y)/\sqrt{\sigma_x^2 + \sigma_y^2} \qquad (7)$$

Where L_x and L_y are the length of the longest stroke in X direction and Y direction respectively. Thus the larger C is the more complex the character is. If $|C_i - C_j| \leq 7$, then the character i and j are considered to be in the same complexity degree range, where the retrieval function works on.

Table 1. Comparison of average retrieval time of three approaches

Approach	Time
Earth Movers' Distance	16.6 minute
Projecting	5.31 minute
Shape Corresponding	1.52 minute

The number of sampled points dominates the computing time of each shape matching process. So dimensionality reduction is needed. The Number of Connected Points (NCP) is defined as the number of contour points existed in its 8-neighbourhood as introduced in [13]. If $NCP \geq 2$ and three consecutive points are in the same direction, then they are considered as parts of the same stroke. The middle point was taken out, and the reminder two points keep the structure information.

In order to measure the efficiency of these three speeding up approaches, we compare our proposed Shape Corresponding approach [7] (after implemented speeding approaches) with Projecting approach [11] and Earth Movers' Distance approach [14], as shown in Table 1. All of the tests are performed on a regular Intel(R)/256RAM personal computer. Compared with [7], the database in this paper is enlarged from 336 individual calligraphy characters to 1650 calligraphy characters, which segmented from works of about 60 calligraphists living in different dynasties. Table 1 indicates that an average single calligraphy character matching takes about 640ms (336 characters, 3.6minute) in [7], while here only 55 ms (1650 characters, 1.52 minute).

5.2   Dynamic Writing Process Simulating

After an individual calligraphy character is displayed before the learners, together with the information of where it comes from and who wrote it. The next service is to offer a visualization of how such a calligraphy character was written step by step, which may help immersion learning.

In order to simulate the dynamic writing process, stroke extraction and stroke sequence estimation should be made. We use contour segments to extract strokes of calligraphy character as introduced in [15]. Strokes in a handwritten calligraphy character are often connected together (see Fig.5). Also strokes of handwriting are not necessary corresponding to strokes of well printed character. Yet it's doesn't matter if several connected strokes are extracted as one stroke, so long as right writing sequence can be estimated. One assumption for estimating the order of the stroke sequence is based on the traditional writing rule:a calligraphy character was written from the left to the right, from the top to the bottom, and from the outside to the inside (see [11], page 14). The other assumption is that people always write a calligraphy character as fast and convenient as possible. So if strokes are connected, total distance travelled in the writing process should be minimized as introduced in [13]. Therefore when a cross corner encountered, we choose to follow the most straightforward contour segment. Because it has

Fig. 5. A calligraphy character example and the corresponding video simulating its writing process

the biggest angle, and comply with the rule that "people write it as convenient as possible"

Based on above observation, we extract the strokes and estimated their sequence. Then develop a video to simulate how a calligraphist wrote a calligraphy character step by step, as show in Fig.5.

6   Implementation and Evaluation

In the experiment, approaches described above are used and tested with the database consists of 1650 individual calligraphy characters. Most of these characters are segmented from 3 volumes of a book named "Chinese calligraphy Collections". Fig.6 shows a retrieval example.

If a learner is interested in one style of the character, for example the last one in the second row in Fig.6, then the learner can click this particular calligraphy character and a new web page (see Fig.7) will pop up showing its original scanned page with a minimum-bounding box marked out where it is, and also who wrote it. In Fig.7, when the name of the author is clicked, a portrait of the author accompanied by a brief resume will be shown. And if the individual character is clicked, a plug-in video (see Fig.5) will show up playing the estimated and visualized writing process.

Recall and precision are the basic measures used to quantitatively speculate the effectiveness of retrieval approach. Recall is the ratio of the number of relevant records retrieved to the total number of relevant records in the database, and precision is the ratio of the number of relevant records retrieved to the total number of irrelevant and relevant records retrieved. Here, we use average recall and average precision. They are defined as:

$$recall_{average} = \frac{1}{C} \times \sum_{i=1}^{c} recall_i / n_i \tag{8}$$

$$presicion_{average} = \frac{1}{C} \times \sum_{i=1}^{c} precision_i / n_i \tag{9}$$

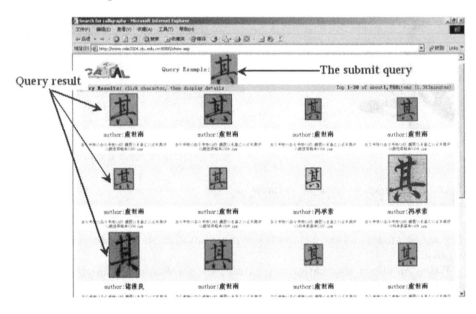

Fig. 6. Screen shot of a retrieval example

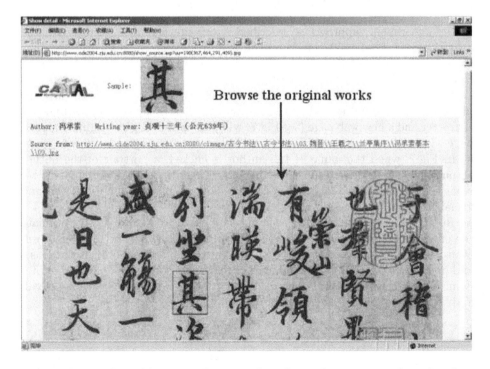

Fig. 7. Screen shot of browsing the original works, with a minimum-bounding box mark out where the interested individual character is

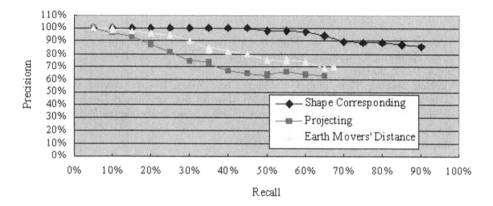

Fig. 8. Comparison of 3 approaches of their average recall and precision ratio on 20 characters with each has more than 6 different styles

Where c is the number of characters, n_i is the number of total styles of the same character i. We randomly chose 20 characters (each has more than 6 different styles) from the database, that is to say when $C = 20$ and $n_i \geq 6$, then Fig.8 can be drawn. It is obvious that the recall ratio is higher than traditional content-based image retrieval.

7   Conclusion and Future Work

We proposed a new system to help people who are interested in calligraphy to enjoy the beauty of different styles of the same Chinese character, to learn the detailed information of a particular character style (such as who wrote it, and in what environment), and also to learn how it can be written step by step. While the experiment is somewhat preliminary, it works efficiently and clearly demonstrates the applicability of our system to web-based Chinese calligraphy learning.

Our further development of this system will include continuing to speed up the retrieval service, developing more large database, and offering more convenient ways for query submitting, such as scratching a query or type in a text query by keyboard.

Acknowledgements

This research is supported by the China-US Million Book Digital Library Project (see http://www.cadal.net), and the National Natural Science Foundation of China (No. 60272031).

References

1. Yueting Zhuang, Xiang Liu, Multimedia Knowledge Exploitation for E-Learning: Some Enabling Techniques, *1st International Conference on Web-based Learning*, pp. 411-422, 2002.
2. Yueting Zhuang, Congmiao Wu, Fei Wu and Xiang Liu, Improving Web-Based Learning: Automatic Annotation of Multimedia Semantics and Cross-Media Indexing, *Third International Conference on Web-based Learning*, pp. 255-262, 2004.
3. http://www.wenyi.com/art/shufa
4. http://www.shw.cn/93jxsd/jxsd.htm
5. S. Belongie , J. Malik , J. Puzicha, Shape Matching and Object Recognition Using Shape Contexts, *IEEE Transactions on Pattern Analysis and Machine Intelligence*, vol.24, pp.509-522, No. 4, April 2002.
6. Jong-Seung Park, Visual Information Retrieval Based on Shape Similarity, *The 7th International Conference on Asian Digital Libraries*, LNCS 3334, pp. 458-461, 2004. 1336-1342.
7. Yueting Zhuang, Xiafen Zhang, Jiangqin Wu, Xiqun Lu: Retrieval of Chinese Calligraphic Character Image. 2004 *Pacific-Rim Conference on Multimedia*, LNCS 3331, pp. 17-24, 2004.
8. Jihai Zhao and Chen Huang, Technical Issues on the China-US Million Book Digital Library Project, *7th Int'l Conf. On Asian Digital Libraries*, LNCS 3334, pp. 220-226, 2004.
9. Thomas M. BreuelRepresentations and Metrics for Off-Line Handwriting Segmentation, *8th International Workshop on Frontiers in Handwriting Recognition*, pp.428 - 433,2002.
10. R. Manmatha, Chengfeng Han,E. M. Riseman,W. B. Croft, Indexing handwriting using word matching, *Proceedings of the 1st ACM international conference on Digital libraries*, pp.151 - 159,1996.
11. Wu You-Shou and Ding Xiao-Qing, Chinese character recognition: the principles and the implementations. Beijing: Advanced Education Press, 1992.
12. http://homepages.inf.ed.ac.uk/rbf/HIPR2/canny.htm
13. Lau K.K., Yuen P.C., Tang Y.Y, Stroke extraction and stroke sequence estimation on signatures, *16th Int'l Conf. On Pattern Recognition*, vol. 3, pp: 119 - 122,2002.
14. S. Cohen and L. Guibas. The Earth Mover's Distance under Transformation Sets. In *Proceedings of 7th IEEE International Conference on Computer Vision*, Corfu, Greece, September 1999, pp. 173-187.
15. Chungnan Lee, Bohom Wu, Wen-Chen Huang, Integration of multiple levels of contour information for Chinese-character stroke extraction, *4th Int'l Conf on Document Analysis and Recognition*, vol.2, pp.584 - 587,1997.

Computer-Assisted Item Generation for Listening Cloze Tests and Dictation Practice in English

Shang-Ming Huang[†], Chao-Lin Liu[†], and Zhao-Ming Gao[‡]

[†] Dept. of Computer Science, National Chengchi University, Taipei, Taiwan
[‡] Dept. of Foreign Languages and Literatures, National Taiwan University, Taipei, Taiwan
chaolin@nccu.edu.tw, zmgao@ntu.edu.tw

Abstract. We take advantages of abundant text resource on the Internet and information about English phonetics for assisting human teachers to prepare test items for listening and dictation in English. In this preliminary exploration, we built an environment in which teachers choose words that they want to have test items for, and teachers compose the final test items based on the test items that are algorithmically generated by our system. The output of the current system indicates that computers can play active roles in assisting the composition of test items, though we have not done a field test over the usability issues.

1 Introduction

Traditional wisdom dictates that listening, speaking, reading, and writing are four major components in learning a language. Listening is a very important input channel for everyday communication, and so for learning languages. Listening is not just an important channel for learning languages, but also a skill that needs to be learned [1]. As a result, both teachers and learners need to have ways to evaluate the competence in listening. A dominant way of evaluating competence in listening is the listening comprehension tests [2], in which examinees answer questions that are related to a spoken segment of story or conversation. Tests of this form allow test administrators to evaluate students' high-level understanding of the spoken passage. In contrast, listening cloze tests (cf. [3]) examines students' capabilities in comprehending the sounds of particular words, and is a mechanism for evaluating students' low-level listening capabilities. Although few will deny the importance of gauging students' high-level and low-level competence in listening [4, 5], there is an imbalance in the availability of practice test items for listening comprehension and listening cloze. This is probably due to the fact that most real-world examinations employ listening comprehension tests rather than listening cloze tests, and the market has a much stronger demand on the practice material for listening comprehension.

Computer-assisted item generation [6] is not a brand new idea for the study of educational technologies. Although test items constructed by human experts are highly preferred for their quality, it is also costly to create such high-quality items while keeping the security of the item pools. When relying on a limited number of human experts to construct test items, the coverage of the constructed test items may be confined to the

R.W.H. Lau et al. (Eds.): ICWL 2005, LNCS 3583, pp. 197–208, 2005.
© Springer-Verlag Berlin Heidelberg 2005

interests and views of these item creators, consequently impairing the quality of the test items. For computer assisted language learning, the Web serves as a good source of text files, and is already helping language learners around the world. Given the ample text files on the Web, we can extract sentences from the Web, compile the extracted sentences into candidate test items, and allow the teachers to select and edit the candidates before delivering the test items for students' practice and evaluation.

Not surprisingly, researchers have applied techniques of natural language processing in this computer-assisted language learning task. For instance, Stevens [7] applies the concept of concordance and Coniam [8] considers the concept of word frequency in generating vocabulary test items from corpora. Wang et al. [9] consider multiple linguistics-based techniques, including selectional preferences and word sense disambiguation [10], in assisting the generation of high quality multiple-choice cloze items. In addition to finding better ways for providing learning material, researchers have also explored the possibility of conducting higher level analyses of learners' language proficiency with computer techniques. Michaud et al. [11] propose methods for analyzing the grammatical structures of written English, and Burstein et al. [12] implement a system for evaluating essays of examinees of the TOEFL tests.

We propose computational methods that help teachers of English to prepare test items for listening cloze, and hope to offer learners of English a middle ground for diagnosing their own deficiency in listening capabilities. A listening cloze item is similar to an ordinary cloze item, except that the test item is delivered in the audio form. Hence, in addition to constructing a sentence for a test item, our system must also recommend distractors for the keywords that are deleted from the main sentences. In addition, we report exploration of classifying errors found in learners' dictation of English sentence. Dictation is relatively more difficult than multiple-choice test items, and implementing this type of testing environment grants ourselves the possibility of constructing a practice environment that may provide appropriate material that adapts to students' different levels of proficiency in English [13]. Similar to Coniam's Text Dictation system [14], we employ the concept of partial dictation [15], in which students are required to put down part of the spoken sentences. Unlike Coniam's rule-based method for giving partial credits to students' dictations, we classify students' answers in order to help students identify their weakness in the dictation task.

We provide an overview of our system in Section 2, elaborate on how we apply phonetics to generate listening cloze test items in Section 3, and present a way to evaluate student's dictation using some linguistics-related criteria in Section 4.

2   System Overview

At the current stage, we consider three different levels of learning English vocabulary. The most popular form of multiple cloze tests, illustrated below, should be the easiest form. In this type of cloze tests, examinees will choose the best candidate from the pro-vided alternatives for the deleted word in the given sentence. As the examinees can read all the available information in the test item, this form of tests is considered to be relatively easier than the listening cloze and dictation tests.

All the flights to and from Hong Kong were ___ because of the heavy thunderstorm.
(A) advised   (B) disclosed   (C) cancelled   (D) benefited

In previous work [9], we build a system that takes advantages of resource available on the Web for assisting teachers to compose multiple-choice cloze items. Figure 1 shows the block diagram for this system. We download and preprocess text files from the Web, augment such information as part-of-speech and root forms of inflected words with the words, and save the results in the tagged corpus. Applying techniques for word sense disambiguation, our system allows teachers to request sentences that include a specific word with a specific meaning in the sentence, and choose appropriate distractors for the keyword to form a multiple-choice cloze item, while ensuring that there is only one correct answer to the composed item.

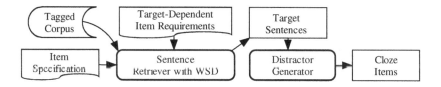

Fig. 1. Block diagram for generating multiple-choice cloze items [9]

We use our Web crawler to obtain raw material from the Internet [16]. The text fragments are segmented into sentences and saved into the database. The corpus has 163,719 sentences, which include a total of 3,077,474 words that comprise 31,732 different words. Recognizing the current choice of the text sources may not be the best possible choice, we use them simply because they offer satisfactory quality of articles and free accessibility. Our main goal is to demonstrate the viability of our system architecture. Whenever necessary, we can replace the text corpora with better ones.

In this work, we continue to use the tagged corpus as the source of sentences for ex-tending our system to assist the tasks of dictation and multiple-choice listening cloze tests. In Section 3, we focus on how we choose distractors for the listening cloze tests. In Section 4, we turn our attention to how we may evaluate students' competence in dictation.

We look forward to a vertically integrated system that is capable of adaptively interacting with students for assisting the evaluation of competence in English vocabulary, putting the resulting components together. The previous work on cloze tests allows learners to examine their English vocabulary in reading form, and the results re-ported in this paper extend the scope to listening and active production in dictation.

3 Generating Multiple-Choice Listening Cloze Items

Our system helps teachers create multiple-choice listening cloze test items. First, teachers request sentences for a selected keyword, and our system will search the corpus for sentences that include the keyword. Our system will arrange the sentences to facilitate the selection of sentences by aligning the keywords in the same column.

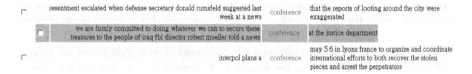

Fig. 2. Teachers select appropriate candidate sentences from the list

This is the same as a concordancer, which is shown in Figure 2. In addition, our system attempts to put sentences that have "similar phonetic environment" around the keyword, which will be explained in Section 3.1. Teachers then select appropriate sentences from these arranged sentences, and our system will automatically select the distractors from our databases and compile the multiple-choice problems.

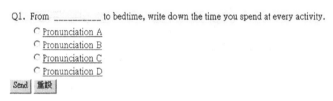

Fig. 3. A format of the multiple-choice listening cloze item

There are two different types of multiple-choice problems in our system. The first type tests on individual keywords, while the other type removes the keyword and the words that immediately precedes and follows the keyword. Figure 3 shows one format of the generated multiple-choice listening cloze items. The keyword in the test item is replaced with underscores, and there are four options for the test item. Clicking on the hyperlinks, students will hear the audio for each distractor. At this moment, we create the audio for the words and sentences with the AT&T Natural Voice [17], and can replace the audio files with human-recorded files for test items of higher quality. There is only one correct option among the alternatives, and the other distractors are automatically generated by our system. Students can click on one of the four checkboxes. and submit their answers.

A more difficult format of the listening cloze tests, which is not shown here, does not show the whole sentences immediately. Instead, students check a button to listen to the whole sentence for a test item up to three times, but they do not have to listen to the whole sentence three times before answering the question. Students will not see the printed form of the test item, which are in the same format as the one shown in Figure 3, until entering the answering mode. After entering the answer mode, the audio for the whole sentence will not be repeated. This format is more difficult because students have to listen to the whole sentence before they answer. In contrast, the test item shown in Figure 3 allows students to focus solely on the sounds of the keywords.

In addition to controlling the item difficulty by manipulating how and when students can listen to the recordings, modulating the playing speeds of the recordings is another conceivable alternative. With appropriately supported software techniques, we can change the speeds of both human-articulated and machine-synthesized recordings. Our current choice of using the AT&T voice synthesizer is a result of an arbitrary decision, though the synthesizer does produce satisfactory recordings for short text segments.

For facilitating the selection of distractors, we employ two metrics for measuring the similarity between words. We consider the features of phonemes that are contained in words for computing the distances between words, and construct a database based on our definition of the *phonetic distance* (**PD**). Words that are similar in terms of the phonetic distance are clustered in the PD database. We also construct a database based on our definition of the consonant-vowel patterns (**CVP**s). Words that have the same consonant-vowel patterns are clustered for future use. We provide more details about the PD and CVP databases in Sections 3.2 and 3.3, respectively.

When composing a test item, our system randomly chooses from the PD database those words that are similar to the keyword first. If there are less than three words available in the PD database, more words will be retrieved from the CVP database. If more distractors are needed, our system will create words to make up the distractors. Disregarding whether the words do exist, we randomly replace vowels of the keyword with other vowels to make a new word. Consider the word "structure" which has two vowels 'u'. We may select the first vowel 'u' and randomly replace it with other vowels like 'a', 'e', 'i' or 'o', and come up with candidate distractors like "stracture", "strecture", "stricture" and "strocture", respectively. Although these distractors may not be appropriate in a reading cloze test, the synthesized sounds of these created words may be quite distracting to students who are not good at listening.

3.1 Phonetic Concordance

The actual sound of words may be influenced by its context, so we try to put candidate items whose keywords have similar phonetic contexts near each other. For example, the sentence "You can get them at the drugstore". The sound of the word "get" is influenced by the phoneme /□/ of the word "them" so that the phoneme /t/ may not be pronounced clearly, and students may get confused by these variations. Considering this situation, we believe that it is useful to arrange candidate items that have similar phonetic environments together to better serve the item preparation process.

To this end, we consider the syllables that are immediately before and after the keyword in determining whether a keyword has similar phonetic contexts in two sentences. For each candidate item, we obtain these syllables from the words that immediately precede and follow the keyword, and concatenate the syllables with the phoneme sequence of the keyword. We compute the similarity between two phoneme sequences with a minimum edit distance (MED) algorithm [cf. 18], which employs the definitions of phonetic distance that we explain in Section 3.2. We consider sequences similar if their phonetic distance is no larger than 50.

For example, consider two sentences: "The sergeant simply abandoned his position", and "This myth was effectively abandoned in the 1990s". The phonemic environments of the word "abandoned" in these sentences are: "-ly abandoned his" and "-ly abandoned in". The corresponding phoneme sequences are: "-ly-a-ban-don-ed-his" and "-ly-a-ban-don-ed-in". After computing the phonetic distances between the sequences, our system will find that the phonemic environments of "abandoned" are similar in these sentences, and will put them together in the interface that looks like Figure 2. In Figure 2, the phonetic environment of the word *conference* in the indented sentence (in red background) is similar to that in the first sentence.

3.2 Phonetic Distance

Each phoneme has its phonetic features [19, 20]. The number of common features determines the similarity between phonemes. We have selected two features which are commonly used to

Table 1. Phonetic features of three phonemes

Phoneme	Place of Articulation	Manner of Articulation
/m/	bilabial	nasal
/n/	alveolar	nasal
/d/	alveolar	stop

differentiate phonemes: the place of articulation and the manner of articulation, although it requires more than two features to completely tell all the phonemes apart. Table 1 shows selected phonetic features of the phonemes /m/, /n/, and /d/: /m/ and /n/ share a common feature, and /m/ and /d/ differ in both features. Perceptually, /m/ is more similar to /n/ than to /d/. This example suggests that the number of different phonetic features reflects our perception about different phonemes.

Hence, we define the *phonetic distance*, PD, between two phonemes based upon the number of the different phonetic features between them as follows. According to the definition, the phonetic distance between /m/ and /n/ is 2, while the phonetic distance between /m/ and /d/ is 3. Distances are defined as 1 for different phonemes which share the same place and manner of articulation.

- PD is 0 if the consonants are exactly the same.
- PD is 1 if both the place and the manner of articulation are the same.
- PD is 2 if either the manner or the place of the articulation is different, but not both.
- PD is 3 for all other cases.

Similarly, we select three features for defining the distances between vowels: the position of the tongue, vowel height (the highest part of the tongue), and the shape of the lips. The definition for phonetic distance between two vowels follows.

- PD is 0 if the vowels are exactly the same.
- PD is 5 if the three features are exactly the same.
- PD is 10 if one of the three parameters is different.
- PD is 15 if two of the parameters are different.
- PD is 20 if all of the three parameters are different.

For example, the phonetic features of the vowel /i/ are: the tongue is high, the tongue position is toward the front, and the mouth is unrounded [20]. The phonetic features of /□/ are: the tongue is semi-high, the tongue position is toward the front, and the mouth is unrounded. There is only one different feature, so the phonetic distance between /i/ and /□/ is 10. For another vowel /u/, the phonetic features are: the tongue is high, the tongue position is toward the back, and the mouth is rounded. There are two different features between /i/ and /u/, so their phonetic distance is 15.

Perceptually, the difference between vowels is much more obvious than that between consonants. Most of the time, vowels are also pronounced louder and more prominent than consonants. To reflect these facts, we amplify the distances between vowels. As consonants are very different from vowels, we define the phonetic distance between any vowel and any consonant as 50.

We define the distance between two words as the minimum edit distance [cf. 18] that is calculated with the phoneme sequences of the words. We first convert the words into their phonemes by looking into the Merriam-Webster online dictionary [21] and grapheme-phoneme-conversion rules, and split the phonemes into individual symbols with standard techniques of lexical analyzers in Computer Science [22]. We then apply the standard MED algorithm for computing the phonetic distance between the words. We apply the aforementioned phonetic distances when encountering insertion, deletion, and substitution of phonemes in the calculation. (It is understood that the actual sound of an individual phoneme may change because of its contextual phonemes [19]. The fact that we use the dynamic algorithm-based MED algorithm is tentative to ignoring such contextual influences.)

Figure 4 shows the process of computing the phonetic distance between *intercately* and *intricately* with the MED algorithm. The leftmost column and the bottom row in the *edit-distance matrix*

□	285	159	154	112	62	78	43	69	67	17
1	285	109	104	62	103	28	75	19	17	67
t	235	107	102	60	53	25	67	17	19	69
ə	185	105	102	58	23	67	17	67	111	79
k	170	55	52	8	55	17	67	61	64	114
□	120	52	50	5	17	67	59	109	154	122
t	100	2	0	2	52	54	104	104	107	157
n	50	0	2	4	54	57	107	109	111	161
□	0	50	100	150	150	200	215	265	315	315
	□	n	t	r	□	k	ə	t	l	□

Fig. 4. PD between intricately and intercately

show the phoneme sequences of he words being compared. In Figure 4, phonemes of *intercately* and *intricately* are on the leftmost column and the bottom row, respectively. Each cell in the matrix reflects the minimum phonetic distance between the corresponding phoneme sequences which appear on the leftmost column and the bottom row, e.g., PD(intricately, intercately)=17 and PD(intricately, inter)=122. The underlined bold cells show the shortest distances between substrings of *intercately* and *intricately*.

In an earlier attempt, we arbitrarily set 50 in PD as the boundary for similar words. When there are two extremely different vowels and three extremely different consonants between the words being compared, the phonetic distance will be 2*20+3*3=49. Hence, a phonetic distance that is larger than 50 indicates really different words. This absolute threshold may not work very well for short words, though.

In the most recent experiments, we have found that a good choice of threshold should depend on the number of syllables in the words being compared. Using a large threshold will admit very different phones to be treated as similar phones, and makes the resulting test item less challenging. Using a very small threshold might cause two kinds of problems. There could be insufficient similar words for each entry in the PD database for even one single test item. Worst yet, when the previous situation does occur, these very few candidates will be repeatedly used, making the resulting test items less useful in practice. Making the threshold a function of the number of syllables is more flexible, but has not been implemented in the most recent version of our system.

Using the phonetic distance, we construct the PD database. We compute and save a list of similar words for each word, except for the function words (such as articles, prepositions, conjunctions, auxiliary verbs and pronouns, etc.). Words that are less than sitions, conjunctions, auxiliary verbs and pronouns, etc.). Words that are less than 50 apart in terms of the phonetic distance are considered similar. The wordlist for each word in the database will be used in the selection of distractors for the multiple-choice items.

3.3 Consonant-Vowel Patterns

In addition to the phonetic distance, we also compare the consonant-vowel patterns (CVPs) of two words to determine their similarity. After converting words into phoneme sequences by consulting the on-line dictionary, we convert a vowel into the symbol "+" and a consonant into the symbol "-". Hence the consonant-vowel pattern of the word "follow" is "-+-+-", and the pattern of "hollow" is also "-+-+-".

Words that have the same CVP may have similar pronunciations, e.g., "follow" and "hollow", and can be used as distractors for each other. However, there are words that have the same CVP, but they have a large phonetic distance, e.g., "absolute" and "organic". Some words have different CVPs, but their phonetic distance is close, e.g., "absolute" and "calculate". Therefore, the information about the consonant-vowel patterns does not guarantee the similarity between words.

Nevertheless, for having a fallback for the PD database, we cluster words that have the same consonant-vowel pattern into groups in the CVP database. We convert each word in the corpus into their consonant-vowel patterns. Words with the same consonant-vowel patterns are clustered, and the information about the consonant-vowel clusters is used in generating the multiple-choice items when necessary.

4   Dictation Error Analysis

Teachers create items for dictation with a procedure that is similar to that for creating multiple-choice listening cloze items. Figure 5 shows a format of the created dictation test item. The sentence with a blank text field is the test item, where students are supposed

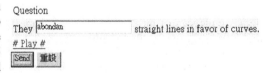

Fig. 5. An item for dictation

to fill out the missing word. Clicking on the hyperlink "#Play#" below the test item, students will hear the whole sentence. Similar to how we create audio for the listening cloze items, we rely on the AT&T Natural Voice for synthesizing the audio for the dictation items. Also similar to the listening cloze items, there is a corresponding, more difficult format of the test, in which students will have to listen to the whole sentence before they can see the sentence with the deleted word as is shown in Figure 5. After filling out the text, students submit their answers by clicking on the "Send" button. Our system will save the answers and deliver the next item.

As an attempt to formulate a principled model of the errors committed by real-world students in dictation, we collected and analyzed actual students' dictations from the English classes of the last author. Unfortunately, we must admit that it is rather hard to come up with a list of well-founded explanations for the observed errors. Sometimes, students put down the correct words in wrong tenses or inflected forms. Sometimes, students seemed to know what they heard but could not spell the words correctly.

Although we cannot establish psycholinguistic foundations for the committed errors, we try to classify the errors purely from the linguistic viewpoints. Specifically, we observed three types of errors, and refer these types as *syntactic errors*, *spelling errors*, and *phonetic errors* for convenience. Section 4.1 explains how we classify the errors, and Sections 4.2 provides details about how our system provides feedback to the students based on their types of errors.

4.1 Three Types of Errors

Students' answers that included **morphological errors** are actually very close to the correct answers. For instance, students may have put down "maps" and "combine", respectively, for "map" and "combined." Errors of this type can be detected with a lemmatization technique [cf. 10]. Lemmatization is the process of converting inflected words to their original forms. For instance, results of lemmatizing "combined" and "maps" are "combine" and "map", respectively. We employ the Porter's Stemmer [23] to lemmatize students' answers and the correct answers, and compare the resulting strings. **Morphological errors** are indicated if some words in these strings become matched only after the lemmatization step, while these words do not match before being lemmatized.

We call the second type of errors **spelling errors**. Students may have heard the phones of the words, but cannot reconstruct the spellings of the pronounced words. It is common that, in this case, the dictation is similar to the correct spelling, but contains a few missing and/or redundant characters. We measure the similarity between such misspelled and correct words from two related perspectives: Maximum Common Characters (MCC) and Minimum Edit Distance (MED). Here we use the Levenshtein cost function for the MED algorithm [cf. 18], i.e., 1 for both insertions and deletions, and 2 for substitutions.

Table 2 shows the MCC and MED for some samples. The leftmost two columns show the correct answers and students' dictations. The third and the fourth columns show the MCC and MED values between the word pairs. Take "intricately" and "intercately" for example. Their MCC value is 10 because of the 10 common characters 'i', 'n', 't', 'r',

Table 2. The MCC and MED of some word pairs

Answer	Dictation	MCC	MED
intricately	intercately	10	2
interwoven	interwoved	9	2
with	intercately	2	11
civilizations	interwoved	2	10
inter	retni	5	8
inter	in	2	3

'c', 'a', 't', 'e', 'l', and 'y'. The MED value is 2 because of 1 deletion ('e') and 1 insertion ('i').

Let L be the number of characters in the correct answer, A and D be the correct answer and the dictation, respectively. After observing the collected data, we consider D is a misspelled form of A if **MCC(A, D) > L/2 and MED(A, D) < L**. The first two instances in Table 2 show examples that meet the conditions, but the other instances do not.

Words that are considered to be a misspelled form of the correct words will be further analyzed for possible **phonetic errors**. As mentioned in Section 3.2, we use the MED algorithm to compute the phonetic distance between two words. By tracing back this optimal path from the upper right corner, we can identify the different phonemes between the words. Consider the edit-distance matrix of PD(intercately, intricately) in Figure 4. The optimal path is "17-17-17-17-17-17-2-0-0-0". Drops in the numbers in the path reveal the different phonemes between the word pair. By this way, the different phonemes between two similar words can be found.

Recall, however, that the words that we compare in Section 3.2 are all correct words in English. Therefore, we can look up the online dictionary for their phones and produce corresponding phoneme sequences. When processing students' dictations, it is not uncommon that students would put down *non*-existent words. It is not directly obvious how one can find the phones of these wrong words. To do as much as we can, we rely on word formation rules [24] and grapheme-to-morpheme rules [25] for converting students' dictations into phoneme sequences. Although the correspondence between graphemes and phonemes are not perfectly regular [19, page 562], existing rules are not completely useless for converting non-existent words into phoneme sequences.

4.2 Item Feedback

A satisfactory feedback system should first identify the actual weakness in students' competence, and provides the material that will really remedy the problems. Given that it is not easy to classify students' errors in dictation, our exploration into providing feedback items for students is nothing but preliminary, if not bold. After classifying students' errors based on the aforementioned three criteria, it is natural that our system responds to students' dictations according to the classified error types.

- Level 1: the dictation is extremely different from the correct answer in spelling, suggesting that the student has no idea about the testing material
- Level 2: (spelling errors): the dictation is a misspelled form of the correct answer and the phonetic distance is larger than 50, suggesting that the student may have some idea about the testing material
- Level 3: (phonetic errors): the dictation is a misspelled form of the correct answer and the phonetic distance is no larger than 50, suggesting that the student has roughly caught the testing material
- Level 4: (morphological errors): the dictation is an inflected form of the correct answer, suggesting that the student may have exactly known the testing material
- Level 5: the dictation is exactly the same as the correct answer

In the prototype for assisting students to practice dictation, after classifying students' answers, our system records the transactions in the students' profiles, and continues to interact with the student. Figure 6 shows such a correspondence. In this example, our system determines that the dictation is not correct, and feedback this evaluation to the student. When necessary or requested, for level 3 errors, our system can show the phonemes that are correctly dictated. If students want to do more practice, the system will deliver more test items that are appropriate for the students' competence levels.

If the entered word is not perfectly correct, our system will continue the previous test item, and may repeat the same item for up to three times. After receiving three incorrect answers, our system will simply show the correct answer. If the entered

Question

they pick up [   ] so naturally and easily

Level 4: The grammar form of your dictation is not correct.

Play

[Send] [重設]

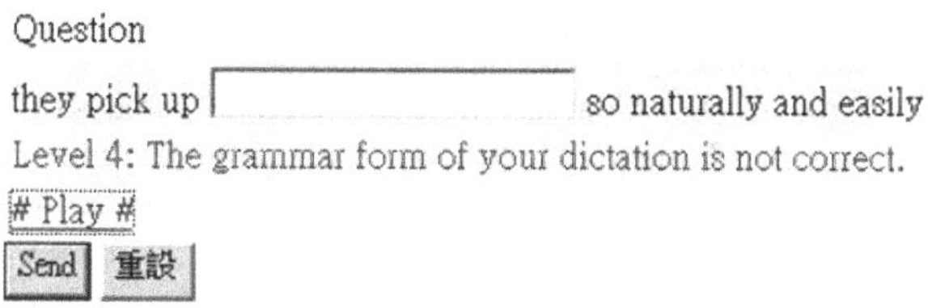

Fig 6. Our system responds to a level 4 dictation

is correct, i.e., level 5, our system allows the student to choose different types of new test items. Students can choose more items which test on the same keyword, items which test on keywords that have the same consonant-vowel pattern with the tested keyword, items which test on other keywords that have small phonetic distance with the tested keyword, or items which test on other items which have similar phonemic environments with the tested item.

5 Conclusions

We proposed a computer-assisted item generation system for helping teachers to create practice items for learning English vocabulary, and report the design of our system for generating listening cloze and dictation practice in this paper. We believe such functions will facilitate the construction of a Web-based test system for a large population. The current system offers aids in constructing test items in different levels of difficulty, including reading cloze, listening cloze to dictation, so our system is posed to support adaptive interaction with the students. Although the current efforts are preliminary, we believe that this is an important step toward realizing adaptive interaction with students in computer-assisted language learning.

We have identified some future work. As pointed out by reviewers, the system should be evaluated by teachers. Technically, we should consider contextual influence on the pronunciation of individual words, so MED is an imperfect method for computing difference between two words. Using a voice synthesizer, it should be possible to add more intermediate steps between listening cloze to dictation tests.

Acknowledgements

The authors thank Professor Maw-Kae Hor, Professor Berlin Chen, and anonymous reviewers for comments on improving a previous version of this manuscript. This work was supported in part by Grants 92-2213-E-004-004, 92-2411-H-002-061, 93-2213-E-004-004, and 93-2411-H-002-013 of the National Science Council, Taiwan.

References

1. Vandergrift, L.: Listen to learn or learn to listen, Annual Review of Applied Linguistics **24** (2004) 3–25
2. Mendelsohn, D.: Teaching Listening. Annual Review of Applied Linguistics **18** (1998) 81–101

3. UBC English Language Institute: http://www.eli.ubc.ca/teachers/lessons/speaking/presentation_skills/expository.html#c

4. Coniam, D.: Computerized dictation for assessing listening proficiency. Computer Assisted Language Instruction Consortium Journal **13**(2-3) (1996) 73–85

5. Ross, S.: Self-assessment in second language testing: A meta-analysis and analysis of experiential factors. Language Testing **15**(1) (1998) 1–20

6. Irvine, S. H., Kyllonen, P. C. (eds.): Item Generation for Test Development, Lawrence Erlbaum Associates (2002)

7. Stevens, V.: Classroom concordancing: Vocabulary materials derived from relevant authentic text. English for Specific Purposes **10**(1) (1991) 35–46

8. Coniam, D.: A Preliminary inquiry into using corpus word frequency data in the automatic generation of English cloze tests. Computer Assisted Language Instruction Consortium Journal **16**(2-4) (1997) 15–33

9. Wang, C.-H., Liu, C.-L., Gao, Z.-M.: Using lexical constraints for corpus-based generation of multiple-choice cloze items. Proc. of the Seventh IASTED Int. Conf. on Computers and Advanced Technology in Education (2004) 351–356

10. Manning, C. D., Schütze, H.: Foundations of Statistical Natural Language Processing, MIT Press (1999)

11. Michaud, L. N., McCoy, K. F., Stark, L. A.: Modeling the acquisition of English: An intelligent CALL approach, Proc. of the Eighth International Conf. on User Modeling (Lecture Notes in Computer Science 2109) (2001) 14–23.

12. Burstein, J., Chodorow, M., Leacock, C.: Criterion[SM]: Online essay evaluation: An application for automated evaluation of student essays. Proc. of the Fifteenth Annual Conf. on Innovative Applications of Artificial Intelligence (2003) 3–10

13. Brusilovsky, P.: Adaptive and Intelligent Technologies for Web-based Education. Künstliche Intelligenz, **13**(4) (1999) 19–25

14. Coniam, D.: Interactive evaluation of listening comprehension: How the context may help. Computer Assisted Language Learning **11**(1) (1998) 35–53.

15. Oller, J.: Language Tests at School: A Pragmatic Approach, Longman, London (1979)

16. China Post, http://www.chinapost.com.tw/; Studio Classroom, http://www.studioclassroom.com/; Taiwan Journal, http://taiwanjournal.nat.gov.tw/; Taiwan Review, http://publish.gio.gov.tw/fcr/

17. AT&T Natural Voice, http://www.naturalvoices.att.com/

18. Jurafsky, D., Martin, J. H.: Speech and Language Processing, Prentice Hall (2000)

19. Fromkin, V., Rodman, R., Hyams, N.: An Introduction to Language, Thomson Learning (2002)

20. International Phonetic Association: Handbook of the International Phonetic Association: A guide to the use of the International Phonetic Alphabet. Cambridge Univ. Press, (1999)

21. Merriam-Webster OnLine: http://www.m-w.com/dictionary.htm

22. Levine, J. R., Mason, T., Brown, D.: Lex & Yacc, O'Reilly (1992)

23. Porter, M. F: An algorithm for suffix stripping. Program **14**(3) (1980) 130–137

24. Sinclair J. (ed.): Collins CoBuild English Guides: Word Formation, HarperCollins (1990)

25. Divay, M., Vitale, A. J.: Algorithms for grapheme-phoneme translation for English and French: Applications for database searches and speech synthesis. Computational Linguistics **23**(4) (1997) 495–523

The Gong System: Web-Based Learning for Multiple Languages, with Special Support for the Yale Representation of Cantonese

David Rossiter, Gibson Lam, and Vivying Cheng

Department of Computer Science,
Hong Kong University of Science and Technology (HKUST), Hong Kong
{rossiter, gibson, vivying}@cs.ust.hk

Abstract. This paper introduces the Gong system, an Internet-based voice board system designed primarily for language learners which includes special support for Cantonese. The Gong system is a client/server design which may be used to complement or, in some contexts, to replace face to face learning. The system supports Unicode input, storage and display of multiple character sets. Furthermore, we have developed a unique storage and display method for the Yale romanized representation of Cantonese, which is the most popular written method used for teaching Cantonese.

1 Introduction

A tool called Gong has been developed that supports Internet-based text and audio communication [1]. It allows students and teachers to participate in discussion groups using their computers. Teachers and students can leave text and voice messages on voice boards. They can listen to and reply to other text and voice messages left by other people. This software is currently used each semester at the author's institution by 300 to 700 undergraduate students, as part of their language course requirements.

2 The Gong System

2.1 Overview

The Gong system is an Internet-based communication tool for language learners. Students and teachers can participate in different discussion boards by reading and writing messages on a board. A message is comprised of a text component and/or a recorded voice component. Fig. 1 shows an example screen display of the system in use by a student. The screen is divided into two parts. The top part shows the message threads of the currently selected discussion board. A user can read or listen to a particular message by selecting the message in the board. The second part contains the content of the selected message. When a message is selected, its text content is displayed in the text area at the bottom while the voice message can be played by using the audio controls. Asynchronous voice discussion on a topic can take place in the board by posting messages in the same message thread.

R.W.H. Lau et al. (Eds.): ICWL 2005, LNCS 3583, pp. 209–220, 2005.
© Springer-Verlag Berlin Heidelberg 2005

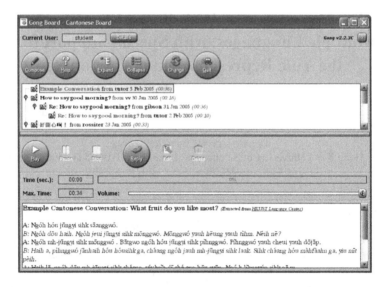

Fig. 1. Screenshot of the Gong system showing a discussion board for a Cantonese course

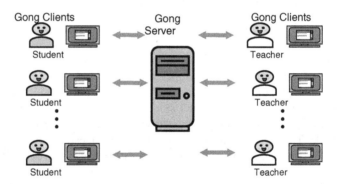

Fig. 2. A basic overview of Gong system usage

The Gong system is currently based on a client and server architecture. It is developed using the Java™ technology so that the system is platform-independent. To be able to use the system, students and teachers use client software to connect to a server on the Internet. If they want to read messages on a board, the client software will download the board data from the server. Similarly, if they post a new message on the discussion board the client software will send a request to modify the data in the server. In summary, the server acts as a communication center and centralized store of data.

2.2 XML Storage and Communication

XML is one type of syntax for expressing data structure. The Gong system has adopted XML as the basis for data storage in the server and also for communication between the clients and the server.

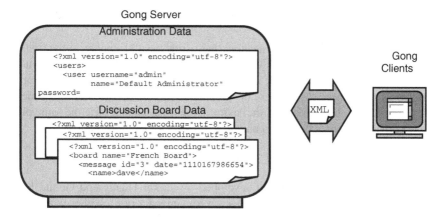

Fig. 3. The XML storage and communication in the Gong system

There are mainly two types of XML data stored in the server. The first type is administration data such as user information, group information and server configuration data. The second one is the content of each discussion board. Each board contains a collection of messages organized in a tree structure.

2.3 Unicode

Unicode [2] is an international encoding standard that provides a unique number for every character, regardless of the platform, program, or language. It has been adopted by the Gong system. This has meant many different languages such as English, Traditional Chinese, Simplified Chinese, French and Japanese can be stored and displayed together.

Although Unicode is able to represent different international languages, it is not specifically designed for displaying romanized languages. A romanized language is an alternative form of a written language which does not use a Latin based alphabet, such as Chinese and Japanese. These types of language are especially important for helping teachers and students in learning the proper pronunciation of foreign languages. Therefore we have created a generic solution for displaying one form of romanized language called the Yale system, with implementation specifically for the Cantonese version of Yale.

3 The Yale Romanization System for Cantonese

3.1 Cantonese

Cantonese is spoken by some 60 million people in many southern parts of China, including the Special Administrative Regions of Hong Kong and Macau. Technically, Cantonese is not a language in itself, but is a dialect of Chinese. However, there are major differences in pronunciation, lexicon and culture which distinguish Cantonese from other dialects.

Cantonese is a tonal language, meaning that words must be spoken at the right pitch to convey the correct meaning. Essentially, Cantonese uses 6 different tone 'structures' for the pronunciation of a word. There are three tones where the pitch does not vary. There are a further three tones where the pitch does vary. Although it is sometimes said that that Cantonese has nine tones, the 'extra' three tones actually use the same pitch as the three unvarying tones described and do not use additional tone patterns.

3.2   The Yale Romanization of Cantonese

The Yale romanization system was developed by Parker Huang and Gerald Kok [3] for learners of Cantonese. The system uses a romanized word together with a marker to indicate the tone which must be used when the word is pronounced.

The romanization of a Cantonese word is generally divided into an initial and a final part. The initial is a combination of one or more consonants. In the Yale system, the initials are restricted to the following set.

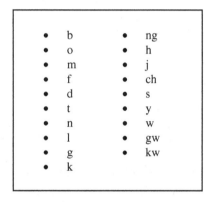

- b
- o
- m
- f
- d
- t
- n
- l
- g
- k
- ng
- h
- j
- ch
- s
- y
- w
- gw
- kw

Fig. 4. The nineteen initials of the Cantonese Yale system

A final starts with at least one vowel letter and may end with different choices of consonants. The range of possible finals is shown in Table 1. However, in some cases, the syllable does not have an initial, which means the syllable starts with a vowel instead of a consonant.

Together with the romanization, there are six different Cantonese tones used in the Yale system. When a tone is one of the three low tones an extra h is added after the vowels of a word. This extra h does not affect the pronunciation of the word at all. It is only used as an indicator of a low tone. For example, the Yale representation of the low level tone of the word lei is leih. Some of the tones are further distinguished by adding a diacritic mark on the first vowel of the word. A diacritic is a mark drawn above a vowel letter to indicate special phonetic information. Diacritics are added to denote a specific tone pattern for several of the Yale tones. Table 2 shows tones together with their corresponding romanized form in the Yale system.

Table 1. The fifty three finals of the Cantonese Yale system

Vowel Base		Finals	Vowel Base		Finals	Vowel Base		Finals
aa	•	aai	a	•	a	e	•	e
	•	aau		•	ai		•	ei
	•	aam		•	au		•	eng
	•	aan		•	am		•	ek
	•	aang		•	an			
	•	aap		•	ang			
	•	aat		•	ap			
	•	aak		•	at			
				•	ak			
i	•	i	o	•	o	u	•	u
	•	iu		•	oi		•	ui
	•	im		•	ou		•	un
	•	in		•	on		•	ung
	•	ing		•	ong		•	ut
	•	ip		•	ot		•	uk
	•	it		•	ok			
	•	ik						
eu	•	eu	ü	•	yu	nasal sound	•	m
	•	eui		•	yun		•	ng
	•	eun		•	yut			
	•	eung						
	•	eut						
	•	euk						

Table 2. The Yale representation of the six Cantonese tones

Tone Number	Tone Description	Yale Example	Cantonese Example
1	High Level	wāi	威 (powerful)
2	High Rising	wái	毀 (destroy)
3	Middle Level	wai	慰 (comfort)
4	Low Falling	wàih	唯 (only)
5	Low Rising	wáih	偉 (great)
6	Low Level	waih	胃 (stomach)

4 The XML Extension for the Yale Romanization System

4.1 Representation of Yale Romanization in XML

An XML representation is proposed for the Yale romanization system. We use two XML tags to denote a structural representation for Cantonese sentence. The first tag,

Cantonese Sentence with
Yale Representation:

Structural Representation:

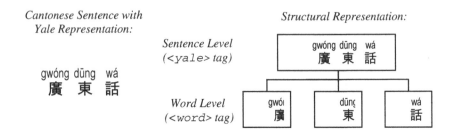

Fig. 5. An example of the structural breakdown of a Cantonese sentence using the XML tags

<yale>, is used to enclose a sentence which represents Yale romanizations of this sentence. Inside the <yale> tag we further divide the sentence into separate Cantonese words by putting each word into a <word> tag. An example is shown in Fig. 5.

We have not implemented a complete grammatical representation because the romanized form of a Cantonese sentence typically has a wide range of possible interpretations.

Other Languages Using the Yale System. Cantonese is not the only language which employs some form of Yale romanization. There are also representations of Japanese, Korean and Mandarin which use a Yale system. To distinguish between these we have defined a lang attribute. By reference to the RFC3066 standard [4] and the Internet Assigned Numbers Authority [5], we use a language code of zh-yue to indicate the Cantonese system. The corresponding language code for Japanese, Korean and Mandarin are ja, ko and zh-guoyu respectively. The lang attribute of the <yale> tag is used to specify which one is being used.

The Tone Numbering System. We have created a tone attribute in the <word> tag so that each word can be associated with the correct tone. We start with six tones in the Yale system. To distinguish between the tones we can make use of tone numbers one to six to represent the tones. However, some variations of the Cantonese Yale system include three or four more tones. Specifically, these include short instantiations of the high level tone, middle level tone and low level tone as well as a high-falling tone. When these are used they are called tones although in the case of the latter three they actually share the same tone structure of tones one, three and six. The high-falling tone is now commonly pronounced as a high-level tone in Cantonese although there are a few exceptions. We use tone zero to represent a high-falling tone and tones seven, eight and nine to represent the three short instantiations. In summary, Table 3 shows the tone numbering system we have adopted.

Combining the XML tags and attributes, we form a general representation of a Cantonese sentence. Two examples are shown in Fig. 6.

4.2   Validation with XML Schema

In order to ensure the correctness of the XML content being stored we have defined an XML Schema. This XML schema not only describes the structural information of the Yale XML but also validates the correctness of the Yale Cantonese words.

Table 3. The tone numbering system used in the Gong system

Tone Number	Name	Tone	XML Example using `lei`
0	High Falling	╲	`<word tone="0">lei</word>`
1	High Level	───	`<word tone="1">lei</word>`
2	High Rising	╱	`<word tone="2">lei</word>`
3	Middle Level	───	`<word tone="3">lei</word>`
4	Low Falling	╲	`<word tone="4">lei</word>`
5	Low Rising	╱	`<word tone="5">lei</word>`
6	Low Level	───	`<word tone="6">lei</word>`
7	Short Instantiation - High Level	─	`<word tone="7">lei</word>`
8	Short Instantiation - Middle Level	─	`<word tone="8">lei</word>`
9	Short Instantiation - Low Level	─	`<word tone="9">lei</word>`

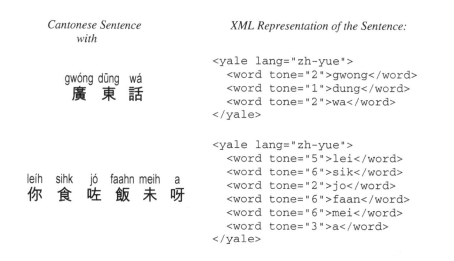

Cantonese Sentence with

gwóng dūng wá
廣　東　話

XML Representation of the Sentence:

```
<yale lang="zh-yue">
  <word tone="2">gwong</word>
  <word tone="1">dung</word>
  <word tone="2">wa</word>
</yale>
```

leíh　sihk　jó　faahn meih　a
你　食　咗　飯　未　呀

```
<yale lang="zh-yue">
  <word tone="5">lei</word>
  <word tone="6">sik</word>
  <word tone="2">jo</word>
  <word tone="6">faan</word>
  <word tone="6">mei</word>
  <word tone="3">a</word>
</yale>
```

Fig. 6. Two examples of XML representation of a Cantonese sentence

The schema validates a Cantonese word by breaking it down into three separate parts: the initial, the final and the tone. Fig. 7 shows three examples. The full listing of the XML Schema used to validate the Yale representation of Cantonese can be found in Appendix A.

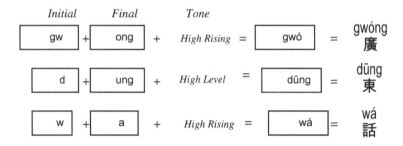

Fig. 7. The combination of initial, final and tone to define Cantonese words in Yale representation

4.3 Visual Presentation of the Yale XML Extension

XSL Transformations of the XML Extension. An XSL transformation is one of the most common methods used for the visualization of XML data. We have created an XSL stylesheet so that the Yale XML extension can be viewed in the form of a Scalable Vector Graphics (SVG) document. SVG is an XML language for describing two-dimensional graphics. Fig. 8 shows an example Cantonese sentence together with the resulting SVG display. The XSL stylesheet used can be found in Appendix B.

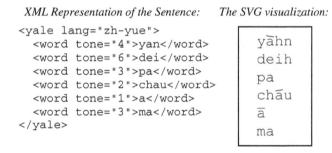

Fig. 8. An example of the visualization of a Cantonese sentence using XSL transformations. The visualization takes the form of an SVG document

Visual Presentation in the Gong System. The Gong system supports the Yale diacritic display and a specially designed stronger depiction of the diacritic display. We have added this visually 'stronger' display because the display of diacritics on different systems is often weak and inconsistent in appearance. We have also adopted a numbering display system for the Yale representation. This display system adds the tone number to the end of a Cantonese word according to the tone numbering system shown in Table 3.

There are three display modes in the Gong system. They are *Tones with Lines*, *Tones with Diacritics* and *Tones with Numbers* as shown in Fig. 9. An example of each is shown in Table 4.

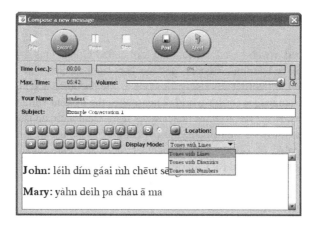

Fig. 9. An example of Yale representation using discrete lines in the Gong system. There are three choices for the display method of the Cantonese words, as shown in the selection box

Table 4. A Cantonese sentence displayed using three different modes in the Gong system

Mode	Cantonese Example
Tones with Lines	yàhn deih pa cháu ā ma
Tones with Diacritics	yàhn deih pa cháu ā ma
Tones with Numbers	yan4 dei6 pa3 chau2 a1 ma3

4.4 Input System for the Yale Romanization in the Gong System

In the Gong system seven buttons are provided to assign a tone to a particular Cantonese word. Visually, we try to help the users in identifying the tone by showing the corresponding tone levels on the buttons. Fig. 10 shows these buttons in the Gong system.

Fig. 10. The input system of the Cantonese Yale representation in the Gong system. The buttons use an image of the corresponding tonal representation

With these buttons a user can input a Cantonese word by first typing in the romanized form of the word, selecting the word and then clicking on one of the buttons representing the desired tone.

5 Conclusion

We have developed a web-based educational tool called Gong. This system is primarily designed for language learning. Students and teachers can participate in discussion groups through the use of the Internet. By using Unicode as the encoding scheme the system can support all major languages in the world. This makes the system suitable for courses of different languages. However, to have better support for Cantonese courses we have added an XML extension for the Yale romanization system. With the use of this XML extension the system is capable of storage and display of the Yale representation of Cantonese sentences which is very helpful for Cantonese learners.

Acknowledgements

This project has been supported wholly or in part by Continuous Learning and Improvement (CLI) grants, as well as a grant from the Vice President for Academic Affairs Office (VPAAO) of the author's University. The CLI project is funded by a Hong Kong Teaching and Development grant. Our thanks go to John Milton of the Language Centre of the Hong Kong University of Science and Technology for his enthusiastic and continuing support for the Gong project.

References

1. The Gong Project, http://www.cs.ust.hk/gong
2. Unicode, http://www.unicode.org/
3. Huang, P. Kok, G.: Speak Cantonese sounds, vols 1-3., Newhaven Yale University Press, 1970.
4. Alvestrand, H.: Tags for the Identification of Languages, RFC 3066, BCP 47, January 2001, http://rfc.net/rfc3066.html
5. Internet Assigned Numbers Authority, http://www.iana.org/

Appendix A   The XML Schema for the Yale Representation

```
<?xml version="1.0" encoding="utf-8"?>
<xs:schema xmlns:xs="http://www.w3.org/2001/XMLSchema">
  <xs:simpleType name="tonetype">
    <xs:restriction base="xs:integer">
      <xs:minInclusive value="0"/>
      <xs:maxInclusive value="9"/>
    </xs:restriction>
  </xs:simpleType>
  <xs:simpleType name="syllable">
    <xs:restriction base="xs:string">
      <xs:pattern
        value="(b|p|m|f|d|t|n|l|g|k|ng|h|j|ch|s|y|w|
               gw|kw)?
```

```
                    (aai|aau|aam|aan|aang|aap|aat|aak|
                     a|ai|au|am|an|ang|ap|at|ak|
                     e|ei|eng|ek|
                     i|iu|im|in|ing|ip|it|ik|
                     o|oi|ou|on|ong|ot|ok|
                     u|ui|un|ung|ut|uk|
                     eu|eui|eun|eung|eut|euk|
                     yu|yun|yut|m|ng)"/>
        </xs:restriction>
      </xs:simpleType>
      <xs:complexType name="wordtype" mixed="true">
        <xs:simpleContent>
          <xs:extension base="syllable">
            <xs:attribute name="tone" type="tonetype"
                          use="required"/>
          </xs:extension>
        </xs:simpleContent>
      </xs:complexType>
      <xs:element name="word" type="wordtype"/>
      <xs:complexType name="yaletype" mixed="true">
        <xs:sequence>
          <xs:element ref="word" maxOccurs="unbounded"/>
        </xs:sequence>
        <xs:attribute name="lang" type="xs:string"
                      fixed="zh-yue" use="required"/>
      </xs:complexType>
      <xs:element name="yale" type="yaletype"/>
    </xs:schema>
```

Note: The regular expression shown above is broken into separate lines to improve the ease of viewing. It is in a single line in the original document.

Appendix B   The XSL Transformation File for the Conversion of Cantonese Yale XML into SVG

```
    <?xml version="1.0" encoding="utf-8"?>
  <xsl:transform xmlns:xsl="http://www.w3.org/1999/XSL/Transform"
                 version="1.0">
    <xsl:output indent="yes"/>
    <xsl:template match="yale[@lang='zh-yue']">
      <svg width="640px" height="480px"
           style="font-family: Courier New; font-size: 25">
        <xsl:for-each select="word">
          <xsl:variable name="initial"
            select="replace(., '[a|e|i|o|u].*', '')"/>
          <xsl:variable name="final"
            select="replace(., '^[^a|^e|^i|^o|^u]+', '')"/>
          <xsl:variable name="vowels"
            select="replace($final, '^([a|e|i|o|u]+).*', '$1')"/>
          <xsl:variable name="consonants"
```

```
          select="replace($final, '^([a|e|i|o|u]+)', '')"/>
      <xsl:element name="g">
        <xsl:attribute name="transform"
          select="'translate(10,',position()*30,')'"/>
        <text>
          <xsl:value-of select="$initial"/>
          <xsl:value-of select="$vowels"/>
          <xsl:choose>
            <xsl:when
              test="@tone='4' or @tone='5' or @tone='6'">
              h
            </xsl:when>
          </xsl:choose>
          <xsl:value-of select="$consonants"/>
        </text>
        <xsl:element name="g">
          <xsl:attribute name="transform"
            select="'translate(',
                     string-length($initial)*15+1,',-17)'"/>
          <xsl:choose>
            <xsl:when test="@tone='1'">
              <rect width="14" height="4" style="fill: white"/>
              <line x2="13" y1="2" y2="2" style="stroke: black"/>
            </xsl:when>
            <xsl:when test="@tone='0' or @tone='4'">
              <rect width="14" height="4" style="fill: white"/>
              <line x2="13" y1="1" y2="3" style="stroke: black"/>
            </xsl:when>
            <xsl:when test="@tone='2' or @tone='5'">
              <rect width="14" height="4" style="fill: white"/>
              <line x2="13" y1="3" y2="1" style="stroke: black"/>
            </xsl:when>
          </xsl:choose>
        </xsl:element>
      </xsl:element>
    </xsl:for-each>
  </svg>
  </xsl:template>
</xsl:transform>
```

A Novel Multi-agent Community Building Scheme Based on Collaboration Filtering*

Yu Sun[1], Peng Han[2], Qian Zhang[1], and Xia Zhang[1]

[1] National Engineering Research Center for Computer Software, Northeastern University,
Shenyang 110004, China
{sun.yu, zhangqian, zhangx}@neusoft.com
[2] Department of Computer Science and Engineering, Shanghai Jiao Tong University,
Shanghai 200030, China
phan@mail.sjtu.edu.cn

Abstract. Research on e-learner community building has attracted much attention for its effectiveness in sharing the learning experience and resources among geographically dispersed e-learners. While collaborative filtering proves its success as one of the most efficient methods in finding similar users in e-commerce domain, it does meet special challenges in e-learning areas. In this paper, we incorporate multi-agent techniques into collaborative filtering and propose a novel community building scheme. By doing so, we manage to collect useful information from the learner behaviors and thus increase the scalability and flexibility of traditional collaborative filtering methods. The experiment on a standard benchmark shows that our scheme has reasonable community building quality and e-learners can make better recommendations to each other inside the community.

1 Introduction

Recently, the research on *e-learner community building* has attracted much attention which tried to group learners with similar background and interests into communities so that they can share their learning resources and experiences efficiently. In this paper, we propose a novel e-learner community building scheme by integrating the collaborative filtering [1-3] with multi-agent architectures. The experiment shows that our community building scheme enables the learners to locate potential neighbors efficiently and eventually self-organize similar users into learning communities.

The rest of this paper is organized as follows. In Section 2, some basic concepts and algorithm framework on CF are presented and discussed. In Section 3, we give the design and key features of our e-learner community building scheme and present the experimental results in Section 4.Finally we conclude the paper and provide an outlook on future research work in Section 5.

---

* Supported by the National High-Tech Research and Development Plan of China under Grant No 2003AA4Z3020.

R.W.H. Lau et al. (Eds.): ICWL 2005, LNCS 3583, pp. 221–225, 2005.

2 Memory-Based Collaborative Filtering

Generally, the task of CF is to predict the votes of active users based on the data in the user database which consists of a set of votes corresponding to the vote of user i on item j. The memory-based CF algorithm calculates this prediction as a weighted average of other users' votes on that item using the following formula:

$$P_{a,j} = \overline{v_a} + \kappa \sum_{i=1}^{n} \varpi(a, j)(v_{i,j} - \overline{v_i}) \tag{1}$$

Where $P_{a,j}$ denotes the prediction of the vote for active user a on item j and n is the number of users in user database. $\overline{v_i}$ is the mean vote for user I and I_i is the set of items on which user i has voted. The weights $\varpi(a, j)$ reflect the similarity between active user and users in the user database. κ is a normalizing factor to make the absolute values of the weights sum to unity.

3 Strategy of Learner Community Self-organization

3.1 Learner Profile Generation

Describing the interest and intention of learners is the first and vital step of e-learner community building. Here, we divide the interest into *explicit* interests and *implicit* interests. In this paper, we name the set of explicit interest as Int^e and the set of implicit interest as Int^i. So for each resource the learner accessed, we can generate a tuple $< u_i, \mathrm{Int}_i^e, \mathrm{Int}_i^i >$. Here $u_i \in U$ is the identity of the resource accessed, Int_i^e is the explicit interests and Int_i^i is the implicit interests. Each tuple has either Int_i^e, Int_i^i or both depend on their availability. In order to decrease the complexity of matching and avoid the traffic overload, we further merge the Int_i^e and Int_i^i into a single Int_{u_i} as following:

$$\mathrm{Int}_{u_i} = \mathrm{g}(\mathrm{f}^e(\mathrm{Int}_j^e), \mathrm{f}^i(\mathrm{Int}_j^i)) \tag{2}$$

Where f^e and f^i are the uniform functions for the explicit and implicit interest respectively while g is the function to combine the two kinds of interests. We implemented these functions as a weighted arithmetic average where each attributes has a weighted assigned.

3.2 Distributed Learner Profile Management Scheme

In order to find similar learners using collaborative filtering algorithm, the LAs should share the profile they generate for learners to each other. So we propose a distributed learner profile management scheme by introducing another kind of agent called Group Agent (GA) which serves as the broker for LAs and responsible for forwarding this information to potential neighbor learners.

Distributed learner profile management has two key steps: *Division* and *Location*. In our scheme, we wish to divide the whole learner profile space into fractions which are called *bucket* in the following of this paper. We make each bucket hold a group of learners' records who has a particular *<Unit_ID, Int>* tuple. It means that learners in the same bucket have the same interest on at least one unit. Figure1 illustrates our division strategy:

Each GA will be responsible to store one or more buckets and later when the LA wants to make prediction for a particular user, we only need to contact special GA to retrieve those buckets which the active user's profile is in. This strategy is based on the heuristic that learners with similar interests will at least rate one item with similar votes. As we can see in section 4.2.1, this strategy has a very high hitting ratio.

3.3 Community Building Scheme

In this section, we provide formal definitions on which we will rely upon for describing our community building scheme presented later.

Let **G** and **L** be disjoint sets of GAs and LAs.

Definition 1: A learner agent *l* is a tuple A_l=*<Learner_ID, **Unit_Int, Local_Neighbor_list**>*, where *Learner_ID* is the uniform ID of *l* and **Unit_Int** is the vote vectors of *l* as described in section 3.2. **Local_Neighbor_list** is the list of similar neighbors with the form of *<Learner_ID, Trust_award>*, where *Trust_award* is the evaluation of interest similarity between *l* and the learner in the local neighbor list.

Definition 2: A group agent *g* is a tuple A_g=*<Local_Learner_List, Unit_Int_List, Neighbor_List>*, where *Local_Learner_List* is the LAs list registered on and managed by *g*. *Unit_Int_List* maintains the *<Unit_ID, Int>* tuples cashed in *g*, *Neighbor_List* contains the *bucket* related to the *<Unit_ID, Int>* in the *Unit_Int_List*.

When a LA generates a new *<Unit_ID, Int>* for the e-learner it monitors, it will send a notification message to the GA which is in charge of storing the bucket corresponding to the tuple. By doing so, the LA can retrieve the profiles in the buckets back which then can be used to make recommendations by CF algorithms. Still, the GA can register the LA in its Local_Learner_List and inform other LA in the list about the updating. The other users can then use this information to update their neighbor list so that later they can make recommendation directly to the LA in their neighbor list.

4 Experimental Results

4.1 Data Set and Metrics

We use EachMovie data set [4] to evaluate the performance of improved algorithm. The EachMovie data set is provided by the Compaq System Research Center as a standard benchmark on the evaluation of collaborative filtering algorithms and contains 2,811,983 *<Unit_ID, Int>* tuples from 72,916 users on 1,628 resources.

We use Mean Absolute Error (MAE), a statistical accuracy metrics, to report prediction experiments for it is most commonly used and easy to understand:

$$MAE = \frac{\sum_{a \in T} |v_{a,j} - p_{a,j}|}{|T|} \tag{3}$$

Where $v_{a,j}$ is the interests given to item j by user a, $p_{a,j}$ is the predicted value of user a on item j, T is the test set, $|T|$ is the size of the test set.

We select 5000 users and choose one user as active user per time and the remainder users as his candidate neighbors, because every user only makes self recommendation locally. We use ALL-BUT-ONE strategy [1] and the mean prediction accuracy of all the 5000 users as the system's prediction accuracy.

4.2 Experimental Result

We design several experiments for evaluating our algorithm and analyze the effect of various factors by comparison. All our experiments are run under Windows 2000 on an Intel Pentium 4 PC with a CPU speed of 1.8 GHz and 512 MB of RAM.

We compare the prediction accuracy of traditional CF algorithm and our Multi-agent based CF algorithm and the results are shown as Figure 1. We can see that our algorithm has better prediction accuracy than the traditional CF algorithm.

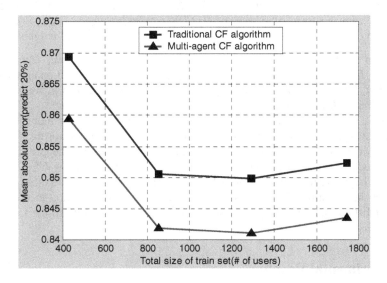

Fig. 1. Multi-agent based CF vs. Traditional CF

5   Conclusion

In this paper, we propose a novel e-learner community building scheme by integrating the collaborative filtering and multi-agent techniques. By using the intelligent agents, are able to monitor the whole dynamic learning behaviors of e-learners and automatically learn the interest of knowledge-oriented resources, then generate the learner profile which can be used by collaborative filtering algorithm. The agents can also accelerate the profile sharing in the distributed environment. Based on this, we extend the traditional collaborative filtering algorithm to make it operational decentralized by proposing a distribute user profile management scheme. The experiment shows that our community building scheme enables the learners to locate potential neighbors efficiently and eventually self-organize similar users into learning communities.

Acknowledgement

The work described in this paper is supported partially by National High-Tech Research and Development Plan of China under Grant No 2003AA4Z3020

References

1. Breese, J., Heckerman, D., and Kadie, C.: Empirical Analysis of Predictive Algorithms for Collaborative Filtering. Proceedings of the 14th Conference on Uncertainty in Artificial Intelligence, p.43-52, 1998.
2. J. L. Herlocker, J. A. Konstan, A. Borchers, and J. Riedl.: An algorithmic framework for performing collaborative filtering. In Proceedings of the 22nd annual international ACM SIGIR conference on Research and development in information retrieval, p.230-237, 1999.
3. G. Linden, B. Smith, and J. York, Amazon.com Recommendations Item-to-item collaborative filtering, IEEE Internet Computing, Vo. 7, No. 1, p.7680, Jan. 2003.
4. Eachmovie collaborative filtering data set.: http://research.compaq.com/SRC/eachmovie

Semantic Caching for Web Based Learning Systems

Xiao-Wei Hao, Tao Zhang, and Lei Li

Software Research Institute, SUN YAT-SEN University,
Guangzhou, 510275, PRC
haoxw70@126.com, zhangtaometeor@tom.com

Abstract. For overcoming the existing problems in Web based learning system when network blocking or disconnection happens, a new architecture of the Web based learning system based on semantic caching is proposed; also, the model and the query processing mechanism of semantic caching are described in detail. Furthermore, this paper proposed and proved 11 simplification rules, which can be used to optimize the query processing of semantic caching, and the optimized query-processing algorithm is thoroughly described.

1 Introduction

Recently, educationalists pay much attention to the World-Wide Web as a learning environment [6]. Comparing to other traditional education pattern, Web based learning is an ideal solution, which can deliver highly efficiently course materials, and access study resources from any location at any time, as well as is potential for widening access—for example, to part time, mature, or work based students. However, Web based learning also faces many difficulties at the same time. Now the solutions supporting Web based learning generally are distributed system ([7], [8]), some are even based on wireless network. The performance of network becomes the bottleneck of these systems. It is significant that Web based learning systems can keep providing available service for teaching and learning when network blocking or disconnection happens.

Semantic caching maintains both semantics and data of previous queries in the cache [1], which is an appropriate caching strategy to implement applications under distributed or wireless environments. Comparing to traditional page caching and tuple caching technology, semantic caching has distinguished virtues, such as saving communication cost and cache space overhead, supporting parallelism and disconnection.

The eLSc proposed in this paper is a new kind of Web based learning system, which includes a middleware-client based on semantic caching, semantic caching component (ScC). When learners want to access course resources, the new learning requests are firstly submitted to ScC. ScC executes some implying computation to judge whether the new requests can be processed locally. It is only necessary to connect the learning server to get correlative data when the new requesting data are not completely stored in local semantic caching. In this way, the learning client can reliably serve for learners even when network blocking and disconnection happens.

R.W.H. Lau et al. (Eds.): ICWL 2005, LNCS 3583, pp. 226–235, 2005.

The main contributions of this paper including: firstly, it proposed a new architecture of the web based learning system, which was based on semantic caching; secondly, it formalized defined the model and thoroughly described the query processing mechanism of semantic caching; thirdly, it gave and proved 11 simplification rules, which can optimize the query evaluation of semantic caching, also it produced a query processing algorithm that only the remainder query needs to be evaluated.

2   The eLSc Architecture

The eLSc is a client/server system. Comparing to other Web based learning systems, the eLSc client includes a semantic caching component (ScC), which is a middleware-client. The kernel of ScC is an embedded rational database Ebase, which stores user's historical learning data and their semantics. In addition, the ScC includes another five modules. These five modules and the Ebase cooperate to serve the learning client. The five modules, as depicted in Fig1, respectively are:

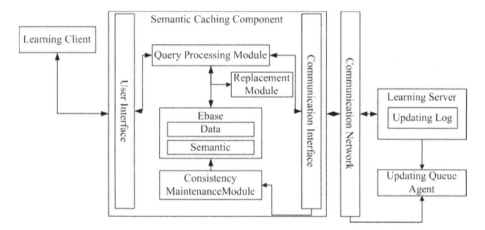

Fig. 1. The eLSc architecture

1. *Ebase.* This Ebase is an embedded rational database management system. It can provide similar data storing and query processing mechanism as other DBMSs, which is used to store the data and the semantic of history learning requests.
2. *Query Processing Module (QPM).* The QPM does the query trimming, submits the learning requests to the Ebase, and then accepts the returning data; also when the query is not completely contained by the cache, it submits the remainder query processing requests to the communication interface, and creates a new relation segment after obtaining the result set.
3. *Consistency Maintenance Module (CMM).* This module is in charge of maintaining the consistency of the learning resources between the learning client and the learning server. The consistency strategy of the *CMM* is a loose consistency

strategy, and is based on updating propagation. Those updating commands will be sent to client to execute as long as the learning resources in server are changed.

4. *Replacement Module (RM)*. When the capacity of semantic caching achieves the utmost of the storage space, if more useful data want to be inserted, then cache space must be evacuated by replacing a portion of useless data from the original semantic caching. The RM uses a special algorithm to choose the least useful items to be replaced, and preserve the information that is most possible used by learners in the future in cache.

5. *Communication Interface (CI)*. This interface encapsulates the communication between the semantic caching component and the learning server. It submits remainder query processing requests to the learning server, and receives the returned result data.

6. *User Interface (UI)*. This module encapsulates the interface between the semantic caching component and the learning client. It standardizes the learning requests and the learning resources.

3 Query Processing of Semantic Caching

Following, the model of the ScC is defined in detail. Based on the model, the processing procedure of the learning request is completely discussed.

3.1 Related Concepts

Definition 1 Query (Q). Query Q appears in the form of $<Q_R, Q_p, Q_c>$, in which Q_R represents the queried relations; Q_P represents the query semantic which is expressed as a conjunct; $Q_c = \sigma_{Qp}(Q_R)$; operations in Q doesn't include the projection operation.

Definition 2 Relation Segment (RS). Relation segment RS appears in the form of $<S_{RSR}, S_{RSp}, S_{RSc}>$, in which S_{RSR} represents the relation of the caching result set; S_{RSp} represents the result set semantic which is expressed as a disjunctive normal form; $S_{RSc} = \sigma_{SRSp}(S_{RSR})$.

Definition 3 Disjointed. Relation segment $S_i = <S_{RSiR}, S_{RSip}, S_{RSic}>$ and $S_j = <S_{RSjR}, S_{RSjp}, S_{RSjc}>$ is disjointed, if $S_{RSiR} \neq S_{RSjR}$ or $S_{RSip} \wedge S_{RSjp}$ is unsatisfiable.

Definition 4 Relation Cache (RC). Relation cache RC is the set of all RS_i, in which, if $i \neq j$, then RS_i and RS_j is disjointed and $S_{RSiR} = S_{RSjR}$; RC appears in the form of $<S_{RC}, S_{RCp}, S_{RCc}>$, $S_{RC} = S_{RSi}$, $S_{RCp} = \vee S_{RSip}(1 \leq i \leq n)$, $S_{RCc} = \sigma_{SRCp}(S_{RCc})$.

Definition 5 Semantic Caching (SC). Semantic caching SC is the set of all RC; The SC is defined as $\{RC_1, \ldots, RC_n\}$.

3.2 Query Processing Algorithm

When the learning client submits a new learning request, the basic thought of the request processing in the semantic caching is: first judges whether it exists exact or contained match[2] relation between the RS and the query of the request; if it does, the request can be processed in local cache; If it does not exist, but exists intersection match[2] relation between the RS and the query, then it is necessary to execute the query trimming to get the probe query which is answered locally and the remainder query which is unanswerable in local; the remainder query will be send to the server for processing. The result set is composed of the result sets of the probe query and the remainder query.

After receiving the Query Q of the learning request (in the form of $<Q_R,Q_q,Q_c>$), the semantic caching firstly carries on the query trimming to obtain the probe query Q_{pq} (in the form of $<Q_{pqR},Q_{pqp},Q_{pqc}>$)) and the remainder query Q_{rq} (in the form of $<Q_{rqR},Q_{rqp},Q_{rqc}>$), obviously it satisfies: $Q_{pqc} \cup R_{rqc}=Q_c$, and $Q_{pqc} \cap Q_{rqc}=\emptyset$. The solution space of the probe query Q_{pq} is $Q_c \cap RC_c$. The solution space of the remainder query Q_{rq} is Q_c - RC_c. Hence, Q_{pqp} and Q_{rqp} are respectively $Q_p \wedge SC_{RCp}$ and $Q_p \wedge \neg SC_{RCp}$. We will use the following example to explain this computation process.

Example 1. Supposes the RC in semantic caching is in the form of $<R,$ $(A>=30 \wedge S>6000) \vee (A<22 \wedge S<=6000) \vee (A>=22 \wedge S<3000), S_{RCc}>$, Now the user sent out the query Q of a request which is $<R, (A>20) \wedge (S<2000), Q_c)$. Then the probe query and the remainder are:

Probe Query:
Q_{pqp}=(A>20 $\wedge$ S<2000) $\wedge$ (A>=30 $\wedge$ S>6000 $\vee$ A<22 $\wedge$ S<=6000 $\vee$ A>=22 $\wedge$ S<3000)
=(A>20 $\wedge$ S<2000 $\wedge$ A>=30 $\wedge$ S>6000) $\vee$ (A>20 $\wedge$ S<2000 $\wedge$ A<22 $\wedge$ S<=6000) $\vee$ (A>20 $\wedge$ S<2000 $\wedge$ A>=22 $\wedge$ S<3000)

Remainder Query:
Q_{rqp}=(A>20 $\wedge$ S<2000) $\wedge \neg$(A>=30 $\wedge$ S>6000 $\vee$ A<22 $\wedge$ S<=6000 $\vee$ A>=22 $\wedge$ S<3000)
= A>20 $\wedge$ S<2000 $\wedge$ A<30 $\wedge$ A>=22 $\wedge$ A<22 $\vee$ A>20 $\wedge$ S<2000 $\wedge$ A<30 $\wedge$ A>=22 $\wedge$ S>=3000 $\vee$ A>20 $\wedge$ S<2000 $\wedge$ A<30 $\wedge$ S>6000 $\wedge$ A<22 $\vee$ A>20 $\wedge$ S<2000 $\wedge$ A<30 $\wedge$ S>6000 $\wedge$ S>=3000 $\vee$ A>20 $\wedge$ S<2000 $\wedge$ S<=6000 $\wedge$ A>=22 $\wedge$ A<22 $\vee$ A>20 $\wedge$ S<2000 $\wedge$ S<=6000 $\wedge$ A>=22 $\wedge$ S>=3000 $\vee$ A>20 $\wedge$ S<2000 $\wedge$ S<=6000 $\wedge$ S>6000 $\wedge$ A<22 $\vee$ A>20 $\wedge$ S<2000 $\wedge$ S<=6000 $\wedge$ S>6000 $\wedge$ S>=3000

When the user query is a conjunct with the length of m, the semantic of a relation segment is a disjunction of n conjuncts with the length of m. Under the worst situation, the probe query is a disjunctive normal form of n conjuncts with the length of 2m, and the remainder query is a disjunctive normal form of m^n conjuncts with the length of 2n. The time and space complexity of computing the probe query all are O(n*m), while the time and space complexity of computing the remainder query are respectively $O(m^n)$ and $O(m*m^n)$.

This remainder query, which is the disjunction of m^n conjuncts with the length of 2n, will be sent to the server for processing and returning data. At last, it will be inserted into semantic caching as the semantic of a new relation segment. Well then, the semantic information in semantic caching is a disjunctive normal form with the length of $m*n+2n*m^n$. It is obviously that the scale of semantic caching will become so huge that the time and space consumption of the query trimming is extremely considerable, and that the resources of limited mobile equipment can not load it. This reduces the practicability of semantic caching in a great extent. Therefore, it is necessary to produce an optimized technology to optimize the query trimming procedure and the trimming result.

4   Optimization of Query Processing

The performance of the eLSc system depends on efficiency of the ScC, and the efficiency of the ScC mainly rests with the time-complexity of the query processing. However, the key technology in the query processing of semantic caching is query trimming. Following, this paper firstly gave and proved 11 simplification rules, which can be used to optimize the query evaluation of semantic caching.

4.1   Simplification Rules

6 simplification rules and their proving are given in details as below, in which the rule1 and the rule2 are basic rules; the rule3 and rule4 may be used in the computation process of trimming probe query; the rule5 and rule6 may be used in the computation process of trimming remainder query.

Rule 1   if $A \rightarrow B$, then $A \wedge B \leftrightarrow A$.

Rule 2   if $A \rightarrow B$, then $A \vee B \leftrightarrow B$.

Rule 3   if $A \rightarrow B_i$, in which i=1,2,…,n, then $A \wedge (B_1 \wedge C_1 \vee B_2 \wedge C_2 \vee … \vee B_n \wedge C_n) \leftrightarrow A \wedge (C_1 \vee C_2 \vee … \vee C_n)$.

Rule 4   if $A \wedge B_i$=false, in which i=1,2,…,n, then $A \wedge (B_1 \wedge C_1 \vee B_2 \wedge C_2 \vee … \vee B_n \wedge C_n) \leftrightarrow$ false.

Rule 5   if $A \rightarrow B_i$, in which i=1,2,…,n, then $A \wedge [(B_1 \vee C_1) \wedge (B_2 \vee C_2) \wedge … \wedge (B_n \vee C_n)] \leftrightarrow A$.

Rule 6   if $A \wedge B_i$=false, in which i=1,2,…,n, then $A \wedge [(B_1 \vee C_1) \wedge (B_2 \vee C_2) \wedge … \wedge (B_n \vee C_n)] \leftrightarrow A \wedge C_1 \wedge C_2 … \wedge C_n$.

Rule3 Proves:

$$A \wedge (B_1 \wedge C_1 \vee B_2 \wedge C_2 \vee … \vee B_n \wedge C_n) \leftrightarrow A \wedge B_1 \wedge C_1 \vee A \wedge B_2 \wedge C_2 \vee … \vee A \wedge B_n \wedge C,$$

From Rule1, we can obtain :

$$A \wedge B_1 \wedge C_1 \vee A \wedge B_2 \wedge C_2 \vee … \vee A \wedge B_n \wedge C_n \leftrightarrow A_1 \wedge C_1 \vee A \wedge C_2 \vee … \vee A \wedge C_n \leftrightarrow A \wedge (C_1 \vee C_2 \vee … \vee C_n)$$

Rule5 Proves:

$$A \wedge [(B_1 \vee C_1) \wedge (B_2 \vee C_2) \wedge … \wedge (B_n \vee C_n)] \leftrightarrow A \wedge (B_1 \vee C_1) \wedge A \wedge (B_2 \vee C_2) \wedge … \wedge A \wedge (Bn \vee Cn) \leftrightarrow (A \wedge B1 \vee A \wedge C1) \wedge (A \wedge B2 \vee A \wedge C2) \wedge … \wedge (A \wedge Bn \vee A \wedge Cn)$$

From Rule1, we can obtain:

$$(A \wedge B_1 \vee A \wedge C_1) \wedge (A \wedge B_2 \vee A \wedge C_2) \wedge \ldots \wedge (A \wedge B_n \vee A \wedge C_n) \leftrightarrow (A \vee A \wedge C_1) \wedge (A \vee A \wedge C_2) \wedge \ldots \wedge (A \vee A \wedge C_n) \leftrightarrow A \wedge (true \vee C_1) \wedge (true \vee C_2) \wedge \ldots \wedge (true \vee C_n) \leftrightarrow A$$

The proofs of Rule1, Rule2, Rule4 and Rule6 are ignored here.

During the query trimming of semantic caching, some of the conjuncts in the middle results, which are disjunctive normal formulas, can be merged. For example: suppose that there is a formula: A>20□S<2000 □A<=20□S<2000, then the two conjuncts can be merged into S<2000. The follow 5 simplification rules can be used to merge some conjuncts in disjunctive normal formulas. The proofs are ignored because they are obvious.

Rule 7   **if c and d are constant, and c<d, then** $\exists A(A>c \vee A<d) \leftrightarrow$ **true**

Rule 8   **if c and d are constant, and c<=d, then** $\exists A(A>c \vee A<=d) \leftrightarrow$ **true**

Rule 9   **if c and d are constant, and c<=d, then** $\exists A(A>=c \vee A<d) \leftrightarrow$ **true**

Rule 10   **if c is constant, then** $\exists A(A>c \vee A=c) \leftrightarrow \exists A(A>=c)$

Rule 11   **if c is constant, then** $\exists A(A<c \vee A=c) \langle \rangle \exists A(A<=c)$

4.2 Optimized Remainder Query Trimming

Remainder query cannot be answered from local cache, and needs to be sent to the server for processing, whose solution space is Q_c - SC_{RCc}. Therefore, the computation procedure of the remainder query is to simplify $Q_p \wedge \neg SC_{RCp}$. The detailed algorithm of optimized remainder query evaluation is described in algorithm 1.

Algorithm 1

```
Optimized_Remainder(Predicate C_q, Predicate C_c, Predicate C_r)
\\Input:Query's semantic C_q=A_1 ∧ A_2… ∧ A_n,
\\Input:RC's semantic C_c=C_1 ∨ C_2 ∨ … ∨ C_m, C_i= B_i1 ∧ B_i2… ∧ B_ij
\\Output: Q_rq's semantic C_r=R_1 ∨ R_2 ∨ … ∨ R_k, R_i= D_i1 ∧ D_i2… ∧ D_ij,
{
        C_c= ¬ C_c
        for(each C_i in C_c)
                for(each B_ij in C_i)
                        if ∃ S, S= A_i, i∈{1,2,…,n}, and S→B_ij
                                delete C_i from C_c;      break;
                        if ∃ S, S= A_i, i∈{1,2,…,n}, and S ∧ B_ij=false
                                delete B_ij from C_i
        C_t= ALL
        for(i=1; i<=m; i++)
                if C_t=ALL then C_t=C_i
                else
                        C_t=C_t ∧ C_i, transform C_t to a disjunctive normal form
                        if C_t is empty then C_r=NULL, and exit
                        for(each C_j in C_t)
                                for(each C_t in C_t, t>j)
                                        if C_j=C_t or C_j→C_t
                                                delete C_t from C_t
                                        else if C_j= ¬ C_t
```

$$C_t=ALL$$
$$\text{else if } C_j \text{ and } C_t \text{ can be merged}$$
$$\text{merge } C_j \text{ and } C_t$$
$$C_r= C_q \wedge C_t, \text{ transform } C_r \text{ to a disjunctive normal form}$$
}

4.3 Optimized Query Processing

The optimized query processing only needs to evaluate the remainder query, does not need to consume resources on the probe query. This thought based on the Theorem 1 is described below.

Theorem1 if $A \wedge \neg B$=false, then $A \rightarrow B$

Proves:

When A=true, based on the condition $A \wedge \neg B$=false, then obviously B=true, therefore the proposition is proved.

According to the Theorem 1, The following conclusion may be drawn: If the remainder query, which is evaluated through optimized remainder trimming, is an unsatisfied formula, then the user query is completely contained by the cache. Here, the new query can be completely processed in local without needing to connect the server.

If the trimmed remainder query is a satisfiable formula, how to process the new query? Firstly, execute the new query using local cache; also send the remainder query to the server to get data. Secondly, merge the result sets of the local cache and the remainder query, and then return them to the user. Finally, use the remainder query and its result set to create a new relation segment, and then add this new relation segment into semantic caching. Detailed algorithm is shown in Algorithm 2.

Algorithm 2

```
Processing_Query (Query Q, SemanticCache SC)
//Input:  Query's semantic Qq=A1∧A2...□An
//Input:  semantic cache SC=RC1∨RC2∨...∨RCm, i=1,2,...,m
{
    find RC meeting QR= SCRCR in SC;
    Initialize variable Qrq:<QrqR,Qrqp,Qrqc>;
  //Trim query Q using RC, get Remainder Query
    Optimized_Remainder(Qp, RCp, Qrqp)
    if Qrqp≠NULL{
        Send Qrq to server to process, get the record set Qrqc
        create a new relation segment RSnew(QrqR, Qrqp, Qrqc)
        insert RSnew into RC
    }
    process Q using relation cache RC
}
```

5   Performance and Study

We designed a simulation experiment to test the performance of the eLSc, and respectively compared the optimized learning request processing without caching and the one without optimization to the method proposed in this paper, and then demonstrated the benefits that the optimization brought from many aspects.

5.1   System Parameters

Main parameters of the simulation system are given in Tab1, in which MaxBrandwidth describes the maximum communication bandwidth in eLSc; WarmUp describes the quantity of query to warm up the cache; GroupCount represents the query quantity of each group; SleepTime describes the interval between two queries.

Table 1. Main parameters of the simulation experiments

Parameter	Val	unit
MaxBrandwidth	56	KB
WarmUp	500	Piece
GroupCount	100	Piece
SleepTime	10	Second

5.2   Performance Comparison

Time Efficiency of Semantic Caching. In order to demonstrate the benefits of semantic caching proposed in this paper, in Fig2 we contrasted the time cost of non-caching query processing and the optimized query processing.

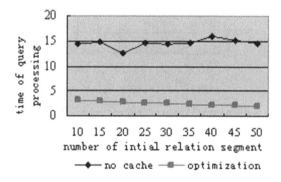

Fig. 2. Effects Analysis of optimized query process

The query processing without caching is stable, and it is because under this strategy all queries are sent straight to the database server for processing. The time cost of optimized query processing is less than the one without caching, and decreases along with the quantity of relation segment increases. That is because the data that the user needs are completely or partially contained by the local cache more and more often as the quantity of pre-existing relation segment increases, then the time cost of network communication is little, hence the processing efficiency is improved.

Optimized Time Efficiency and Space Efficiency of Query Processing. We have chosen two major parameters, namely the time and space consumption of trimming, to analyze the performance of the optimized query trimming. The Fig 3 and Fig 4 show the contrast with the non- optimization.

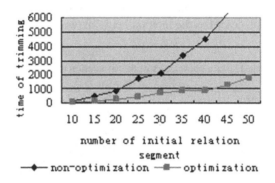

Fig. 3. Time effect analysis of optimized query trimming

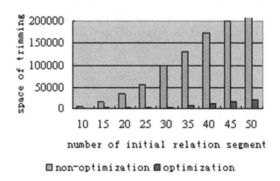

Fig. 4. Space effect analysis of optimized query trimming

Overall speaking, when the quantity of pre-existing relation segment increases, the time and space cost to trim the query increases. It is because the more of the pre-existing relation segments, the more of the semantics participating in the trimming computation. Nevertheless, very obviously: the speed of the time and space cost without optimizations increases far more quickly than the one proposed in this paper. Even when it needs a great amount of time and space to trim without optimization, the one with optimization is stable, and can quickly complete the trimming.

In summary, the eLSc proposed in this paper satisfied very good performance under poor network environment. Therefore, the eLSc based on the optimization query processing strategy in semantic caching is effective and reliable.

6 Conclusion

Aiming at the problems that existing in Web based learning system when network blocking or disconnection happens, a new architecture of the Web based learning system based on semantic caching is proposed in this paper; also, the model and the query processing mechanism of semantic caching are described in detail. Furthermore, this paper proposed and proved 11 simplification rules, which can be used to optimize the query evaluation of semantic caching. Comparing to other query processing technologies of semantic caching, this paper produced a query trimming method that only needs to evaluate the remainder query. The performance analysis of the simulation test also indicated that the eLSc is more valid and effective in the two parts of time and space complexity.

Reference

[1] Qun Ren, Margaret H. Dunham, Vijay kumar. Semantic Caching and Query Processing, In: IEEE Transaction on Knowledge and Data Engineering Vol.15, No.1,2003, 192-210

[2] Wu Ting-ting, Zhou Xing-ming. Extracting query results from semantic cache, In: Chinese J.Computer, Vol.25, No.10, 2002, 1104-1110

[3] Wu Ting-Ting, Zhang Wen-Song, Zhou Xing-Ming, Answering query through cache during disconnection, In: Chinese J.Computer, Vol.26, No.10, 2003, 1393-1399

[4] Wu Ting-Ting, *etc*, Mobile query through semantic cache, Journal of computer research and development, 2004, 41(1), 187-193

[5] Zhang Tao, etc, Consistency maintenance mechanism of semantic caching based on downwards update, Journal of computer research and development, 2004, 41. Suppl. 28-34

[6] T.Reeves and P.Reeves, The effective dimension of interactive learning on the WWW, In: B.Khan(ed). Web-based instruction, Englewood Cliffs, NJ: Education Technology, 1997, 59-66

[7] Robert H.Jackson, Web based learning resources library, http: // www. knowledgeability. biz/ weblearning, 2004.2

[8] Judy McKimm, CarolJollie, Peter Cantillon, ABC of learning and teaching Web based learning, http://bmj.com/cgi/content/full/326/7394/870, 2003

[9] Yatchou, R.; Nkambou, R.; Tangha, C.; An approach to reduce transactional distance: semi-synchronous distance monitoring of learners, In: the Proceeding of the FIfth International Conference on Information Technology Based Higher Education and Training, Page(s):10 - 14

[10] Chih-Ming Chen, Ling-Jiun Duh, Chao-Yu Liu, A personalized courseware recommendation system based on fuzzy item response theory, In: the Proceeding of the 2004 IEEE International Conference on e-Technology, e-Commerce and e-Service, Page(s):305 - 308

An Approach to Acquire Semantic Relationships Between Words from Web Document[1]

Xia Sun, Qinghua Zheng, Haifeng Dang, Yunhua Hu, and Huixian Bai

Shaanxi Provincial Key Laboratory of Satellite and Terrestrial Networks Tech,
School of Electronics and Information Engineering, Xi'an Jiaotong University, Xi'an, China
sx@mailst.xjtu.edu.cn
{qhzheng, yunhuahu}@mail.xjtu.edu.cn
{xjtu_hfdang, baihuixian}@163.com

Abstract. In this paper, we focus on the semantic relationships acquisition from Chinese web documents motivated by the large requirement of web question answering system in e-Learning. With our scheme, we dwindle in numbers of text to be analyzed and obtain initial sentence-level text in pre-process phase. Then linguistic rules, which are broken down into unambiguous and ambiguous, designed for Chinese phrases are applied to these sentence-level text to extract the synonymy relationship, hyponymy relationship, hypernymy relationship and parataxis relationship. Lastly, candidates are refined using two heuristics. Compared to other previous works, we apply not only strict unambiguous linguistic rules but also loose ambiguous linguistic rules to extract relationships and proposed efficient approach to refine the outputs of these rules. Experiments show that this method can acquire semantic relationships efficiently and effectively.

1   Introduction

Web question answering is one of key issues in e-Learning due to the rapid growth of network education [1]. They provide direct answers to e-Learning users' questions during the leaning process of courseware, as well as associational learning through expanding keywords semantically. For instance, when users submit "network protocols" to a question answering system, they may expect to know some information about "FTP" or "HTTP" (hyponymy expansion); when users submit "operator system" to a question answering system, they may want to know some information about "computer software" (hypernymy expansion); When users submit "HTTP" to a question answering system, they may know some information about "FTP" (parataxis expansion). Through communicating with users, system can offer better services and induct users' learning. Practical experiences show that this ways of associational learning can advance the users' learning efficiency significantly. Thus, we proposed a method of acquiring semantic relationships between words from web documents to implement semantic expansion and provide associational learning.

---

[1]   Funding for this work was provided by NSF grant 60373105 and 60473136.

R.W.H. Lau et al. (Eds.): ICWL 2005, LNCS 3583, pp. 236–243, 2005.

There have been several approaches to discover semantic relationships between words from text [2~6]. WordNet [7] describes semantic relationships between words, such as synonymy, hypernymy, hyponymy and antonymy. However, manually constructed repositories are time and manpower consuming, furthermore, have the limitation of broad-coverage lexicon. Researchers prefer to (semi-)automatic approaches of acquiring semantic relationships between words. Pantel and Lin proposed an algorithm, called CBC, for automatically extracting semantic classes by computing the similarity between words based on their distribution in a corpus. The output of this program is a ranked list of similar words to each word. A problem of such approach is that it only shows the degree of similarity between words, rather than differentiates the synonymy, hyponymy and hypernymy. Yuan obtained semantic relationships relying on HowNet, which is a large Chinese semantic lexicon. Because HowNet describes the semantics of common words, it misses many domain words, which results in the limitation of this method.

2 Architecture of Semantic Relationships Acquisition

We focus in this paper on acquiring semantic relationships between words from Web documents, including synonymy relationship, hyponymy relationship, hypernymy relationship and parataxis relationship. Figure 1 shows the architecture of semantic relationships acquisition.

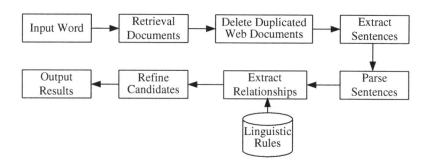

Fig. 1. the architecture of semantic relationships acquisition

As illustrated in Figure 1, our basic idea is as follows: collect the corpus that contain the potential semantic relationships using search engine; then delete duplicated Web documents and wipe off the sentence that have no relevancy with the word, which is submitted to search engine, in order to acquire fine initial data; next, match each sentence to be parsed against linguistic rules to extract relationships; finally, compute the candidates' scores and output the results. Following is description of every module.

Input Word (*IW*): Considering abundant information on the Web, we decide to make use of search engine to gain the documents that contain semantic relationships.

Retrieval Documents: The search engine Google [8] is used to return and rank the top 500 documents.

Delete Duplicated Web Documents: Reprinting of information between websites produces a great deal redundant web documents. If we extract relationships from duplicated Web documents, the statistic value of association between words is invalid. Therefore, string of feature code based algorithm [9] is adopted to remove the duplicated web documents.

Extract Sentences: To decrease the amount of text to be processed and make the procedures of relationships extraction easy, the documents are broken into sentences that contain *IW*.

Parse Sentences: For each sentence to be extracted, following processes are performed. Word segmentation is the first step, since there are no blanks to mark word boundaries in Chinese text. After segmentation, *POS* (Part Of Speech) tagging and shallow parser should be run. Interested reader can refer to our previous works [10~12].

Linguistic Rules Database: It stores many linguistic rules, which are deduced from expressions linked by semantic relationships by manually.

Extract Relationships: We match each sentence to be parsed against linguistic rules to extract words (Output Word, *OW*) that associate with *IW*. Different semantic relationship corresponds a set of linguistic rules.
Refine Candidates: Two heuristics are applied to refine the candidates (see section 3.2).

Output Results: The format of ultimate results are defined as:

Results:={*Syn* (*IW*, *OW*) | *Hypon* (*IW*, *OW*) | *Hyper* (*IW*, *OW*) | *Par* (*IW*, *OW*)}

Where *Syn*, *Hypon*, *Hyper* and *Par* denote the synonymy relationship, hyponymy relationship, hypernymy relationship and parataxis relationship respectively.

3 Semantic Relationships Acquisition

3.1 Description of Linguistic Rules

Expressions that reflect specific semantic relationships are either explicit or implicit, depending on whether exists the distinct characteristic. For examples, "door knob" is an implicit expression, while "water consists of hydrogen and oxygen" is an explicit expression with a characteristic term "consist of". The explicit ones are further broken down into unambiguous and ambiguous. Correspondingly, linguistic rules are divided into unambiguous rules and ambiguous rules.

Unambiguous rules always convey a specific semantic relationship. The illustrations of unambiguous rules are list below.

IF *Unambig* < *Syn* (*IW*+ ([punctuation] CT_{Usyn} [punctuation])+ *OW*) > THEN *Syn* (*IW*, *OW*)

CT_{Usyn}:={ "又称 ▪ (in other words)" | "或称 (alias)" | " ▪ 称(abbreviate)" …}

Where, *Unambig* denotes the type of rules, i.e., unambiguous rule. Identifying a specific semantic relationship according to a set of terms (Characteristic Term, *CT*) is an efficient way. CT_U denotes a set of characteristic terms in unambiguous rules. And CT_{Usyn} indicates a set of characteristic terms to recognize synonymy relationship. A pair of bracket denote optional item. The meaning of this rule is: if a term that belongs to CT_{Usyn} follows the *IW*, then subsequent noun to CT_{Usyn} is the target. An example is: "Hyper Text Transmission Protocol is commonly *abbreviated* to HTTP". A simple matching against the rules leads to the discovery of synonymy relationship, *Syn* (Hyper Text Transmission Protocol, HTTP).

IF *Unambig* < *Hypon* (*IW*+([punctuation | quantifier] CT_{Uhypon} [punctuation | quantifier])+*OW*) > THEN {*Hypon* (*IW*, *OW*), *Hyper* (*OW*, *IW*), [*Par* (*OW*$_i$, *OW*$_j$)]}

CT_{Uhypon}:={ "包括(such as)" | "分 ▪ (divide into)" | "由... ▪ 成" (consist of)...}

We take an example to demonstrate the rule 2. The example sentence is: "*such animals as* cats and dogs". The rule 2 is applied to extract the hyponymy relationship from this example sentence. Two relationships are acquired: *Hypon* (animal, cat), *Hypon* (animal, dog). It is noteworthy that hyponymy relationship and hypernymy relation is relative. If word A is hyponymy relationship of word B, then word B is hypernym relationship of word A. Thus, two hypernym relationships are produced: *Hyper* (cat, animal), *Hyper* (dog, animal). Considering "cat" and "dog" have the hypernymy relation with the same word "animal", we gain a parataxis relationship additionally, *Par* (cat, dog).

IF *Unambig* <*Par* (*JOP*(*IW*, *OW*) + CT_{Upar} > THEN *Par* (*IW*, *OW*)

CT_{Upar}:= {" ▪ 系(relate to)" | "区 ▪ (discriminate from)" | "相比 ▪ " (compare with)...}

The expression of *JOP*(*IW*, *OW*) means a juxtaposition of phrases containing *IW* and other noun words, which are targets. For instance, "*discriminate* HTTP *from* FTP", a parataxis relationship additionally is derived: *Par* (HTTP, FTP).

Ambiguous rules often express several distinct semantic relationships by equal opportunity. That is to say, the same ambiguous rule reflects different relationships in different contexts. Except for different *CT*, the formats of ambiguous rules and unambiguous rules are quite similar. CT_A denotes a set of characteristic terms in ambiguous rules. Different from the elements of CT_U, the elements of CT_A are identifications of a certain semantic relationship, as well as another semantic relationship in some contexts. For instance, "connects two cities, *namely*, New York and Chicago" is hyponymy, whereas "Hyper Text Transmission Protocol, *namely*, HTTP" is synonymy. Thus, it is inconsistent because a pair of words has several kinds of semantic relationships. The following heuristics is applied to eliminate the inconsistency.

3.2 Heuristics

Heuristics 1 is designed to filter out the noisy candidates acquired using the unambiguous rules. This noise is primarily due to overgeneralization of the unambiguous patterns. Some sentences match a certain unambiguous rule, but extracted pairs of terms take none of pre-definitional semantic relationships (synonymy, hyponymy, hypernymy and parataxis). For the purposes of removing these false pairs occurring in this circumstance, we compute the semantic association degree of each pair of candidate, *SUP*, and retain only the pairs that the number of times occurred in collects is bigger than the value of *SUP*. Finally, calculate the value of *CON* of the each rest candidate, and get rid of potential false pairs.

Definition 1

SUP is the minimal value that determines whether a pair of terms takes on a certain semantic relationship. If $f(R(w_1, w_2)) \geq SUP$ then delete $R(w_1, w_2)$. Where, $f(*)$ is the number of times a pair of terms occurred in text that are consistent with a rule, and we set *SUP* to 2.

Heuristics 1

If a pair of terms, such as $R(W_p, W_q)$, was extracted using more than one specific rule, then the bigger the number of rules and the value of $f(R(W_p, W_q))$ are, the more possible $R(W_p, W_q)$ is a correct relationships pair.

Definition 2

According to the heuristics 1, *CON* is defined as:

$$CON(R(W_p, W_q)) = SUM + \frac{M \times SUM}{M + SUM} \tag{1}$$

$$SUM = \sum_i^M f(R(W_p, W_q)) \tag{2}$$

M is the number of rules. We set *CON* to 15. If the value of *CON* of each candidate is less than 15, then this pair is regard as false one and is deleted.

Heuristics 2 is designed to filter out the noisy candidates extracted using the ambiguous rules. There have mainly two kinds of noisy candidates: i) since the same ambiguous rule reflects different relationships in different contexts, some extracted pairs are marked wrong relationships. That is, we acquire a pair of terms using a specific ambiguous rule, such as hyponymy, but this pair of terms actually reflects other pre-definitional relationship; ii) some extracted pairs of terms take on none of pre-definitional semantic relationships, as a result of overgeneralization of the patterns. In order to remove these false candidates, the following operation will be applied.

Heuristics 2

IF $Set^A \cap Set^U = C \neq \varnothing$ THEN $\tilde{Set}^A = Set^A - C$

Where, Set^A and Set^U are the set of pairs that are extracted using ambiguous rules and unambiguous rules respectively. $\tilde{Set}$ is the set of pairs that have been refined. The heuristics 2 means: If there exists some extracted pairs that match against not only unambiguous rules but also ambiguous rules, then these extracted pairs are removed from Set^A. Because refined pairs that were extracted by unambiguous rules are more desirable. After that, we adopt the heuristics 1 to remove the rest false candidates.

4 Experimental Results and Analysis

To verify the validity of the proposed approach, we design three experiments. 50 nouns were selected from a lexicon at random, and then were submitted to Google. Top 500 documents were returned for each selected noun. After deleting duplicated Web documents and wiped off the sentences that have no relevancy with the selected word, the following matching strategies were performed:

Unambiguous rules and ambiguous rules are applied to extract the relationships, as well as the candidates were refined with heuristics. The experimental results are in Table 1.

Only unambiguous rules are applied to extract the relationships. We recorded the two sets of experimental results respectively according as candidates were refined or unrefined with heuristics, shown as Table 2.

Only ambiguous rules are applied to extract the relationship. We recorded the two sets of experimental results respectively according as candidates were refined or unrefined with heuristics, shown as Table 3.

The *precision* performance metrics is defined as:

$$precision = \frac{M}{N} \tag{3}$$

Where, M is the number of correct retrieved relations (human annotator judge the correctness of results provided by system). N is the number of retrieved relations.

The *recall* performance metrics is not computed. Because the goal of our approach is to extract as many valid pairs as possible from the text collection. We do not attempt to capture every instance of such pairs. Instead, we exploit the fact that these pairs will tend to appear multiple times in the collections. As long as we capture one instance of such a pair, we will consider the system to be successful.

Table 1. Results of the First Matching Strategy

Type	Number of retrieved relations N_1	Number of correct retrieved relations M_1	Precision P_1
Synonymy	28	24	85.7%
Hyponymy	73	65	89.0%
Parataxis	32	26	81.3%

The results in Table 1 illustrate that our approach can acquire the most semantic relationships correctly. Hyponymy and hypernymy is a relative relationship. The precisions of these two relationships are same. So we only list the experimental results of hyponymy.

Where, P_{r2} is the precision when candidates were refined with heuristics in experiment 2. P_{u2} is the precision when candidates were unrefined in experiment 2.

As shown in Table 2, the average precision of $(95.2\%+92.3\%+94.4\%)/3$ is exciting, which is increase of 7.9% than the P_{u2}. This indicates the heuristics to refine the candidates is effective. Nevertheless, comparing M_{r2} with M_1, we conclude that some correct relationships were failed to extract if only unambiguous rules were applied.

Table 2. Results of the Second Matching Strategy

Type	Number of retrieved relations		Number of correctly retrieved relations		Precision	
	N_{r2}	N_{u2}	M_{r2}	M_{u2}	P_{r2}	P_{u2}
Synonymy	21	24	20	20	95.2%	83.3%
Hyponymy	52	58	48	49	92.3%	84.5%
Parataxis	18	19	17	17	94.4%	89.5%

Table 3. Results of the Third Matching Strategy

Type	Number of retrieved relations		Number of correctly retrieved relations		Precision	
	N_{r3}	N_{u3}	M_{r3}	M_{u3}	P_{r3}	P_{u3}
Synonymy	10	13	7	8	70.0%	61.5%
Hyponymy	23	26	17	17	73.9%	65.4%
Parataxis	15	19	9	11	60.0%	57.9%

Where, P_{r3} is the precision when candidates were refined with heuristics in experiment 2. P_{u3} is the precision when candidates were unrefined in experiment 3.

Similarly, from the results of P_{r3} and P_{u3}, we can see that the heuristics can delete the most incorrect relationships, while legitimate ones maybe be eliminated sometimes, e.g. M_{r3} and M_{u3} in the first row and the third row of table 3.

5   Conclusions

We present an approach of semantic relationships acquisition from Chinese Web documents. We don't analyze every sentence in documents, but wipe off the sentences that have no relevancy with the *IW* to dwindle in numbers of text to be analyzed and obtain initial sentence-level text. For a distinct semantic relationship, corresponding unambiguous rules and ambiguous rules designed for Chinese phrases are applied to the initial sentence-level text. Lastly, candidates are refined with two heuristics according to different traits of rules. Compared to other previous works, we apply not only strict unambiguous rules but also loose unambiguous rules to extract relationships and proposed efficient approach to refine the outputs of these rules.

Although linguistic rules we used almost cannot cover all instances, we believe that there are many expressions that convey the same relationships on the Web. So the most semantic relationships can be recognizes through these rules.

The main shortcoming of our approach is that acquisition of rules. At present, these rules are derived from large number of corpus by human, which is inefficient. So we intend to the detection of extraction rules and to discover constrains for all the rules.

References

1. Xia Sun, Qinghua Zheng.: Semantics-based Answers Selection in Question Answering System. In: Proceedings of the 3rd International Conference on Web-Based Learning (ICWL2004), Tsinghua University, Beijing, China (2004)
2. Girju. R., Badulescu. A., Moldovan. D.: Learning Semantic Constraints for the Automatic Discovery of Part-Whole Relations. In: Proceedings of HLT-NAACL (2003)
3. Gildea. D, Jurafsky. D.: Automatically Labeling Semantic classes. In: Proceedings of Annual Conference of the Association for Computational Linguistics, ACL (2004)
4. Pantel. P., Lin, D.: Discovering Word Senses from Text. In: Proceedings of ACM Conference on Knowledge Discovery and Data Mining, CIGKDD (2002)
5. Matthew. B., Eugene. C.: Finding Parts in Very Large Corpora. In: Proceedings of the 37th Annual Meeting of the Association for Computational Linguistics, Maryland (1999)
6. Li. Y., He. Q., Zhongzhi Shi.: Association Retrieve Based On Concept Semantic Space. Journal of University of Science and Technology, Beijing (2001)
7. WordNet. http://www.cogsci.princeton.edu/~wn/index.shtml
8. Google. http://www.google.com/
9. Wu. P, Chen.Q., Ma. L.: The Study on Large Scale Duplicated Web Pages of Chinese Fast Deletion Algorithm Based on String of Feature Code. Journal of Chinese Information Processing, Beijing, (2003)
10. Qinghua Zheng, Sunjuan Zhang.: A Novel Algorithm of Eliminating the Chinese Word Segmentation Ambiguities for Web Answer. Computer Engineering and Applications (2004)
11. Zhaojing Wang, Qinghua Zheng.: An Approach of POS Tagging for Web Answer. Computer Engineering and Applications (2004)
12. Xia Sun, Qinghua Zheng.: A Method of Special Domain Lexicon Construction Based on Raw Materials. Mini-Micro Systems (2005)

Grounding Collaborative Knowledge Building in Semantics-Based Critiquing

Anders I. Mørch[1], William K. Cheung[2], Kelvin C. Wong[2], Jiming Liu[2], Cynthia Lee[3], Mason H. Lam[2], and Janti P. Tang[2]

[1] InterMedia, University of Oslo, Norway
anders.morch@intermedia.uio.no
[2] Department of Computer Science, Hong Kong Baptist University, Hong Kong
{willliam, kcwong, jiming, mason, janti}@comp.hkbu.edu.hk
[3] Language Centre, Hong Kong Baptist University, Hong Kong
cfklee@hkbu.edu.hk

Abstract. In this paper we investigate the use of Latent Semantic Analysis (LSA), Critiquing Systems, and Knowledge Building to support computer-based teaching of English composition. We have built and tested an English Composition Critiquing System that make use of LSA to analyze student essays and compute feedback by comparing their essays with teacher's model essays. LSA values are input to a critiquing component to provide a user interface for the students. A software agent can also use the critic feedback to coordinate a collaborative knowledge building session with multiple users (students and teachers). Shared feedback provides seed questions that can trigger discussion and extended reflection about the next phase of writing. We present the first version of a prototype we have built, and report the results from an informal experiment. We end the paper by describing our plans for future work.

1 Introduction

English is the preferred second language for many people and learning it occurs in many ways. For example, young people are quite apt in learning spoken English phrases when watching TV, browsing the Internet and communicating with peers on mobile phones (e.g. SMS). However, previous studies have shown these influences may have negative effect on vocabulary development [19, 27]. As a consequence, students' reading and writing skills do not keep pace with listening and speaking. Furthermore, English composition is primarily taught in the classroom and practiced in homework assignments, supported by qualified teachers and parents. These are important but scarce resources, creating an imbalance of textual and oral language exposure. We address this dilemma by augmenting classroom-based composition training integrated with computer support.

The paper is organized as follows. We start by characterizing English composition as a design activity and identify the components of a computer-based design environment to support it. Next, we explain how latent semantic analysis (LSA) can be

R.W.H. Lau et al. (Eds.): ICWL 2005, LNCS 3583, pp. 244–255, 2005.
© Springer-Verlag Berlin Heidelberg 2005

used to provide feedback on student compositions within this context, and how we have incorporated LSA as part of system architecture. We show a prototype of a critiquing system we have built, discuss our efforts in integrating it with a knowledge-building environment (FLE) and report the preliminary findings by comparing LSA with manual teacher feedback on a set of essays.

2 Related Work

Essay writing can be viewed as a design activity, producing a textual artifact - a document. A document consists of words and sentences. It has structuring (abstraction) and content production (composition) elements [28]. These are key aspects of any design process. Structuring defines the organization of the document in terms of sentences, paragraphs and sections (i.e. levels of abstraction); whereas content production is about finding words and phrases, and sequencing them into readable sentences, which again become part of paragraphs, and so on. A well-composed essay will communicate certain ideas, topics or themes about some area of shared concern. Intermediate level abstractions, such as paragraphs and sections, serve as placeholders for complex ideas extended over multiple paragraphs, so that the writers and readers can focus on one idea at a time while suppressing unimportant details.

Creative design is said to consist of two sub-activities, action and reflection, supporting composition and abstraction, respectively. Action means to create an artifact by selecting and combining building blocks into functional arrangements and reflection means to evaluate the artifact from multiple viewpoints [16]. When this occurs without external disruption other than situation-specific feedback, it is referred to as reflection-in-action [23]. In a good process of design, the designer will rapidly cycle between action and reflection until the design is completed. During this process, the "back talk" of the situation signals to the designer when there is a need to switch to the other mode. This is communicated by e.g. an incomplete drawing, inconsistency in arrangement of parts, a need for restructuring the task, etc.

2.1 Design Critiquing

Computational support for reflection-in-action is provided with the critiquing approach [7, 18, 21]. Critiquing is defined as "presentation of a reasoned opinion about a product or action" created by a user with a computer [7]. A Critiquing System integrates computational support for design-as-action and design-as-reflection and operationalizes Schön's notion of "back talk" with computational critics [7, 20]. Critics make the situation talk back so that non-expert designers can understand it, giving them task-specific feedback about the artifact-under-construction. Examples of critiquing systems are Janus [16], ArgoUML [20], and The Java Critiquer [18]. These systems were developed for the domains of kitchen design, UML (Unified Modeling Language) and Java programming, respectively. For example Janus allows designers to model kitchen designs at different levels of abstraction (from appliances to work centers), ArgoUML knows about the elements and relations of UML and can tell the designer when a software architecture diagram violates the rules of UML [21]. Similarly, the Java Critiquer identifies statements in a program code that can be improved by readability and best practice [18]. These critics provide feedback on partially completed software artifacts, pointing out inconsistency and incompleteness in the design.

We believe the critiquing approach can be useful for computer-supported English composition for the following two reasons. First, writing can be modeled as a design activity [28], and second, critic feedback can supplement teacher feedback on student essays in certain situations (after school hours, in distributed environments). In this context we propose to integrate collaborative knowledge building and LSA with critiquing- Knowledge building to support collaborative reflection and LSA to compute the critic feedback. This is different from past work on critiquing systems and educational applications of LSA. The previous work on LSA has focused on individual learning by integrating it with Intelligent Tutoring Systems [24]. A goal for us is to provide computer support for both action and reflection, and individual and collaborative learning.

2.2 Collaborative Knowledge Building

Knowledge building [22] requires that new knowledge is not simply assimilated with the help of a more knowledgeable person or mediated by a computer system, but also jointly constructed through solving problems with peers by a process of building shared understanding. This type of teaching and learning takes its inspiration from pedagogical models such as problem-based learning and case-based instruction. These are models for teaching that require students to explore open-ended problems and generalize from exemplary cases. The basic idea of knowledge building is that students gain a deeper understanding of a knowledge domain through engaging in a research-like process by generating or responding to problems or questions, proposing tentative answers (personal explanations) and searching for deepening knowledge collaboratively.

Knowledge building and its subsequent refinement, Progressive Inquiry [8] are well suited to be supported by Internet technologies such as web-based discussion forums and have received considerable attention in the Computer Supported Collaborative Learning (CSCL) community. A reason for this is that the regularity of knowledge building, which is modeled after scientific discourse, provides students with a well-defined scaffolding structure built into the online learning environments. Knowledge building environments are pedagogically designed discussion forums and include CSILE [22], Knowledge Forum, and Future Learning Environment (FLE) [10]. They are used in schools in Canada, Hong Kong and Scandinavia, as well as elsewhere in the world.

The reason for our wish to integrate collaborative knowledge building with a critiquing system is twofold. First, critiquing systems do not provide full support of design-as-reflection because they address primarily individual designers' needs, inspired by Schön's notion of reflective practice [23]. Knowledge building, on the other hand, can add a multi-user dimension by supporting "collaborative reflection," even though knowledge building was not originally conceived as such. Collaborative reflection occurs during "talk with peers" [e.g. 15] in meaningful contexts, i.e. jointly addressing problems or questions shared by a community of stakeholders in which shared understanding can emerge [2]. Knowledge building thus becomes an important part of the integrated collaborative learning and problem-solving environment.

Second, one of the authors has previously participated in a study to evaluate a knowledge-building environment (FLE) to support problem-based teaching of natural science in two high school classes in Norway [14, 17]. One of the results of this study was that students found knowledge building difficult. In particular they did not properly understand how to use the message categories to post messages in the forum. This was manifest in that interaction over time became less knowledge-building intense and more task-specific (localized), revolving around the respective schools' local situations, thus grounding the interaction. In the current project we address the grounding problem [2, 3, 4] computationally by integrating a knowledge-building environment with an LSA-based critiquing system.

2.3 Latent Semantic Analysis

Latent Semantic Analysis (LSA) is a mathematical technique for computing the semantic similarity between words and text segments with the help of a large corpus. The corpus can be a set of related documents. It can also be one document broken down into smaller text segments such as paragraphs or even sentences, as in our case. The input to LSA is the set of text segments, which may need processing by the computer in various ways.

LSA computes the similarity of two input texts (student and teacher) as follows. First, both input texts are segmented to form the corpus. Then, the word-segment association matrix D is constructed. In the matrix D, each row stands for a unique word and each column stands for a text segment. Each cell entry can be the frequency of a given word in a given text segment. As an example, consider the segment "The 2004 IEEE International Conference on Electronic Technology, Electronic Commerce and Electronic Service." If the jth column corresponds to the aforementioned segment and the ith row corresponds to the word "Electronic", then the value in D_{ij} would be 3 as "Electronic" occurs three times in the segment. As weighting the words based on their individual importance is known to be effective in obtaining better matching results, we use entropy values instead of computing D_{ij} given as

$$D_{ij} = \log\left(f_{ij} + 1.0\right) * \left\{1 - \frac{1}{\log(N)}\sum_{j=1}^{N}\left[\frac{f_{ij}}{gf_i}\log\frac{f_{ij}}{gf_i}\right]\right\}$$

$$gf_i = \sum_{j=1}^{N} f_{ij}$$

where N: number of text segments in the stored corpus

f_{ij} : frequency of the ith word in the jth text segment

Once the matrix D is computed, it is decomposed using Singular Value Decomposition (SVD) [25]. The matrix D is expressed as a unique product of three matrices: $D = P\lambda Q'$ such that P and Q have orthonormal columns and λ contains the singular values on the diagonal. By comparing the diagonal elements of λ, we only need to keep those elements with large values and can set the others to zero, with the effect that the dimension of λ will be reduced. This is equivalent to removing the corresponding columns from P and rows from Q. The new P and Q then define the revised "semantic space." Words that have appeared in similar segments, and segments with similar semantic content, will be positioned near one another [24]. Words that do not co-occur (e.g. bicycle and bike), but occur in similar contexts will also be grouped together.

After the semantic space has been computed the new D can be "reconstructed" based on the new P and Q. The similarity between two text segments can then be computed by calculating the geometric cosine between their corresponding vectors in D, given as

$$\cos \theta = \frac{X \bullet Y}{\|X\| * \|Y\|}$$

where $X \bullet Y$ is the inner product of vectors x and y and defined as follows

$X \bullet Y = x_1 y_1 + x_2 y_2 + \ldots + x_n y_n$, and $\|X\|$ is the length of a vector X,

defined as $\|X\| = (X \bullet X)^{1/2} = (\sum_{i=1\ldots n} x_i^2)^{1/2}$

Remark. In order to allow the latest submitted essays to be compared with the corpus in the derived semantic space; one can project them by the SVD results. These are referred to as pseudo documents [5]. This has the advantage that we only need to compute the SVD once instead of per submission. Additional technical details on LSA can be found in [9].

3 Components of a Learning Environment for Essay Writing

We have incorporated *LSA* together with *critiquing* and *knowledge building* to form an integrated learning environment for English Essay Writing. The LSA-based critiquing component of this environment allows us to compare student and model essays and provide critic feedback to the students when they submit their work in progress, whereas the knowledge building component provides support for collaboratively resolving critic feedback that is not well understood by the students on their own, grounding it in a relevant context. The overview of this environment is shown in Figure 1 and the workings of its components are explained below.

The teacher first decides on the topic to be taught and writes and/or collects a set of samples articles and essays that represent the domain in some detail. These samples are then input into the system so that the LSA analyzer can build a semantic space for the domain. Student model essays, suggested answers by teachers, as well as articles from external sources (which could be anything from on-line newspapers to scanned essays of textbooks) constitute this set.

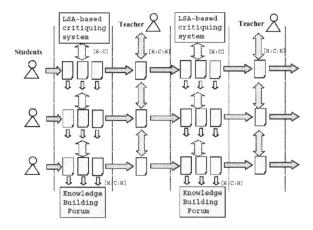

Fig. 1. English composition integrated learning environment system architecture

The students write their essays using the English Composition Critiquing System (see below). When they require assistance they can request automated feedback (critique), which points out missing items in their text (compared with the corpus essays). Before the text can be input into LSA all the articles are broken down into sentences and preprocessed by techniques such as stop-word removal and stemming as described above. The Analyzer then computes the word-segment association matrix. Singular Value Decomposition [25] is performed on the matrix and the semantic similarity between all possible sentence pairs, one from the student and the other from the model samples, is computed. This allows the system to identify the sentences in the model essays that contain themes that are missing in the students' submissions.

The final steps are semantic matching and summarization. The identified sentences containing the missing themes can be summarized as a trunk of keywords or short phrases preset by the teacher or automatically by the system, using computational text summarization techniques. This will result in a summary that is reported as critic feedback in the user interface. In the prototype we describe below, we have modeled our critics' feedback based on the phrasing and organization of Hong Kong English teachers' marking schemes. When the critique is presented as feedback immediately after the students have completed a part of their essay, it will allow them to revise their essays in a meaningful context.

The roles of teachers and students could be much more active than merely providing model samples and improving essays based on the predefined critic feedback. Teachers can monitor how well the different themes are handled by the students. They may provide more insight into how individual students incorporate missing themes, and participate as facilitators of student collaboration sessions to provide feedback when the students run out of ideas [11]. Their participation serves the purpose of supportive interaction through which an expert assists a group of learner to develop a higher level of understanding [e.g. 15] and pushes the learner's zone of proximal development [26]. A recent large-scale language learning survey has confirmed the observation that most students in East Asian and European countries have a positive attitude towards cooperating in groups in order to achieve common goals, and they would like to see themselves as active participants in the classroom learning process [12].

The LSA-based critiquing and knowledge building environment marks the contours of a "double-loop" learning process (see Figure 1), alternating between inner (individual) and outer (collaboration) phases. The process can be repeated several times before the students submit their final essay for grading or commenting on by the teacher. In a good process of writing, we anticipate this learning environment will support reflection-in-action at two levels: 1) individual (inner loop) activity when students switch between essay composition and modification by responding to well understood critique and 2) collaborative (inner + outer loop) activity by entering a collaborative mode of interaction through responding to critique that is not well understood or where the understanding can be broadened or made more interesting for the students by sharing their ideas with others. Whether or not our computational environment can provide adequate scaffolding for reflection-in-action in English essay writing at these two levels is currently a hypothesis. Its conceptual basis and technological platform are provided in this paper.

3.1 System Prototypes

In order to support English essay writing as a design activity based on the models and techniques presented above we decided to reuse and integrate existing systems, making modifications when necessary. When selecting the critiquing component we considered both ArgoUML [21] and the Java Critiquer [18]. The latter has the advantage that it supports the design of a textual artifact (program code), but ArgoUML has the advantage it is a freely downloadable, open source system. We decided on ArgoUML due to its accessibility. However, we had to modify the system extensively, with the effect its UML features are no longer visible (see Figure 2).

The system building approach we took was to start with the existing system, removing all the features we did not need and adding the features that are unique to our domain. In retrospect we could have built the equivalent functionality from scratch in about the same time. However, some of the Argo features we have hidden, such as the building block palette and to-do list we anticipate to be useful in future versions of our system. For example, the current version requires students to input their essays in terms of characters and words (i.e. the composition area is a text processing window), whereas LSA Analyzer requires sentences as input. Furthermore, we know from previous studies that designers work at multiple levels of abstraction [1], which in the context of essay composition means words, sentences, paragraphs, sections, and other higher level structures [28]. Therefore, providing support for direct manipulation of intermediate-level building blocks is another way to extend the current system. It will allow the students to acquire skills in organization as well as composition, and it may simplify LSA preprocessing by reducing the need for sentence segmentation. Furthermore, to-do lists that can keep track of overlooked critic messages and suggest when they should be attended to, can help students to manage multiple missing sub-themes. This is part of future work.

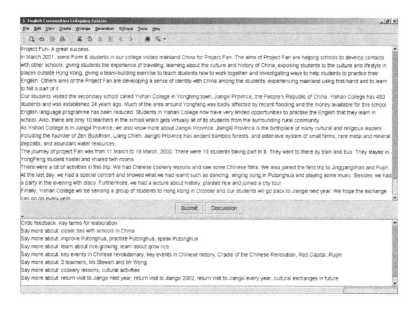

Fig. 2. The English composition critiquing system has a "Submit" button to generate LSA-based critique and a "Discussion" button to trigger a knowledge building session (Figure 3)

For the knowledge-building component we decided on another open source system, FLE (Future Learning Environment) [10]. FLE is a knowledge building environment developed in accordance with the progressive inquiry model [8]. It is an asynchronous, web-based groupware for computer-supported collaborative learning. It is designed to support collaborative learning in the form of a discussion forum with message categories (knowledge types) named after the stages of the progressive inquiry model. These stages and corresponding categories can help students improve their collaboration and ability to solve open-ended problems. The categories that are provided with the system (Fle3) are *"problem," "my explanation", "scientific explanation", "summary"* and *"comment."* Two of these categories are displayed in Figure 3.

Figure 3 shows the reader's interface of the knowledge-building forum of Fle3 from a simulated session involving two students who have been invited to join the forum by a coordinator agent to resolve a missing essay topic. The missing essay topic is picked up by the agent and serves as a seed question. In knowledge building these initial questions are often formulated by teachers, based on their knowledge of the subject to be taught. In this case it is handled by a software agent based on its ability to identify students who receive the same feedback, and a belief that two students receiving the same feedback have something in common that they can resolve by information sharing and discussion. The reason why discussion may be the appropriate form of resolving the feedback is based on the fact that missing sub-themes define open-ended questions, i.e. they can be addressed in many different ways. We have not yet tested these claims, but it builds on our previous (empirical-based, system building) work on integrating agents with FLE [6] and adaptive user interface agents [13].

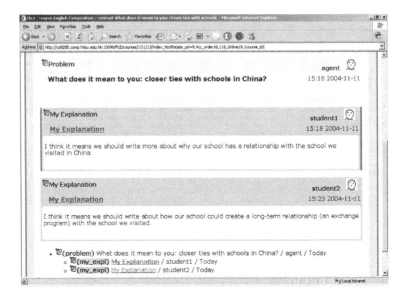

Fig. 3. The Fle3 Web-based knowledge-building forum shows a persistent storage of discussions related to students' missing essay topics. An agent initiates a thread when it discovers an essay topic that is missing by more than one student. The KB forum has not yet been fully integrated into our environment and it has not yet been tested with students

4   Evaluation and Preliminary Results

In order to assess the feasibility of our system regarding its ability to suggest missing themes for students to consider when revising their essays, we conducted an experiment. Seven high school students in Hong Kong were invited to write a 400 to 500-word essay on the topic "Write an essay about the experience of traveling to China". At the same time, a teacher was asked to provide a number of sub-themes (25 in this study) of this topic, which the students were expected to include in their essays.

The teacher assessed the finished essays to identify the sub-themes that were missing, based on the set of predefined sub-themes. Then the essays were assessed by our system. Each text segment in the student essay was compared with each sample segment suggested by the teacher. If the semantic similarity (which was represented by the cosine value calculated by LSA) was below a preset threshold, we considered the sub-theme of the sample segment to be missing in the student essay. Finally, the missing sub-themes identified by the teacher and our system were compared to evaluate the performance of the system. The system identified 35 missing sub-themes in the 7 student essays, 22 of them were judged to be correct (i.e., also identified by the teacher as missing sub-themes), whereas the remaining 13 were considered inappropriate. Based on this we get a tentative precision rate of 63%. A reason for this low number is the small size of the corpus.

We used a corpus of about 3,000 words to build the semantic space. This is smaller corpus than what has been used in related studies, such as TASA-all (a large knowledge space consisting of text samples from the K12 (grade 1-12) curriculum in the United

States) [24]. The TASA-all corpus comprises approximately eleven million words. We believe that a larger corpus for constructing our semantic space will further improve the accuracy of our system in identifying missing sub-themes. We will explore this hypothesis by varying corpus size for different domains in our further work

5   Conclusions and Directions for Further Work

Many students find essay writing stressful because they do not have sufficient ideas to fully cover the topic they are asked to write about. They usually run out of ideas before they have completed their essays. When the class size is large and when running in-class writing exercises, it is difficult for teachers to give proper feedback to individual students on missing topics to address in their rewrite, because it requires considerable amount of teachers' time.

We believe the use of our semantic-based critiquing system can support students by autonomously suggesting what missing sub-themes they should pay attention to when revising their essays. Students can submit their draft essays to the system for feedback whenever they are running out of ideas. If the feedback is incomplete or poorly understood (e.g. due to LSA truncation steps) the students can enter a system-initiated, contextualized discussion forum that provides support for collaborative knowledge building using the pedagogically informed progressive inquiry model. We believe that this can help students to enrich their essay content with more vocabulary in a context that is meaningful to them, thus grounding their learning activity. We are also interested in how the students view the critiquing system and to what extent the knowledge-building forum will be used. On the technical (algorithmic) side, we want to investigate the factors that will affect the performance of LSA in the essay-writing domain. For instance, how to determine both the optimal number of dimensions of the semantic space and the optimal threshold value for similarity matching are questions that require further research to answer.

Acknowledgments

This work was partly supported by Faculty Research Grant of Hong Kong Baptist University-FRG/02-03/II-38 and Group Research Grant of Research Grant Council (RGC) - HKBU 2/03/C. The first author was as a Visiting Research Scholar at CS department, Hong Kong Baptist University while this paper was written, and he thanks InterMedia and Faculty of Education, University of Oslo for a sabbatical leave.

References

1. Akin, O: How Do Architects Design? In: Latombe, J. (ed.): Artificial Intelligence and Pattern Recognition in Computer Aided Design. North-Holland, New York, NY (1978) 65-104
2. Arnseth, H. C., Solheim, I: Making Sense of Shared Knowledge. In G. Stahl (ed.): Proceedings of CSCL 2002 – Conference for Computer Support for Collaborative Learning (Boulder, 2002) 102-110

3. Baker, M.J., Hansen, T., Joiner, R., Traum, D: The Role of Grounding in Collaborative Learning Tasks. In: Dillenbourg, P. (ed.): Collaborative Learning: Cognitive and Computational Approaches. Pergamon/Elsevier Science, Amsterdam, The Netherlands (1999) 31-63

4. Brennan, S.E.: The Grounding Problem in Conversations with and through Computers. In: Fussell, S.R., Kreuz, R.J. (eds.): Social and Cognitive Approaches to Interpersonal Communication. Lawrence Erlbaum, Mahwah, NJ (1998) 201-225

5. Deerwester, S., Dumais, S.T., Furnas, G.W., Landauer, T.K., Harshman, R.: Indexing by Latent Semantic Analysis. Journal of the American Society for Information Science 41, 6 (1999) 391-407

6. Dolonen, J., Chen, W., Mørch, A.: Integrating Software Agents with FLE. In: Wasson, B., Ludvigsen, S., Hoppe, U. (eds.): Proceedings of Conference of Computer Supported Collaborative Learning (CSCL 2003). Kluwer Academic, Dordrecht, The Netherlands (2003) 157-161

7. Fischer, G., Lemke, A.C., Mastaglio, T., Mørch, A. I.: The Role of Critiquing in Cooperative Problem Solving. ACM Transactions on Information Systems 9, 3 (1991) 123-151

8. Hakkarainen, K., Lipponen, L., Järvelä, S.: Epistemology of Inquiry and Computer-Supported Collaborative Learning. In: T. Koschmann, Hall, R. and Miyake, N. (eds.): CSCL 2: Carrying Forward the Conversation. Lawrence Erlbaum, Mahwah, NJ (2002) 129-156

9. Landauer, T.K., Foltz, P.W., Laham, D.: An Introduction to Latent Semantic Analysis. Discourse Processes 25 (1998) 259-284

10. Leinonen, T: Fle3 > Future Learning Environment. Website hosted by UIAH Media Lab, University of Art and Design Helsinki, Finland, http://fle3.uiah.fi/ (retrieved May. 2nd, 2005).

11. Littlewood, W.: The Use of Collaborative Interaction Techniques in Teaching EAP. HKBU Papers in Applied Language Studies, Language Centre, Hong Kong Baptist University, Kowloon Tong, HK (2001)

12. Littlewood, W.: Students' Perception of Classroom Learning in East Asia and Europe. HKBU Papers in Applied Language Studies, Language Centre, Hong Kong Baptist University, Kowloon Tong, HK (2003)

13. Liu, J., Wong, K.C., Hui, K.K.: An Adaptive User Interface Based on Personalized Learning. IEEE Intelligent Systems 18, 2 (2003) 52-57

14. Ludvigsen, S., Mørch, A.: Categorization in Knowledge Building: Task-specific Argumentation in a Co-located CSCL Environment. In: Wasson, B., Ludvigsen, S., Hoppe, U. (eds.): Proceedings of Conference of Computer Supported Collaborative Learning (CSCL 2003). Kluwer Academic, Dordrecht, The Netherlands (2003) 67-76

15. Maybin, J., Mercer, N., Stierer, B.: Scaffolding Learning in the Classroom. In: Norman, K. (ed.): Thinking Voice. Hodder & Stoughton, London, UK (1992) 186-195

16. McCall, R., Fischer, G., Mørch, A.: Supporting Reflection-in-Action in the Janus Design Environment. In: McCullough, M., Mitchell, W.J., Purcell, P. (eds.): The Electronic Design Studio, MIT Press, Cambridge, MA (1990) 247-259

17. Mørch, A., Omdahl, K., Ludvigsen, S.: Knowledge Building in Distributed Collaborative Learning: Organizing Information in Multiple Worlds. Proceedings of the Human Factors in Computing Systems (CHI 2004) Workshop on Designing for Reflective Practitioners, also Technical Report UCI-ISR-04-2, Institute for Software Research, University of California, Irvine, CA (2004) 31-33

18. Qiu, L., Riesbeck, C.K.: Making Critiquing Practical: Incremental Development of Educational Critiquing Systems. Proceedings of the 2004 International Conference on Intelligent User Interfaces. ACM Press, New York (2004) 304-306

19. Rice, M.L., Huston, A.C., Truglio, R.T., Wright, J.C. Words from Sesame Street: Learning Vocabulary while Viewing. Developmental Psychology 26, 3 (1990) 421-428

20. Robbins, J.E.: Design Critiquing Systems, Technical Report UCI-98-41, Department of Informatics, University of California, Irvine, CA (1998)
21. Robbins, J.E., Redmiles, D.F.: Software Architecture Critics in the Argo Design Environment. Knowledge-Based Systems 5, 1 (1998) 47-60
22. Scardamalia, M., Bereiter, C.: Computer Support for Knowledge-Building Communities. The Journal of the Learning Sciences 3, 3 (1994) 265-283
23. Schön, D.A.: The Reflective Practitioner: How Professionals Think in Action. Basic Books, New York, NY (1983)
24. Steinhart, D.J.: Summary Street: An Intelligent Tutoring System for Improving Student Writing Through the use of Latent Semantic Analysis. Ph.D. thesis, Dept. of Psychology, University of Colorado, Boulder, CO (2001)
25. Strang, G.: Linear Algebra and Its Application, 2nd edition. Academic Press, London, UK (1980)
26. Vygotsky, L.: Mind in Society – The Development of Higher Psychological Processes. Harvard University Press, Cambridge, MA (1978)
27. Weizman, Z.O., Snow, C.: Lexical Input as Related to Children's Vocabulary Acquisition: Effects of Sophisticated Exposure and Support for Meaning. Developmental Psychology 37, 2 (2001) 265-279
28. Yamamoto, Y., Takada, S., Gross, M., Nakakoji, K.: Representational Talkback – An Approach to Support Writing as Design. Proceedings of the Asia Pacific Conference on Computer Human Interaction (Kanagawa, Japan), IEEE Computer Society (1998) 125-131

Real-Time Adaptive Human Motions
for Web-Based Training

Frederick W.B. Li[†], Becky Siu[‡], Rynson W.H. Lau[‡], and Taku Komura[‡]

[†] Department of Computing, The Hong Kong Polytechnic University, Hong Kong
[‡] Department of CEIT, City University of Hong Kong, Hong Kong

Abstract. Web-based training offers many benefits over instructor-led training environments. It provides a time, class size and geographical location independent learning platform to students. To enable active learning and enhance the effectiveness in students' understanding of the training materials, multimedia cues, like 3D graphics, animation and sound, have been employed in web-based training systems to achieve these goals. However, if a training system involves a large amount of 3D animation, such as crowd animation in an emergency evacuation training system, the requirements for rendering capability and network bandwidth may become too high to meet. In this paper, we propose an adaptive human motion animation method to support real-time rendering and transmission of human motions in web-based training systems. Our method offers a mechanism to extract human motion data at various levels of detail (LoD). We also propose a set of importance factors to allow a web-based training system to determine the LoD of the human motion for rendering as well as the LoD for transmission, according to the importance of the motion and the available network bandwidth, respectively. We demonstrate the effectiveness of the new method with some experimental results.

Keywords: Adaptive motion synthesis, adaptive motion transmission and Web-based training.

1 Introduction

The Internet provides a rich environment for constructing interactive, intelligent and collaborative learning environments. It offers certain distinguished advantages over the traditional learning environment. First, unlike traditional learning that requires students to gather at certain time and at specific place to attend a lesson, web-based learning allows students at different geographical locations to join a lesson without physically travel. Second, web-based learning also allows the consolidation and distribution of e-Learning contents from a vast amount of Internet web sites to students. Third, web-based learning natively supports the presentation of various types of media, such as 3D graphics, animation and sound, to help students visualize and understand some ideas. For example, [Canó04] proposes a multimedia-enabled emergency evacuation training system for an underground metropolitan transportation environment. The system made use of text, images, audio, video and simple 3D graphics to construct the user interface and present evacuation training materials. Results show

R.W.H. Lau et al. (Eds.): ICWL 2005, LNCS 3583, pp. 256–266, 2005.
© Springer-Verlag Berlin Heidelberg 2005

that such arrangement could effectively improve students' understanding of complex procedures.

To allow students to be actively trained in various emergency situations, a virtual environment of different situations could be built using 3D animation [Sims95]. While it is important for students to fully visualize the emergency situations and learn to response to them interactively, it is also necessary for the instructors to be able to visually monitor the progress of the students from different angles in the virtual environment. Despite having these benefits, complex 3D animation, in particular when large amount of human motions is involved, can be very demanding in terms of rendering time. If we need to transmit this information over the network, the bandwidth requirement can also be very significant. Hence, a practical web-based emergency evacuation training system with 3D animation is still under exploration.

In this paper, we present an adaptive human motion framework to support real-time rendering and transmission of human motions in web-based training systems. The rest of this paper is organized as follows. Section 2 provides a survey on related work. Section 3 presents the adaptive human motion framework in detail. Section 4 shows some experimental results of our method. Finally, section 5 concludes the work presented in this paper.

2 Related Work

2.1 Formulation of Human Motions

An intuitive way to construct human motions for use in virtual environments is key-framing [Burt76]. This approach requires animators to construct an articulated figure to represent a human, and to define and draw key-frames of a motion sequence of the articulated figure to be animated. However, manipulating and coordinating the limbs of an articulated figure via key-framing is a complicated and tedious task. In addition, using this approach is also hard to produce realistic and natural looking motions. To ease the construction process of human motions, we may alternatively make use of motion capturing devices [Meye92] to acquire the movement of live objects, and then apply the captured position and orientation information on articulated figures to drive their motions. This approach is very impressive and has been widely accepted in real applications as it helps produce realistic and natural looking character animations. In general, regardless of which approach is being used, motion data is often large in size since it comprises a continuous data stream describing the spatial changes of all joints of each articulated figure. This likely poses a significant burden if we need to transmit the motion data over the Internet.

On the other hand, an animator may further edit and combine the motion sequences of an articulated figure to create new motion sequences for using in different applications. Inverse kinematics [Wang91], which is a process for computing the pose of an articulated figure from a set of analytically constrained equations of motion, could be adopted to achieve physical realism in motion editing. For example, [Popo99] suggests a variety of modifications to running and jumping motion data using a low resolution physical model to constrain the search space and trajectory optimization to generate physical realism in motion modifications, while [Rose96] proposes a minimum energy solution for transitions between motion sequences using an inverse kine-matics model.

2.2 Level of Detail of Human Motions

During a 3D interaction, users normally have different perceptions on different ob-jects in the environment. Such differences could be evaluated from a set of viewing parameters [Lau97], including viewer-object distance, viewer's line of sight, viewer's depth of field and object moving speed. To take advantage of this, methods have been developed to adjust the level of detail (LoD) of 3D geometry models, behavior and animation data to achieve better run-time performance for character animations.

In LoD of geometry models, a 3D model of an articulated figure could be simpli-fied by various multi-resolution modeling methods [Hopp96, To99]. Most of these multi-resolution modeling methods construct an edge collapse sequence of a 3D model to allow the model to be rendered with a selected number of polygons during run-time. However, the simplification of an articulated figure does not directly corre-spond to a simplification of its animation. In LoD of human animation, [Endo03] proposes a framework to support the transmission human motion data with different LoD's. In this framework, human motion data is modeled according to the H-Anim specification [H-Anim], which allows an articulated figure to be modeled in several levels of articulation (LoA), in which different LoAs of the articulated figure com-prise different numbers of representative joints. To transmit the human motion data, the server determines an appropriate LoA of the articulated figure for a client based on the importance of the figure and the available bandwidth of the client network connection. It then delivers only the motion data of the representative joints contained in the selected LoA of the articulated figure. However, this method does not consider the optimization of the motion sequence of each joint. In contrast, [Naka99] considers this factor as the primary way to reduce the transmission workload of human motion data. This method proposes to choose only a subset of motion data of each joint for transmission. This is done by regularly discarding motion data of each joint over the motion sequence. However, without analyzing the characteristic of the motion se-quence, the method may likely remove some important motion data. As mentioned in the previous section, since motion data is typically large in data size, lacking of a good method for handling the transmission of human motion data would probably hinder the incorporation of character animations in web-based applications.

3   Adaptive Human Motions

3.1   Overview

In [Li04], we have developed a progressive content distribution framework to handle the transmission of 3D content in web-based learning/training systems. Experimental results show that the framework offers very impressive transmission performance for distributing geometric information of 3D enriched learning materials. We have also built an urban walkthrough system and a Moai study system to demonstrate the func-tionality of the framework. To extend the ability of this framework to support applica-tions that requires large scale 3D animation, such as the emergency evacuation training system, we have developed a method to adaptively transmit human motion data over the Internet. In this method, we maintain human motion data using the data structure as defined in the BVH data format [Land98]. We also propose a method to decompose human motions into different LoD's and a metric to determine the appropriate LoD of the motion data for different parts of an articulated figure.

3.2 Human Motion Decomposition

Technically, it is not a trivial task to efficiently transmit human motion data over the Internet, particularly when a lot of articulated figures are involved, due to the large data size of the human motion data. The motion data is ordered as a sequence of sets of key values. Each set of key values indicate the positions and orientations of individual joints of the articulated figure at a particular frame. Although many data compression methods are available, most of them could not handle human motion data efficiently. It is because motion data is represented by a time-dependent data stream of hierarchically defined and highly co-related spatial information. In addition, human beings are also very sensitive to sudden changes in human motion, which can be produced by compressing the motion data with generic data compression algorithms. On the other hand, human motion may not necessary be restricted to any regular patterns and sudden changes may appear in the motion data.

To address the above problems, we have developed a human motion decomposition mechanism based on wavelets analysis [Stol96]. Wavelets are a mathematical tool for hierarchically decomposing data series into multiple LoD's using wavelets functions. The major advantage of wavelets is that wavelets functions are local in nature. In other words, wavelet could describe data series with a relatively small number of wavelets functions. Hence, the transformed data representation of a data series by wavelets analysis is compact in data size. On the other hand, this also enables wavelets to describe any sharp changes appearing in the data series. Although wavelet analysis has been applied in many applications, such as image compression, it is relatively new in the area of human motion.

To perform human motion decomposition, we read the human motion data from the BVH file for each articulated figure. For each joint of a figure, we handle its motion sequence separately using wavelets analysis. We express the motion sequence of each joint, i.e., $\mathbf{c}^n = \left[c_1^n, c_2^n, ..., c_{2^n+3}^n \right]$, as a linear combination of B-splines basis functions [Pieg95], where each c_i^n in $\mathbf{c}^n$ is assigned as the coefficient of the ith B-splines basis functions and n represents the highest possible LoD of a joint. As B-splines basis functions are semi-orthogonal, this provides a sufficient condition for us to fit the human motion data into the wavelets analysis process. After executing wavelets analysis, we could obtain a coarse representation and a set of refinement records for the human motion data. To transmit human motion data in a web-based training system, we first distribute the coarse motion representation of the required articulated figure to a user. The system may then refine the animation quality of the articulated figure by sending more refinement records of the motion data to the client under the control of our proposed metrics.

When animating an articulated figure, if only a subset of the motion data of an articulated figure is made available at the client, the animation quality of the articulated figure may be affected. To remedy this, we use B-splines to interpolate the low resolution motion data to generate a smooth motion path. In our implementation, for each joint of an articulated figure, we use a cubic B-splines curve to interpolate the motion sequence of the joint. The choice of a cubic degree of B-splines is for its simplicity in run-time computation and ability to provide smooth interpolation of a motion sequence. Another important contribution of applying B-splines interpolation is to ensure that the transition of human motion from one LoD to the next could be presented smoothly to the users.

3.3 Determination of Animation Quality

When animating an articulated figure, different parts of the articulated figure may have different importance values depending on the application as well as on the observer location. For example, the wrist joint may play a more important role, and have a high visual importance, in a punching motion than in a pure walking motion. For a web-based training system to adjust both the transmission and the rendering qualities of human motion data, we consider the motion performing by the articulated figure and the possible contribution of the figure to the user attention [Trei80]. We model these factors by a *joint importance* and a *visual importance*, respectively. They are dedicated as the primitive parameters to construct the metric for selecting the level of decomposition of human motion data, and the details are depicted as follows:

Joint Importance: This parameter measures the importance of each joint of an articulated figure by analyzing the human motion data acquired from the BVH file. Given a motion sequence, we compute the accumulated motion difference for each joint across the sequence. We then determine the degree of influence of a joint by evaluating the ratio of the accumulated motion difference of the joint against the maximum accumulated motion difference among all joints of the articulated figure. Finally, we normalize the degree of influence of a joint by the LoD of the motion data of this joint received by a user to yield the joint importance.

Visual Importance: To model the importance of an articulated figure to a viewer, we measure the run-time viewing parameters of the viewer with respect to the articulated figure as follows:

1. *Distance of the articulated figure from the viewer:* It is obvious that nearby articulated figures could be visualized more clearly and could draw more of the viewer's attention than those articulated figures located farther away from the viewer. So, the closer an articulated figure is to the viewer, the higher its visual importance value.
2. *Viewing direction of animating articulated figure from the viewer:* We notice that if the moving direction of an articulated figure is perpendicular to the viewing direction of the viewer, the motion details of the figure will be more obvious to the viewer than if the moving direction is parallel to the viewing direction. Hence, we can take advantage of this and compute the visual importance of an articulated figure according the orientation of its motion plane with respect to the viewing direction of the viewer.

We may now compute the visual importance of an articulated figure according to the above viewing parameters f_i as follows:

$$\text{Visual Importance Value} = \sum_{i=1}^{n} w_i f_i$$

where n is the number of parameters that we consider and each w_i is an application dependent weight for the corresponding viewing parameter f_i.

4 Results and Discussions

We have conducted experiments to evaluate the performance of our approach on *data error* and *smoothness of transition*.

Table 1. Accumulated movement of each joint on z, x and y axes

Joint Name	Accumulated movement of the joint			Total movement
	Z	X	Y	
Hips Position	5	0	3	8
Hips Rotation	0	1	3	4
Left Up Leg Rotation	105	29	35	169
Left Low Leg Rotation	265	2	6	273
Left Foot Rotation	113	6	45	164
Left Toes Rotation	184	0	3	187
Right Up Leg Rotation	82	17	14	113
Right Low Leg Rotation	218	4	6	228
Right Foot Rotation	111	4	34	149
Right Toes Rotation	160	0	5	165
Upper Back Rotation	4	1	1	6
Chest Rotation	4	10	8	22
Neck Rotation	8	11	11	30
Head Rotation	18	11	14	43
Chest Rotation	0	0	0	0
Left Up Arm Rotation	301	3	315	619
Left Low Arm Rotation	42	8	30	80
Left Hand Rotation	0	9	12	21
Left Fingers Rotation	0	0	0	0
Chest Rotation	0	2	0	2
Right Up Arm Rotation	216	19	285	520
Right Low Arm Rotation	69	4	41	114
Right Hand Rotation	0	12	63	75
Right Fingers Rotation	0	0	0	0

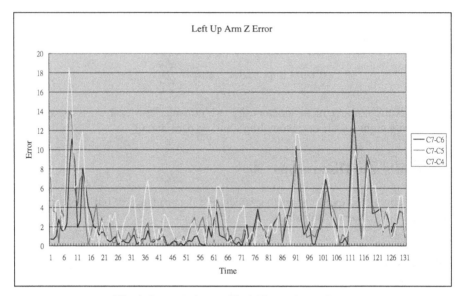

Fig. 1. Data error rate of Left Up arm in z axis

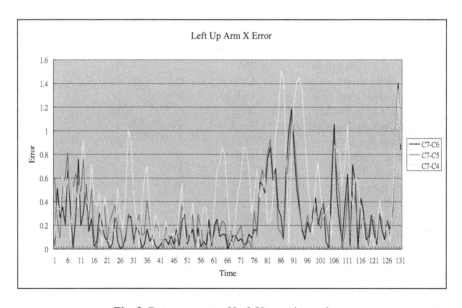

Fig. 2. Data error rate of Left Up arm in x axis

4.1   Experiment 1 – Data Error

In this experiment, we performed a walking animation. The animation consists of 131 frames and is rendered at 30 frames/second. We examine the joint with the highest total movement. Table 1 records the accumulated movement of each joint within the whole animation sequence. From the table, we can see that the Left Up arm has the highest total movement and hence, we examine this joint here.

Figures 1 to 3 illustrate the data error rate of the Left Up arm in x, y and z axes. For the legend shown on the right hand side of each chart, C7 refers to motion of highest detail, i.e., the non-decomposed motion. C6, C5 and C4 refer to the motions after one, two and three levels of wavelets decomposition, respectively. In our implementation, we store the joint positions/orientations in polar coordinate, i.e., we represent each value by two angles, in order to reduce the storage requirement of the motion data. Hence, the error of each joint is expressed in terms of *degrees*.

From table 2, we could see that for the Left Up Arm (with the highest accumulated joint movement), the average data error for C6 is no more than 2.5 degrees, for C5 is less than 2.8 degrees and for C4 is less than 3.7 degrees. This result is very encouraging. As the maximum error is less than 3.7 degrees, the user would not notice the difference. As a comparison, the data error for [Naka99] can reach as high as 8 degrees. Therefore, we are about 1.2 times better than their method.

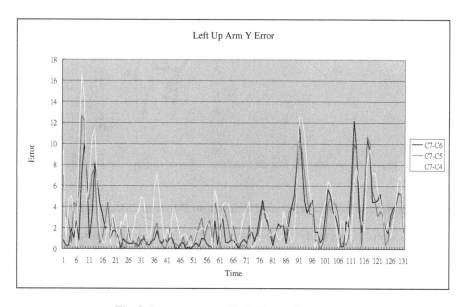

Fig. 3. Data error rate of Left Up arm in y axis

Table 2. Average data error for each level of detail

Axis of joint	Average data error for each level of detail		
	C6	**C5**	**C4**
Left Up Arm Z	2.306°	2.691°	3.655°
Left Up Arm X	0.2596°	0.292°	0.463°
Left Up Arm Y	2.483°	2.782°	3.586°

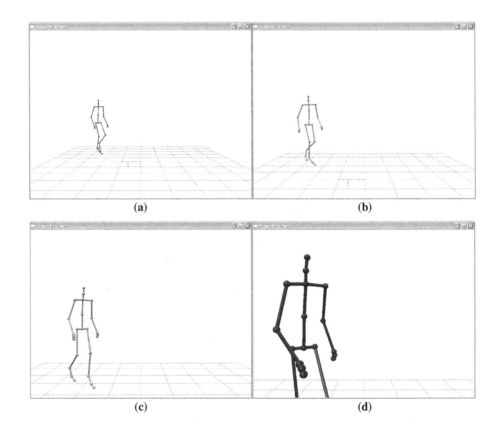

Fig. 4. Screen shots of motion transition between different levels of detail

4.2 Experiment 2 – Smoothness of Transition Between Different LoD's

In this experiment, we study the smoothness of switching between different LoD's of human motion. We start at a distant location from the articulated figure and we gradually move closer and closer to the figure. During this movement, the articulated figure will switch itself to a higher and higher LoD. To make the changes more visible, we use different colors to represent different levels of motion. Figure 4 shows a sequence of four major screen shots showing the motion transitions from a lower LoD to a higher one. If we do not use different colors to separate different LoD's, the user will not easily to notice the changes. In the trial run of our prototype, we could see that the transition is very smooth and natural.

5 Conclusion

In this paper, we have proposed an adaptive human motion animation method to support real-time rendering and transmission of human motions in web-based training systems. Experimental results show that our method could efficiently reduce the size of the human motion data. This is particularly useful to support distributing 3D animation data in web-based training systems. On the other hand, our method could also render human motion at different levels of detail. By taking advantage of this feature, a system could provide a promise between rendering performance and output quality.

Acknowledgements

The work described in this paper was partially supported by two CERG grants from the Research Grants Council of Hong Kong (RGC Reference No.: CityU 1133/04E and PolyU 5188/04E).

References

[Canó04] J. Canós, G. Alonso, and J. Jaen, "A Multimedia Approach to the Efficient Implementation and Use of Emergency Plans," *IEEE Multimedia*, **11**(3):106–110, July-Sept 2004.

[Burt76] N. Burtnyk and M. Wein, "Interactive Skeleton Techniques for Enhancing Motion Dynamics in Key Frame Animation," *Communications of the ACM*, **19**(10):564–569, 1976.

[Endo03] M. Endo, T. Yasuda, and S. Yokoi, "A Distributed Multiuser Virtual Space System," *IEEE Computer Graphics and Applications*, **23**(1), pp. 50-57, Jan.-Feb. 2003.

[H-Anim] H-Anim Specification, Available at: *http://h-anim.org/*.

[Hopp96] H. Hoppe, "Progressive Meshes," *Proc. of ACM SIGGRAPH'96*, pp. 99–108, 1996.

[Körn88] T. Körner, "Fourier Analysis," *Cambridge University Press*, 1988.

[Land98] J. Lander, "Working with Motion Capture File Formats," *Game Developer Magazine*, Jan. 1998.

[Lau97] R.W.H. Lau, D. To, and M. Green, "An Adaptive Multi-Resolution Modeling Technique Based on Viewing and Animation Parameters," *Proc. of IEEE VRAIS*, pp. 20-27, 1997.

[Li04] F.W.B. Li and R.W.H. Lau, "A Progressive Content Distribution Framework in Supporting Web-Based Learning," *Proc. of International Conference on Web-Based Learning*, pp. 75-82, Aug. 2004.

[Meye92] K. Meyer, H. Applewhite, and F. Biocca, "A Survey of Position Trackers," *Presence: Teleoperators and Virtual Environments*, **1**(2):173–200, 1992.

[Naka99] T. Naka, Y. Mochizuki, T. Hijiri, T. Cornish, and S. Asahara, "A Compression/Decompression Method for Streaming Based Humanoid Animation," *Proc. of Symposium on VRML*, pp.63-70, 1999.

[Pieg95] L. Piegl and W. Tiller, "The NURBS Book," *Springer*, 1995.

[Popo99] Z. Popović and A. Witkin, "Physically Based Motion Transformation," *Proc. of ACM SIGGRAPH'99*, pp. 11–20, 1999.

[Rose96] C. Rose, B. Guenter, B. Bodenheimer, and M. Cohen, "Efficient Generation of Motion Transitions Using Spacetime Constraints," *Proc. of ACM SIGGRAPH'96*, pp. 147–154, 1996.

[Sims95] D. Sims, "See How They Run: Modeling Evacuations in VR," *IEEE Computer Graphics and Applications*, **15**(2):11–13, Mar., 1995.

[Stol96] E. Stollnitz, T. Derose, and D. Salesin, "Wavelets for Computer Graphics: Theory and applications," *Morgan Kaufmann Publishers*, 1996.

[To99]   D. To, R.W.H. Lau, and M. Green, "A Method for Progressive and Selective Trans-
           mission of Multi-Resolution Models," *Proc. of ACM VRST*, pp. 88-95, Dec. 1999.

[Trei80]   A. Treisman and G. Gelade, "A Feature-Integration Theory of Attention," *Cognitive
           Psychology*, **12**:97–136, 1980.

[Wang91]   T. Wang and C. Chen, "A Combined Optimization Method for Solving the Inverse
           Kinematics Problems of Mechanical Manipulators," *IEEE Trans. on Robotics and
           Automation*, **7**(4):489– 499, Aug. 1991.

Experiences in Using an Automated System for Improving Students' Learning of Computer Programming*

M. Choy, U. Nazir, C.K. Poon, and Y.T. Yu

Department of Computer Science, City University of Hong Kong
{csmchoy, usmann, csckpoon, csytyu}@cityu.edu.hk

Abstract. Practical exercises and assignments are an integral part of programming course, which is a core basic skill required in computer science and best learned by doing. For effective learning, assignments have to be inspected and graded carefully but quickly so that students may benefit from the useful and timely feedback. This can be facilitated by automating the process using a specifically designed software system. PASS is such a system being developed in our department. A first version has been pilot run, with very encouraging responses from tutors and students. We observed that with this automated system, students can have their programs tested anytime, anywhere. They are encouraged to practice more without hesitation or embarrassment about their programming mistakes, and thus this learning environment can boost up their motivation to continue the practice of their programming skills. This paper aims at sharing the initial experiences we gained in using this system.

1 Introduction

Practical exercises and assignments are an integral part of courses in computer programming, which is a core skill required in Computer Science and best learned by doing. Calif and Goodwin [3] described their experiences of students who considered computer programming simply as a course of hurdle. There were severe motivation problems that inhibited them to practice more, and many students relied on memorization of program codes to pass the course.

From our experiences in teaching first year undergraduate students programming courses, we observed a significant discrepancy between the coursework marks and the programming skills actually gained by the majority of the class. It is becoming a common phenomenon for university students to submit a friend's work, a program with part of the code copied from others', a fusion of several programs, a joint effort group work, or even paid work as their own work in programming assignments. Using these tricks, getting a reasonable or even high mark might not be so difficult. Besides programming assignments, the other major contribution in assessment comes from the end-of-course examination. According to our statistics from the years 2000

---

* The work described in this paper was partially supported by Teaching Development Fund (project no. 6980041) from City University of Hong Kong.

R.W.H. Lau et al. (Eds.): ICWL 2005, LNCS 3583, pp. 267–272, 2005.

to 2003, the style of computer programming examination questions for first year undergraduate students is composed of writing small program segments (36.6%), tracing program for outputs (21.2%), completing a program statement or a program definition (20.4%), essay questions (10.6%), finding program errors (6.2%), and writing a complete program (5%). We note that it is rare to require students to write a complete program on their own. Thus, it is possible for students to get a good grade in the course even if they cannot write computer programs without assistance. These observations are similar to the findings in universities elsewhere [1, 2].

This year, we have introduced an automated programming assessment system, known as PASS, in several programming courses so that students may learn from the system by testing their programs. This way, we hope that students will feel that writing a correct program is within their reach and hence be encouraged to practice more on their programming skills instead of relying on plagiarism or code memorization to pass the course, thereby boosting their motivation in learning computer programming.

2   Using an Automated Programming Assessment System

A Web-based automated Programming Assignment aSsessment System (PASS) is currently used by several teaching staff at the Department of Computer Science, City University of Hong Kong. A preliminary prototype version [4] was initially built for demonstration purposes in early 2004, now it has been used in several programming courses. With PASS, everything is done on-line: setting up user accounts by the administrator, uploading exercises or assignments together with testing data by the tutor, downloading the exercises, and on-line program testing by the students.

For assignments, students are required to submit their programs to the system on line. Marking will start automatically when the tutor initiates the process by clicking a button. As soon as the assignments are marked, the tutor will receive the assessment report, and the students can get to know their results together with the feedback added by the tutor. Fig. 1 shows the interactions between a tutor and a student through the system. Detailed descriptions of this system can be found in [4]. PASS is used in laboratory sessions too. Each week, students will be writing 3-5 programs during the laboratory session. For laboratory exercises, there is no submission, but the system still provides test cases for selected exercises and a testing environment so that students can work with the exercises anytime, anywhere.

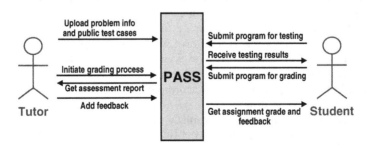

Fig. 1. Interactions between the tutor and student through PASS [4]

2.1 Using PASS for Assignment Assessment

When the problem given is an assignment, only a few test cases are made publicly available in PASS for students to test their programs before submission. These test cases belong to a subset of the complete set of test cases used in the assessment of this assignment. The rest of the test cases are hidden from the students in order to prevent any attempt to hard code the results into the submitted programs.

The automated testing environment makes possible the testing of students' programs with a lot more testing data than in the past when the programs were executed by hand. Hence, a more complete checking of correctness can be done. In addition, the assessment becomes more objective and consistent compared to manual marking.

2.2 Using PASS for Guidance to Learning

For laboratory exercises, the system will make available all test cases for students' own testing. Students can test their programs online, and use the instant feedback to improve their work and retest to check their progress. Students can continue to work on the exercises and have them checked by PASS even after their laboratory session.

We understand that there are many ways to define the logics to solve a programming problem. With the high degree of creativity of students, they might come up with a lot more ways to write a program than experienced programmers normally do. A large number of test cases are needed to test each program in order to uncover as many faults in their work as possible.

With the arrangement of weekly laboratory exercises and the automated testing of programs, PASS is able to help students in their learning of computer programming. Instead of waiting for the tutor to check their programs one by one, students can obtain instant feedback on the correctness of their programs. On a number of programming problems, by repeated usage of the system, students are able to develop better awareness of program correctness, and hence they will write programs more carefully. This has been observed by the tutors in our trial-run. By providing such continuing feedback to students who use PASS for their laboratory exercises, students are encouraged and motivated to practice more.

2.3 A Comparison Between Teaching Programming With and Without PASS

Before PASS was developed, during laboratory sessions, the tutor had to manually go through students' program codes to make sure they were correct. Testing programs with many test cases during a 1-2 hours laboratory sessions is not quite feasible. Therefore, usually the tutor would only use a few predefined test cases to test the students' programs. Sometimes the tutor might have to help students in debugging. With only a few test cases, it is likely that the program still contained errors even after being checked by the tutor. With this approach, not much could be done within the laboratory session, and it was almost always impossible to check everyone's work. Students would then be responsible to test their own programs with additional test cases they created, and consult the tutor after class if they encountered problems. Unfortunately, most students did not know how to create adequate test cases on their own. In this way, students had to be adequately self-motivated to continue working with the exercises outside the laboratory session. Without further supervision outside the class, it was not surprising to see that motivation usually dropped dramatically when students started to lag behind in the scheduled weekly exercises.

Now, students can learn under the provision of feedback from PASS, and more exercises than before are given to students each week. Besides, the manual checking of programs by the tutor is now changed to automatic checking by PASS with a lot more test cases, allowing more thorough checking. PASS is responsible for the testing, and the instant feedback given to students provide them with informative clues about how to make corrections. It was observed that students were more motivated under this environment, and with extended supervision, there were fewer excuses to lag behind.

3 Effectiveness of Learning with PASS

Learning computer programming is best done by practice. As the tutor has made the weekly exercises with test cases available in PASS, students can work with the exercises anytime, anywhere. Besides, since instant feedback is available as students test their programs with PASS, they can make use of the feedback information to revise their programs and submit for testing again. In this way, learning to write programs is more effective within such an interactive and progressive learning cycle [4].

A number of similar automated programming assignment assessment systems have been described in the literature [5, 6]. Some of these systems emphasize on system performance and reducing manual work of the tutor and do not elaborate on the effectiveness of learning from the students' perspective [5]. Some other systems such as Online Judge [6] aims at challenging the users: the test cases are hidden and the users are only informed of whether their programs are correct or not. The system does not tell the user on which test cases the program works correctly and on which test cases the program fails. In contrast, PASS is expressly designed to help beginners to discover any problems in their programs. In the first pilot run of PASS, there was a response of "correct" or "wrong" for each execution of the program with respect to a test case. With a thoughtful design of test cases, we believe that each test case may help the students to pin-point to some possible logical faults in the program that cause the error. By adding annotations to each test case in the next release, the feedback returned to students will better help them understand their logical errors and thereby make the appropriate corrections.

During the semester, a tutor has closely observed two students in their laboratory sessions. Both students were slow learners and had no programming experience prior to taking the course. These two students worked on every laboratory exercise and used the feedback from PASS to revise their programs. Their progress was slow, but steady and encouraging. They found the availability of PASS suited their learning pace, and the testing environment provided by PASS provided them with useful feedback when revising their programs. Towards the end of semester, both students were able to write long programs on their own. We believe that this would not have been possible without an automated assessment system such as PASS.

PASS has been in operation for two semesters in four computer programming courses. A survey was conducted at the end of the first semester to evaluate the usefulness of this system from the perspective of students in two courses (the other two courses are still ongoing). The results are summarized as follows.

- The majority of the students reported that they used PASS about 5 times a week to check their lab exercises. On average, a student uses the system about 7 times a week, and a few students used the system more than 30 times a week.

- About 70% of the students reported that PASS did help them to reveal bugs.

- When asked to compare their understanding of lab exercises with PASS and without PASS, more than 80% of students considered PASS quite helpful or very helpful in their lab exercises, and about one out of four students requested to have PASS available for every program in the lab exercises. (We had intentionally left out some lab exercises which were not made available in PASS.)

- Students were asked to rate PASS on a scale of 1 to 5, and the distribution of their ratings is shown in Table 1. We note that about two-third of the students gave PASS a rating of 4 or above. It is encouraging to know that most students appreciated the assistance from PASS in their learning of computer programming.

Table 1. Distribution of students' rating of PASS (5 being the best rating)

Rating	1	2	3	4	5
Percentage (%)	3.0	8.9	24.4	50.4	13.3

- In their written comments, most students expressed their view that PASS was very helpful in facilitating their learning process. Below are some comments from students extracted from the survey (minimally grammatically edited):
  - I can work more independently and it gives me confidence when I got all correct. Little by little, I build up my own reliance!
  - Very good, the fast response can help me to follow up errors at once.
  - Build up my confidence.
  - Make the correctness of our programs higher, even without tutor's help.
  - Sometimes I thought my program was correct and actually it is incorrect and PASS helps me to know more about my program, so that I can revise again.
  - It's very useful because the test cases sometimes can notify me to think more carefully when coding.
  - It can help me to check my lab exercises by myself. It can encourage me to do all the lab exercises. So it is very useful.
  - We can know the bugs immediately; it increases the rate of learning.
  - It lets me know that my program still has bugs even after I tested it carefully.
  - I can check the answer and see any flaws in my algorithm or implementation.

These comments demonstrate that PASS has been well accepted by the students in assisting their learning in computer programming.

4 Conclusion and Further Work

This paper has reported the effective use of PASS in assisting the progressive learning of computer programming. PASS allows a tailor-made learning pace and style for students. It has provided a quick and convenient channel for students to test their work without manual involvement. Instant feedback to students encourages them to enhance their programming skills. Tutors observed that during laboratory sessions, some students simply used the system as a compiler and debugger without first test running the programs themselves, even when their program still had syntactic errors.

The introduction of PASS has made the learning of computer programming more rewarding than before. Both tutors and students are encouraged to witness the mobility and flexibility of learning supervised by PASS. We have used PASS in four programming courses with favourable student responses. In view of this, we plan to extend the use of PASS in more programming courses.

Currently, PASS performs the checking of outputs by simple textual comparison. Therefore, students must adhere to a fixed input and output format when writing their programs in order to satisfy the checking requirement. Working with such formatting constraints can be quite a hassle, as negligible differences between the outputs can result in the program being treated as "incorrect". Some students found such a restriction frustrating, and a number of them requested for higher flexibility. Presently, to circumvent this limitation, the tutor manually compared the outputs when such a claim is raised by students. We plan to improve this aspect of the system in the next release of the system. Moreover, we plan to attach annotation to each test case so that the feedback will become more informative and provide more concrete assistance for students to revise their programs, and debugging will become more interesting.

References

1. Woit, D., Mason, D.: Effectiveness of Online Assessment. SIGCSE Bulletin, Vol. 35.1 (2003) 137-141
2. Sheard, J., Dick, M., Markham, S., Macdonald, I., Walsh, M.: Cheating and Plagiarism - Perceptions and practices of first year IT students. Proc. 7th Annual Conference on Innovation and Technology in Computer Science Education, Denmark (2002) 183-187
3. Califf, M., Goodwin, M.: Testing Skills and Knowledge - Introducing a Laboratory Exam in CS1. SIGCSE Bulletin, Vol. 34.1 (2002) 217-221
4. Chong, S.L., Choy, M.: Towards a Progressive Learning Environment for Programming Courses. Int Conf of Web Learning: New Horizon in Web-based Learning, (2004) 200-205
5. Luck, M., Joy, M.: A Secure On-line Submission System. Software Practice and Experience, Vol. 29(8) (1999) 721-740
6. Kurnia, A, Lim, A., Cheang, B.: Online Judge. Computers & Education, Vol. 36(4) (2001) 299-315

Automatic Leveling System for E-Learning Examination Pool Using Entropy-Based Decision Tree

Shu-Chen Cheng[1], Yueh-Min Huang[2], Juei-Nan Chen[2], and Yen-Ting Lin[1]

[1] Department of Computer Science and Information Engineering,
Southern Taiwan University of Technology, Tainan 710, Taiwan
kittyc@mail.stut.edu.tw, ricky014789@yahoo.com.tw
[2] Department of Engineering Science,
National Cheng Kung University, Tainan 701, Taiwan
huang@mail.ncku.edu.tw, nan@www.mmn.es.ncku.edu.t

Abstract. In this paper, we propose an automatic leveling system for e-learning examination pool using the algorithm of the decision tree. The automatic leveling system is built to automatically level each question in the examination pool according its difficulty. Thus, an e-learning system can choose questions that are suitable for each learner according to individual background. Not all attributes are relevant to the classification, in other words, the decision tree tells the importance of each attribute.

1 Introduction

Due to the rapid growth of information and communication technologies, the education environment has being enriched with those technologies and become more diversified. Obviously, the Internet-based environment has been rapidly replacing the traditional lecture-based one due to the factor of providing the multimedia-enhanced learning anytime and anywhere. Nowadays, there are more and more instructors who have been making Internet-based courseware or even curriculum of distance learning for extending education purpose. In fact, many research works have focused on employing multimedia and Internet technologies to produce more attractive or effective course contents. Besides the effective courseware, we believe that developing an effective learning assessment is another key for quality-assured e-Learning. Due to its important role, some researchers have developed some techniques for the area, such as automatic classifier for assessment items [7], question databases [8], assessment items for cooperative items [9], etc. In [7], they design an automatic classifier for Chinese assessment items in terms of particular keywords. Sumitomo et al. also employed keyword search to analyze data in their designed question-answer database. In [9], he further divided the assessments into self and peer parts for collaborative learning purpose. However, how to design an assessment with an individual background involved is still an open issue.

Many studies have been working on the development of individual course content by using artificial intelligence (AI), data mining, as well as agent technologies [1][2]. Their common purpose is to correctly assist a learner to achieve an optimal learning effectiveness according to his/her current background. Similarly, the design of an effective assessment must be able to examine an individual learning status so that an

R.W.H. Lau et al. (Eds.): ICWL 2005, LNCS 3583, pp. 273–278, 2005.

instructor can properly progress his/her teaching. In other words, it is desired to design an individual assessment which can explore the capability of an individual student. In 2004, Büchner and Patterson suggested platforms to keep track of learners' activities including content viewed, time spent and quiz results [3]; Kuo et al. proposed a real-time learning behavior mining algorithm [4].

Over the last years, we have witnessed an explosive growth of e-learning. Internet has been widely used in various fields. More and more learning contents have been published and shared over the Internet. Therefore, how to progress an efficient learning process becomes a critical issue. For example, there are various applications to facilitate learners, especially for distance education. However, general learning system cannot provide suitable learning materials to achieve efficient learning. More and more people try to apply the artificial intelligence techniques, such as the agent technology [1][2], to the application of distance learning. In 2003, Fei et al. designed the question classification for e-learning using artificial neural network [5]. In 2004, Merceron et al. proposed a question answering mining platform [6]. In this paper, an automatic leveling system for e-learning examination pool is proposed.

The remainder of the paper is organized as follows. In Section 2, the function of e-learning examination pool is described. In Section 3, we propose the automatic leveling system for e-learning examination pool using the algorithm of the decision tree. Finally, the conclusions are made in Section 4.

2 E-Learning Examination Pool

An example is described by the values of attributes and Boolean values for the classification of the examples. In Table 1, learners with individual backgrounds are divided

Table 1. An example of learners with individual backgrounds

Learner	Attributes						
	Educational background	Department	Institution	Hobby	Occupation	Answer
No.1	University	CSIE	TKU	Computer	Student	Correct
No.2	Vocational school	ME	LIT	Playball	Doctor	Wrong
No.3	Institute of technology	AI	NTCB	Internet	Civil servant	Wrong
No.4	Institute	EE	NCKU	Swimming	Student	Correct
No.5	Vocational school	TI	TKCVS	Shopping	Service trade	Wrong
No.6	University	ME	NCCU	Reading	Student	Wrong
No.7	University	AI	CYCU	Computer	Lawyer	Correct
No.8	University	CDIE	PU	Shopping	Service trade	Wrong
No.9	Academic	EE	NTU	Fishing	Teacher	Correct
No.10	Institute	EE	FJU	Movie	Student	Correct
⋮	⋮	⋮	⋮	⋮	⋮	⋮

into two groups. One is for learners whose answer is correct and the other is for those whose answer is wrong. For each question in the examination pool, all learners' behaviors can be recorded as shown in Table 1. After automatic leveling system is built, each question would be leveled automatically according its difficulty and an e-learning system can choose questions that are suitable for each learner.

3 Automatic Leveling System

The automatic leveling system is built to automatically level each question in the examination pool according its difficulty. If most learners with similar background can answer a question correctly, the question is labeled as "easy", and vice versa. Thus, an e-learning system can choose questions that are suitable for each learner according to individual background. As shown in figure 1, the input of the automatic leveling system is the values of attributes and Boolean values for the classification of the examples. The output of the automatic leveling system is a decision tree. Figure 2 illustrates the automatic leveling system can automatically level each question so that a suitable question can be chosen for a new learner and the new data can feedback the result to the automatic leveling system. How to build the automatic leveling system using the algorithm of decision tree is illustrated in Section 3.1 and Section 3.2.

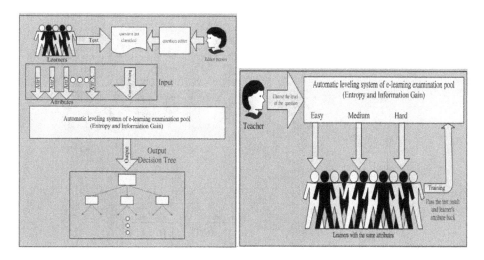

Fig. 1. System Architecture of Automatic Leveling System

Fig. 2. Purpose of Automatic Leveling System

3.1 Entropy

Entropy measures the impurity of a data set S and is defined as:

$$\text{Entropy (S)} = -P_+ \log_2 P_+ - P_- \log_2 P_- \tag{1}$$

where P+ is the proportion of positive examples while P- is the proportion of negative ones. The entropy of S is zero when the examples are all positive or all negative. The entropy reaches its maximum value of 1 when half of examples are positive and half are negative.

3.2 Decision Tree and Information Gain

In Figure 3, we see a tree used to determine whether a learner's answer is correct or wrong. This kind of tree is called a decision tree [10][11]. A decision tree takes in the attribute values and outputs a Boolean decision. Once a decision tree is constructed, we start at the root node to check the attribute value. Based on the attribute value, the branch labeled with the corresponding value is chosen. Continue checking the next attribute value until a leaf node is reached.

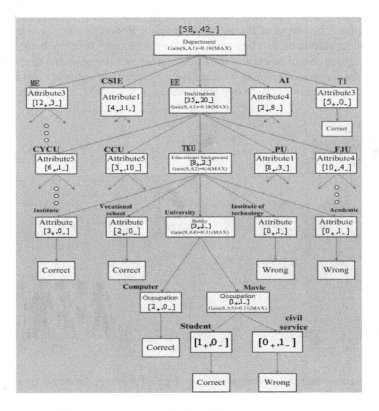

Fig. 3. A decision tree for classifying learners' answers

Decision tree induction involves a set of training data to generate a decision tree that can classify the training data correctly. If the training data represent the entire space of possible data adequately, the decision tree will then correctly classify new input data as well. The best-known decision tree induction algorithm is ID3, which was proposed by Quinlan in 1980s. The algorithm builds a decision tree from top down and finds the shortest possible decision tree to classify the training data correctly. The method used by the algorithm to determine which attribute to be chosen for each node is to select the attribute that provides the greatest information gain at each stage [10][11]. A perfect attribute divides the examples into sets that are all positive or all negative. The information gain of an attribute tells us how close to perfect the attribute is. Information gain is defined as the reduction in entropy and calculated by:

$$Gain(S, A) = Entropy(S) - \sum_{V \in values(A)} \frac{|S_V|}{|S|} Entropy(S_V) \qquad (2)$$

Where Entropy(S) denotes the entropy of a data set S and can be calculated by equation 1. $Gain(S, A)$ is the expected reduction in entropy due to sorting S on attribute A. Looking at the attribute "Department" as shown in figure 3, we can calculate the entropy for the data set and its subsets. The total information gain, $Gain(S, A)$, is defined as the entropy of the set minus the weighted sum of the entropies of subsets. Hence, at this stage, the information gain for the attribute "Department" is 0.16. Considering another attribute "Institution", the information gain for this attribute is 0.02. After considering all of the attributes, we found the attribute "Department" provides the greatest gain; therefore, the attribute "Department" is placed as the root at this stage. Apply the method recursively until a decision tree is constructed.

4 Conclusions

In this paper, we propose an automatic leveling system for e-learning examination pool using the algorithm of the decision tree. After the decision tree is constructed, we can see that not all attributes are relevant to the classification; therefore, the classification might be made by only 2 or 3 attributes. In other words, the decision tree tells the importance of each attribute. Unfortunately, it is quite possible that even when vital information is missing, the decision tree learning algorithm will find a decision tree that is consistent with all the examples. This is because the algorithm uses the irrelevant attributes. In the future, some technique to eliminate the dangers of over-fitting must be developed in order to select a tree with good prediction performance.

References

1. Y.M. Huang, J.N. Chen, K.T. Wang, C.H. Fu, "Agent-Based Web Learning System," IEEE Learning Technology Newsletter, Vol. 6, Issue 2, pp. 38 – 41, April 2004
2. Y.M. Huang, J.N. Chen, S.C. Cheng, W.C. Chu, "Agent-Based Web Learning System Applying Dynamic Fuzzy Petri Net," Proceeding of International Conference on Web-Based Learning, pp. 338 – 345, 2004
3. Alex G. Büchner, David Patterson, "Personalised E-Learning Opportunities", Proceedings of 15th International Workshop on Database and Expert Systems Applications, pp.410 – 414, 2004

4. Y.H. Kuo, J.N. Chen, Y.M. Huang, "Real-time Learning Behavior Mining Algorithm," IEEE Learning Technology Newsletter, Vol. 6, Issue 4, pp. 89 – 92, October 2004
5. Ting Fei, Wei jhy Heng, Kim Chuan Toh, Tian Qi, "Question Classification for E-learning by Artificial Neural Network", ICICS-PCM, 2003
6. Duval, P., Merceron, A., Rinderknecht, C., Scholl, M., "LeVinQam: a question answering mining platform", ITHET 2004. Proceedings of the Fifth International Conference on, 2004
7. Chein B.C. And Liau S.T., "An Automatic Classifier for Chinese Items Categorization", Proceedings of 2004 National Conference on Artificial Intelligence and Its Application, Taiwan, 2004
8. Chisa Sumitomo, Akira Okada and Yahiko Kambayashi, "Design and Evaluation of lecture Support Functions for Question Databases", Proceedings of 1st International Conference on Web-based Learning, ICWL2002, Hong Kong, China, 2002
9. Park C., "Development of Self and Peer Assessment Items in Web-based Cooperative Learning", Proceedings of 3rd International Conference on Web-based Learning, ICWL2004, China, 2004
10. Stuart Russell, Peter Norvig, "Artificial Intelligence: A Modern Approach", Prentice Hall, pp.531-544, 1995
11. Ben Coppin, "Artificial Intelligence Illuminated", Jones and Bartlett, pp.276-286, 2004

A Web-Based Environment to Improve Teaching and Learning of Computer Programming in Distance Education

S.C. Ng, S.O. Choy, R. Kwan, and S.F. Chan

School of Science and Technology, The Open University of Hong Kong
scng@ouhk.edu.hk

Abstract. Learning computer programming is not an easy task. Students need to spend hours doing practical activities in order to comprehend the techniques of writing computer programs and beginners usually face a number of obstacles associated with installing and using a compiler or integrated development environment. This paper introduces an online web-based system that provides an interactive integrated environment for students doing programming activities and coursework in a distance learning institution. The interactive system provides students with timely and effective feedback about programming activities without the need to have instructors and students meet at the same time and the same place. The web-based system provides students with an editing, compiling, testing and debugging environment for learning computer programming on the web. Instructors can monitor the learning progress of students, compile the student's program and view the error messages through the student's workplace in the online system.

1 Introduction

Computer programming courses are core components of many university programmes in Computer Science, Engineering, Information Technology, and other related fields. The Open University of Hong Kong (OUHK) offers three courses on computer programming at different levels for undergraduate programmes. The population of students taking programming courses is also large. In OUHK, a first year programming course enrolled over 400 students in the past academic year.

Teaching computer programming has never been a straightforward process. Programming is a skill that requires practice. In order to strengthen students' programming knowledge, students need to do a lot of programming practice. Therefore, practical activities play an important role in the learning process [1]. Traditional web based learning systems have not made full use of the advanced Internet computing technology to improve the quality of teaching and learning. Many people use technology simply to replicate the existing ways of teaching and learning at a distance, such as posting online teaching materials and providing electronic submission for the students' assignments [2]. These kinds of learning systems do not

R.W.H. Lau et al. (Eds.): ICWL 2005, LNCS 3583, pp. 279–290, 2005.
© Springer-Verlag Berlin Heidelberg 2005

provide added value in improving the quality of teaching and learning computer programming in distance education.

With the increase of students taking fundamental programming courses and increasingly limited teaching resources, the tutoring time spent on each student is reduced. As a result, students may suffer from the lack of timely feedback from their instructors. It may lead to poor results in learning computer programming. In a traditional university education setting where students can often meet their fellow students and instructors, the teaching process is significantly improved by conducting practical workshops in which teachers are present to serve the learning needs. Students can also interact with their fellow students in a computer laboratory to enhance the learning process.

However, in a distance learning setting, the education process is distributed. For most of the time, students and instructors are geographically remote from each other. Students are given a set of study materials that consists of traditional textbooks and printed study units. To enable students to carry out programming activities at home, a set of software including a compiler and program development environment is also provided. However, it is both time consuming and frustrating for beginners to learn how to use the integrated development environment (IDE), set it up, and become familiar with the programming environment [3]. According to Proulx [4], the first course in programming is a major stumbling block for novice programmers. Most beginners find problems in setting the environment variables, such as PATH and CLASSPATH, during the installation of Java Development Kit (JDK) in their machines. Some may fail to manage a suitable Java integrated development environment (IDE). It was not uncommon to find that some students are still unable to install the Java JDK properly even after ten weeks of study in an introductory Java programming course in OUHK.

Besides, distance learners spend most of the time working alone. They usually have little or no contact with their fellow students. When they find a problem during their learning, they usually ask their instructors through the telephone or email. It is difficult for the students to express their programming problem clearly in a textual message or vocal communication with their instructors. This kind of debugging process could be prolonged and ineffective. From an instructor's perspective, it is not easy to keep track of students' study progress and give timely feedback to them in a distance learning setting.

This paper describes how the web-based system adopts the Internet technology in a more efficient way to help both instructors and students to teach and learn computer programming respectively in a distance learning environment. Our web-based system aims to improve the effectiveness of teaching elementary Java programming in a distance learning environment. The system provides a virtual workplace for performing programming activities. It provides an online and integrated environment for writing, compiling and testing programs. Students just need to use an Internet-connected computer to access the system for doing programming activities. They don't need to prepare and set up the whole programming environment and IDE in their own machines. The system's file server stores all the student's intermediate and submitted work. The system allows students to do practical exercises by filling in a template-like programming editing area. When a student wants to compile and run the program, the system will generate the resulting output in Java Archive format (JAR) and return it to the student. The student can run the program in his or her own machine. In case compilation errors occur in the program, the system will generate useful and helpful hints for students to debug the program. The system also includes a communication tool between students and tutors. Whenever a student needs further help, the instructors can directly access the student's workplace, compile the student's program and view the error messages through the online system. All student activities will be recorded in the system so that instructors can use the log data to keep track of the student's progress. In addition, the system provides syntax highlighting in editing program code, which could help novice programmers understand and remember the program code more easily. In short, the new system makes use of the current Internet computing technology to provide an online environment for practical programming activities.

Related work has been found in the literature. CourseMaster [5] was developed as a computer-based tutoring system, which mainly provides features for automatic assessment handling of students' work. Since it is not a web-based system, students still need to learn how to use the IDE first, and that could hinder the students' learning process. ELP [6] provides a web-based interface for students to do programming activities. However, ELP provides limited support for students to edit their programs and get help from the instructors.

The organization of this paper is as follows. Section 2 of this paper shows the system architecture. Section 3 describes the system overview with the functions for both students and instructors. Section 4 discusses the system workflow with the descriptions of user interface generation and compilation result generation respectively. Section 5 discusses the pilot run of the system as a programming learning environment in the presentation of an OUHK course. Finally, conclusions are drawn in section 6.

2   System Architecture

Fig. 1 shows the overview of the architecture of our system. A Content Management System (CMS) runs on the Apache Web Server with MySQL database and provides basic management functions of the website. The system consists of four main sub-modules written by PHP scripts — Activity Parser, Activity Compiler, Student Activity Logger and Activity Log Analyzer — to perform the online programming activities and student performance monitoring service on the web.

There are several interactions between client and server sides. When the client browses an activity, a request will be issued to the server to access a particular programming activity. By using the Activity Parser module, the server parses the Activity XML and loads all the necessary files from the file server. If the request is not a student's first attempt at a particular activity, the Activity Parser module will load the previous work from the Student Activity file. After the parsing and loading

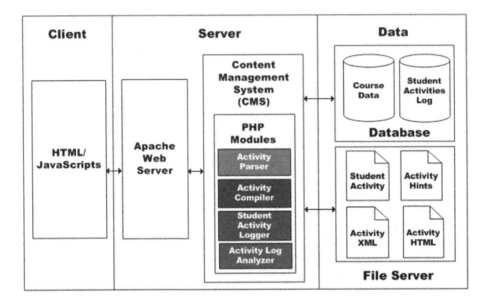

Fig. 1. System Architecture

process, the server will send the activity content in the form of HTML format back to the client. Other than loading the activity, the server also allows the client to compile their programs online. After receiving the client side compilation request, the server compiles the program from the student's working directory. If no error is found, the server will generate a Java Archive (JAR) file for the student to download. Otherwise, an error log will be generated in the current activity, and the error message will be passed back to the client for debugging.

All of the above interactions will be captured by the Student Activity Logger and stored in the Student Activities Log database. By using the Activity Log Analyzer, the tutors are allowed to access the student's performance. The Activity Log Analyzer will make use of the Course Data and Student Activities Log Data to perform those analyses for monitoring the student's progress.

3   System Overview

This section describes how students and instructors interact with our system. Our online system provides both students and instructors with an environment for learning and teaching programming on the web. Instructors can create and upload the programming activities materials to the system through the web browser. The instructors can upload the activities description file, activities template file and the hint files. Activities description file provides the basic description and information about the activities; activities template file provides students with a template to work

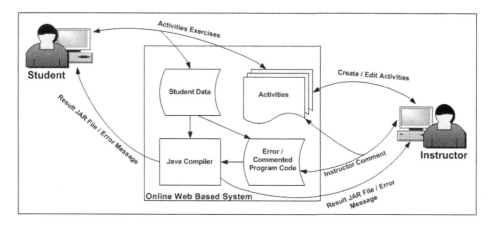

Fig. 2. The Web Based System Overview

on an activity; and hint file provides students with a sample output of the required program for reference.

Fig. 2 illustrates the interaction between the students and instructors on the web-based system. Students can navigate through the activities and attempt each of them. Students are allowed to compile the program at the server side, and the server will send back the resulting ".class" files of the activity packed with other libraries in a Java Archive (JAR) file. In case of syntax errors in the program, the corresponding error messages will be sent back to the student. If a student finds any problem in handling the activities, he or she can send a help message to the respective instructor for help. The system will then copy the student's program code to a temporary directory. When the respective instructor logs into the system, he or she can view the error code directly from the student's temporary workplace. The instructor can compile the program and see the error messages from the online compiler. After fixing the program errors, the instructor can just reply to the student's message and give comments in the program code. The student can view the instructor's comments and suggestions in the reply.

3.1 Student View of the System

Fig. 3 shows how the students walk through and perform the programming activities online. Students can navigate the programming activities by using the web browser. After selecting the programming activity, a text editor is provided for the student to edit the program code. After the student finishes editing the program with the given template, he or she can compile the program by clicking the compile link on the web page. The program code will be sent to the server side for compilation. If there is no error during the compilation process, the system will automatically generate the executable Java Archive (JAR) file back to the student. Otherwise, the system will generate an error message back to the student for debugging. If the student has

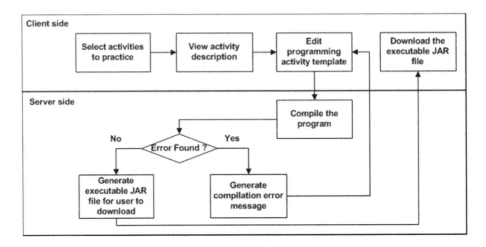

Fig. 3. The flow of performing online programming activities

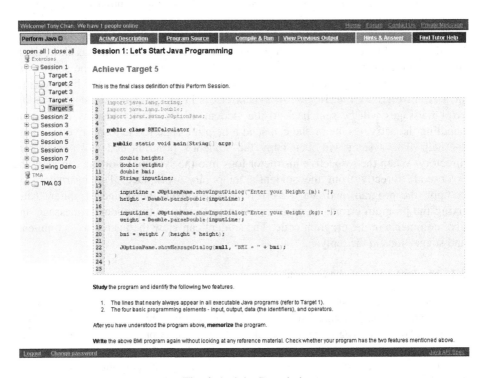

Fig. 4. Activity Description

installed the Java Runtime Environment (JRE) in his or her own machine, he or she can simply click the "Open" button to run the program immediately. In addition, a reset function is also provided for students to reset the activities back to the original programming template.

Fig. 4 shows the "Activity Description" interface — students are provided with detailed information about an activity. Fig. 5 shows the "Program Source" interface —

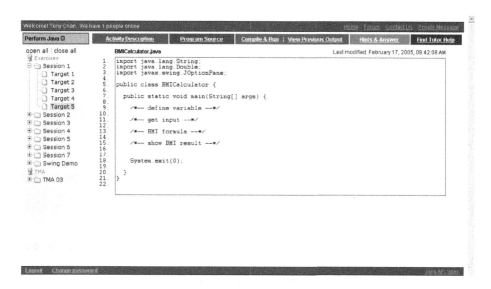

Fig. 5. Program Source Area

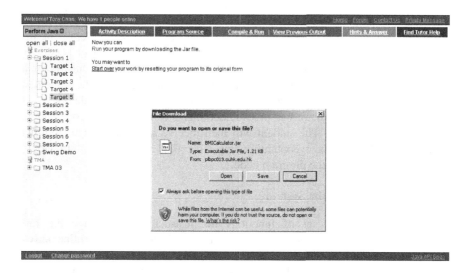

Fig. 6. Compile and Run the program

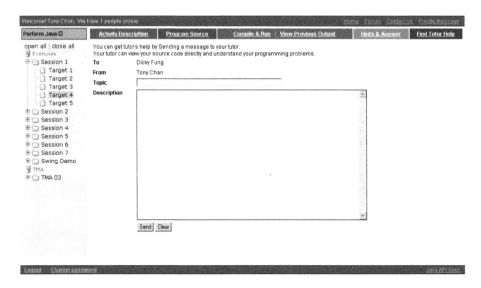

Fig. 7. Find Tutor Help

this area provides a simple editing area for students to write and develop their programs. Fig. 6 shows the "Compile & Run" interface — this area allows students to compile and run their programs directly. The "Hints & Answer" interface provides a sample program output for students' reference.

When a student encounters problems in doing the programming activities, he or she can request help directly through the system. By using the help function, instructors can view the student's program code directly. The student only needs to send a help message to their instructors by clicking the "Find Tutor Help" link in the system. The interface for "Find Tutor Help" is shown in Fig. 7. His or her program will then be copied to a temporary folder inside the server. Once the instructor logs into the system, he or she can directly view the help message from the student with the program codes. The instructor can then compile the program in the system and view the errors. The instructor can provide comments in the program code and reply to the student's message. The student will then receive a reply message from his or her instructor. The message contains a hyperlink that allows student to view the instructor's comments in the program code.

3.2 Instructor View of the System

The system provides a set of functions for instructors to manage the online programming activities. The instructors can create, edit or delete the online activities through our system. It provides a simple interface for instructors to upload the online programming activities files to the server (see Fig. 8). An activity contains three types of file; they are activity description files, activity programming code template files

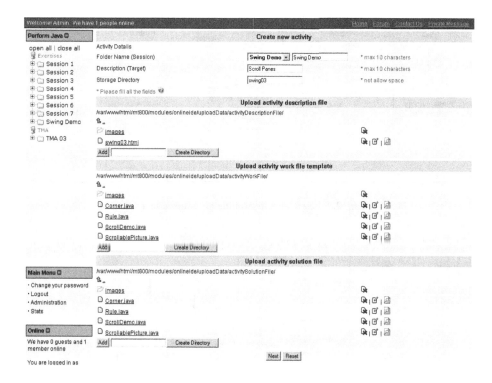

Fig. 8. Interface for instructor to create new activity

and activity hint files. Activity description files are mainly composed of HTML code and related image files. The system also provides a simple HTML text editor for instructors to edit the activity description files online. The activity programming code template files provide students with programming templates to work on as they practice. The files will be loaded into the student data folder when the students first attempts or resets the activity. In order to provide students with a sample output for reference, instructors can upload the activity hints file to the server so that the student can view the activities sample outputs. The hint files then will compile into Java class files and pack into an executable JAR file for students to download.

4 System Workflow

In our system, each activity is described and controlled by an eXtensible Markup Language (XML) file. The Activity Parser module in Fig. 1 is responsible for generating exercises from the XML files and related activities files to be converted into HTML format. Fig. 9 shows the flow of the activity interface that can be generated from the server.

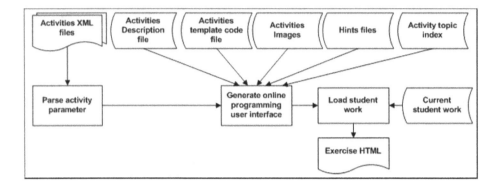

Fig. 9. Steps to generate online programming activity

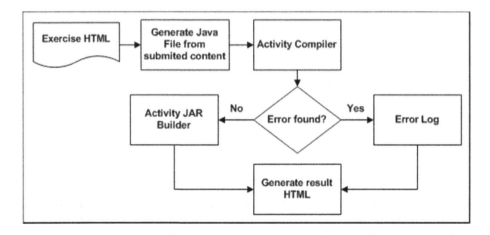

Fig. 10. Generate compilation result

After the students log into the system, there is a tree menu for students to choose which activities to practice. The activities tree menu is generated from the activities XML files. The system will parse the entire activities XML files and then generate the tree menu dynamically.

When the student selects a particular activity to practice, the system will generate the user interface according to the activity XML file information. The activity XML file will provide all the information about the activity such as activity description file name, activity template code file name and main class name. If the student has attempted the activity before, the system will load the student program code back into the simple editor. Finally, the activity HTML will be sent to the student.

The Activity Compiler in Fig. 1 is responsible for compiling, building and making a JAR file from a student's program code. Fig. 10 shows the workflow of how the server generates compilation results. After the student finishes editing the program code, he or she can then click the "Compile and Run" link to send the program to the server side for compilation. When the server receives the student's program code, the server will generate the Java files first. Then the system will rely on the activity XML file instruction to compile the Java files. If no error is found, the system will execute the jar command to make an executable JAR file for the student to download. In order to let the client side computer run the JAR files easily, the executable JAR file, which has been sent back to the student is described by the Multipurpose Internet Mail Extension (MIME) type content type "application/java-archive". The student can then double click the JAR file to run the program and view the output result directly.

5 Discussion

We have piloted the use of this web-based system as a learning tool for the course *MT800 Information Technology and Software Development* in OUHK. Most students in this course do not have prior Java programming experience. We used the system as an online, interactive learning environment for students to learn Java programming. The students were given a set of online activities to work on at their own pace. Since the materials can be assessed easily through the Internet, students can learn programming with greater flexibility, anytime and anywhere. Students are not required to set the environment variables such as PATH and CLASSPATH when installing JDK in their machines. The only requirement is to have the Java Runtime Environment (JRE) — all the programs can be run immediately in students' machines. Ninety percent of students in the course *MT800* had tried the online practical activities and all agreed that the system makes writing and compiling Java programs much easier. It was encouraging to see 100% submission of Java programming assignments, which indicates all students were confident in handling Java programming assessment. In the past, the normal submission rate of Java programming assignments was around 80%.

6 Conclusions and Future Work

The proposed system provides an online and interactive environment for students to learn programming at a distance. Using this online system, students are not required to install Java Integrated Development Environment (IDE) and set up suitable environment variables for program compilation. Students can get hints and extra help easily through the new system. Once the students can gain access to the Internet, they can use this online system to develop their programs and learn programming anytime and anywhere.

This paper reports the progress of the development status of the online and interactive system for teaching and learning programming. Currently, our system provides basic functions for students to do programming activities. In the future, more advanced features will be added to the system. Further investigation will be concentrated on the use of an intelligent software agent [7] that is able to monitor and collect information about students' performance. The software agent works for the instructors and tutors to aid early detection of problems in the course delivery and give suitable advice to students in learning how to program.

Acknowledgments

The authors would like to thank the OUHK and Education and Manpower Bureau (EMB) for the Earmarked Research Grant (Ref: 9004/03H) that allowed that the system to be developed.

References

1. Thomas, P. G. and Paine, C. B. (2000). "How student learn to program: Observation of practical work based on tasks completed", Research Report 2000/03, Department of Computing, The Open University, United Kingdom.
2. Syed, M. R. (2001). "Diminishing the Distance in Distance Education", IEEE Multimedia, July-Sept. 2001, pp. 18-20.
3. Lewis, S. F., & Watkins, M. (2001, 22nd January). "Using Java tools to teach Java, the integration of Bluej and CourseMaster for delivery over the Internet", proceedings of the 5th Java in the Computing Curriculum Conference (JICC 5), South Bank University, UK.
4. Proulx V. K. (2000). "Programming Patterns and Design Patterns in the Introductory Computer Science Course", in SIGCSE Bulletin Conference Proceedings of the Thirty First SIGSCE Symposium on Computer Science Education, Vol. 32, No. 1, pg. 80-84, ACM Press, 2000.
5. Foxley, E., Higgins, C., Tsintsifas, A. and Symeonidis, P. (1999). The Ceilidh-CourseMaster System, The University of Nottingham, UK., available online: http://www.cs.nott.ac.uk/~cmp/more_info/html/CMIntro.htm
6. Nghi Truong, Peter Bancroft & Paul Roe (2003). "ELP – A WEB ENVIRONMENT FOR LEARNING TO PROGRAM", ACM International Conference Proceeding Series archive, Proceedings of the twenty-sixth Australasian computer science conference on Conference in research and practice in information technology - Volume 16 Pages: 255 – 264.
7. Caglayan, A. and Harrison C. (1997). Agent Sourcebook: A Complete Guide to Desktop, Internet, and Intranet Agent. John Wiley & Sons.

The Design and Implementation of Digital Signal Processing Virtual Lab Based on Components*

Jianxin Wang[1], Lijuan Liu[1], and Weijia Jia[2]

[1] School of Information Science and Engineering, Central South University,
ChangSha, 410083, China
jxwang@mail.csu.edu.cn
[2] Department of Computer Engineering and Information Technology,
City University of Hong Kong, Kowloon, HongKong
itjia@cityu.edu.hk

Abstract. This paper proposed the design and implementation of digital signal processing virtual lab (DSPVL) based on components. In the DSPVL, all the virtual instruments are developed as components and implemented as Java Beans, which improve the developing efficiency, the reuse of software and make the system be maintained and expanded easily. This paper also introduces the characters and architecture of user platform and illustrates the key design and implementation technologies. In the DSPVL, we developed a lot of components for the experiments in Digital Signal Processing (DSP) course. In this paper, we also gives an example of designing components of Discrete Fourier Transform (DFT) to show the process of designing, implementing and using the components in the DSPVL.

Keywords: Virtual Laboratory, DSP, components, Java Beans.

1 Introduction

With the rapid development of Internet, modern long-distance education as a new education mode has became an important problem for discussion. Virtual Laboratory (VL) based on the Internet is a key on improving the quality of distance education since experiments are significant for most engineering and application courses [1,3].

Digital Signal Processing (DSP) course is an important course in information science. How to construct a security, powerful and easy-use Digital Signal Processing Virtual Lab (DSPVL) platform is the key part of our research. In order to keep the balance of high efficiency and correctness during developing the DSPVL, we propose a new method that all the virtual instruments are encapsulated in the components based on Java Beans which can keep the platform independent and make users interact with each other well [2]. By choosing the required components to construct an experiment, users can do DSP experiments and deeply understand and consolidate the complex knowledge.

* This work is supported by the Major Research Plan of National Natural Science Foundation of China, Grant No.90304010 and City University Strategic Grant No. 7001587.

R.W.H. Lau et al. (Eds.): ICWL 2005, LNCS 3583, pp. 291–301, 2005.

The rest of the paper is organized as follows. In section 2, we introduce the architecture of DSPVL. Section 3 describes the design and implement of DSPVL modules. Section 4 deals with the design and implementation of the components in DSPVL. Conclusion is given in section 5.

2 The Architecture of DSPVL

The DSPVL is designed based on BS mode [2]. Its client is implemented with components and object-oriented technologies that offer users with applet embed in HTML files. The server side mainly includes Web Server to visit DSPVL through browsers. The architecture of the DSPVL is shown in Fig.1.

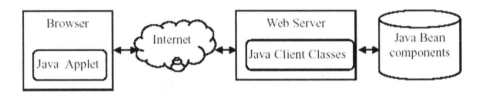

Fig. 1. The architecture of the DSPVL

Its clients contain many components that have two types. The first is to invoke the objects and methods in the server side and run, the second is to run directly in client side. Besides using the components offered in DSPVL to do experiments, users can also submit their self-develop components to the Web Server from the client side. After the system administrator testing the self-develop components strictly, they can be inserted to the system and all the following users can use them. By this way, the DSPVL will be more applicable and scalable.

3 Design and Implementation of DSPVL

The DSPVL is constructed of three modules that are experiment designing, experiment running and submitting components. In design module, users select and connect the virtual instruments to construct an experiment. The default parameters of components are set by the system, if necessary users can reset them. Then the DSPVL will run the experiment and display the result in run module. When users want to use and test their local components developed by themselves, they can add them into the DSPVL in submission module.

3.1 Implementation of Design Module

Fig.2 shows the main modules in the DSPVL. Users connect Web Server through browsers. After entering the DSPVL, browsers automatically download applets from server to clients. There are several classes in the user interface in the DSPVL.

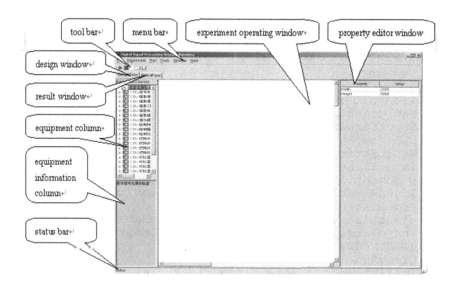

Fig. 2. Main modules in DSPVL

(1) MainWindow Class

This class realized the main frame of the platform. It contains design window, result window, tool bar and menu bar. In menu bar, we set six buttons named file, experiment, run, tools, window and help to do experiment work. All the buttons are defined in MainMenu class by the method of setJMenuBar. In order to trigger and perform the events by pushing the buttons, we set some listeners and actions. The main code is showed as follows:

```
Public class MainWindow extends JFrame{
    mainMenu=new MainMenu(this);
    toolbar=new MainMenu(this);
    designPanel=new DesignPanel(this);
    resultPanel=new ResultPanel(this);
    jTabbedPane=new JTabbedPane();
    jTabbedPane.add(designPanel, "designPane");
    jTabbedPane.add(resultPanel, "ResultPane");
    this.getContentPane().add(StatusBar,BorderLayout.
    SOUTH);
    this.getContentPane().add(jTabbedPane,
    BorderLayout.CENTER);
    this.getContentPane().add(toolBar,
    BorderLayout.NORTH);
    this.setJMenuBar(mainMenu);
    actionPerformed(ActionEvent e);
    }
```

(2) RegisteredClassPanel Class

XML(Extensible Markup Language) is structural, scalable and self-definitional, so that XML can be very useful to create, read, write and save a file. In

RegisterClassPanel class, we define an XML file to register components to the system. By reading this kind of files, we can easily get the parameters and methods of components. The main code of reading components information from XML file is showed as follows:

```
Public void readXML(){
    URL url=null;
    InputStream in=null;
    url=new
    URL((String)csuSystem.getObject("SP_SYSTEMCLASS");
    in=url.openStream();
    Document listXML;
    listXML=XmlDocment.createXmlDocument(in,false);
    NodeList classList;
    classList=listXML.getElementsByTagName("class");
    int classListLength=classList.getLength();
    ClassNode[] classNodes=new
    ClassNode[classListLength];
    for(int loop_class=0;loop_class<classListLength;
    loop_class++)
    {
      Element cur_class;
      cur_class=(Element)classList.item(loop_class);
      DefaultMutableTreeNode cls=null;
      String cls_name=cur_class.getChildNodes().item(1).
            getChildNodes().item(0).getNodeValue();
      String
    cls_title=cur_class.getChildNodes().item(3).
            getChildNodes().item(0).getNodeValue();
      String
    cls_label=cur_class.getChildNodes().item(5).
            getChildNodes().item(0).getNodeValue();
      String cls_desc=cur_class.getChildNodes().item(7).
            getChildNodes().item(0).getNodeValue();
      cls=new DefaultMutableTreeNode(new
        ClassNode(cls_name,cls_title,cls_label,cls_desc,
            classNode.CLASS));
    }
}
```

(3) PropertyEdit Class

PropertyEdit class is used for users to set the parameters of components and check them whether they are appropriate. If not, the editor will catch the exception and cancel the setting and then ask users to reset them. In addition, PropertyEdit class also supplies methods for users to select that are applied by components.

(4) DesignPanel Class

DesignPanel class is the key class in design module. As a container, it lays an instrument column on the left, operating window in the middle and property editor on the right in the platform. The definition of DesignPanel class is as follows:

```
public class DesignPanel extends JPanel implements
   MouseListener, MouseMotionListener, KeyListener
```

It realizes the interfaces of MouseListener, MouseMotionListener and KeyListener. So by listening to the interfaces, we can make components communicate with each other synchronously. In DesignPanel class we also definite an inner class named DrawCanvas to invoke the interface to link the selected components and realize an experiment flow.

hotLeadArea is a property of DesignPanel class that stands for the component legs of mouse current location. Modifer is the legs' property that records the type of transmission data. By comparing the Modifers between input and output components, we can judge whether they can be connected. If they are the same type, we can invoke method of repaint from an object of DrawCanvas class to connect the legs of components. All the connecting lines are put into the object named connectors inheriting from HashMap class. The main code of realization is showed as follows.

```
set entries=carriers.entrySet();
   Iterator iterator=entries.iterator();
   DeviceCarrier car1;
   Lead h1;
   Map.Entry entry;
   while(iterator.hasNext()){
      entry=(Map.Entry)iterator.next();
      car1=(DeviceCarrier)entry.getValue();
      h1=car1.getLead(e.getPoint());
      if(h1!=null){
         Point[] pa=tConnector.getHandler();
         String  inModifer=
               this.selectedCarrier.getLead(new
               Point(pa[0].x,pa[0].y-3)).modifer;}
         if(!h1.modifer.equals(inModifer)){ break;}
   }
```

(5) DeviceCarrier Class and DeviceConnector Class

DeviceCarrier class stands for equipments and Deviceconnector class stands for connecting lines between components. The most important property of DeviceCarrier class is instance. When the equipments are selected and dragged into the operating window, the system will use the instance to build an object of Java Bean and get its information, and then use static method in Introspector class to return an object defined by BeanInfo to save the parameters and methods of components. At last we can build the legs of components based on the information in BeanInfo. This is the application of reflection technology in Java. By using the technology, object is introduced, loaded and created dynamically. The main code of self analyze for Java Bean is showed as follows:

Commenced Publication in 1973

Founding and Former Series Editors:
Gerhard Goos, Juris Hartmanis, and Jan van Leeuwen

Editorial Board

David Hutchison
Lancaster University, UK

Takeo Kanade
Carnegie Mellon University, Pittsburgh, PA, USA

Josef Kittler
University of Surrey, Guildford, UK

Jon M. Kleinberg
Cornell University, Ithaca, NY, USA

Friedemann Mattern
ETH Zurich, Switzerland

John C. Mitchell
Stanford University, CA, USA

Moni Naor
Weizmann Institute of Science, Rehovot, Israel

Oscar Nierstrasz
University of Bern, Switzerland

C. Pandu Rangan
Indian Institute of Technology, Madras, India

Bernhard Steffen
University of Dortmund, Germany

Madhu Sudan
Massachusetts Institute of Technology, MA, USA

Demetri Terzopoulos
New York University, NY, USA

Doug Tygar
University of California, Berkeley, CA, USA

Moshe Y. Vardi
Rice University, Houston, TX, USA

Gerhard Weikum
Max-Planck Institute of Computer Science, Saarbruecken, Germany

296 Publication in 1973 W. Jia

```
if(newClassURL.toUpperCase().startswith("CSU:/")){
    className=newClassURL.substring(5);
    selfClass=Class.forName(className);
    node=selfClass.newInstance();    }
BeanInfo
beanInfo=Introspector.getBeanInfo(selfClass,stopClass);
Property
properties[]=beanInfo.getPropertyDescriptors();
Method getter,setter;
for(int i=0;i<properties.length;i++){
    setter=properties[i].getWriteMethod();
    if(setter==null){
        inCount++;
        l=new lead();
        l.type=lead.PROPERTY_IN;
        l.offsetX=inCount*10;
        l.name=properties[i].getName();
        l.modifer=properties[i].getPropertyType().getName();
        v.add(l); }
```

3.2 Implementation of Run Module

Run module is the key part for the DSPVL to simulate the process of an experiment. Users can freely choose the required virtual instruments and link them to assemble an experiment flow. Output components can be connected with multiple input components as long as their interfaces are matched. System will build a directed chart with no ring based on the simulate process. The chart uses components as its nodes and connecting wires as its sides [4]. Then analyze the data type between the components and get its topology sequence. If the components can run concurrently, the system will build a single thread for computation. At the same time the system will actuate a management thread to make them work together and respond to users' interrupt instruction. The simulation process is shown in Fig.3.

The key part of run module is ResultPanel class. Its method of queueFlow is used to make the components to queue in a line. The main code is as follows:

```
private void queueFlow(){
    notReadyCarriers=new Vector();
    notReadyConnectors=new Vector();
    runQueue=new Vector();
    notReadyCarriers=copyVector();
    while(true){
        String carName=getZeroInCarrier();
        if(carName!=null){
            runQueue.add(carName);
            notReadyCarriers.remove(carName);
            removeConnector(carName);
        }
        else {return;}
    }
}
```

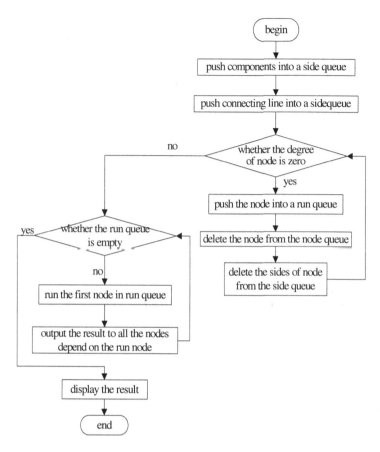

Fig. 3. Flowchart of the simulation process

3.3 Implementation of Submitting Components

This module is used to submit components developed by users. The components must be developed according to the regulations of Java Beans and their interfaces should be matched. Then the users can add their new components into the DSPVL and do experiments with other existent components together.

The process of submission is showed in Fig.4. URLClassLoader class loads the Java Beans to the system and Introspector class gets their information and returns an object defined by BeanInfo class. The object saves the parameters and methods of the components and sent them to another object defined by RegisteredClassPanel class. Then the object will register the new components into the component column. This is the process of how to add the self-developed components by users to the DSPVL. Users can do experiments to test and evaluate them. In order to enhance the function of DSPVL, we use another method to submit components to Web Server by browsers. The administrator checks the correctness and security of components and decides which will be registered. All the qualified components will be added into the system and be offered to all the users.

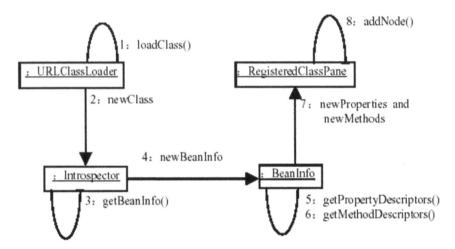

Fig. 4. Submitting components

4   Design and Implementation of DSPVL Components

4.1   General Principle of Designing DSPVL Components

In the DSPVL, we develop many components such as discrete signal generator, signal adder, discrete random signal generator, oscillograph, DSP, discrete Z transform, discrete hilbert transform, amplitude spectrum, angle spectrum, power spectrum and various filters of finite impulse response and infinite impulse response [5]. All the signals are discrete in DSP experiments, so we set the type of transform date among components as a double array. The simulation process is shown in Fig.5. Furthermore, we definite an attribution named sleepInterval to control the run frequency of threads and display the result dynamically.

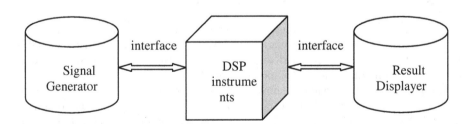

Fig. 5. Simulation process of DSP experiments

4.2   Example for Designing Components

There are many components in the DSPVL. Take the DFT experiment for example to introduce the design and implementation of components.

The algorithm of DFT is Fast Fourier Transform (FFT). FFT algorithm first rearranges the input signals in bit-reversed order and then builds the output to transform based on base-2 select in time domain. The basic idea is to break up a transform of length N into two transforms of length $N/2$.

The signal generator generates 32 discrete signals to keep the number of signals is integrated power of 2 and saves them in a double array. There are 5 Java Beans shown in Table.1 that is used in the DFT experiment.

Table 1. The Java Beans Classes in DFT

Class name	Function
sp_Complex	define a type of complex and construct methods of getting amplitude and angle.
sp_DiscreteFourier	realize FFT algorithm
sp_DFT	realize DFT algorithm
sp_SpectrumAmplitude	draw the amplitude of transformed signals
sp_SpectrumAngle	draw the angle of transformed signals

The 32 discrete signals will be sent to the component of sp_DFT from the signal generator through the interface of a double array. The size of array is 33, which use the last position as a flag to judge whether a group of signals has been transferred into sp_DFT completely. Then in sp_DFT class, we define an object named DFT from sp_DiscreteFourier class to invoke the FFT methods. First we reverse the order of the signals. The result is saved in an array named data1 whose type is double.

```
data1 = DFT.reverse(value);
```

Then we invoke the method in sp_DFT class to transform the signals saved in data1 based on base-2 select in time domain and save the result in an array named data3. The type of data3 is complex which defined by sp_Complex class.

```
data3=DFT. transform (data1, data2);
```

The IDFT is the reverse process of DFT and both are based on FFT algorithm, so we construct an all-purpose Java Bean named sp_DiscreteFourier to realize the two transforms respectively in time domain and in frequency domain. In frequency domain, we will reverse the order of signals whose type is complex. So in the method of transform there are two formal parameters, which data1 stands for the real part and data2 stands for the virtual part. In order to make the method of transform be all-purpose, there are also two formal parameters in DFT, but the value of data2 is zero.

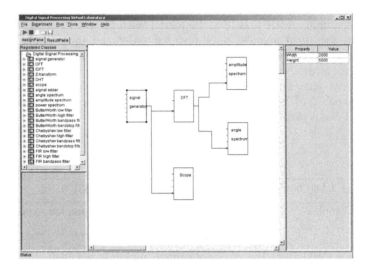

Fig. 6. The simulation process of DFT

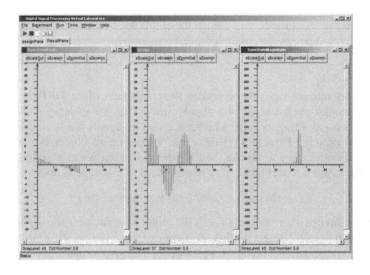

Fig. 7. The result of DFT

Now we get the result of DFT, which the type of data is a complex saved in an array named data3. In order to analyze the result, we send the result into sp_SpectrumAmplitude and sp_SpectrumAngle components by the methods offered in sp_Complex class to get their amplitudes and angles. At last, we'll draw them and see the dynamical result in result window.

```
buffer[i] = data3[i].mod();
buffer[i] = data3[i].arg();
```

The experiment flow is showed in Fig.6 and the result is showed in Fig.7. In Fig.7, from left to right, they are the pictures of angle spectrum of transformed signal, original discrete signal of sine wave and amplitude spectrum of transformed signal.

5 Conclusions

This paper introduces the design and implementation of DSPVL based on components in detail. All the components are developed by pure Java language, which make the system be maintained and extended easily. With the reuse of software and general structure of executing orderly, we can construct various kinds of virtual laboratories (VLs) such as image processing, digital communication and computer network. We still have a lot of work to do to consummate the system and make it more powerful. The VLs will play an important role in the development of remote education, especially for engineering and application courses.

References

1. Wang Jianxin, Peng Bei, Jia Weijia, Design and Implementation of Virtual Computer Network Lab Based on NS2 in the Internet, Proceeding of ICWL 2004, Lecture Notes in Computer Science 3143, 2004, 346-353
2. Wang Jianxin, Chen Songqiao, Jia Weijia, Pei Huiming, The Design and Implementation of Virtual Laboratory Platform in Internet, Proceedings of ICWL 2002 , Hong Kong, 2002.8, 160-168.
3. Jiannong Cao, Alvin Chan, Weidong Cao, and Cassidy Yeung, Virtual Programming Lab for Online Distance Learning, LNCS 2436, First International Conference, ICWL 2002 Hong Kong, China, 2002, P. 216-227.
4. Wang Jianxin, Lu Weini, Jia Weijia, A Web-Based Environment for Virtual Laboratory with CORBA Technology, International Journal of Computer Processing of Oriental Languages, 2003, 16(4):261-274.
5. Steven W. Smith, Ph.D. The Scientist and Engineer's Guide to Digital Signal Processing, California Technical Publishing, 1997, P. 141-168.

A Design for Generating Personalised Feedback in Knowledge Construction

Jude Lubega, Lily Sun, and Shirley Williams

Department of Computer Science, The University of Reading, UK
{j.t.lubega, lily.sun, shirley.williams}@reading.ac.uk

Abstract. As the learning paradigm shifts to a more personalised learning process, users need dynamic feedback from their knowledge path. Learning Management Systems (LMS) offer customised feedback dependent on questions and the answers given. However these LMSs are not designed to generate personalised feedback for an individual learner, tutor and instructional designer. This paper presents an approach for generating constructive feedback for all stakeholders during a personalised learning process.

The dynamic personalised feedback model generates feedback based on the learning objectives for the Learning Object. Feedback can be generated at Learning Object level and the Information Object level for both the individual learner and the group. The group feedback is meant for the tutors and instructional designer to improve the learning process.

1   Introduction

As the learning paradigm shifts to a more personalised learning process, users (learners, tutors and instructional designers) need dynamic feedback from their knowledge path. Learners appreciate real time feedback that helps them improve. Knowing how the students performed in a particular learning scenario is a responsive communication to both tutors and instructional designers. It is particularly emphasised by the learning theories [1] as the important instrument used in a learning process where progress, improvements and achievements are provided in the real-time [2]. The feedback offered to the learner should motivate them rather than demoralise their efforts to learn. Learners who fail to achieve particular learning objectives should be encouraged and advised on achieving the learning objectives.

Feedback generation is considered as an important functionality in e-learning. Many Learning Management Systems (LMS) [3] contain the functionality for offering feedback. For example, the comments and suggestions are pre-defined and associated with the individual assessment questions. The feedback is then generated by consolidating the predefined information after the learner has been assessed [4]. To provide this kind of feedback would satisfy a degree of success for individual questions, but it is difficult to customise feedback according to individual learners' performance and to support continuous improvements during the learning process. Furthermore, there is no mechanism for the feedback to reflect the learning objectives

R.W.H. Lau et al. (Eds.): ICWL 2005, LNCS 3583, pp. 302–310, 2005.
© Springer-Verlag Berlin Heidelberg 2005

set for the overall learning content and achievements at different learning stages. On the other hand, it is impossible for the users, i.e., content designers and tutors, to receive feedback on the quality of learning content designed and delivered. Therefore an effective method is needed that can enhance dynamic generation of feedback for the individual learner, tutor and instructional designer about the learning process.

This paper presents a method for generating personalised feedback. This method considers learning objectives as the criteria for measuring achievements at various learning stages. Feedback should then be generated according to individual users' role and achievements within a learning process. The technical components of the method can be incorporated in the LMS for enhancing the capability of facilitation.

2 Learning Process and Information Required

Learning as a process of knowledge construction involves different users (learners, tutors and instructional designers) participating in several activities like content authoring, assessments, application and feedback generation. The different users aim at achieving different goals depending on the activities carried out within the learning process. As Constructivism states, learners play an active role and take on responsibility to construct their own knowledge and meaning [5], [6], [7]. The learners will act in different ways based on their own judgement hence make meaning out of the learning process. The learners prefer different ways by which information is presented to them because it affects how they act on it. The individual learner's actions become the basis of what feedback should be generated for them. The constructivist theory has been used in the design of constructivist e-learning environments. Within these e-learning environments, learners take on responsibility for their learning process by managing the learning activities and collaboration with others. The constructivist e-learning environments are capable of offering personalised content, track learning activities and offer dynamic feedback to the learners.

Immediate gathering of the learner's actions within a tracking process helps in the generation of constructive feedback. The theory of constructivism enables us to identify important features for the learning process, such as personalisation of content to the individual learner; tracking the learner's activities at each level of the learning process; and generating feedback.

The basis for measuring educational and personal learning requirements achievement is driven by learning goals [8]. The personal learning requirements, e.g., the personal learning style, prior knowledge, the learning needs, are captured in a user profile [9]. This information will be the input for selecting, sequencing and presenting the information content which meets the users' requirements. Figure 1 describes the conceptual model, containing five components: *Overview*, *Summary*, *Information Object*, *Practical Object*, and *Assessment Objects*.

The *Overview* contains general information about the module, such as the module code, level, aims/objectives, pre-requisites, co-requisites, learning outcomes, indicative content, assessment strategy, and credits. Metadata is used to describe the objectives for the different objects within the Learning Object. The *Information Object* component represents a topic within the module. The practical instruction on this topic can be composed in a Practical Object which describes the topic applications. The Assessment Object contains questions that measure the learner's competence against the learning objectives. The assessment questions are designed to test for both application and theory understanding of the topic. The assessment questions assess one or more objectives within the topic/module. The information encapsulated in this object contributes to composing the feedback. The *Summary* contains a review of the module, which assists students in self-assessment and self-reflection through recommendations.

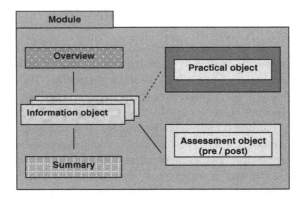

Fig. 1. Template for module package

The learning objectives for each Information Object are sub-objectives for the overall module objectives. Therefore attaining the objectives at Information Object level, reflects that the learner has attained the module learning objectives.

A well designed learning environment should be capable of facilitating learners at the different stages of learning and levels of content. The learners should be able to achieve their learning goals and receive effective feedback on how they can improve so as to attain all learning objectives. The tutors and instructional designers should be able to receive responsive feedback on the content effects to the students. The dynamic feedback acts as a support for learners to improve on their knowledge construction process, for tutors and instructional designers on how they can improve on their content instruction. A model that generates dynamic feedback at each level of the Learning Object content is developed to improve on the personalised learning process.

3 Feedback Process

Feedback may be described as a proactive process in which communication takes place in response to the learners' activities and outcomes. It is believed that feedback has a significant impact on the learning process since it adds value that results in improving quality and success in knowledge construction. Gagne and Briggs [12] stress that there is need for evaluating the student's understanding and offering feedback during evaluation within an effective learning. The feedback is important to the tutors because it reflects how best the student gained in the learning process and may also indicate what instruction content is inadequate.

Feedback can be generated for different purposes depending on a nature of assessment: formative and summative. The feedback for formative assessment puts emphasis on the student's self-reflection and self-direction. The learner can improve their understanding by being continually assessed. The comments in the feedback can be generated from the specific learning objectives associated with the Information Objects. In contrast, the feedback for summative assessment assists the measure on the overall learning objectives at the Learning Object level.

During learning, personalised learning activities are continuously monitored and the data corrected used for feedback generation. The learner-oriented tracking model [10, 13] collects useful information about the learning process which uses it for generating personalised feedback. Personalised information like assessment results is used for generating personalised feedback for learner, tutor and instructional designer.

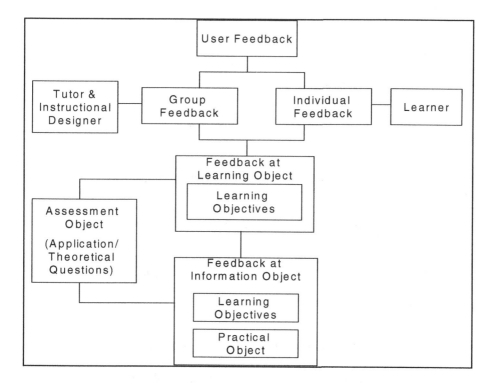

Fig. 2. A Dynamic Personalised Feedback Model

4 Personalised Feedback Model

The personalised feedback model shown in fig. 2 relies on the learning objectives specified in *Overview* of the Learning Object (LO). These learning objectives contain sub-objectives that are contained at the Information Object (IO). At both LO and IO an assessment object that contains a set of both application and theoretical questions is used to assess the achievement of the learning objectives. The feedback generated is based on the results from the assessment that reflect the attainment of the learning objectives. This feedback is generated based on the individual or group assessment results. The individual assessment results are used for generating feedback for the learner. The group assessment results are used for generating tutor and instructional designer feedback.

The model illustrates what feedback can be generated for learner, tutor and instructional designer. The assessment question type on which the model is applied is the commonly used multiple choice. The assessment question results are computed based on the set of application and theoretical questions. Once these results have been computed, a suitable feedback template is chosen, feedback determined and generated. The assessment results are computed at the LO and IO as follows:

Assessment results computed at LO: (Q_G)

$$Q_G = \sum_{i=1}^{n} (P(sa/SA) + T(sa/SA))_i / n \tag{1}$$

Assessment results computed at IO: (S_G)

$$S_G = \sum_{i=1}^{n} (P(fa/FA) + T(fa/FA))_i / n \tag{2}$$

Where:
n = Number of learners who participated in the attempting assessments.
$P(sa/SA)$ = Assessment result ratio of the attained application related questions to the total application related questions within the summative assessment at the LO level.
$T(sa/SA)$ = Assessment result ratio of the attained theoretical related questions to the total theoretical related questions within the summative assessment at the LO level.
$P(fa/FA)$ = Assessment result ratio of the attained application related questions to the total application related questions within the formative assessment at the IO level.
$T(fa/FA)$ = Assessment result ratio of the attained theoretical related questions to the total theoretical related questions within the formative assessment at the IO level.

5 Application of the Model in Feedback Generation

Applying the personalised feedback model to generate feedback is described in this section. A case study that describes an Information Technology module e-Business is used. This module teaches students to design web sites using the Dreamweaver application [14]. A section from the module content is considered for illustration and explains how the personalised feedback can be generated at each level and in different forms.

The student has to learn how to design dynamic web pages using the Dreamweaver application. The module used here is Designing Dynamic web pages (Learning Object). The module contains several objectives including: using dreamweaver windows, dynamic functions and palettes, learning how to set up an ODBC connection, learning how to create a record set, creating a dynamic table, adding repeat region and navigation server behaviours, creating a record insertion web page, creating a master-detail web page, creating a search web page, creating a login web page, creating a delete web page, creating an update web page

A summative assessment is used to assess the achievement of the objectives in both application and theoretic knowledge of the module.

A topic (Information Object) within the module "Using dreamweaver windows, dynamic functions and palettes" is considered during the application. The topic contains the following objectives: being able find and use the different palettes, selecting what window view to use during design, the dynamic functions that may be used to design dynamic pages, how to save the dynamic pages without using the HTML extension.

An assessment containing a set of application and theoretical multiple choice questions is presented to the learner for assessing their knowledge construction. Figure 3 describes the sample questions that may be used for assessing the learner at different levels within the Learning Object.

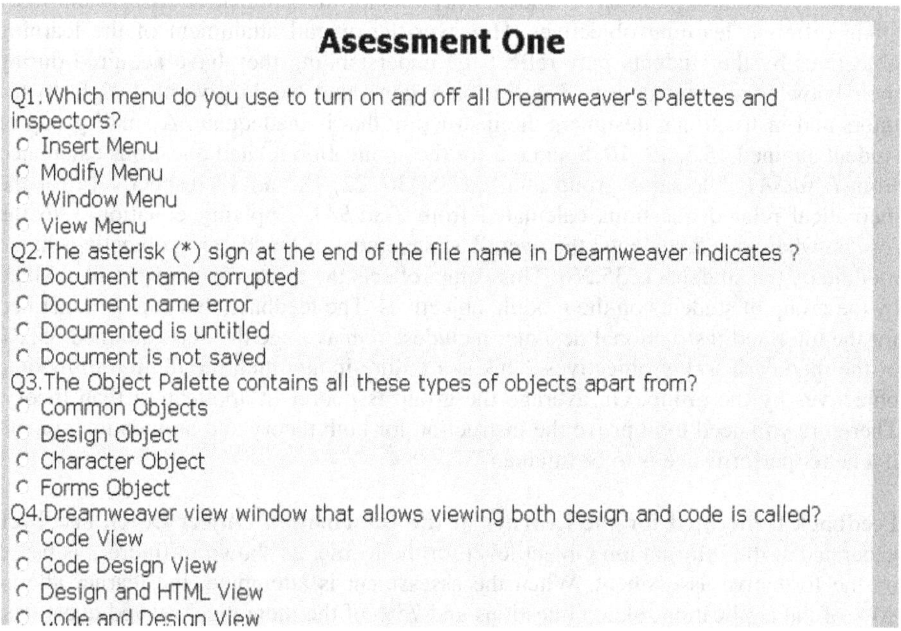

Asessment One

Q1.Which menu do you use to turn on and off all Dreamweaver's Palettes and inspectors?
- Insert Menu
- Modify Menu
- Window Menu
- View Menu

Q2.The asterisk (*) sign at the end of the file name in Dreamweaver indicates ?
- Document name corrupted
- Document name error
- Documented is untitled
- Document is not saved

Q3.The Object Palette contains all these types of objects apart from?
- Common Objects
- Design Object
- Character Object
- Forms Object

Q4.Dreamweaver view window that allows viewing both design and code is called?
- Code View
- Code Design View
- Design and HTML View
- Code and Design View

Fig. 3. Description of an assessment containing multiple choice questions

If we consider the assessment in figure 3 as containing 30% application related questions (Q1, Q3, Q4, Q6) and 70% theoretical related questions (Q2, Q5, Q7, Q8, Q9, Q10). These rates reflect the achievement that can be obtained of the learning objectives. This achievement can then be used for generating feedback depending on level at which the assessment is taken. Examples of feedback that may be generated from the assessment results are shown below.

Feedback Generated for Learner at the Learning Object Level. Considering figure 2, the feedback that may be generated at the Learning Object level is based on the result from equation 1. When a summative assessment is taken by a learner, the results indicate that 55% of the applications questions set and 50% of the theoretical questions set were attempted right. Calculating for $P(sa/SA)$ we obtain 16.5 and for $T(sa/SA)$ we obtain 35. When equation 1 is evaluated where n = 1 (learner), the overall assessment result is 51.5% total objectives achieved. The feedback that can be generated for the learner at the Learning Object level based on the summative assessment results includes: "You have successfully attained 51.5% of the learning objectives for this module. Both your application and theoretical understanding were relatively good. However for a better achievement of the learning objectives, you need to read carefully the content and probably do more practical work".

Feedback Generated from a Group of Learners. Feedback generated for tutor and instructional designer is based on the group assessment achievement on the learning objectives. Considering figure 2 and assuming n learners have attempted the assessment, the achievement of the learning objective by the group is evaluated using equation 1. When a number of students (n) attempt the summative assessment, they attain different learning objectives. However the overall attainment of the learning objectives by the students may reflect the understanding they have acquired during their knowledge construction. The feedback generated would give an insight to the tutors and instructional designers the instruction that is inadequate. A small group of student attained 16.5, 12, 10, 8 and 6.5 for the application related questions calculated from $P(sa/SA)$. The same group attained 35, 30, 22, 18 and 18 respectively for the theoretical related questions calculated from $T(sa/SA)$. Applying equation 1 to the results, where n is 5 students; the overall achievement of the learning objectives in the module by the students is 35.2%. This value reflects the average achievement attained by the group of students on the module objectives. The feedback that can be generated for the tutor and instructional designer includes: "On average the class attained 35.2% of the module learning objectives. This is a failure in attaining the minimum module objectives by the group. On average the group is poorer in application than theory. Therefore you need to improve the instruction for both theory and application content if a better performance is to be attained."

Feedback Generated for the Learner at the Information Object Level. Feedback generated at the Information Object level for the learner as shown in figure 2 is based on the formative assessment. When the assessment is attempted, the learner attains 80% of the application related questions and 75% of the theoretical related questions. Therefore $P(fa/FA)$ and $T(fa/FA)$ evaluate to 52.5 and 24 respectively. On applying equation 2 the overall learning objective achievement where n (learner) = 1 is 76.5%.

The feedback that may be offered to the learner about this topic includes: "Congratulations you attained 76.5% of the learning objectives. Both your application and theoretical skills were good. You can proceed to the next topic."

During the generation of feedback, the contents may vary depending on what was achieved from both application and theoretical related questions within the assessment. Once the achievement has been determined, a feedback template is selected and the feedback contents determined. The feedback is then generated for the learner to improve their knowledge construction and tutor/instructional designer to improve on the content instruction.

6 Discussion and Future Work

A dynamic personalised feedback model is designed measure the learning achievements. The model is capable of generating feedback of different forms at different levels during the learning process. Feedback generated for students is dynamically delivered to them at the different levels of the learning process. This motivates them to put more emphasis on the areas where improvements are required.

Generation of the feedback during the learning process is to be allocated to a feedback agent that will carry out this work on an independent basis. This agent will link up with another agent that will distribute the feedback to the different users. The feedback templates for the feedback tree will be designed. The feedback templates will be dynamically selected for feedback generation at different levels during the learning process. Related work on learner profiling and Learning Object repositories are underway. These will be used with the learner-oriented tracking model to offer an effective learning process. The dynamic personalised feedback model can be embedded into the learner-oriented tracking model to improve student's support during the learning process.

References

1. Duffy, T.M., Cunningham, D.J.: Constructivism: Implications for the design and delivery of instruction, in Handbook of research for educational communications and technology, D.H. Jonassen (Ed.), New York: MacMillian Library Reference, (1996).
2. Martens, R.L.: The use and effects of embedded support devices in dependent learning, Phd thesis (OTEC), Lemma, (1998).
3. Edu Tools: (2004) at:
   http://www.intranetjournal.com/articles/200110/ic_10_17_01a.html
4. Mory E.H.: Feedback research revisited, in Handbook of research for educational communications and technology, D.H. Jonassen (Ed.), New York: MacMillian Library Reference, (2003).
5. Fosnot, C.: Constructivism: A Psychological theory of learning. In C. Fosnot (Ed.): Constructivism: Theory, perspectives, and practice. New York: Teachers College Press, (1996) 8-33.
6. Steffe, L.P., & Gale, J. (Eds.): Constructivism in Education. Hillsdale, NJ: Erlbaum, (1995).

7. Honebein, P.C., Duffy T. and Fishman B.: Constructivism and the Design of Learning Environment: Context and Authentic Activities for Learning, in T.M. Duffy, J. Lowyck and D. Jonassen (eds.), Design Environments for Constructivist Learning, Springer-Verlag, NY, (1993) 87-108.

8. Sun, L. and Williams S.: An Instructional Design Model for Constructivist Learning, EdMedia 2004 World Conference on Multimedia, Hypermedia and Telecommunication, Lugano, Switzerland, ISBN: 1-880094-53-3, (2004) 2476-2483.

9. Sun, L., Ousmanou, K. and Williams, S.A.: Articulation of Learners Requirements for Personalised Instructional Design in E-Learning Services. In: W. Liu, Y. Shi and Q. Li (ed.): Advances in Web-Based Learning. Lecture Notes in Computer Science, Vol. 3143. Springer-Verlag Heidelberg (2004) 424-431.

10. Sun, L., Lubega, J. and Williams, S.A.: Design for a Learner-Oriented Tracking, In: W. Liu, Y. Shi and Q. Li (ed.): Advances in Web-Based Learning. Lecture Notes in Computer Science, Vol. 3143. Springer-Verlag Heidelberg (2004) 155-162.

11. Lubega, J. and Williams, S.: Patterns of Use when Interacting with a Managed Learning Environment, EdMedia 2004 World Conference on Multimedia, Hypermedia and Telecommunication, Lugano, Switzerland, (2004) 5001-5005.

12. Gagne, R. M. and Briggs, L. J.: Principles of Instructional Design (2nd ed.). New York, NY: Holt, Rinehart and Winston, (1979).

13. Lubega, J., Sun, L. and Williams, S.: An Effective Tracking Model for Personalised e-Learning, in the 3rd European Conference on e-Learning, Paris, edited by Dan Remenyi, ISBN 0-9547096-7-5, (2004)181-188.

14. Macromedia: Dreameaver Application, (2004) at:
    http://www.macromedia.com/software/dreamweaver/

Refining the Results of Automatic e-Textbook Construction by Clustering

Jing Chen[1], Qing Li[1], and Ling Feng[2]

[1] Department of Computer Engineering and Information Technology,
City University of Hong Kong, 83 Tat Chee Avenue, Kowloon, Hong Kong
{jerryjin, itqli}@cityu.edu.hk
[2] Department of Computer Science,
University of Twente, PO Box 217, 7500 Enschede, The Netherlands
ling@ cs.utwente.nl

Abstract. The abundance of knowledge-rich information on the World Wide Web makes compiling an online e-textbook both possible and necessary. The authors of [7] proposed an approach to automatically generate an e-textbook by mining the ranking lists of the search engine. However, the performance of the approach was degraded by Web pages that were relevant but not actually discussing the desired concept. In this paper, we extend the work in [7] by applying a clustering approach before the mining process. The clustering approach serves as a post-processing stage to the original results retrieved by the search engine, and aims to reach an optimum state in which all Web pages assigned to a concept are discussing that exact concept.

1 Introduction

The World Wide Web has evolved into one of the largest information repositories. It now becomes feasible for a learner to access both professional and amateurish information about any interested subject. Professional information often includes compiled online dictionaries and glossaries, course syllabus provided by teachers, tutorials of scientific software, overview of research areas by faculties from research institutes, etc. Discussion boards sometimes offer intuitive description of the interested subjects, beneficial for students or beginning learners. All these resources greatly enrich and supplement the existing printed learning material. The abundance of knowledge-rich information makes compiling an online e-textbook both possible and necessary.

The most common way of learning through the Web is by resorting to a search engine to find relevant information. However, search engines are designed to meet the most general requirements for a regular user of the Web information. Use Google ([1]) as an example. The relevance of a Web page is determined by a mixture of the popularity of the page and textual match between the query and the document ([2]). Despite its worldwide success, the combined ranking strategy still has to face several problems, such as ambiguous terms and spamming. In the case of learning, it becomes even harder for the search engine to satisfy the need of finding instructional

R.W.H. Lau et al. (Eds.): ICWL 2005, LNCS 3583, pp. 311–319, 2005.

information, since the ranking strategy cannot take into account the needs of a particular user group, such as the learners.

1.1 Background of Research

Recently, many approaches have been proposed to improve the appearance of Web search engine results. A popular solution is clustering, providing users with a more structured means to browse through the search engine results. Clustering mainly aims at solving the ambiguous search terms problem. When the search engine is not able to determine what the user's true intention is, it returns all Web pages that seem relevant to the query. The retrieved results could cover widely different topics. For example, a query 'kingdom' actually referring to biological categories could result in thousands of pages related to the United Kingdom. Clustering these results by whole pages or their snippets is the most commonly used approach to address this problem ([3][4][5]). However, the structure of the hierarchy presented is usually determined on-the-fly. Cluster names and their organized structure are selected according to the content of the retrieved Web pages and the distribution of different topics within the results. The challenge here is how to select meaningful names and organize them into a sensible hierarchy. Vivisimo [6] is an existing real-life demonstration of this attempt.

The clustering approach works well to meet the needs of a regular user. But when the application is narrowed down to an educational learning assistant, it is possible to provide the learners with more 'suitable' Web pages that satisfy their needs in the pursuit of knowledge. Users seeking for educational resources prefer Web pages with a higher quality of content. Such Web pages often satisfy the criteria of being self-contained, descriptive and authoritative [7]. Limited work has been done to distinguish higher quality data from the Web. An important one is [8], where the authors attempt to mine concept definitions on the Web. They rely on an interactive way for the user to choose a topic and the system automatically discovers related salient concepts and descriptive Web pages, which they call informative pages. They not only proposed a practical system that successfully identified informative pages, but also more importantly pointed out a novel task of compiling a book on the Web.

In [7], the authors proposed an approach to automatically construct an e-textbook on the Web. They extend Liu et al.'s work by adding a concept hierarchy that outlines the user-specified topic. In the concept hierarchy, also called a concept tree, each node corresponds to a concept and the ancestor relationship of nodes represents the containing relation of the concepts. The use of the concept tree is essential and benefits the learning experience to a great extent. The concept tree is used to gather Web pages that are more likely to be of learning importance. It also readily serves as a table-of-content for the final e-textbook. It is easier for the users to understand compared with the cluster hierarchy generated on-the-fly, thus saves time for browsing. The approach is described concisely in the following:

1. Dataset collection: The concepts in the concept tree are used to generate a query phrase for each node. The query terms indicate the relationship of concepts. Web pages that cover more concepts in the query are more likely to be ranked high in the list.

2. Mining process: "Suitable" pages from the retrieved list of each concept tree node are mined and re-ranked according to a combined ranking strategy.
3. Expansion: For some nodes that do not have sufficient "suitable" pages, an expansion process is activated.
4. Result presentation: Remaining Web pages are presented to users with the concept tree in the left area of the screen, serving as a navigation guide.

In the approach, the mining process is performed on the retrieved result of the search engine. However, the ranking strategy of the search engine cannot guarantee that the main theme of a highly ranked Web page is actually about the query. Often, a Web page describing an ancestor or offspring concept is ranked high in the list. For instance, for a query "infinite series", a Web page actually discussing a sub-topic "geometric series" is ranked high in the list. The phrase "infinite series" appears several times in the Web page, since "geometric series" is a sub-topic of the broader "infinite series". The search engine only notices to what extent this page is related to the search term, but cannot determine the main theme of the page. It should not be blamed for such a relevance measure, but in our scenario it is better that the page about "geometric series" is considered a candidate page for the node "geometric series" rather than for "infinite series". The algorithm proposed in [7] tries to stress on the search terms by giving higher priority to them, but is too simple and not sufficient to successfully identify a Web page's main theme. So the quality of the mining process is affected by these "noises" that could have been "hits" for other concept tree nodes.

1.2 Paper Contribution and Organization

In this paper, we add a clustering procedure before the mining process to adjust the distribution of the Web pages in the concept tree. The performance of the mining process is improved because Web pages are associated with the appropriate concept tree nodes in the adjusted Web page collection. In our approach, we treat the retrieved results of all nodes in the concept tree as the initial clustering condition, and perform a clustering procedure upon it to optimize the distribution of the documents in the collection. In order to make the clustering process suitable for such an application, we propose a new Web page representation model, which projects a Web page onto the concept tree. The projection is called an instance tree. The new Web page representation model can well describe the distribution and the relationship of the concepts appearing in a Web page, and consequently, characterize its main theme precisely. It also reduces the dimension of the representation and improves the efficiency of the clustering process. Then the corresponding tree distance measure is defined to evaluate the distance between two instance trees. When the clustering process terminates and the optimum status is reached, Web pages are assigned to the appropriate concept tree nodes that match with their main themes.

In the rest of the paper, we first define the new Web page representation model, along with the similarity metric used to measure the distance between two instances of the model. In Section 3, we discuss how the clustering algorithm is applied with Web page representation model. Section 4 gives a case study of our approach. And we conclude our paper in Section 5.

2 Web Page Representation Model

The most popular document representation model in modern information retrieval is the vector space model (VSM [9]). A document is considered as a set of terms and represented as a high-dimensional vector where a term stands for a dimension. A non-binary weight is assigned to each term in the term space. Based on the vector space model, the similarity of Web pages can be measured through computing the cosine distance between the two vectors.

But the vector space model is not very suitable in our scenario. Web pages associated with "close" concept tree nodes are sometimes similar with each other in their distribution of terms, even though they are not describing the exact same concepts. The previous example of "infinite series" and "geometric series" explains why their features can overlap. Thus the similarity between two "close" Web pages cannot be evaluated precisely. In our case, preciseness is required. We must identify the main theme a Web page is describing, at the presence of other "close" concepts in the concept tree. The Web page representation model must be able to record the information of the relationship of the concepts contained in the Web page along with the concept distribution.

2.1 Instance Trees

The central idea of our approach is about a user-specified concept hierarchy, which we call the concept tree. The concept tree should provide a hierarchical outline of the concerned topic, where nodes on the upper part of the tree represent more general concepts and those in lower positions stand for more specific topics. A concept tree is a labeled ordered rooted tree. A rooted tree is a tree with a vertex singled out as the 'root'. The root node of our concept tree represents the main topic the user is interested in. We consider the concept tree as ordered mainly for clarity in description. The concept tree is defined as follows:

Definition 1. Let CT denote a concept tree.

- $|CT|$ represents the number of nodes in the concept tree CT;
- V_{CT} denotes the set of vertexes of CT;
- $V_{CT}[i]$ is the i-ism vertex of CT in a preorder walk of the tree;
- $E[i, j]$ is the edge between two adjacent vertexes $V_{CT}[i]$ and $V_{CT}[j]$. The direction of the edge is ignored in our definition;
- $C(x)$ stands for the corresponding concept to vertex x;
- EdgeDist (x,y) denotes the edge distance between vertex x and y, which is calculated by the minimum number of edges between x and y.

An example of a concept tree is displayed in Figure 1. The edge distance between vertex $V_{CT}[4]$ and vertex $V_{CT}[7]$ is 3 according to the definition of edge distance, where the corresponding edges are E[4, 3], E[3, 1], E[1, 7].

By mapping a Web page onto a concept tree, it is possible to analyze the relationship of the concepts appearing in a Web page, thus further determining the main theme of the document. In our approach, each Web page is represented as a tree structure identical to the concept tree, called an *instance tree*.

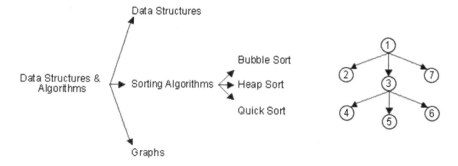

Fig. 1. Example of a concept tree

Definition 2. Let T_x be an instance tree from a Web page W_x to the concept tree CT. $|T_x|$ denotes the number of nodes in T_x. Let V_{Tx} be the set of vertexes in T_x, and $V_{Tx}[i]$ be the i-ism vertex in a preorder walk of T_x. Let $C(x)$ be the corresponding concept to vertex x in T_x. Function $\phi: V_{Tx} \rightarrow V_{CT}$ is a projection from the vertexes in an instance tree T_x to vertexes of the concept tree CT such that the i-ism vertex in T_x is mapped to the i-ism vertex in CT in preorder. The value of a vertex $val(V_{Tx}[i])$ is denoted as the number of occurrences of the concept $C(V_{CT}[i])$ in Web page W_x.

The following conditions are held for instance tree and the concept tree:

- $|T_x|=|CT|$;
- $\phi(V_{Tx}[i]) = V_{CT}[i]$ for any $1 \leq i \leq |T_x|$;
- $C(V_{Tx}[i]) = C(V_{CT}[i])$ for any $1 \leq i \leq |T_x|$.

Figure 2 depicts three different instance trees corresponding to the concept tree in Figure 1. The numbers on the right side of each concept tree node stands for the value of that node.

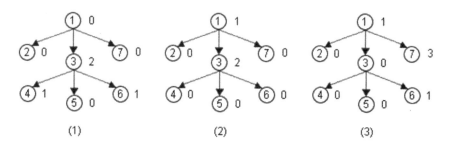

Fig. 2. Three different instance trees

2.2 Distance Measure

In k-means clustering and many other clustering approaches, it is necessary to calculate a "distance" between two objects or an object and a cluster centroid. In our approach, an object is an instance tree. A popular means to compare the difference between two trees is the edit distance. This method tries to convert one tree into the other, and analyzes the distance by counting the number of steps needed for the transformation. [10] gives a general description about edit distance, and the measure is widely used in many tree comparing tasks ([11][12][14]). However, edit distance is mainly for evaluating structural similarity in two different tree structures, while the instance trees are all of the same structure. In addition, the instance tree not only reflects the distribution of the concepts in a Web page, but also records the relationship of the appearing concepts. The relational information is important and should not be ignored.

To take the relational information into account, given a vertex x in an instance tree T_1, we are first interested in its "closest" vertex y in T_2. The "closeness" is measured by the EdgeDist(ϕ (x), ϕ (y)) defined above. Such a distance is called the distance between the vertex x in T_1 and the instance tree T_2. We also define the following function σ which indicates whether a concept has occurred in a Web page:

$$\sigma(x) = \begin{cases} 1, & \text{if } val(x) > 0; \\ 0, & \text{elsewise} \end{cases}$$

Definition 3. Let x be a vertex in a tree distance T_1, the distance between x and instance tree T_2 is defined as:

$$dist(x,T_2) = \sigma(x) \times \left(min\{EdgeDist(\phi(x),\phi(y)) \mid \sigma(y) = 1, y \in T_2\} + 1 \right)$$

The σ (x) in the equation above guarantees that the distance makes sense only when the value of vertex x is not zero.

Given the distance of a vertex in T_1 and another instance tree T_2, the distance between two instance trees T_1 and T_2 can then be defined:

Definition 4. The distance between two instance trees T_1 and T_2 is:

$$treedist(T_1,T_2) = \frac{\sum_{i=1}^{|T_1|} |val(V_{T_1}[i]) - val(V_{T_2}[i])| \times dist(V_{T_1}[i], T_2) + \sum_{j=1}^{|T_2|} |val(V_{T_2}[j]) - val(V_{T_1}[j])| \times dist(V_{T_2}[j], T_1)}{\sum_{i=1}^{|T_1|} \sigma(V_{T_1}[i]) + \sum_{j=1}^{|T_2|} \sigma(V_{T_2}[j])}$$

It can be easily proved that for any two instance trees T_1 and T_2, the instance tree distance satisfies the following constraints:

- treedist(T_1, T_1)=0;
- treedist(T_1, T_2)$\geq$0;
- treedist(T_1, T_2)= treedist(T_2, T_1).

However, the instance tree distance is not normalized. In the example of the three instance trees in Figure 2, the following can be easily calculated:

$$treedist(T_1,T_2) = \frac{((2-2)\times1+(1-1)\times2+(1-0)\times2)+((1-0)\times2+(2-2)\times1)}{3+2} = \frac{6}{5}$$

$$treedist(T_1,T_3) = \frac{((2-0)\times 2 + (1-0)\times 3 + (1-1)\times 1) + ((1-0)\times 2 + (1-1)\times 1 + (3-0)\times 3)}{3+3} = \frac{5}{2}$$

$$treedist(T_2,T_3) = \frac{((1-1)\times 1 + (2-0)\times 2) + ((1-1)\times 1 + (3-0)\times 2 + (1-0)\times 2)}{2+3} = \frac{12}{5}$$

3 Clustering Process

K-means clustering is a well-known member of the family of clustering algorithms ([2]). The user first defines a preset number k of clusters. Initially, the objects can be arbitrarily divided into k clusters. Each cluster is represented as the centroid of the documents within it. Thereafter, an iterative process begins by assigning objects to the closest cluster. A detailed implementation of the k-means clustering algorithm can be found in [13]. This approach is especially useful when the k clusters are already formed by some other algorithm. For the ranking lists provided by the search engine, Web pages are naturally clustered to the concept tree node used to generate the queries. The k-means clustering algorithm can then be applied as a postprocessing stage to move the misplaced points to the appropriate cluster.

The centroid of a cluster of instance trees is represented by a tree structure similar as the concept tree and the instance trees. The value of its vertexes is defined as follows:

Definition 5. Let C_i denote the centroid of the cluster corresponding to the concept tree node V $_{CT}$[i]. N is the number of instance trees that belong to cluster C_i. The value of the i-ism vertex in C_i is calculated as:

$$Val(V_{C_i}[k]) = \frac{\displaystyle\sum_{T_j \in C_i} val(V_{Tj}[k])}{N}$$

A distortion metric is minimized during the clustering process. We choose to minimize the total distance between all objects and their centroids for simplicity. The minimal distortion and the instance tree distance together determine the shape of the optimum clusters.

4 Case Study

In this section, we provide a case study of how our algorithm works. The following concept tree (Figure 3) is used to generate queries and obtain the corresponding Web page set:

The following snippets in Figure 4 are provided by the search engine for the concept tree nodes "data mining" and "association rules" respectively. (a) is an abstract of a paper about mining association rules. It was mistakenly retrieved for the concept tree node "data mining" because the term "data mining" appeared several times in the Web page. (b) is someone's publication list, mainly in the area of data mining. Besides his contribution in "association rules", the author had many other publications in classification, clustering, etc.

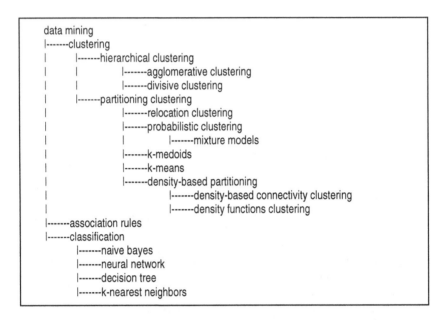

Fig. 3. Concept Tree for "data mining"

32. An efficient **cluster** and decomposition algorithm for **mining ...**
... Sampling Large Databases for **Association Rules**, Proceedings of **...**
Database applications Subjects: **Data mining** I. Computing **...**
I.5.3 **Clustering** Subjects: Algorithms. **...**

http://portal.acm.org/citation.cfm?id=986453

(a)

4. Rakesh Agrawal's Publications
... Srikant, H. Toivonen and AI Verkamo: "Fast Discovery of
Association Rules", Advances in Knowledge Discovery and
Data Mining, Chapter 12, AAAI/MIT Press, 1995. **...**

http://www.almaden.ibm.com/cs/people/ragrawal/pubs.html

(b)

Fig. 4. Snippets from the SE results. (a) 32nd result for node "data mining"; (b) 4th result for node "association rules"

In our approach, (a) was moved to the concept tree node "association rules", while (b) was assigned to the correct ancestor concept tree node "data mining". The movement from a node to an ancestor or an offspring is the most common action taken by our algorithm.

5 Conclusion

In this paper, we target at improving the results of an automatically generated online e-textbook. We propose a new Web page representation model, which we call the instance tree, to highlight the relationship of concepts contained in the Web page as well as their numerical appearances. A clustering algorithm is introduced to cluster the instance trees, and obtain an optimum state where all Web pages are assigned to their appropriate concept tree node. In the future, we will carry on more extensive experiments to evaluate our proposed clustering algorithm thoroughly.

References

[1] S. Brin, L. Page, "The Anatomy of a Large-scale Hypertextual Web Search Engine", in Proceedings of International Conference on World Wide Web, 1998.

[2] S. Chakrabarti, Mining the Web: Discovering Knowledge from Hypertext Data, Morgan Kaufmann Publishers, 2002.

[3] Oren Zamir, Oren Etzioni: Grouper: A Dynamic Clustering Interface to Web Search Results. Computer Networks 31(11-16): 1361-1374, 1999.

[4] Hua-Jun Zeng, Qi-Cai He, Zheng Chen, and Wei-Ying Ma. Learning To Cluster Web Search Results. In Proceedings of the 27th annual international conference on research and development in information retrieval (SIGIR'04), pp. 210-217, Sheffield, United Kingdom, July 2004.

[5] Paolo Ferragina, Antonio Gullí: The Anatomy of a Hierarchical Clustering Engine for Web-page, News and Book Snippets. ICDM 2004: 395-398, 2004.

[6] Vivisimo, http://vivisimo.com/html/index

[7] Jing Chen, Qing Li, Liping Wang, Weijia Jia: Automatically Generating an e-Textbook on the Web. ICWL 2004: 35-42, 2004.

[8] B. Liu, C-W. Chin, H-T. Ng, "Mining Topic-specific Concepts and Definitions on the Web", in Proceedings of International Conference on World Wide Web, 2003, pp. 251-260, 2003.

[9] Salton. G. and McGill, MJ., Introduction to Modern Information Retrieval McGraw Hill, New York, 1983.

[10] K. Zhang and D. Shasha. Simple fast algorithms for the editing distance between trees and related problems. SIAM Journal of Computing, 18(6):1245-1262, 1989.

[11] Yuan Wang, David J. DeWitt, Jin-yi Cai: X-Diff: An Effective Change Detection Algorithm for XML Documents. ICDE 2003: 519-530

[12] Andrew Nierman, H. V. Jagadish: Evaluating Structural Similarity in XML Documents. WebDB 2002: 61-66

[13] Tapas Kanungo, David M. Mount, Nathan S. Netanyahu, Christine D. Piatko, Ruth Silverman, Angela Y. Wu: An Efficient k-Means Clustering Algorithm: Analysis and Implementation. IEEE Transaction on Pattern Analysis and Machine Intelligence, 24(7): 881-892, 2002.

[14] Davi de Castro Reis, Paulo Braz Golgher, Altigran Soares da Silva, Alberto H. F. Laender: Automatic web news extraction using tree edit distance. WWW 2004: 502-511

ANTS: Agent-Based Navigational Training System

Yu-Lin Jeng[1], Yueh-Min Huang[1], Yen-Hung Kuo[1], Juei-Nan Chen[1],
and William C. Chu[2]

[1] Department of Engineering Science, National Cheng Kung University,
Taiwan No. 1, Ta-Hsueh Road, Tainan 701, Taiwan, R.O.C
{jack, keh, nan}@www.mmn.es.ncku.edu.tw
huang@mail.ncku.edu.tw
[2] Department of Computer Science and Information Engineering,
TungHai University, No. 181, Taichung-Kang Road, Sec. 3, Taichung 40744, Taiwan
chu@csie.thu.edu.tw

Abstract. There is an explosive growth of e-learning trend during the last few years. More and more learning resources are generated by different purposes in the world. How to make the learning resources to be sharable and reusable is a key factor in e-learning environment. This paper presents a system framework of Agent-based Navigational Training System (ANTS) to facilitate lecturers and learners achieving their works. Besides, we apply the model of Dynamic Fuzzy Petri Net (DFPN) and the intelligent agent into the system to assist learners. The intelligent agent can dynamically generate the learning path for each learner. Moreover, the system is compatible to Sharable Content Object Reference Model (SCORM) which is the most acceptable e-Learning system developing standard. Accordingly, the learning resources could be sharable and reusable in any platforms which are compatible to SCORM standard.

1 Introduction

Due to the appearance of Internet, many people use computer networks to accomplish a plenty kinds of tasks. In last few years, lots of lecturers put the teaching materials to the Web and define a term – e-Learning. It provides a convenient channel to gain information without going to school.

Web services are web applications consisting of eXtensible Markup Language (XML), Universal Description Discovery & Integration (UDDI), Simple Object Access Protocol (SOAP) and Web Services Description Language (WSDL). Based on Web services, the learning resources can be integrated and share with other e-Learning systems. UDDI provides two basic functions: registration and searching. All the requests and responses are contained in the UDDI registry and all partners are transmitted by SOAP messages. SOAP contains message layout specifications, which defines a uniform way of passing XML-encoded data [1]. WSDL applies multiple XML schemas defining the specific web services structure. The advantage of using web services architecture could make useful learning resources sharable and reusable.

Intelligent agents as a concept have been around for more than a decade, and it has gained popularity as a marketable product in the recent times. The proposed agent has

R.W.H. Lau et al. (Eds.): ICWL 2005, LNCS 3583, pp. 320–325, 2005.
© Springer-Verlag Berlin Heidelberg 2005

aptly described intelligent agent as "e-assistant" that is basically responsible for carrying out various requests for each learner [2]. In [3] [4], they described the concept of agent applying in e-learning, and the agent suggests possible actions or web resources based on its understanding of the learner's behavior. In [9], the authors proposed the concept of Dynamic Fuzzy Petri Net (DFPN) applying to e-learning. In this paper, we apply DFPN model to be expert agent's knowledge guiding learner achieving his learning target. Expert agent is a connector between the system and learner, and it can judge what the next course should provide to the learner based on DFPN model [15].

The rest of this article is organized as follows. Section 2 describes the features of ANTS with web services. Section 3 shows the component WSMS of ANTS. Section 4 outlines expert agent features and its related methodology. Then, there is a system presentation introduction in the Section 5. Finally, section 6 draws conclusions.

2   Agent-Based Navigational Training System (ANTS)

2.1   System Architecture

The main system framework of ANTS is shown in Fig 1. Authoring tool provides lecturers a convenient tool and edits several learning assets into a course [10] [11]. It produces standard Sharable Content Object (SCO) for database and Web Service Management System (WSMS). With the help of authoring tool, lecturers can use their learning resources like video or MS-PowerPoint slides to organize a SCO. Consequently, the easiness and convenience is the goal of this authoring tool.

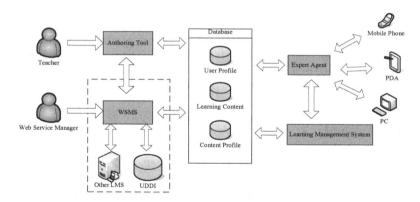

Fig. 1. Agent-based Navigational Training System Framework

The ANTS system databases are built in relational database schema, which include learner profile, learning content and content profile. Learner profile keeps learner's personal data and learning status. By keeping those data, system can analyze learner's behavior to find out learner's learning pattern and provide learner with some useful suggestions. Learning content keeps data about learning resources which include documents, pictures, video, and some other multimedia data. Content profile database is responsible to record information of learning content.

LMS extracts data from database and provides information for learners. It is a learning platform which gives the channel for lecturers and learners to communicate with each other. It also provides three roles which is administrator, lecturer and learner. Administrator manages the registration and certification of the learners. Lecturer could place a course in LMS and register it, and then learners can read the course online. Learner has several useful functions in LMS; they can read courses, write down their notes of certain courses, assign their personal calendars, and so on.

Eventually, the rule of expert agent in this system is to provide learning suggestion based on learner's behavior by using DFPN model [9]. This agent operates its job according to learner's learning process, and this operation does not visible for the learner. The system just suggests the learner what is the next course to learn by agent's arrangement. The full description is written in the third section of this paper.

2.2 Web Services Management System (WSMS)

The concept of WSMS combines traditional authoring tool with web services technique. Using web services technique integrates the digital learning resource into service oriented architecture. If the learning resource content provider wants to provide their content on web services architecture, they can simply register their content by the UDDI server which is built by the system. Therefore, lecturers can find the course by UDDI searching and directly use the resources provided by the UDDI server.

With the usage of web services, WSMS can integrate the other LMS resources registered on the UDDI server. By this framework, lecturers or learners can obtain online courses not only from the local LMS but also the other LMS. WSMS would classify the different resources from different LMS by a classification method. Thus, lecturers and learners could find the resources easily.

According to SCORM, the web services architecture applies to the SCORM fully. That is, SCORM wants digital resources to be sharable and reusable, and WSMS does the same work. When lecturers search courses by UDDI server, they can download the course and re-organized the course which is claimed as free.

3 Expert Agent

Regarding the expert agent, the system use the method Dynamic Fuzzy Petri Net (DFPN) proposed by [9]. The architecture of the expert agent applies the DFPN to the learning path by generating the learning path dynamically for the learner. The method of DFPN model applying in e-learning is proposed in [9].

In our framework, the DFPN model is setting in the course by authoring tool. The information about the learning history would be delivered to DFPN model which can generate dynamic learning path according to the learning history. During the learning processing, the expert agent shows the best learning path for the learner by the learner's learning behavior. There is a diagram for DFPN in Fig 2. The real line represents the static learning path, and the dotted line represents the dynamic learning path. Circle A, B, and C represent different course respectively. There is a threshold value set by the content provider or the lecturer between course A and course C. When a learner finishes course A, there is an exam. If the learner cannot get the score value over the threshold value, the dotted line would transform into real line. Then, the learner is guided to the course B which probably is an assisted course or a low level course. Once the learner finish the course B and pass the threshold value, he can go on to learn course C. This mechanism makes sure that every learner would understand what he learns online.

There is an example for DFPN process shown in Fig 3. Assume that the threshold value is set to be 0.6. And after a learner finishes a course, his exam score is 50. Using intensity function [8] to transform this score would get a value between 0 and 1. Accordingly, the score 50 is transformed to 0.5, the value is little than 0.6 (threshold value). Therefore, the dotted line becomes real line. That means the learner could not learn the course C until he pass the course B. On the contrary, if the learner gets score 0.7 which is bigger than the threshold value, the dotted line disappear. And the learner can directly learn the course C. The description is shown in Fig 3.

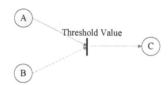

Fig. 2. Dynamic Fuzzy Petri Net

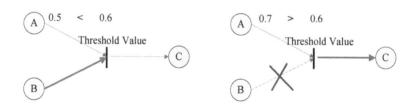

Fig. 3. The Sample of Dynamic Fuzzy Petri Net

4 System Presentation

This part of the paper introduces the presentation of the course and what guideline would the expert agent suggests. A learner may click the course of data structure Stack to learn as shown Fig 4. After the learner clicks the hyperlink, the course presentation provides the learner with the course video streaming, the course indexing terms and the course slides. If a learner finishes a course, he may have an exam or a simple test. Then, the score of the exam gives the expert agent for reference of the learner's ability. According to the DFPN, if a learner fails a course, he would be guided to low level course or assisted course. Otherwise, the learner would be guided to higher level course.

After the exam of the course, the learner could get a score. If the score is lower than 60 (threshold value), he fails the course. Then he is guided to low level course like Link List for advice (Fig 5(a), 5(b)). The reason of the learner cannot understand the course Stack may be that he didn't learn Link List well. Consequently, after the learner learns the course Link List well, he may pass the course Stack. Thus, the data structure course of Link List is called assisted course here.

In addition, when a learner finishes an assisted course Link List, he is expected to pass the course Stack. The expert agent then guides him to learn higher level course Tree (Fig 5(c), 5(d)). This process is operating by expert agent automatically.

Different course may be different degree for every learner. Some learners with powerful ability may learn chapter 3 without learn chapter 1 before. But the other learners may learn courses step by step otherwise they might get confused. Accordingly, DFPN which dynamically generate the learning path for every learner is a good solution applies to e-learning environment.

Course Name	Teacher	Score
Data Structure - Stack	Yueh-Min Huang	*

Fig. 4. View the Course – Stack

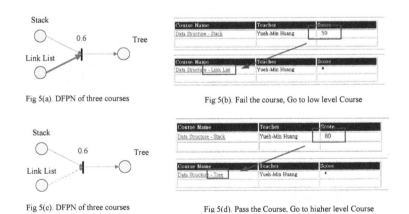

Fig 5(a). DFPN of three courses

Fig 5(b). Fail the course, Go to low level Course

Fig 5(c). DFPN of three courses

Fig 5(d). Pass the Course, Go to higher level Course

Fig. 5. DFPN Example

5 Conclusions and Future Works

This investigation proposes a framework – ANTS, which includes web services and DFPN technique. Therefore, ANTS can provide the learning suggestions to an individual learner. Moreover, ANTS is compatible to SCORM which is most accepted e-learning standard in the world. This study also illustrates the system architecture and some detail system functions. Finally, a system presentation introduction is given to demonstrate the expert agent with different score value. The authors believe that this work provides lecturers and learners with a convenient way to learn online.

The further work would be the problem of the testing system which includes setting the questions online and publish them. A good testing system can evaluate the ability of learners even if their ability is unknown. This is important for us to understand learners' learning performance. Accordingly, by the testing score, we can improve the recommendation mechanism with more precision degree.

Acknowledgment

The authors would like to thank the National Science Council of the Republic of China for financially supporting this research under Contract No. NSC 93-2524-S-006-001.

Reference

[1] N.H. Michael, "Agent as Web Services," *IEEE Internet Computing,* Vol. 6, Issue: 2, July/August, 2002, pp. 93 – 95.

[2] VIRTUALLY HELPFUL, Telephony, 2/11/2002, Vol. 242 Issue 6, p56.

[3] O.R. Zaiane, "Building a Recommender Agent for e-Learning Systems," *Proceedings of the International Conference on Computers in Education,* 2002, pp. 55.

[4] F. Arriaga, M.El Alami, A. Arriaga, "Multi-Agent Architecture for Intelligent E-Learning," *IEEE International Conference on Electronics, Circuits and System (ICECS),* 2003, pp. 53 – 55.

[5] Z. Shen, C. Miao, "Agent Mediated Grid Services in e-learning," *IEEE International Symposium on Cluster Computing and the Grid,* 2004, pp. 210 – 211.

[6] R. Agarwal, A. Deo, S. Das, "Intelligent agents in E-learning," *ACM SIGSOFT Software Engineering Notes,* Volume 29, Issue 2, 2004, pp. 1.

[7] W. Quesenbery, "The Logic Underlying the Intelligent Technologies Used in Performance Support," *Technical Communication,* Vol. 49, Issue 4, 2002, pp. 449.

[8] J.N. Chen, Y.M. Huang, W.C. Chu, "Adaptive Multi-Agent Decision Making Using Analytical Hierarchy Process," *Proceedings of 15th Australian Joint Conference on Artificial Intelligence,* 2002, pp. 203 – 212.

[9] J.N. Chen, Y.M. Huang, "Using Dynamic Fuzzy Petri Net for Navigated Learning," *Proceeding of International Conference for Engineering Education and Research (iCEER),* 2005.

[10] Y.M. Huang, J.N. Chen, S.C. Cheng, W.C. Chu, "Agent-Based Web Learning System Applying Dynamic Fuzzy Petri Net," *Proceeding of International Conference on Web-Based Learning,* 2004, pp. 338 – 345.

[11] Y.M. Huang, C.C. Chang, P.Y. Chiu, S.C. Huang, and William C.C Chu, "Applying Multimedia Authoring Tool and XML Techniques to Standardized Knowledge Management for Web-based Learning," *Proceeding of International Conference on Web-Based Learning,* 2002.

An Educational Virtual Environment for Studying Physics Concept in High Schools

Ruwei Yun[1], Zhigeng Pan[2], and Yi Li[1]

[1] Educational Technology Department, Education Science College,
Nanjing Normal University, Nanjing, 210097, China
[2] State Key Lab of CAD&CG, Zhejiang University, Hangzhou, 310027, China

Abstract. Virtual Reality has been applied in many fields such as scientific visualization, manufacturing, architecture, entertainment, education and training. In this paper, we present a virtual educational environment for studying some abstract concept in physics. With this environment, middle school students are able to study the abstract concept such as relative motion, and to make themselves construct their knowledge of the field. Experimental results show the efficiency of our method.

1 Introduction

Virtual Reality (VR) is a three-dimensional, participatory, multi-sensory, computer-based simulated environment occurring in real time. It has been defined as a highly interactive, computer-based, sensory experience by using computer graphics, sounds, and images to reproduce electronic versions of real-life situations.[1]

VR has been applied in many fields such as scientific visualization, manufacturing, architecture, entertainment, education and training[2]. The application of VR system in education field is called VR-based Education, or educational virtual environments. In recent years, growing emphasis on VR-based education technology brings forward the potential of developing constructivist 3D virtual learning environment[3]. It can extend the classroom via new windows into other realities. By reflecting the real world, the simulation provides the participants the chance to try different options without the dangers, expense, or time consumption which may happen when the users do the 'real thing'[1]. One may also try out scenarios that are actually impossible to do in real world and determine which scenarios present the best chance of accomplishment. Therefore, VR technology has been widely accepted as a major technological advance that can offer significant support for education field.

2 Learning Scheme in Visual Educational Environment

Based on above constructivist learning theory, we put forward our learning scheme. Figure 1 shows our 3D virtual learning scheme. The symbols used in the figure are:

R.W.H. Lau et al. (Eds.): ICWL 2005, LNCS 3583, pp. 326–331, 2005.

LA------learner A
LB-----learner B
UI-----User Interface
3DVLE-----3D Virtual Learning Environment
CDI-----Courseware Design Interface
CD------Courseware Designer
IH-----Instructional Hint

Learning or designing flow can be achieved by following steps:

(1)----Start to learn through interacting with UI
(2)----Request exploring learning resources
(3)----Get needed learning resources from 3DVLE
(4)----Complete learning action online
(5)   Establish meaning in mental brain
(6)----Co-operating with other learners
(7)---- Synchronization with other learners
(8)----Analysis teaching target
(9)----Designing 3DVLE with CDI
(10)---Upload 3D environment
(11)---Upload Hint Information
(12)---Get instruction from IH
(13)---Put instruction into IH

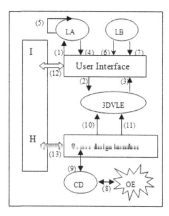

Fig. 1. 3DVLE Learning Scheme

Learning part in Figure 2 shows 5 steps of completing a learning process. It starts with learners' intension to learn and ends up with establishing meaning in learners' human brain. This learning mode supports co-operative learning mechanism. Several learners organized in a group can use communication tools such as chat, sound, whiteboards etc to explore the shared learning environment in synchronization. Course designing part shows if courseware designer have got a clear teaching target (through a lot of analysis such as what he teaches, where he teaches, whom he teaches, which kind of way he teaches etc), he can design the courseware by himself. That means, the learning mode should provide a common courseware designing interface defined by CDI in Figure 2. According to exogenous constructivism, in a problem-based learning environment, learners rely much on instructional hints to complete their learning process[4]. Instructional hint designed in IH help learners in several ways. Also, agent-based hint system implemented for the requirements of learners' individual mental model and learning activity.

3   Creating the Virtual Environment of Relative Motion

In this section and Section 4, we will discuss the implementation techniques for the educational virtual environment. To simplify the introduction, we will use the "relative motion", a very important concept in physics, as an example.

3.1 Creating Virtual Objects

In order to obtain realistic scene composed of virtual objects like cars, trucks in motion, we need produce 3-D presentation model with better visual effect, which in the end decides the sense of whether being real[4]. There are three methods of using OPENGL to create 3-D solid models[5]. In this paper, the authors will make full use of the advantage of OPENGL as well as 3DMAX's modeling function.

3.2 Creating the Reference Scene of Relative Motion

For those virtual scenes (trees, streets or lawns) in the relative motion, they can be designed directly using VRML 2.0. Firstly, we need create a set of textures for scene of maps, including trees, streets, lawn set al. This can be done with help of the tool of PhotoShop. Then these images ought to be saved as transparent PNG pattern that can be adopted by web files. Secondly using VRML to create the reference objects. VRML provides 54 nodes, which cab be easily employed to build every virtual reference objects, and save them as "wrl" pattern files.

3.3 Using VRML to Control the Motion of Viewpoint

In the study of relative motion, the key point is to choose different reference object, that is to say, changing viewpoint to the observation of objects. And this can be implemented in the VRML by viewpoint node. For a viewpoint, we can create a corresponding space viewpoint in the virtual space, with which we can change the space position of the space viewpoint by setting values of position as well as changing the direction of space viewpoint by setting value of orientation.

Fig. 2. A virtual scene observed in a position of space

4 Study Relative Motion and Construct Field Knowledge

4.1 Study Relative Static and Relative Motion

The system can set up three viewpoints in above-mentioned scenes: Viewpoint 1 is set up at the truck facing the car, and makes it move with the truck through setting up the route; Viewpoint 2 is set up at the car facing the truck, and makes it move with the car through setting the route; viewpoint 3 is set up above meadow, and it can see the car, the truck, and most roads in front of the car at the same time (fig 3). Regarding viewpoint 3 as the current viewpoint, start the car and the truck, making them advance with the uniform velocity at the same speed, and we can see that the car and the truck all go fast on the road. Click the truck and make viewpoint 1 as the current viewpoint, we can see the car is static while the road and wayside trees moving backward fast.

This proves that the car is static to the truck, and the road and trees by the road is movable to the truck. Click the car and switch over the current viewpoint to viewpoint 2, we can see the truck is static, but the road and wayside trees is moving backward fast.

4.2 Study Relative Curvilinear Motion

Set up three viewpoints with the steps described in Section 4.1. Regarding viewpoint 3 as current viewpoint, and let the car go right with acceleration in crossroad and the truck go down the road at the uniform velocity. At this moment, we can see that the car and the truck are both in rectilinear motion, and the speed of the car is faster and faster. Click the truck, viewed from viewpoint 3, we can see the car is in accelerated motion on the horizontal road surface, and the road is going upward at the uniform velocity. Hiding other objects of reference besides car, we can see the car is in curvilinear motion on the screen, that is to say, the car is in curvilinear motion to

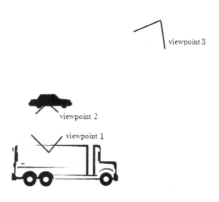

Fig. 3. Scheme of viewpoint

the truck. Click the car, switch the current viewpoint to viewpoint 3, and hide other objects of reference besides the truck, we can see the truck is in curvilinear motion on the screen too. That means the truck is in curvilinear motion to the car too.

4. 3 Study the Relative Accelerated Motion

Set up three viewpoints as described in Section 4.1. Regarding viewpoint no 3 as the current viewpoint, the car is going along right direction with acceleration a, initial velocity 0, and the truck is going along right direction with uniform velocity. It is obvious that the car and the truck are both going right, and the speed of the car is faster and faster. Click the truck and make viewpoint no1 as the current viewpoint, restart the car and the truck, we can see the car goes left at first, and the speed is slower and slower, then goes right faster and faster. Click the car and switch over the current viewpoint to the viewpoint 2, restart the car and the truck; we can observe the motion state of the truck.

4.4 Construct Elementary Knowledge of Relative Motion

The meaning constructing is the final purpose to study[6]. It refers to the characteristic, rules, and inner relationship of things. To help students gain the thorough comprehension of the characteristic, rules, and inner relationship of things is the goal of construction in learning. Followed with such a research, students can know initiatively that static and moving of objects are all relative to the observing object, which is called a reference object. Authors designed two questions for students on constructing the knowledge of relative motion. One is how does the object move if the reference object is static? The other is how does the object move when the condition changes for the reference object is moving (static and moving here is relative to the earth surface)? Students use their communication and cooperation to construct the knowledge of relative motion initiatively.

4.5 Construct Deep Knowledge of Relative Motion with Virtual Experiment

In the constructional point of view, students do not only comprehend and memorize conclusions, but also internalize them by critically analyzing the rationality of conclusion on the base of their experience[6]. Therefore, besides leading students to discuss examples in daily life, teachers should ask imaginary questions for their thinking and discussion in order to further their comprehension.

However, students might be confused at some imaginary questions since they cannot be experimented actually due to restricted conditions. Under such circumstances, teachers can design a virtual experiment according to scientific theory for students to observe and then to make the conclusions. For example, when teaching the relative motion of objects, collaborating with a middle school physical teacher the authors designed a question about a top moving on the North Pole. Students are asked to answer: 1) Observed straight over the North Pole, how do the top and the earth move; 2) Observed from a certain point near the North Pole on the earth surface, how do the top and the earth move? A few of them gave the correct answer to the first question and nobody answer the second one. Then, the author asked them to study with the help of virtual experiment. This time all of them got the answer to the first question, 80% of the students answered the second question, 12% of the students raised the question that how the top and the earth move when observed from the point straight over the North Pole that rotating with the angular speed of the earth and succeeded in answer it by virtual experiment.[7]

Fig. 4. Observed from a point straight over the North Pole

Fig. 5. Observed from a point near the North on the earth surface

5 Conclusions and Future Work

Educational virtual environment is an important application of VR techniques. In this paper, we present our experience in design and implementation of such an environment using relative motion as a case study. Relative motion is difficult for middle school student to learn and for people to understand in daily life, even college students majoring in physics make mistakes about it. The primary reason is that when observing a moving object people usually unconsciously take objects near it, which are relatively static to the earth surface (such as road, trees and furniture along roads) as reference objects. Thus they are unable to make clear the relation between moving objectives.

With VR, we can change the observing point by changing the viewpoint, which making it be possible to observe from the earth surface or a moving object. Moreover, it is possible to conceal the interfering surroundings for pure study and then to come back into reality by uncovering the surroundings. In this way, VR helps students learn relative motion easily and construct their knowledge about it.

References

[1] David, The why and how VR in schools: a preferred future pedagogic mission by a group of worldwide experts in VR and education, The International Journal of Virtual Reality, Vol.5, No. 1 ,pp1-12,2001

[2] Zhigeng Pan, Jiaoying Shi, Virtual Reality Technology Development in China: An Overview, *The International Journal of Virtual Reality*, 2000,Vol.4, No.3, pp2-10

[3] Weihua Hu, Jiejie Zhu, Zhigeng Pan, Yanfeng Li, Cunhui Ju: Learning by doing: A Case for Constructivist 3D Virtual Learning Environment. EUROGRAPHICS 2003

[4] Zhigeng Pan, Weiwei Xu, Jin Huang, Mingmin Zhang and Jiaoying Shi. Easybowling: a small bowling machine based on virtual simulation. *Computers & Graphics*, 27(2):pp231-238, April 2003

[5] Haijun Zhu, Cao Tian, The study of boat driving simulation based on VR, Navigation Engineering (in Chinese),VOL.27,No.2,pp34-37,2003

[6] David H Jonassen□Instructional Design Models for Well-Structured and Ill-Structured Problem-Solving Learning Outcomes□Educational Technology Research and Development□Vol 45□No.1□pp.65-94, 1997

[7] Ruwei Yun, VR for explaining the concept " relative motion in physics", Eurographics/ACM SIGGRAPH Workshop on Computer Graphics Education 2004, Hangzhou, China, June 2-4, 2004

Mobile Learning with Cellphones and PocketPCs

Minjuan Wang[1], Ruimin Shen[2], Ren Tong[2], Fan Yang[2], and Peng Han[2]

[1] Educational Technology, San Diego State University,
5500 Campanile Dr. North ED 280, San Diego, CA 92182
mwang@mail.sdsu.edu
[2] E-Learning Lab of Shanghai Jiaotong University,
Haoran building 6th Floor, Shanghai
{rmshen, tongren, fyang, phan}@sjtu.edu.cn

Abstract. Mobile Learning (mLearning), having drawn a great deal of attention and application in the US and European countries, is just entering China's K-12 and higher education. Although the use of mobile devices in education is still in its infancy, there have been a few exemplary cases of successful use in schools. Several K-12 schools participated in a mobile inquiry program about birds; and several others use mobile devices for students and teachers to exchange short text-messaging. In higher education, leading institutions have attempted to create mobile virtual classrooms. The E-learning Lab of Shanghai Jiaotong University (SJTU), for instance, has successfully delivered sample broadcast of its online courses onto cell phones and PDAs. Here we report the mobile technological success of this Lab, and we describe learning settings that might benefit from mobile learning, including a college-level English course of about 50 campus and 30 online students.

1 Introduction

Mobile learning (mLearning), defined as learning with mobile devices such as Palms, PocketPc, Wireless Cameras, Web Tablets, Cell phones, and any other handheld devices [1-3], has drawn a great deal of attention in the U.S. and European Countries. Several exemplary projects are noteworthy. The Mobile Inquiry Technology conducted at the Stanford Research Institute provides science and math inquiry for K-12 students through portable accessible computing. The Institute currently is piloting the project with teachers from four Massachusetts public school districts who are leaders in math, science, and technology [4]. In higher-education, the ActiveCampus Project of the University of California at San Diego aims to increase communication and collaborations among its large "nomadic" undergraduate population through the use of PDAs and an extensive suite of mobile services such as instant messaging, ActiveClass, and ActiveResearch, so as to build and sustain learning communities [5].

Aiming to integrate mobile communication and network technologies with education, mobile learning is more advantageous than online learning in China for its mobility, universality, personalization, and efficiency. Until recently, China's mobile phone users largely outnumbered wired PC users. Even mobile users who are not

R.W.H. Lau et al. (Eds.): ICWL 2005, LNCS 3583, pp. 332–339, 2005.

familiar with computers can easily access the network through cell phones. This easy accessibility has greatly encouraged personalized, anytime-anywhere, and lifelong learning [6]. Technologically, General Packet Radio Service (GPRS) and Code Division Multiple Access (CDMA) enable users to be "always connected/online," which helps learners acquire and process information and thus better supports their learning.

Mobile computational devices currently used in China include mobile phones, pagers, Palms, PocketPCs, wireless cameras, and small notebooks. Along with the development of data communication technologies and the broad application of mobile terminal units in China, mobile devices were first used in disciplines such as finance, telecommunications, mass media, business, transportation, and health care. The unprecedented success of cell phone text messaging inspired the telecommunication industry to develop additional multimedia applications. With their sophisticated features and great capacity to facilitate communication and collaboration, mobile devices finally entered the field of education in the past two years and therefore launched China's new era of mobile learning or education (m-Education) [7]. Although the use of mobile devices in education is still in its infancy, there have been a few exemplary cases of successful use in K-12 schools and higher educational institutions. For instance, the Bird-Watching Learning (BWL) program, aiming at supporting students' learning about bird watching, was implemented in several schools in China [8]. Through this BWL system, the experimental group of a class was able to gain access to information instantly, apply the information quickly, communicate with experts, integrate various informational resources, and use it anytime, anywhere, in everyday life. From PDAs, BWL broadcasts bird pictures and videos, offers a bird-search system, builds local bird databases, and allows the instructor to trace all learners' actions on the system. Comparing to the control group of the class that used binoculars and guidebook for the same activities, the BWL group achieved significantly higher test scores at the end. In other cases, several experimental K-12 schools use mobile devices for students and teachers to exchange short text-messaging, such as mobile e-mail, text meeting, activity notice, and grade query. These exchanges greatly facilitated two-way communication between students and their teachers, and increased students' better participation in the learning process.

2 Description

Recently, the educational technology communities in China have initiated research about the principles and practices of mobile learning. China's Ministry of Education has recently established a "mobile education" program. However, the current use of mobile devices is still limited to student-teacher and student-student communications. For instance, several experimental K-12 schools use mobile devices for students and teachers to exchange short text-messaging: mobile e-mails, text messaging, activity notices, and grade queries. Several leading institutions of higher education have attempted to create mobile virtual classrooms. The E-learning Lab of Shanghai Jiaotong University (SJTU), for instance, has successfully delivered its undergraduate-level courses through mobile devices such as cell phones (e.g. Nokia 6600 see Figure 1) and PDAs (e.g., PocketPC 2003, see Figure 2). Here we report their technological success and describe learning settings that might benefit from mobile learning, including the Hope Elementary Schools Project and online courses that require more learner interactions.

The mobile learning system developed by the E-learning Lab supports three types of learning access: tuning into live broadcast, Video-on-demand (VOD), and downloading archived broadcast to mobile devices. The application (i.e., SjtuPlayer) on the mobile phones are developed using the Nokia S60 Software Development Kit (SDK), and then implemented on Nokia 6600 and Nokia 7610 Smart Phones. The application on PocketPC is developed using PocketPC 2003 SDK.

Before mobile learning was developed, all classroom courses supported by the E-learning lab could be accessed live online. While an instructor teaches in a traditional classroom, his or her presentations are simultaneously converted by the SjtuRecorder to online streaming learning content or courseware. Meantime, the recorder on the instructor station also saves the instructor's class activities on its local hard drive. Learning materials used for mobile learning are further compressed by the SjtuRecorder, to better adapt the live presentations for mobile delivery. Thus, the SjtuRecoder will generate three types of streams: a) an instructor's presentation screen, with the output size being 240*340, b) the video stream that captures an instructor's facial expressions, with the final output being 80*60, and c) the audio stream of an instructor's voices, with the final output being Mono-mp3. (Please see Figures 1-2 for a visual representation of the three streams). The bandwidth of the wireless connection (i.e., GPRS & CDMA) is about 40-60kbps. To accommodate this narrow bandwidth, each of the three streams is compressed to 8kbps, which can better support user access. And learning content is further optimized with engineering techniques to preserve video qualities. The live broadcasts and their archived recordings are then transmitted to the Lab's server (CastServer) located in China telecom, which then sends information to students, who in turn connect to this server and gain access to learning content with their mobile phones or PocketPCs. Upon receiving the streams transmitted by the CastServer, the Mobile Phones or PocketPCs decode the encoded screen, video, and audio using a proper decoding scheme such as mp3 and divX. Figure 3, an overview of the mobile learning production, delivery, and access system, displays the overall flow of the learning content generation and transmission.

It is worth mentioning an inconsistency between the screen size of the S60 mobile phones (176*208) and the output screen (240*320) of the courseware produced. Despite the mis-match, the larger output size will make the teaching screen more legible on the mobile phones. On the other hand, users will have to scroll around to read the rest of the screen. The instructor screen can be further zoomed in, if it is set as 320*480 or even higher, 600*800; user navigation will be more challenging, however, and they might lose the zoom-out feeling of a presentation.

In the near future, our mobile learning system will also enable instructor monitoring of students' learning activities. Students' mobile phone screens are to be transmitted through the socket connection between the phones and the server that will be used to monitor student activities. The monitoring system will rely on Direct Screen Access technology developed by Symbian, Inc. to capture the students' mobile device screens and to periodically send them to the monitor server through the socket.

The server will then reassemble students' mobile screens and display them on a larger projection screen for the instructor's easy viewing.

2.1 Figures and Tables

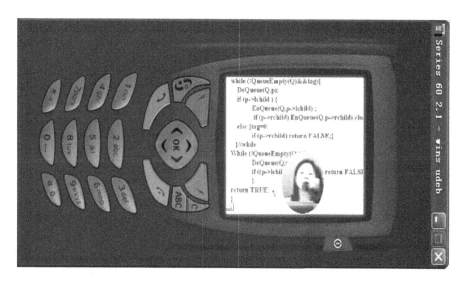

Fig. 1. Screen Shot of Learning Content Delivered onto a Cell Phone

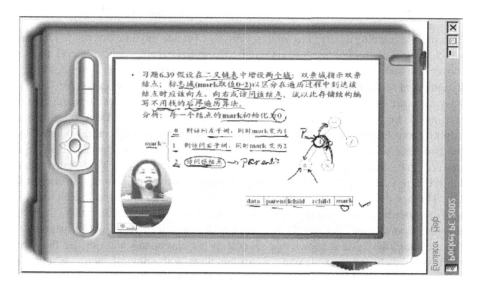

Fig. 2. Course Delivery onto a Handheld Device through Code Division Multiple Access (CDMA) 1X Technology

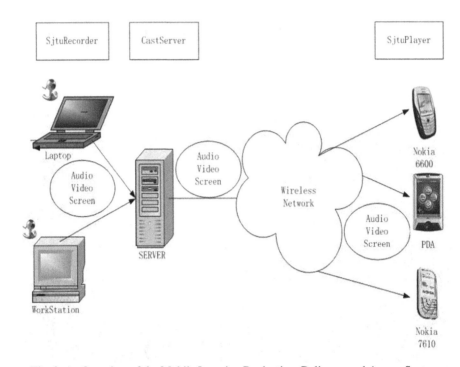

Fig. 3. An Overview of the Mobile Learning Production, Delivery, and Access System

2.2 Application Scenarios of Mobile Learning and Their Great Benefits

This mobile learning system has great potentials to create anytime-anywhere learning, which is one of the course delivery goals of the E-Learning Lab. Students will no longer be tied to a seat in front of a networked computer. Here we describe a hypothetical scenario of mobile learning by current SJTU online students. Mr. Tong, a busy manager of an international corporation in Shanghai's new development area, is waiting for his flight to Hong Kong at a quiet terminal of the Pu Dong International airport. Unfortunately the flight is delayed because of the pouring rain. To better use his two-hour waiting time, he takes out his mobile phone and connects to the Sjtu server. First, he looks for live broadcast that is part of his MBA curriculum. Unfortunately, none of the courses being broadcast at that moment are of interest to him. He then decides to review the learning content from an online course he tuned in to live yesterday. This time he selects the VOD (Video-on-demand) option, finds the recorded courseware, and scrolls to a section he needs to review. While listening to the recoding, the system shows that several of his classmates are viewing the same segment as well. After exchanging warm greetings with some of them, he sent text messages to one of them, attempting to discuss the content. Two hours seem to fly by and it is time to board the plane. Yet, he is eager to complete reviewing part of that courseware. He says good-bye to his classmates and starts to download the recordings (presentations and exercises) to his PDA-size cell phone, so that he can continue his study in air. Before the flight takes off, he switches his phone to "flight mode", continuing his reading and exercising. By the time the plane reaches Hong Kong, Mr. Tong has made great progress with that lesson and is very satisfied with his productivity on an airplane.

Secondly, the E-Learning Lab plans to pilot implement mobile learning activities with its several large-size classes; and all of them can greatly benefit from mobile interaction and communication. Each student will receive a PocketPC and be able to communicate more easily with their instructors and classmates. This easy communication will help them get instructor's proper attention and have their questions answered promptly. Because of the high costs of watching videos on cell phones, the E-learning Lab will reimburse students for their cell phone times used in mobile learning. The final goal is to build mobile virtual classrooms (MVClassroom), where classroom and online students can share electronic whiteboards and other presentation tools, interact more often among themselves, and engage in dialogue more often with the instructors. Courses that are delivered in MVclassrooms will need to be redesigned with more student-centered learning activities and multiple assessment methods such as team projects, discussions, participation, and tests. Currently, college-level courses in China predominantly feature teacher's one-way lecturing, students' silent note-taking, and then a final "fate-determining" test. It is our hope that mobile learning can bring bottom-up pedagogical changes to China's higher education, by placing students at the center of instruction and by encouraging more interaction and collaborative learning.

We also plan to conduct associated research to assess the effect of mobile learning on students' learning satisfaction, sense of community, and learning outcomes. In addition, we will examine and compare students' learning outcomes (test scores and quality of essays) to assess the impact of mobile learning. At present, the E-learning lab is developing a learning management system for instructors to monitor students' course-related activities. In the near future, we plan to further develop the system to track which courses or videos a student has taken. The tracking data can be used in more quantitative analysis of students' performance. For instance, we can correlate the frequency of their usage with their learning outcomes (grades).

Finally, the E-learning Lab hopes to contribute to the nationwide Project Hope, which is launched by the Chinese government and aims to help improve primary education for children in many poor and isolated countryside areas of China. Project Hope mobilizes Chinese and foreign materials and financial resources to help bring dropouts back to school, to improve educational facilities and to promote primary education in China's poverty-stricken areas [8]. In many of these areas, children live far away from their schools and need to hike through hills, rivers, or mountains to attend classroom instruction. Also in these areas, mobile phone ownership is much higher than computers. We hope to donate more cell phones and PDAs to help Project Hope schools deliver some of their courses to these mobile devices, so that children can still attend school in unusual circumstances such as busy harvest season or bad weather.

3 Conclusion

Here we provide a glimpse of China's mobile learning and mobile education development in the past two to three years. China's mobile phones users are growing rapidly every year and thus create ample opportunities for further designing, developing, and implementing mobile learning. However, mobile learning is still in its infancy and enjoys only limited use in both K-12 and higher education. In particular, the K-12 school use is confined to instant-messaging type of communication. By contrast, several higher educational institutions such as Shanghai Jiaotong University (SJTU) and Peking University are leading the trend in creating mobile virtual classrooms. Because their efforts are still underway, we focus on reporting the technological success and the flow in mobile learning delivery at the E-learning Lab of SJTU. We also provide hypothetical scenarios--online students, mobile virtual classrooms (MVclassrooms), and Project Hope--, where mobile learning can be used to improve teaching, learning, and course delivery.

The learning activities described in this paper are still hypothetical and need to be pilot tested with real users. We plan to conduct rapid prototyping with potential users in the near future, so as to improve course design, development, and delivery. In addition, we plan to collect learner feedback and further evaluate the impact of mobile course delivery on learner motivations and learning outcomes.

With the rapid technological development, mobile learning in China will have enormous opportunities in the near future. The traditional teacher-centered curriculum, however, is urgently in need of redesign so to make the best of the advantages of mobile devices. For instance, several of the distance education departments of institutions of higher education are actively seeking ways to adapt their current curriculum for successful delivery to mobile devices. Thus, we hope that the development of mobile learning can also facilitate the pedagogical changes to higher education in China. Finally, because of the lack of large-scale implementation in education, little research addresses the dynamic issues associated with mobile learning. More research needs to be conducted to explore the impact of mobile learning on students' learning motives, their course performance, and their mastering of information technology skills.

References

1. P. Harris (2001). Goin' Mobile. Learning Circuits, (http://www.learningcircuits.org/2001/jul2001/harris.html)
2. J. S., Kossen (2001). When e-learning Becomes M-Learning. Palmpower Magazine. (http://www.palmpowerenterprise.com/issues/issue200106/elearning001.html)
3. C. Quinn (Fall 2000). mLearning: Mobile, Wireless, In-Your-Pocket Learning. Linezine: Learning in the New Economy, (http://www.linezine.com/2.1/features/cqmmwiyp.htm)
4. S. Shi (2004). Supporting Integrated Science Learning with Pocket computers (http://www.concord.org/~sherry/cilt/index.html)
5. M. Ratto et al. (June 2003). The ActiveClass Project: Experiments in Encouraging Classroom Participation. In Computer Support for Collaborative Learning 2003: Kluwer.

6. S.Q., Yu, M.J., Wang, & H.Y., Che (2004). Critical Issues of Educational Informatization in China. Unpublished manuscript.
7. G. Cui (2004). MVClass: Mobile Virtual Class for Open and Distance Education, (http://www.metc.pku.edu.cn/melab/publications/mepaper09.pdf)
8. Chen, Y.-S., et al. A mobile scaffolding-aid-based bird-watching learning system. in IEEE International Workshop on Wireless and Mobile Technologies in Education (WMTE'02). August 29, 2002. Växjö, Sweden.
9. Project Hope. Today's Hope is China's Future. (http://www.nacef.org/english/ehope982.htm)

A Novel Mobile Learning Assistant System[*]

Ren Tong, Zuwei Hu, Peng Han, and Fan Yang

Department of Computer Science and Engineering, Shanghai JiaoTong University,
Shanghai, 200030, China
{tongren, huzw, phan,fyang}@mail.sjtu.edu.cn

Abstract. The growth of wireless networking and the maturing of online learning have created an environment in which students are mobile and leaning is no longer tethered to the classroom or the laboratory. We have developed a mobile learning platform, which supports multi-media courses delivery and has applied in Network Education College of Shanghai Jiaotong University. Based on the platform, this paper mainly proposes an assistant system to solve the learning status monitoring issue which is becoming a challenge of learning effect control in mobile learning. This assistant system can enable teachers to monitor the students' mobile phone screen synchronously thus know the learning state of the students, and it also supports real time interaction with the students by instant messages. Meanwhile, the students can view the status of other online peers, interact with each other and ask for remote assistance by sharing their own screens to those willing to help.

1 Introduction

The combination of wireless technology and mobile computing is resulting in escalating transformations of the educational world [1]. Mobile Learning is becoming more and more popular these days, which enables people to learn anytime and everywhere so that they are no longer tethered to the classroom or the laboratory. Many researchers are conducting researches in this domain, to produce a pedagogically sound set of guidelines for learners; teachers and policy makers are considering adopting m-learning technology [2]. Many mobile learning applications are also booming and several of them are noteworthy. Distance learning through mail exchange by mobile phone is developed in Japan [3], which also provides a management system to promote competitive behavior between students, and to maintain their interest and motivation. The mCLT project [4] allows students to participate in a knowledge building process via mobile devices. The students can interact among themselves according to the model defined by the teacher. It also allows students to browse the list and the detailed information of the courses. A Mobile Learning Organizer for University Students [5] is conducted to make use of existing mobile applications as well as tools designed specifically for the context of learning. In particular, City University of Hong Kong incorporates 3D content in web-based learning systems and allows students to visualize various types of complicated structures or certain difficult conceptual ideas [6]. The E-Learning Lab of Shanghai

[*] Supported by National Natural Science Foundation of China under Grant No.60372078.

R.W.H. Lau et al. (Eds.): ICWL 2005, LNCS 3583, pp. 340–348, 2005.
© Springer-Verlag Berlin Heidelberg 2005

Jiaotong University has developed a mobile learning platform, which supports multi-media courses delivery; with mobile phones, the students can simultaneously view online broadcasts when the teacher is instructing in the traditional classroom.

Great progress has been made in mobile learning field; however most of these approaches or systems ignore the learning status monitoring issue, which is becoming a challenge of learning effect control in mobile learning. And the lack of interaction among students will make them feel lonely during the learning process. The purpose of this paper is to propose an assistant system which enables the teacher to monitor all the online students' learning status and make the communication between teacher and students with unprecedented flexibility and convenience.

The rest of this paper is organized as follows: Section 2 briefly relates the background and architecture of the Mobile Learning Assistant System. The implementation details of the system and a case study of this system is described in Section 3 and Section 4 respectively. Finally we make a conclusion and give an outlook of future work.

2   System Description

The main contribution of this paper is to introduce a new methodology to support the mobile learning process by monitoring the student's screens, and to enable all kinds of interactions between the students by providing the capability of sharing one student's screen to another.

2.1 Backgrounds

Our E-Learning Lab has designed a learning platform for mobile phones which supports three types of learning access: tuning into live broadcast, Learning-on-demand (LOD), and downloading archived broadcast to mobile devices.

While a teacher instructs in a traditional classroom, his or her presentations are simultaneously converted to online streaming learning content by a Recording program which will generate three types of streams: a) an instructor's presentation screen from his desktop b) the instructor's facial expressions from a video camera, and c) the audio stream of an instructor's voices from a microphone. These streams are transmitted to a Cast Server. And for mobile phones to retrieve these learning materials, they have to get access to the Internet by GPRS (General Packet Radio Service) which is a technology allows mobile phones to be used for sending and receiving data over an Internet Protocol (IP)-based network. Yet the bandwidth of GPRS is quite limited, which is approximately 28.8kbps for downloading, and 10kbps for uploading.

To successfully deliver the Learning materials to mobile phones, it is further compressed. Each of the three streams are reduced to as low as 8kbps, so that it can better adapt to the bandwidth of GPRS, Figure 1 shows the application on mobile phones (SjtuPlayer) running on the actual devices, which are Nokia 7610 and Nokia 6600.

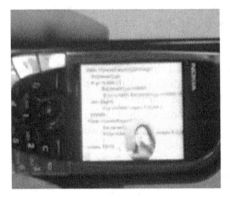   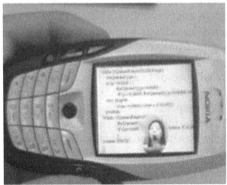

(a) SjtuPlayer on Nokia 7610   (b) SjtuPlayer on Nokia 6600

Fig. 1. SjtuPlayer on Actual Nokia Mobile Phones

After deploying this system to the Network Education College (NEC) in Shanghai Jiaotong University (SJTU) for two weeks, we encountered several problems: The teacher did not know how many students was actually learning, not to mention knowing their learning state or to interact with them for the problems which were encountered in the learning process. Also the students were lonely, they didn't know how many of their peers were learning too, and could not exchange ideas with them. To solve these problems, we developed the Mobile Learning Assistant System to facilitate the mobile learning process.

2.2 Architecture

This system consists of two parts as shown in Figure 2: (1).MobileServer runs on a Server which can be directly accessed on the Internet, Its main purpose is to display the screens of the connected students, and to transmit communication data (screen sharing data, text messages) between students; (2).SjtuAssistant runs on the S60 phone [7] which was based on Symbian Operating System [8], connects to the Internet via GPRS and work as a background agent, Sending screens to the MobileServer, and collecting information from the server, then shows the details such as online lists to the students.

The main idea of this system is to capture the mobile phone's screen periodically and then transmit the screen data to the MobileServer, while the MobileServer display those received screen data on a teacher's desktop, it also enables the teacher to directly control one of the connected phones from his desktop. If there is any interaction between students, the Mobile Server transmits the communication data which can be short messages or screen sharing data between the interacting students.

The whole system is based on the SOCKET connection: there is a SOCKET connection between each mobile phone and the Mobile Server; due to the unreliability of the wireless connection, we use the TCP protocol to achieve a reliable transmission channel between them.

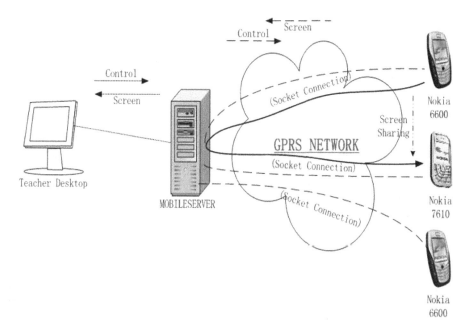

Fig. 2. Architecture of the Mobile Learning Assistant System

3 Implementation

The application on the mobile phone (SjtuAssistant) is developed using Series 60 SDK 2.1 for Symbian OS. The application on the server (MobileServer) is developed by Microsoft Visual C++ with a Skin++ package to make the User Interface look prettier.

Currently, we only support Series 60 phones, which include almost all modern phone types: Nokia 6600, 7610, 6630, N-Gage; Siemens SX1, Panasonic X700, and Sendo X etc.

There are four important aspects of the system: 1. "Screen Data Transmitting" is about how to effectively sending the phone's screen data to the MobileServer. 2. "Rendering the Screens" discusses how to display all the connected phone screens to the teacher's desktop; 3."Teacher-Student Interaction" concerns about how the teachers can communicate with the students by sending short text messages or directly operating on the students' mobile phones; 4."Student-Student Interaction" explores how the students can discuss among themselves via short text messages or sharing their screens with each other. We will discuss the details in the following sections.

Here we defined a common data structure, which is used for communication between SjtuAssistant and MobileServer:

```
typedef struct {
            int     type;     //0:screen, 1:control, 2:text
            int     toWhom;  // 0: teacher; X: Xth peer
            int     length;  // The Length of the data
} MSGHEAD;
```

3.1 Screen Data Transmitting

To get access to Internet on mobile phones, we use GPRS, and as mentioned above the bandwidth of GPRS is quite limited, which is approximately 10kbps for uploading. To successfully transmit the mobile phones screens to the server in an acceptable interval, we should transmit as little data as possible.

To capture the mobile phone's screen to a bitmap, we use the API provided by the S60 SDK:

```
CFbsBitmap scrBitmap;
CEikonEnv::Static()->ScreenDevice()-
>CopyScreenToBitmap(scrBitmap);
```

As the phone's color depth is 16bit(2Byte) which can display 65535 colors, and the screen size is 176*208, so the total data size of the screen shot will be as large as 176*208*16= 585728(bits) which is approximately 73KB, so it will take more then 1 minute to transfer the screen data (because the upload bandwidth is 10kbps) which is obviously too long for the monitoring purpose. To resolve this problem, we applied the Symbian's ICL (Image Converter Library) [9] to encode the resulted screen bitmap; the following code skeleton shows how to encode the bitmap data to jpeg format. We used an 85% quality factor and the resulting data is about 5KB to 15KB according to the content of the screen currently displays. So that we can update the screen of students' mobile phones every 10 sec.

```
HBufC8* iJpegData = 0; //a buffer to store JPEG data...
CImageEncoder* iImageEncoder =
CImageEncoder::DataNewL(iJpegData,
CImageEncoder::EOptionAlwaysThread, KImageTypeJPGUid,
KNullUid, KNullUid);
TJpegImageData* imageData = new (ELeave)TJpegImageData;
imageData->iSampleScheme = JpegImageData::EColor444;
imageData->iQualityFactor = 85;    //quality factor
iFrameImageData = CFrameImageData::NewL();
User::LeaveIfError(iFrameImageData-
>AppendImageData(imageData));
TRequestStatus Status;
iImageEncoder->Convert(&Status, *scrBitmap,
iFrameImageData);
User::WaitForRequest(Status);
```

To transmit the phone screen to the MobileServer, it first sends the message head to the server, and then sends the whole screen data to the server. As the screen data length is varied each time, the MSGHEAD will make it easier for the MobileServer to render the screen to the teacher's desktop:

```
MSGHEAD head;
head.type = 0;    //screen data
head.length = iJpegData->Length(); //screen data length
head.toWhom = 0; //to teacher
TPtrC8 ptrd;
ptrd.Set((unsigned char*)&head, sizeof(head));
// First send the head to the server
iSocketsEngine->WriteL(ptrd);
//Writing the actual data
iSocketsEngine->WriteL(*iJpegData);
```

3.2 Rendering the Screens

When the MobileServer receives data from the each of the students' phone, it first copies the data to a local buffer, after receiving the whole message head (MSGHEAD), the server will know the length of the screen data from the length tag of the MSGHEAD; Then, after receiving all the screen data, it will call "DispScrns" to render the screen data to the screen. The first parameter was the pointer to the actual screen data, the second parameter is a "this" pointer, which was used by the DispScrns function to determine which client is sending the data; the third parameter determined the position to show on the screen, and the last parameter is the length of the screen data.

```
void CClientSocket::OnReceive(int nErrorCode)
{
int nLen = 0;
nLen = Receive(m_pRecvBuf, BUFLEN);
if (cnt+nLen>=BUFLEN)
        return; //m_pscrData: buffer for screen data
memcpy(m_pscrData+cnt, m_pRecvBuf, nLen);
cnt+=nLen;    //cnt: actual data length in m_pscrData
while (cnt > sizeof(MSGHEAD)) {
MSGHEAD* head = (MSGHEAD*)m_pscrData;
int proLen = head->len + sizeof(MSGHEAD);
if (proLen <= cnt) {   //proLen: length to render screen
        m_pDlg->DispScrns(m_pscrData+sizeof(MSGHEAD),
this, m_SIndex, head->len);
            cnt-=proLen;
            if (cnt > 0) {
               memmove(m_pscrData, m_pscrData+proLen,
cnt);
            }
}
else {
        break;
}
}
CSocket::OnReceive(nErrorCode);
}
```

3.3 Teacher-Student Interaction

When the student encounters some unclear points, he can ask the teacher for help by selecting the "Q&A" function provided by our application (SjtuAssistant) on his mobile phone. We set the type of MSGHEAD to 2, and then send the student's question the MobileServer. Once upon receiving the question on the server, the teacher will be notified and then can select that student to be the ACTIVE user, and then type in some answers to be sent to the student and displayed in the Q&A section of SjtuAssistant. All the communication is based on the socket connection too. As the text input on the phone is not very convenient, we are planning to provide some Voice Q&A functionalities in our next version.

3.4 Student-Student Interaction

The teacher may become too busy if every student asks him for help when encountering any problem, so we provide some mechanism to assist student-student interaction. When the student logged on to our system with his mobile phone, SjtuAssitant will send his IMEI(International Mobile Equipment Identity) to MobileServer, which is an unique 15 digital number assigned to each GSM mobile phone and can be obtained by pressing *#06# on the phone. We have a database with student's name and his phone's IMEI, so we can easily maintain an online student list on our MobileServer, and we will send this information periodically to the current online students, so that they can see how many of their classmates are currently online. Also they can choose from their online lists to start a text conversation or ask for remote assistance by sharing their screens to the students they choose. The scenario of sending text messages to each other is similar to 3.3 Q&A with teacher. Here we discuss the situation of share their screens to other students' mobile phones.

The screen data is first sent to the server, but set the MSGHEAD's toWhom = X; (X is the internal representation of the students name), so that when the MobileServer received this stream data, it will retransmit to the selected students' mobile phone via the socket connection, if the other student accepted the incoming screen, we again use the ICL in a converse process, to first encoding the received JPEG screen data to the CFbsBitmap representation inside the S60 phones and then render it to the receiver's screen, so that they can solve the problem cooperatively.

4 Case Study

Here we describe a scenario of our mobile learning assistant system. As the SjtuAssistant may intrude the students' privacy by monitoring all the activities on their mobile phones, we are authorized by the students in advance to install this application on their mobile phones. Figure 3 is a screenshot of our running system on the server, which can be divided into two panels. The left panel is a set of online students' mobile phone screen. The right one is the Active Focus Screen which can be stimulated by double clicking one of the students' screen shot in the left panel, then the display of the simulated mobile phone image is changed to the Active student's screen. Once a student becomes active, the teacher can directly control the student's mobile phone by operating on the simulated phone image, or interact with the student by sending instant text messages.

Shown as Figure 3, we can see that there are four students online, three are studying, but one is playing a game. As the teacher can monitor all the online students, he/she can first double click the screen playing game and make this student as the Active student, then type in a note "Hi, You should not play game when having class" and press "Enter". Immediately, the active student's phone will pop up a note with the contents the teacher typed in. If the student ignored the teacher's notice, the teacher can operate on his phone by manipulating on the mobile phone image to make sure that the student is studying when he is supposed to.

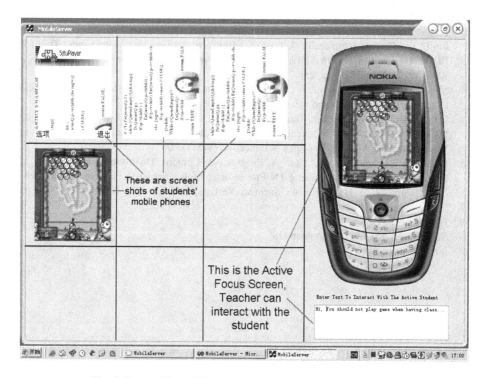

Fig. 3. Screen Shot of Teacher's desktop monitoring the online students

5 Conclusion and Future Work

Great progress has been made in mobile learning field; however most of these approaches or systems ignore the learning status monitoring issue, which is becoming a challenge of learning effect control in mobile learning. And the lack of interaction among students makes them feel lonely during the learning process. This paper proposed an assistant system which enables the teacher to monitor all the online students' learning status and make the communication between teacher and students with unprecedented flexibility and convenience. The next step in our work is to add more interaction functions into this assistant system, such as voice Question and Answering component, which can facilitate the interaction process as it would be more convenient than typing text messages on mobile phones.

References

1. Bryan Alexander Going Nomadic: Mobile Learning in Higher Education. IN: EDUCAUSE Review, vol. 39, no. 5 (September/October 2004): 28–35.
2. Giasemi N.Vavoula, Paul Lefrere, Claire O'Malley, Mike Sharples, Josie Taylor: Producing guidelines for learning, teaching and tutoring in a mobile environment IN Proceedings of the The 2nd IEEE International Workshop on Wireless and Mobile Technologies in Education (WMTE'04)
3. Kouji Yoshida1, Kouiti Matsumoto1, Kazuhiro Nakada1, Tomonori Akutsu1, Satoru Fujii2 and Hiroshi Ichimura3: A Trial of a Bidirectional Learning Management Tool for Promoting Learning by Mobile Phone IN V. Palade, R.J. Howlett, and L.C. Jain (Eds.): KES 2003, LNAI 2774, pp. 756-763, 2003.
4. Marco Arrigo, G. Chiappone: mCLT: an application for collaborative learning on a mobile telephone IN http://www.mobilearn.org/mlearn2004/
5. Dan Corlett, Mike Sharples, Tony Chan, Susan Bull: A Mobile Learning Organiser for University Students IN Proceedings of the The 2nd IEEE International Workshop on Wireless and Mobile Technologies in Education (WMTE'04)
6. Frederick Li and Rynson Lau: A Progressive Content Distribution Framework in Supporting Web-based Learning IN Proceedings of International Conference on Web-based Learning 2004, LNCS 3143, Springer-Verlag, pp. 75-82, Aug. 2004.
7. http://www.series60.com/
8. http://www.symbian.com/
9. Series 60 SDK Help for Symbian OS
10. http://forum.nokia.com/

Context-Sensitive Content Representation for Mobile Learning

William C. Chu[1], Hong-Xin Lin[2], Juei-Nan Chen[3], and Xing-Yi Lin[4]

[1,2,4] Department of Computer Science and Information Engineering, TungHai University,
No. 181, Taichung-Kang Road, Sec. 3, Taichung 40744, Taiwan
chu@csie.thu.edu.tw
{hxlin, bowji}@itlab.csie.thu.edu.tw
[3] Department of Engineering Science, National Cheng Kung University,
No. 1, Ta-Hsueh Road, Tainan 701, Taiwan
nan@itlab.csie.thu.edu.tw

Abstract. Mobile learning means that the learning contents can be displayed any-time, anywhere, and with any kind of presenting device. Learning Content Management Systems (LCMSs) usually provide convenient authoring tools to help instructors to construct their learning contents, which may include static document such as powerpoint, word, pdf document and dynamic multimedia document such as video and audio files, and then integrate these learning contents to provide learners with proper contents rendering through access devices. However, most of LCMSs are based on desktop computer environments, rather than mobile devices. Context-Sensitivity is an application of software system's ability to sense and analyze context from various sources. In this paper, we develop a Context-Sensitive Middleware (CSM) for LCMS to transform the same learning contents to different mobile devices, so mobile learning can be supported.

Keywords: Mobile Learning, Learning Content Management System (LCMS), Context-Sensitive.

1 Introduction

The purpose of learning is to absorb knowledge efficiently. In tradition, studying habits may be affected by the restriction of time and space to decline the learning quality. Mobile learning means that the learning contents can be gotten anytime, any-where, and with any kind of devices.

Many Learning Content Management Systems (LCMSs) [1] were developed, which offer convenient authoring tools help instructors to construct their learning contents, which may include static document such as powerpoint, word, pdf document and dynamic multimedia document such as video and audio files, and then integrate these learning contents to provide learners with proper contents rendering through access devices.

However, most of LCMSs are based on desktop computer environments, rather than mobile devices. Context-Sensitivity is an application of software system's ability

R.W.H. Lau et al. (Eds.): ICWL 2005, LNCS 3583, pp. 349–354, 2005.

to sense and analyze context from various sources. In this paper, we develop a Context-Sensitive Middleware (CSM) for LCMS to transform the same learning contents to different mobile devices, so mobile learning can be supported.

The rest of this article is organized as follows. In section 2, we discuss the related technologies applied in mobile learning. The complete system architecture and approaches are described in section 3. Finally, the conclusion and future works are described in section 4.

2   Related Works

2.1   SCORM

SCORM (Sharable Content Object Reference Model) is a set of standards proposed by ADL (Advanced Distributed Learning). The purpose of its development lies in online teaching and web-based learning, and it composes reusable learning object with the techniques of framework [2][3]. SCORM defines a set of related specifications to enable the learning content and system to conform to the high-level requirement model. In addition, the multimedia teaching materials were extensively applied to e-learning applications, so that learning objects no longer confine to texts. In the transmission of information, the multimedia teaching materials usually have more expressiveness than texts. Liu et al. have presented methods in automatically producing SCORM-based multimedia learning material [4].

SCORM defines a whole set of system structure. Learners can extend the system functions to exchange information and share the teaching materials with other systems. However, SCORM was not designed to take care of context-sensitivity issues. In order to efficiently and effectively achieve mobile learning, context-sensitivity issues need to be solved. A relevant research called Pocket SCORM which has discussed about context-sensitivity to mobile devices [5]. Our approach focuses more on solving problem on rendering standard SCORM contents in different mobile devices.

3   Context-Sensitive Mobile Learning Environment

The mobile computing environment consists of LCMS, rendering devices, and Context-Sensitive Middleware (CSM), as shown in Fig. 1. The major functionality of CSM is to provide learners with proper content format when they access contents from different mobile devices, so the content rendering is appropriate.

In our approach, we have applied MVC pattern to the design and implementation of our mobile e-learning environment. In order to promote the reusability of mobile contents, we follow SCORM 1.3.1 [3], in which learning content is subdivided into Asset, SCO, SCA and Content Packaging; meanwhile, the linking relationship of these elements is defined by XML description. In this paper, our work has been based on the design and implementation of Context-Sensitive Middleware (CSM).

In the following sections, we will focus on discussing about the detail of *XML Profile Generator* and *View Adaptor*. We leave out the other subsystems since their designs are straight forward.

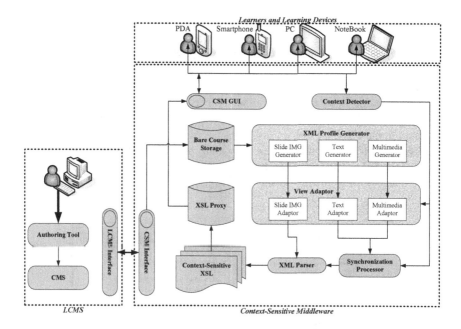

Fig. 1. System Architecture of the Context-Sensitive Mobile Learning

3.1 XML Profile Generator

Due to the limitation of the resources of mobile devices, such as the smaller screen size, the learning content, e.g. slides in powerpoint format which were originally designed for PC environment, can not be properly rendered in mobile devices and need to be analyzed and transformed to the appropriate format. In order to make learners acquire learning contents by their mobile devices, all learning resources are transformed to XML profiles via XML Profile Generator.

XML Profile Generator classifies the learning content into three categories: Slide IMG, Text, and Multimedia. Slide IMG is the image and picture, Text is the text, and Multimedia is the attached multimedia files from slides. These three types of content will be extracted from original slides and transformed into their corresponding profiles in XML format. Based on these profiles, *View Adaptor* then can adapt them into appropriate format for different devices.

3.1.1 Transformation of Learning Content

The steps of the transformation of learning content into XML profile are the following:

I. *Parse and Analyze the slide.* When an mobile learning content (MLC) is acquired from *LCMS*, we can parse and analyze the slide element according to the Slide Element Table (SET).

II. *Extract the text and image from slide.* After parsing and analyzing the slide, one of the slide templates is selected. Then, we must extract the text and image from slide. Since powerpoint supports Text mode (shown in Fig. 2), this problem can be solved. In addition, if there exists some images in the slide, we can extract it directly since powerpoint regards images as independent objects. The process to extract image is by discarding other objects in the slide, as shown in Fig. 3. As mentioned above, the elements of the slide can be extracted effectively and re-used in our *CSM.*

III. *Generate the XML profiles based on analyzed result.* Finally, since the text can be extracted successfully, we transform Text into XML profiles by Text Generator. The complete process is shown in Fig. 4.

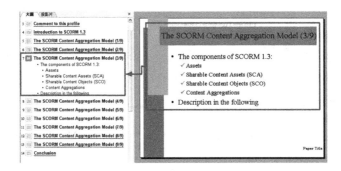

Fig. 2. Extract Text from PowerPoint

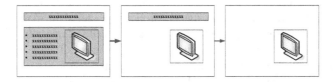

Fig. 3. Image Extraction Process

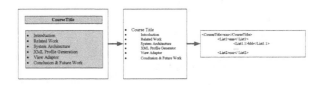

Fig. 4. Slide Transformation Process

3.1.2 Transformation of Slide IMG and Multimedia

The purpose of generating Slide IMG is to make learners hold the full view of the content when learning in mobile devices. "Slide IMG Profiles" are transformed via

Slide IMG Generator, as shown in Fig. 5. Besides, if mobile devices support multimedia playing (detected by Context Detector), learners can switch Slide IMG Mode or Multimedia Mode by this button, " 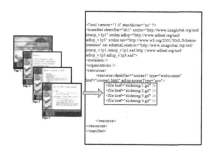 " in Fig. 5.

Fig. 5. Transform Slide IMG to XML Profiles

3.2   View Adaptor

In section 3.1, we know how to generate the XML profiles of the three learning resources - Slide IMG Profile, Text Profile, and Multimedia Profile. Next, we describe how to transform the three XML profiles into adaptive ones by Context Detector and View Adaptor, and then integrate these into a customized learning content.

3.2.1   Context-Sensitive Content Rearrangement

Based on the representation of Slide IMG, learners can hold the full view of the content, rather than the detail. This problem can be solved by the connection of Slide IMG and Text. When learners select one Slide IMG, the Text of the image is matched to Text Mode. The technique to attain this is to use a "Double Anchor Hyperlink" between Text and Slide IMG, as shown in Fig. 6.

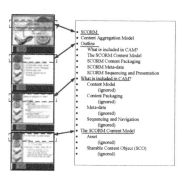

Fig. 6. Relationship of Slide IMG vs. Text

3.2.2 Context-Sensitive Content Transformation

Some XSL which describe device context are stored in Context Detector. When learners study online, Context Detector selects the proper XSL and then integrates this with XML profiles generated by XML Profile Generator. Finally, we transform the customized mobile learning content according to the browsers that mobile devices support, this is called Context-Sensitive XSL. We put Context-Sensitive XSL into XSL Proxy, so that it is convenient for learners to learn by the same mobile device.

4   Conclusion and Future Works

Most of LCMS can integrate static and dynamic files, but they only pay attention to develop systems based on desktop computer environments, rather than mobile devices. In this paper, the XML profiles of the three learning resources are generated by XML Profile Generator. Then, adaptive XML profiles are transformed via View Adaptor and Context Detector that detect device context of mobile devices. Finally, a customized mobile learning content is packaged to enhance the reusability of learning resources successfully. In the future, we will extend "Context-Sensitive Content Representation" to include "Interactive Learning" and "Offline Learning".

References

[1] Advanced Distributed Learning (ADL), "SCORM 2004 2nd Edition Overview," *Available at ADLNet.org*, July, 2004.
[2] Advanced Distributed Learning (ADL), "SCORM Content Aggregation Model Version 1.3.1," *Available at ADLNet.org*, July, 2004.
[3] J. T. David Yang and C. Y. Tsai, "An Implementation of SCORM-compliant Learning Content Management System – Content Repository Management System," *Proceedings of the 3rd IEEE International Conference on Advanced Learning Technologies* (ICALT' 03), 2003, pp.453.
[4] P. Liu, L. H. Hsu and A. Chakraborty, "Towards Automating the Generation of SCORM-Based Multimedia Product Training Manuals," *Proceedings of 2002 IEEE International Conference Multimedia and Expo* (ICME' 02), 2002, pp. 397-400.
[5] N. H. Lin, T. K. Shih, H. H. Hsu, H. P. Chang, H. B. Chang, W. C. Ko and L. J. Lin "Pocket SCORM," *Proceedings of the 24th International Conference on Distributed Computing Systems Workshops* (ICDCSW'04), March, 2004, pp. 274-279.

Managing Student Expectations Online

D.A. Newlands and J.M. Coldwell

School of Information Technology, Deakin University,
Geelong, VIC, 3217, Australia
{doug, jojo}@deakin.edu.au

Abstract. In contrast to other studies of students in online environments, which examine the skills and attitudes that students bring to an online university learning environment, we are interested in the expectations with which students come to online university study. Four expectational barriers, which arise from students' background and cultural history, are identified as being: who is responsible for learning, who is responsible for student interaction with content, who is responsible for the use of appropriate learning strategies and who is responsible for required ancillary skills. There is a discussion of how these barriers arise and how one might attempt to manage the students' expectations and ameliorate their effects.

1 Introduction

The American Psychological Association has identified a number of factors which are associated with success in a course of study (APA, 1997). The students' motivational and emotional state regarding the study on which they are embarking, their intrinsic motivation to learn, their curiosity, insightfulness and their perception that the learning tasks are designed to be interesting and to engage them in personally useful, real-world situations are all important contributors to outcomes. Students also bring their differing familial and societal backgrounds with them and these will affect their interpersonal interactions in group tasks, their opportunities for seeing different perspectives, their feelings of self-respect and perceived sexual stereotypes. Through these various influences the student has to deal with learner-content, learner-learner and learner-instructor issues (Chou, 2004) as well as learner-interface difficulties (Hillman et al., 1994). They also have a set of expectations based on their educational experiences to date. The disparity between their expectations and the actuality of online learning in a university environment will greatly affect how they deal with these difficulties and, ultimately, affect educational outcomes.

This paper explores some of these potential disparities and identifies how the difficulties, which arise, have been or might be addressed in the context of a fully online presentation of a computer ethics course in our university

2 The Changing Setting of the Educational Experience

The student body enrolled in the course being discussed come from a wide range of previous educational experiences. Local students include those who have completed

R.W.H. Lau et al. (Eds.): ICWL 2005, LNCS 3583, pp. 355–363, 2005.
© Springer-Verlag Berlin Heidelberg 2005

high school, others who have completed a post-secondary diploma and have transferred into university, and yet others who are mature age students who have entered on the basis of some experience other than formal education. Overseas students all have completed high school in their home country. Some commence their tertiary studies directly after completing high school, some have completed a suitable post-secondary diploma course in their home country, and some have completed the first, and possibly second, year of our degree in an overseas partner institution.

Courses at our university are presented in a mixture of modes (Coldwell and Newlands, 2004). On-campus students will encounter traditional, face-to-face teaching, but it is supported by online technologies. Typical, individual, off-campus students enrolled in this course have all materials delivered by online technologies supplemented by online contact and discussion forums. Overseas partner institutions have materials supplied by online technologies but students are supported by local tutors. The university endeavours to provide as similar a learning experience as possible to all students, regardless of mode of study or physical location. This is supported by our current learning management system (LMS), which is implemented using WebCT Vista. As part of the University's commitment to preparing students for lifelong learning, it has prescribed that every student must experience at least one wholly online course as part of their undergraduate degree programme (Deakin University, 2003). The computer ethics unit being discussed here is one such course.

The computer ethics course is a final year core unit for all students enrolled in the Bachelor of Information Technology (BIT). It is unusual for this unit to be given as advance standing, so essentially every student has to complete it. This has resulted in very large class size (500+ students in 2004). Students have different levels of local learning experiences when they encounter this course. On the one hand, there is the traditional student who is in their last semester of study having completed 5 or more full-time equivalent semesters at Deakin already. At the other extreme, there is the student who is just commencing their studies at Deakin with 2 years equivalent of advance standing and encountering the computer ethics unit as one of their first courses in this new environment.

As the computer ethics course is compulsory in the BIT, the students are thrust into university studies in an online mode without any options. They *must* access materials online, submit assignments online, collaborate with group members online and take an active part in online discussions. They have very different levels of experience of using the online environment from never having encountered any online learning environments through to those who may have already encountered a wholly online unit in their studies. The subsequent sections of this paper explore the expectations of students and the faculty in this environment.

3   What Expectations?

3.1   Faculty Expectations

Faculty expectations of students are varied and some are reflected in the Student Responsibilities section of our University's Student Charter (Deakin University, 2004), viz.:

1. students are expected to be self-motivated and self-directed learners;
2. students are expected to prepare for and to participate appropriately in the range of experiences which make up their course of study;
3. students are responsible for ancillary skills such as use of technology (although that might be implied in above);
4. students are expected to ensure regular electronic contact with the university via StudentConnect, (providing students access to enrolment, administrative and support services).

These may be reasonable expectations but they offer little guidance on how to satisfy them. There is an implicit expectation that strategies to satisfy them are known to all students but this expectation takes no cognisance of the wide variety of social, cultural and educational backgrounds from which the students come. It is, then, unsurprising that some, perhaps many, students are not ready for online university study.

3.2 Student Expectations

Surveys of student expectations (for example Bolliger and Martindale, 2004) reveal that students expect:

1. staff to be available at flexible times;
2. good response times for queries and marking;
3. easily accessible help with technology;
4. easy to navigate web sites;
5. course content to be perceived to be real-world and relevant to their future;
6. facilitation of collaboration in tasks.

The first three items are concerned with expectations of the staff which appear to be reasonable. However, the first item, in particular, is often assessed poorly in student surveys as the students do not realise that faculty are expected to devote time to research as well as teaching, have a life away from the university, and cannot be available 24/7 as some students expect. The fifth item appears to be entirely reasonable but student perceptions of what is meaningful and real-world does not necessarily correspond with that of faculty. This is, perhaps, particularly true in the early stages of a programme of study when the students are unfamiliar with the subject matter and the distinctions drawn

4 The Disparity in Expectations

The high school learning environment is different from a university learning environment for a number of reasons, some of which are:

1. high school teaching takes place in small groups (25-30 in a class, 15-20 in a lab) compared to lectures with groups of 50 to several hundred and compared to online where it may appear to be a group of one;
2. interactivity may be entirely driven by the instructor in high school but in an online university setting, it is expected to be largely student driven, particularly in group-oriented activities;

3. the social interactivity and maturity of students at high school is variable and they may not be ready for interaction with an heterogeneous group of strangers, far less students from other cultures and countries;
4. students may have used computers in a variety of settings but purely as a tool to complete discrete tasks and not as the primary communication tool as is required in online learning environments.

The cultural baggage which students carry relates to their:

1. attitude to others, elders, those with higher perceived social standing, strangers;
2. likelihood of interacting with the above;
3. likelihood of initiating such interaction;
4. ability to use the language of instruction and the sophistication of such use.

Problems arising from the above can be examined under a number of separate headings).

4.1 Who Is Responsible for Learning?

Disparity of expectations appears to stem from the perception of who is responsible for what. High school is traditionally an *instructivist* environment (Burford and Haggis, 2000) where teachers are responsible for teaching the material and for the students' learning. At the tertiary level, the rate of presentation of content is much greater and the lecturer cannot present all of the relevant content but will be more concerned with the overall structure rather than dealing with detail in every area. Since the students are now responsible for at least some of their learning, the large scale structure of the syllabus content is an important concern for the academic and a *constructivist* approach, showing the structure of the syllabus content, is attractive. The academic is now responsible for ensuring that students are provided with the means to learn rather than instruction per se. The responsibility for learning rests squarely on the students' own shoulders. This forms the first barrier due to the differing expectations as to who is responsible for learning.

4.2 Who Is Responsible for the Student Interacting with the Syllabus Content?

Our experience of students learning behaviour at the level of this course suggests that they are assessment driven and this colours the manner in which they deal with requirements. They also seem hesitant to take on the responsibility for their learning and would rather that it be shouldered by academics. This disparity often causes major problems for both staff and students particularly in online courses as the online learning environment is a *pull* technology as opposed to the face-to-face classroom situation which is more congruent with *push* technology. What do we mean by this? In the classroom students may, if they wish, simply absorb what is being said to them by the teacher. They have little option but to listen to what is being said. However, in the online environment, the best that the teacher can achieve is to make available the information that they require the student to access. It is then up to the student to access and read that information. This forms a second barrier due to differing expectations as to who is responsible for student interacting with the syllabus content.

4.3   Who Is Responsible for Use of Appropriate Learning Strategies?

Students may not understand the difference between surface or superficial learning and deep learning approaches to study. They may not realise that rote learning often leads to superficial learning rather than deep learning (Richardson, 1994). Rote learning may be implicit in high school learning, perhaps driven by assessment methods. These may be such that subjects in which assessment modes emphasise recall, like history or English literature, encourage surface learning whereas subjects such as mathematics and physics encourage deep learning strategies. Asian high schools appear to teach from an authoritative position rather than encourage experiment, discussion and insight (Smith, S., Miller, R., and Crassini, B. 1998). The students' lack of understanding of the inappropriateness of some learning modes form a third barrier.

4.4   Who Is Responsible for Ancillary Skills in the Online Environment?

Student attitudes to computers, networks and online communications are often that detail of use should be explicitly taught rather than made available and expect students to self learn. Bearing in mind that the students we are discussing here are all BIT students and have reasonable levels of computer literacy, this is somewhat surprising! The students' lack of ancillary skills and their expectation as to who is responsible for these skills is a fourth barrier to student learning since it interferes with their ability to easily access syllabus content, particularly as online learning environments are inherently constructivist and collaborative in nature.

5   Strategies to Manage the Disparities

5.1   Responsibility for Learning

Although the online learning context is student-centered, it is not entirely so. The lecturer *does* interact with the students via messaging and discussion forums as well as via the online syllabus content. However, the student expectation, arising from their past experiences, may lead them to believe that only face-to-face contact is important and that all secondary, indirect contact is optional and ignorable. Other face-to-face strategies such as timely reminders and follow-up on items become less immediate in the online environment since we cannot force students to find or read these. This can be seen as a consequence of the contrast between the immediacy of an on-campus presentation compared with the hypermediacy, but lack of immediacy, of the web-based presentation (Richards, 2002).

One solution is to use an effective tracking mechanism embedded in the LMS. Tracking statistics can show various levels of detail of individual student activity including.

1. when have they logged into the system;
2. when have they accessed (but not necessarily read!) announcements, subject materials etc.;
3. when have they accessed assignments,
4. when have they attempted to submit their solutions.

Use of this tracking information allows one to react to students who are not engaging with the material on an individual and person-to-person basis. For instance, enrolled students who have failed to submit the first assignment can be identified and contacted through channels other than the LMS in a time-frame permitting remediation of their behaviour. This can, to some extent, replace the immediacy of face-to-face contact so that the instructor can identify non-engaging behaviour and try to remedy it. It may even be an easier problem to handle the online student who does not read than the on-campus student who doesn't turn up.

5.2 Interacting with Syllabus Content

In the classroom situation academics are able to use various means to encourage students to engage with syllabus content, such as verbal discussions, providing readings, asking questions and so on. What is different about online learning environments? It is still possible to encourage engagement through discussion forums, content delivery and posing questions. The problem here is the intervening technology interface. Although the technology infrastructure layer of an LMS should play an invisible supporting role, as suggested by Harris (1999), it inevitably intervenes in the interactions between LMS users, be they staff or students. Rather than communication being direct, it is being facilitated by a software artifact, introducing the issues related to human-computer interactions rather than human-human interactions. It is no longer possible to view students' reactions for example, identify whether their attention has lapsed or they have become distracted.

However, there are additional tools and functionality in an electronic environment that are not necessarily available in the face-to-face situation. It is possible to send regular reminders regarding upcoming deadlines, work requirements and other key events. This can be done in various ways such as:

1. global announcements to the class which, in WebCT Vista, take the form of pop-up windows that appear when students access their online classroom;
2. messages on discussion boards providing information and advice. Unlike verbally provided advice, the message is permanently on the board for students to view and review;
3. individual or global emails sent to the students' preferred email address.

There is opportunity, however, for these forums to be overused and the resultant dissemination of information being viewed by students as spam. A survey of students enrolled in the computer ethics course in 2003 indicated that providing information using these various forums was deemed useful by those who were well-motivated, and simply a nuisance factor by those who were not! In 2004, staff minimised the number of different forums that were used regularly to disseminate the same information. However, a different problem arose as some students did not bother to read the information and messages, rather taking the easy route and simply posing a question to elicit the required response. This had the effect of increasing the number of messages on discussion boards unnecessarily as many students who *had* read the information proceeded to reply suggesting, politely and sometimes not so politely, that the questioner should "read the previous messages/appropriate document/announcement".

5.3 Appropriate Learning Strategies

Salmon's studies (Salmon, 2002; Salmon, 2003) suggest that online communities need to develop to enhance communication and hence learning. But where do students learn interactive discussion habits, even face-to-face, if not online, ones other than by absorption? Many students appear comfortable with using electronic means of communication. For example they can be found SMSing during lectures, or communicating in a variety of chat rooms during laboratory sessions. However, place academic overtones on the online discussion and they appear to become much less communicative. Anecdotal evidence suggests that students are concerned, in such an environment, with being right or wrong. This could stem from their assessment driven learning style. They perceive themselves as being judged, perhaps more so than they actually are. This is evidenced by students' concerns with how many marks they achieved each week for their online contributions.

Online facilitation and moderation are skills staff need to acquire. Staff need to be quick to respond to online enquiries to avoid mole hills escalating quickly into mountains. One strategy to overcome the escalation problem is to publish guidelines as to what level of service students can expect. As mentioned previously, students can be quite unreasonable when it comes to 24/7 service particularly at times of increased stress such as around assignment due dates. As in the case of cancelled face-to-face classes, students need to be informed if staff are unavailable at times they expect.

Assessment tasks need to be explicit and be directed at a specific goal or outcome so that student expectations can be set appropriately. Active participation needs to be perceived by students as valuable. To many this translates to contributing to their overall mark. The perceived value bears a strong relationship to the relative value of the task to the overall assessment. Contrariwise, one should not over specify the introductory tasks. We have seen an example where students were directed to a) post a message, b) respond to at least one other message, and c) respond to one message that was posted in response to yours! Do we have to teach students how to hold a conversation?

5.4 Ancillary Skills

Research agrees that orientation tasks are an essential component allowing students to familiarise themselves with the environment, become familiar with course requirements and to develop a relationship with other participants (Salmon, 2003; Smith et al., 2004). Salmon suggests however that the orientation and support needs to occur only in the early stages of the online activity, with students being able to take on more of the responsibility for learning as they progress. Smith et al. (2004), however, recommends that orientation and support activities may need to continue throughout the students' tenure in the online environment. The main difference here is that Salmon's students appear to be more mature and self-motivated, and have chosen the course as it is online thus better meeting their learning requirements. The students that Smith et al. are discussing did not chose to study online, come from very different backgrounds, as discussed earlier, and are not self-motivated or mature.

These orientation tasks should exercise the ancillary skills required *by design* and the students should understand that this is how they become familiar with new technologies and new learning skills. Our experience suggests that even those students who have passed a class specifically using such technologies appreciate a revision. Faculty, of course, worry about student compartmentalising of knowledge as belonging to this or that unit but this seems to be a trait in all but the best students

6 Conclusions

This paper has looked at the management of student expectations rather than at the technology used or at the course content or methods of teaching. It is asserted that one has to be aware of the students' expectations as they approach online, university study and where these expectations arose. To present a course which will be engaging for the students, one has to ensure that they have realistic expectations. We have identified four areas where students may have inappropriate expectations: who is responsible for their learning, who is responsible for how they interact with the syllabus, who is responsible for their using appropriate learning strategies and who is responsible for their having appropriate ancillary skills to learn in the online environment. Methods to manage expectations and methods of monitoring the effect of the management have been discussed in the light of our experience using an LMS to deliver a computer ethics course. Efforts should also be made to ensure expectations are continuously cultivated to allow students to achieve a positive outcome when experiencing online learning.

A recent development that may overcome some of the current limitations of electronic online learning systems, which appear to be aggravating the barriers to engagement, is the new generation of synchronous communication tools which allow more than just online chat and whiteboard facilities. Modern technologies provide functionality for online chat and whiteboard as well as video, application sharing, desktop control and voice. Voice and video functions in particular, would overcome the inability to *see*, and the desktop control and application sharing could usefully assist in technical support, but these are reliant on the technology being present at both ends of the communication channel. Although we have relied on asynchronous communication in the computer ethics unit to date, the new generation of synchronous tools may go some way to minimising some of the barriers described here.

References

1. APA (1997). Learner centered psychological principles: a framework for school design and reform. American Psychological Association, Board of Educational Affairs.
2. Bolliger, D.U. and Martindale, T. (2004). Key factors for determining student satisfaction in online course. International Journal on E-Learning, January-March:61-67.
3. Burford, S. and Haggis, J. (2000). Multicultural awareness: issues for online education. In Sims, O'Reilly and Sawkins (Eds.), Learning to Choose – Choosing to Learn. Short Papers and Works in Progress presented at the 17th Annual Conference of the Australasian Society for Computers in Learning in Tertiary Education (ASCILITE) December 10th - 13th, 2000.
4. Chou, C.C. (2004). A model of learner-centered computer-mediated interaction for collaborative distance learning. International Journal on E-Learning, January-March:11-18.

5. Coldwell, J. and Newlands, D. (2004). Deakin online: an evolving case study. Issues in In-
    forming Science and Information Technology, 1:1-10.
6. Deakin University (2003). Online technologies in courses and units - operational policy.
    http://theguide.deakin.edu.au.
7. Deakin University (2004). Student charter. http://theguide.deakin.edu.au.
8. Harris, D. (1999). Creating a complete learning environment. In French, Hale, Johnson,
    and Farr, editors, Internet Based learning: an introduction and framework for higher edu-
    cation and business, Sterling, VA. Stylus Publishing.
9. Hillman, D., Willis, D., and Gunawardena, C. (1994). Learner-interface interaction in dis-
    tance education. The American Journal of Distance Education, 8(2):31-42.
10. Richards, C. (2002). Distance education, on-campus learning, and e-learning conver-
    gences. International Journal on E-Learning, July-September:30-39.
11. Richardson, J. (1994). Cultural specificity of approaches to studying in higher education:
    A literature survey. Higher Education, 27:449-468.
12. Salmon, G. (2002). E-tivities: the key to active learning online. Kogan Page.
13. Salmon, G. (2003). E-moderating: the key to teaching and learning online. Routledge Fal-
    mer.
14. Smith, P.J., Smith, S.N., Coldwell, J., and Murphy, K. (2004). Patterns of engagement in
    CMC: comparisons between Australian and Chinese students. In Pioneers 2004 Confer-
    ence, Toronto.
15. Smith, S., Miller, R., and Crassini, B. (1998). Approaches to studying of Australian and
    overseas Chinese university students. Higher Education Research and Development,
    17(3):261-275.

Collaborative Virtual Learning Environment Using Synthetic Characters

Zhigeng Pan[1,2], Jiejie Zhu[2], Mingming Zhang[2], and Weihua Hu[1]

[1] Hangzhou Dianzi University, Hangzhou, 310027, P.R. China
[2] State Key Lab of CAD&CG, Zhejiang University, Hangzhou, 310027, P.R. China
zhujiejie@cad.zju.edu.cn

Abstract. This research work not only proposes a deep insight to initiative and vivid concept modeling which makes use of several techniques like flash animation, rolling image-based introduction, virtual experiment, etc., but also explores the potential integration of synthetic characters with virtual learning environment to better simulate the social interaction and social awareness. Through analysis of constructivist learning theory, we present a new learning strategy with pedagogical agent. Based on this strategy, we take CG course in practice as an example to implement our multi-user application for individual learning and collaborative learning. Experiment results show that learning attraction, especially some difficult concept understanding, is very inspiring, and learning result is hopefully improved.

Keywords: Collaborative Virtual Learning Environment; Synthetic Character; Social Interaction; Constructivist Learning Theory; Knowledge Visualization.

1 Introduction

Virtual Reality (VR) has been proposed as a technological breakthrough that holds the power to facilitate learning. Knowledge visualization for learning materials and social interaction among learners are two critical factors for advanced learning on web-based immersive education. The application and development of VR technology in education has enriched the form of teaching and learning in current educational strategy. VR teaching system not only provides rich teaching patterns and teaching contents, but also helps improve learners' ability of analyzing problem and exploring new concepts.

Web-based learning environment characterized by its significant feature of convenience has shown its remarkable usage and advantages in distance education. Using a network supported computer, learners can learn everywhere at any time. At the same time, efforts from the development of communication and collaborative technology on international level[1,2] promotes open learning greatly. However, open curricula in world wide universities remains a big problem on knowledge sharing. Real

R.W.H. Lau et al. (Eds.): ICWL 2005, LNCS 3583, pp. 364–374, 2005.

experience of sharing learning resource and exploring deepened knowledge are seldom implemented in traditional collaboration learning environment which overlooks the importance of the right visualization for different concepts and seeks seldom efforts for social interaction in learning activity. The objective of this paper proposes a potential technique to improve this situation using collaborative virtual learning environment (CVLE).

Knowledge visualization and social interaction among learners are two critical factors for advanced learning on web-based learning. Excellent first concept understanding is very important for learners to learn new concepts. Correct first understanding not only helps avoid mistakes in deepen learning, but also save time. Thus, the skill of correct visualization knowledge concept is particularly important. To achieve this goal, modeling concepts from existing textbooks is not adequate for lack of related knowledge understanding. In our experiment, we seek help from computer graphic experts both from local university and educational bureau to gain right advice on modeling concepts.

The social context of the learner is a factor in determining the success or otherwise of study [3]. We believe there are two important factors in social interaction. One is communication and the other is cooperation. Communication is particularly effective over the net for educational purpose that helps learners exchange ideas and share information. Through communication, each learner's thoughts, experiences, knowledge resource and knowledge result can be shared to the whole learning group. Cooperation [4] is a method by which small groups of students incorporate a co-operative task structure, a co-operative incentive structure and a collaborative motive to produce collaborative behavior. Realistic simulation of social interaction and social awareness in such environment enhance learning attraction and help learners construct deepen understanding for new concept.

An overview and brief evaluation to previous research work, theoretical foundation from constructivist learning theory and using synthetic character to implement social interaction are presented in Section 2. Section 3 introduces the implementation of CoVLE system, a virtual learning environment running on local university network for CG study. Some important feedbacks from students are reported in Section 4 and planned improvements according to these feedbacks are described. Finally we draw a conclusion for collaborative virtual learning environment.

2 Collaborative Virtual Learning Environment

2.1 Objective o CVLE

E-Learning is now popular accepted among young generation. Present open courses or instructional resources are organized in 2D forms, such as text-based instruction, meaningful images and simple flash animation for concept meaning which are all simply redesigned from traditional textbook. New improvements for present E-Learning application includes following points:

Diverse Showcases of Concept
Learning is an active process in which the learner uses sensory input and constructs meaning out of it [5]. Different showcases of knowledge provide an all-aspect view of new concepts for learners.

Natural and Meaningful Visualization of Knowledge
Learning is contextual. People do not learn isolated facts and theories in some abstract ethereal land of the mind separate from the rest of their lives. A correct reflection for specified concept and its related knowledge help learners grasp concepts in a contextual environment.

Learning by Doing
There is really only one way to learn how to do something and that is to do it. For training courses, collaborative virtual learning environment overcome the unpractical situation for learners by actually performing.

Social interaction and Social Awareness Simulation
Learning is a social activity. Collaboration in virtual learning environment provides a shared space for different learners study together, thus learning activities can be acted intimately associated with connection to other participants.

We summarized a well-modeled 3D learning environment featured as followings that meets items 1, 2, 3.

a. Honest 3D concept representation in a learning world.

b. Exploring and interacting with the learning environment.

c. Real-time feedback.

d. Multi-media assisting for interesting learning.

e. Pedagogical methods for knowledge mental construction.

f. Offering plentiful learning program as well as providing meaning construction tool.

An honest collaborative learning environment meets the requirements of item 4, which provides a virtual place where learners can *meet* and support space communication in realistic simulation among dispersed learners.

2.2   Theoretical Foundation from Constructivism

J.Piaget defines constructivism as a cognitive theory of objectivism [6,7]. Cognitive theory believes that knowledge is separated from the learner, and study is the result of stimulation and response.The relationship of virtual learning environment to constructivist learning theory is that the theory provides a theoretical analysis for

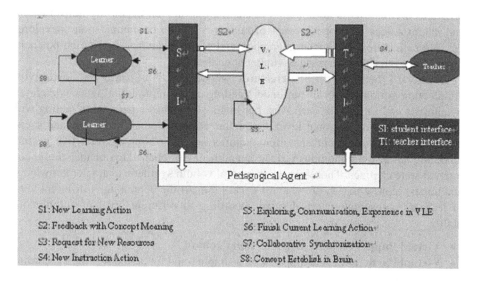

S1: New Learning Action

S2: Feedback with Concept Meaning

S3: Request for New Resources

S4: New Instruction Action

S5: Exploring, Communication, Experience in VLE

S6: Finish Current Learning Action

S7: Collaborative Synchronization

S8: Concept Establish in Brain

Fig. 1. Learning pattern based on constructivist learning theory

designing immersive 3D learning environment [8].Figure 1 shows the pattern we build for constructivist learning theory.

Learner Module: Individual learner gets learning resources from virtual learning environment, acquiring knowledge by meaningful construction. Group learners can also communicate with each other in synchronous or cooperative mode. Student interface offers support for various activities.

Teacher Module: The teacher sets teaching target and designs teaching content with the help of Teacher Interface. It also helps them enrich specified learning materials which will be represented in the VLE.

Virtual Learning Environment: This 3D learning environment is an abundant knowledge library which embodies the course principle. Components are including simulated entity, motion entity, artistic processing entity, information entity and self-adapting assistor.

Pedagogical Agent: Pedagogical agent helps learners experience learning actions in a learning environment. It finds out the right condition that intentionally interested by learners and decides which condition to notify. Pedagogical agent remains active once it has been assigned to specific learner. A common procedure for a pedagogical agent's state change can be divided into five steps: state analysis, goal generation, motivation generation, action selection and execute.

2.3   Integration with Synthetic Character for Social Interaction

Human beings are social creatures. Much of our intelligence derives from our ability to manipulate our environment through collaborative endeavors. Most exsist computer programs and interfaces do not explore advantages of such manifestly human talents and interests, leaving broad avenues of human-computer communication unexplored [9]. We believe realistic social interaction and social awareness can enrich potencial possibilities for virtual learning envionment on the web.

Kline [10] believes virtual creatures whose behavior, form and underlying architecture not only informs our understanding of the natural intelligence displayed by animals and ultimately ourselves, but that also touches a person interacting with them on a profound personal level. Communication in social interaction and social awareness for learner representation requires not only simple avatar-like gesture modeling but also autonomous reflection and behavior change to outside stimuli and internal state changes. Therefore, we can employ both synthetic character knowledge and honest representation of behavior generation. At the beginning, 4 different level of learner representation are divided according to different level of autonomous ability.

- **Virtual Puppet** supports simple gestures control.
- **Virtual Participant** is equipped with a simple mind for action selection according to outside stimuli.
- **Virtual Character** enables both outside stimuli and internal perception.
- **Advanced Character** can do learning.

Robert [11] present thoughtful brain architecture for synthetic character which can adopt to above division assigning different level of skill. It is composed of six sub-systems with one internal memory. (see table 1)

Table 1. Virtual Brain Concept Sub-systems

Sub-System	Functions
Sensor	Acting as the enforcer of sensory honesty.
Perception	Helping each character assign a unique "meaning" to events in the world.
Proprioception	Emulating proprioception and extend it to include many forms of self-awareness, including awareness of emotional state and of self-action.
Memory	Maintaining a list of persistent *PerceptMemory* objects that constitutes the character's "view" of the current context.
Action	Deciding which action(s) it is appropriate to perform.
Navigation& Motor	The Navigation System typically functions by overriding the motor commands passed down by the Action System. In some cases this command is for an explicit Navigation task, such as "APPROACH."

The advantage of this architecture is that data flow can be processed correctly and efficiently in a top-down model like a real brain working flow. World events take the form of a uniformed data record. Interpretation to each data record depends entirely on the sensory and perceptual abilities of character. However, how to choose the right level autonomous for learner in a collaborative virtual learning environment remains unexplored, although we know that virtual puppet attracts most learners' interests, this level of capacity on autonomous do not meet the requirements of social interaction. Further research results should gain from pedagogy theory and psychology learning theory.

3   CoVLE: Implemented System Using VRML and Java Techniques

3.1   System Architecture

Bowser-based technique is first implemented for learners' convenient access using VRML and JAVA [12,13,14,15].A web-based system architecture is implemented to support the functions such as: active learning process, text-based communication, white board as a shared cyberspace, collaborative mechanism, friendly user interface, extra learning tools and an online CG material database. In addition, tools enabling students and teachers to choose or upload additional CG material are also provided by this platform. CoVLE adopts client/server type architecture. VRML browser plug-in is used to render 3D scene using Blaxxun Contact plugin [16]. Java graphic interface is a human-machine interface designed according to constructivism learning tool kit, which includes personal Information, upload resource, course maker, course modify, learning course, 3D chat room, shared whiteboard etc. Communication tool supports synchronized message delivering. Event Dispatcher dispatches all the request events to server (such as

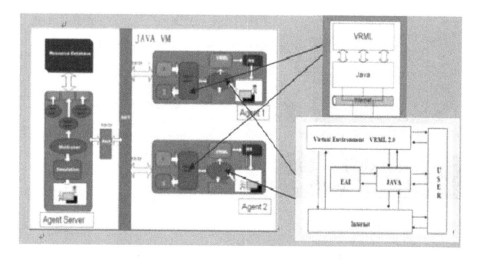

Fig. 2. Collaborative VLE architecture using VRML

request for login, request for download resource, request for synchronization) or get event from server (such as get user information, get resource etc).

Limitation includes following points:

- Compatible difficulty: Since Microsoft and IBM have a long way to cooperate, VRML plug-in embedded in Microsoft IE is not fully supported and sometimes we meet run-time errors for unknown reason.
- Debug difficulty: Present free toolkit for debug Java Applet is not available.
- Low Quality on rendering: Though VRML has an advantage on net-worked 3D environment, the low quality breaks away from the honest rule to visualize knowledge.

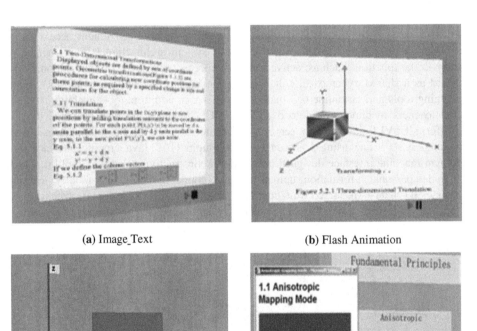

(a) Image_Text   (b) Flash Animation

(c) Virtual Experiment   (d) Interactive Aalgorithm

Fig. 3. Implemented four showcases in CoVLE

3.2   System Implementation and Feedback

Four Showcases:
Image text: Narrative text is converted to images. Learners can control the sequence of the image by up/down button. First room of each chapter house contains image text of each chapter. Some pictures are also showed in this way.

Flash Animation: Animation is used to clearly show the results of the instruction resource. It can also be used to substitute page rolling. Learners standing before the animation window are greatly impressed.

Virtual Experiment: Virtual experiments give learners an opportunity to experience. CG course virtual experiment can mimic a real situation of interest.

Interactive Algorithm: Computer graphic algorithms are the most difficult part to learn. Representation of direct algorithm results after learners' interaction with the interface gives learners another chance to enjoy what they are studying..

User Interface

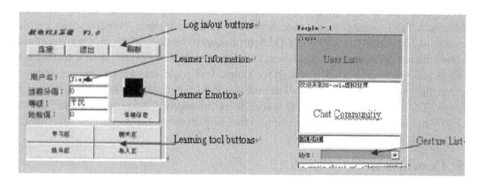

Fig. 4. Chinese Interface for control learning process in CoVLE using Java Applet

Nonverbal Communication
Nonverbal communication is essential for understanding learning and experience among the group learners. As we interact with people, we are interpreting what they are saying verbally and nonverbally in order to understand what they are communicating. Gestures and facial expressions are two important nonverbal communication tools for communication process. At present, we implement gesture control for expressing common feelings. 4 gestures are supported according to common usage in learning process. They are: nodding, disagreement, approve, laugh. Further research on nonverbal communication in learning actions should be analyzed.

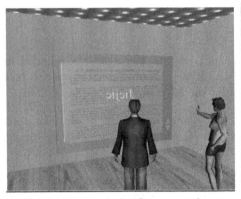

(a) Gesture expression for concept deny   (b) Three avatars are exchange ideas

Fig. 5. Two Nonverbal communication examples

4 Feedback

Most of the learners show a big interest in the learning environment we built, except for those that feel dizzy while experiencing of controlling character acting in a 3D environment. Learning results are hopefully improved since learners focus on the excellent four showcases of the CG algorithm introduction, theoretic simulation and algorithm results interaction. However, learning effectiveness from learner's feedback is not as good as we expected. Through the simple web pages and Java examples, learners grasp the concepts well and with short time, while in the virtual CG world they are not so better. The reasons are that in 3D world, there are many things users can do such as chatting, walking. They are not willing to focus much more attention to their learning.

5 Conclusion

Web-based learning environments are becoming very popular. How to integrate VR technique into Web-based learning environment seems a big challenge. Constructivist learning theory, as a philosophy of practical online learning, provides a theoretical analysis for designing honest collaborative learning environment on the web. This paper centers on knowledge visualization for learning materials and social interaction among learners. We take CG algorithm course in practice as an example to implement our multi-user application supporting both individual learning and collaborative learning. We summarize following points that should improved in future work:

a. Support concept visualization
b. Limiting learner's unnecessary activity in order to reinforce learning effectiveness.
c. Improving synchronization in virtual experiment to simulate social interaction.
d. Providing virtual sound for immersive sound call and instruction.
e. Performing psychological and pedagogical analysis according to CVLE.

Evaluation to learning result is a hard job for us. We planned to seek help from local educational researchers to give an investigation and make use of their results. Further theoretical research on educational strategy should get through this experiment. We plan to add an online feedback from each learner's positive response and these feedbacks will be delivered to local psychological experts.

Acknowledgements

This research project is co-supported by 973 project (grant no: 2002CB312103), ELVIS project, and Excellent Youth Teacher Program of MOE in China. In addition, we would like to express our thanks to Prof. Shijie Cai who provide the teaching materials on computer graphics, and to Tian Hu, Rong Gao, Bin Xu, Yanfeng Li, Dr. Yigang Wang, Hongwei Yang who showing their kindness to help us during the whole work.

References

[1] De Abreu A., Rodriguez O., Matteo A. "Analysis and Design of Virtual Reality Applications in the WEB: A Case of Study" In the Proceedings of IV (1999) p.322-327

[2] Andrew, C., Rob, V. "Exchange Learning to share learning: an exploration of methods to improve and share learning" A report prepared for the UK Commission for Health Improvement. 2003

[3] McInnerney, J.M., Roberts, T.S. "Online Learning: Social Interaction and the Creation of a Sense of Community" Educational Technology & Society (2004) 7 (3) p.73-81

[4] Slavin, Robert E. "Cooperative Learning" New York: Longman, 1983.

[5] Brooks, M., Brooks, J. "In Search of Understanding: the Case for Constructivist Classrooms", Alexandra, VA:ASCD, 1995.

[6] El-Hindi, Amelia, Jr.Leu, J.Donald, "Beyond classroom boundaries: constructivist teaching with the Internet" Reading Teacher (1991) p.694-701.

[7] He, K.K. "Constructivism – The basic theory of innovate traditional teaching" Subject education, 1998 (In Chinese)

[8] Hu. W.H., Zhu,J.J., Pan, Z.G. "Learning By Doing: A Case for Constructivist Virtual Learning Environment" In the Proceedings of Eurographics Education Program (2003) p.6-15

[9] Clark, E., Jacek, B. "Autonomous agents as synthetic characters" AI Magazine (1998)

[10] Bruce B., Marc D., Yuri A.I., etc. "Integrated learning for interactive synthetic characters" In the Proceedings of SIGGRAPH (2002) p.417-426

[11] Burke, R., D. Isla, M. Downie, etc. "Creature Smarts: The Art and Architecture of a Virtual Brain" In the Proceedings of GDC (2001) p.147 – 166

[12] ISO/IEC1 4772-1:1997, VRML97 International Standard. http://www.vrml.org

[13] External Authoring Interface Working Group. 1998
http:://www.vrml.org/WorkingGroups/vrml-eai.html

[14] Pan Z.G., Shi J.Y. "Virtual Reality Technology Development in China: An Overview" The International Journal of Virtual Reality (2000) 4(3) p.2-10

[15] Massakuni, K.M., Kirner,C., Serique M., etc. "Collaborative Virtual Environment of Teaching using VRML and JAVA" In the Proceedings of SCI 2001

[16] Blaxxun Company http://www.blaxxun.com

[17] Pan, Z.G., Zhu, J.J., Hu, W.H. "Interactive Learning of CG in Networked Virtual Environments" Computers & Graphics (2005) 29(2)

[18] VNET, A Multi-user system on the Internet Introduction
http://www.csclub.uwaterloo.ca/u/sfwhite/vnet/

[19] Allan, C. "Situated Learning and the Culture of Learning" Education Researches (1989) 18(1) p.32-42

[20] Fisher, S.S., Fraser, G. "Real-time interactive graphics: Intelligent virtual worlds continue to develop", Computer Graphics (1998). 32(3)

[21] Carlsson C., Hagsand, O. "DIVE- A Multi User Virtual Reality System" In the Proceedings of IEEE VRAIS (1993) p.394-400.

[22] Zhu J.J., Hu W.H., Pan Z.G. "Design and implementation of Virtual Multimedia Classroom" Journal of CAD&CG (2004) 16(1) p.73-79 (in Chinese)

[23] Michael L., Mark D.I. "A Conceptual Framework for Agent Definition and Development" The Computer Journal (2001) 44(1) p.1-20

[24] Shi J.Y., Pan Z.G. "China: Computer Graphics Education Available at Universities, Institutes and Training Centers" Computer Graphics (1999) 31(3) p.7-9

Devising a Typology of LOs
Based on Pedagogical Assumptions

Emanuela Busetti[1], Giuliana Dettori[2], Paola Forcheri[1], and Maria Grazia Ierardi[1]

[1] Istituto di Matematica Applicata e Tecnologie Informatiche del CNR, Genova – Italy
{busetti, forcheri, ierardi}@ge.imati.cnr.it
[2] Istituto di Tecnologie Didattiche del CNR, Genova – Italy
dettori@itd.cnr.it

Abstract. In this paper, we outline the pedagogical assumptions that underlie the design of a distributed web-based environment, presently under development, devoted to robotics education at university level. We briefly discuss, from an educational point of view, the approach followed to implement these assumptions. In particular, we focus our attention on the methodological choices underlying the design of the Learning Objects (LOs) to be used as didactical materials in the environment. These have been conceived so as to meet the complex requirements of the learning subject considered, and to model the didactical proposal based on a constructive view of the learning process.

1 Introduction

Educational technology offers new possibilities to education, since it puts at learner's disposal complex resources, including several which can be used at a distance. An interesting example of such remote applications is offered by robotics education. In this field, as a matter of fact, most universities put at students' disposal a laboratory where only experiments on some specific class of robots can be carried out. The possibility of sharing such resources at a distance allows students to avail themselves not only of simulation tools which are available in other universities, but also of the very robots located elsewhere, by means of tele-presence.

Exploiting this possibility is the basic idea of the TIGER (Telepresence Instant Groupware for higher Education in Robotics) project, which aims at building a web-based environment to operatively access robot labs distributed in several Italian Universities, hence providing for the students an educational context which transforms the potential of technology into a real opportunity to build up knowledge and experience.

The considered application field is very complex, and is characterized by the need to keep a particularly strict connection between theoretical knowledge and methodological competence necessary for the use of robotic laboratories [6]. Moreover, students need to develop good abilities of self-regulated work, and become able to fully avail themselves of the use of virtual environments on the web. To this end, we worked out the structure of an educational framework where Learning Objects (LOs) [3, 4, 9] are the central tool which keeps a strict connection among

R.W.H. Lau et al. (Eds.): ICWL 2005, LNCS 3583, pp. 375–386, 2005.

theoretical, methodological and operational competence. This is obtained by defining a typology of LOs, apt to meet the variety of requirements which characterize education on robot control.

With our contribution, we aim to propose an approach to the design of educational environments which combine the learning object paradigm with the current pedagogical view of teaching in complex fields.

2 Educational Framework

From a pedagogical point of view, our proposal is based mainly on a constructivist approach to knowledge, where learning is viewed as resulting from personal activity and comparison with the activity of others. We briefly remind here that the constructivist approach relies on active learning, oriented to the acquisition of non-trivial knowledge and skills, to the solution of complex problems, to the focus on constructing knowledge rather than transmitting it, and to the development of self-regulation abilities [1, 2, 10]. In this view, new knowledge is built up, based on the previously acquired one, by means of personal reflection and social interaction, by analysing and combining experiences, by abstracting concepts and consciously applying them to the solution of new problems [5, 12]. Moreover, tools need to be provided and activities suggested, so as to help the learners develop meta-cognitive abilities, that is, awareness and regulation of cognition (which includes planning, monitoring and self-evaluation of learning) [7, 8]. Our view of learning, hence, is essentially learner-centred. Nevertheless, we think that teachers have an important role to play in it, introducing concepts and guiding their deepening, posing problems, organising the overall activity, coaching, monitoring, scaffolding, assessing and keeping up student's motivation. The picture which emerges from this characterization spots learning as developing from activities of three different kinds, that is, individual, teacher-guided, and in collaboration with peers. In this framework, technology can play a meaningful role in every component, by offering non-trivial working tools and individually adaptable hypermedia learning materials, easing communication and collaboration with peers, supporting self-assessment, as well as by performing some functions which were traditionally of teachers, such as scaffolding and problem posing. The educational framework which arises from this articulated pedagogical view is summarised in Figure 1.

3 Implementing the Educational Framework

The TIGER project is developed within the general framework of current education at university level, in particular as concerns robotics education. The design of robot control requires a particularly strict integration between methodological and operational competence, as can be obtained by a learning-by-doing approach. The situation is, however, made particularly difficult by the fact that robots are delicate and expensive devices and students need to undergo a suitable preparation with exploratory activities on recognition of the environment's features before they can materially access the real tools. Moreover, for economical reasons, labs with different

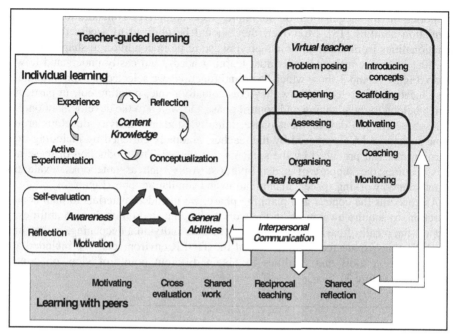

Fig. 1. Educational framework defined by our pedagogical view

equipment are spread across several universities. On the other hand, the physical availability of the laboratories is crucial for suitable learning of robot control, and hence the use of simple simulation programs can not be sufficient. This motivated the need to develop tele-presence environments, including the development of a rich and articulated range of abilities, such as technical, instrumental and methodological competence, meta-cognitive and self-regulatory abilities, relational abilities so to be able to perform collaborative work on complex tasks [6].

Hence, in order to face the complexity of the considered educational situation, we decided to let the TIGER project put at user's disposal a variety of resources apt to help students to take initiative and control of their own learning, as well as to encourage them to interact with their peers and with the tutor. Moreover, we organised and structured the students' work by integrating individual activity with learning guided by the teacher and learning in collaboration, as well as by fostering the acquisition of abilities of autonomous learning. To this end, we devised tools and functions which could be apt to implement this process, and worked out a suitable organization for the educational materials by defining a typology of Learning Objects.

3.1 Devising Tools and Functions

We started from observing that a complex educational activity, though based on an overall design made by the teacher, leaves the students wide space of autonomous choice and conscious reflection on the work to be carried out. This entails that students should be in condition to take autonomous decisions on their work, as well as planning and controlling its development. In their activity, students need to be supported in the acquisition of cognitive, meta-cognitive, collaboration and self-regulation abilities [13]. Moreover, they should be allowed to access the system's functionalities from different points of view, so to be in condition to shape their own learning paths according to individual learning needs, and easily understand how to do so. Figures 2 and 3 show which tools and functions we selected to support and ease the educational activity and how they conceptually relate, pointing out, in particular, which belong to the planning and control phase and which to the development one.

As concerns the development phase, initially, student's activity develops around some structured LOs proposed by the teacher, gradually enriched by including other learning material produced by the students themselves. The production of these new LOs requires the support of general-purpose tools such as notebooks, evaluation forms, shared working spaces, manipulation and simulation tools (Figure 2).

As concerns the control and planning phase, we included materials to plan content selection, to acquire awareness on the work to be done and on one's own abilities, to support the recall of basic knowledge, to stimulate individual deepening, and to limit the difficulties connected with the use of the TIGER environment. We included also communication tools and facilities to obtain different points of view on content knowledge (Figure 3).

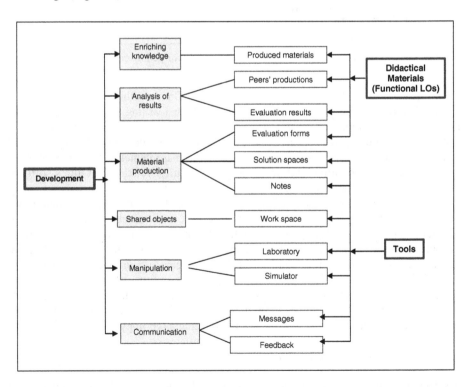

Fig. 2. Examples of tools and functional learning materials for the development of activity

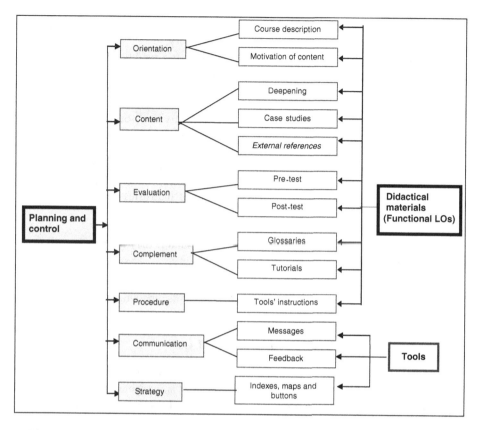

Fig. 3. Examples of tools and functional materials for planning and controlling of activity

4   Structuring the Didactical Activity

4.1   Educational Modules as Initiators of Constructive Learning Processes

Based on the educational framework outlined, we oriented our designing effort by considering Learning Objects from a teacher's point of view. We started from observing the behaviour of a teacher who designs some educational activity. Starting point of this process is devising an overall learning experience, based on previous educational work, as well as on new contents to be learnt and abilities to be acquired. Then, the teacher organises the overall path in a number of educational modules, each focused on addressing a specific topic, either theoretically or by means of some activity. These modules are actually initiators of learning experiences. Thus, they include a specific educational objective, and a pedagogical approach to it. They also make use of general-purpose complementary material, aiming to possibly give different orientations to the learning process they plan. They organise the use of tools so to be functional to the work development and to suggest the interactions among the actors of the educational experience. Following our pedagogical framework, each didactical module include or refer to a combination of the following resources:

- Individual or group activities;
- Simulation tools or actual access to the laboratory;
- Tools which are meaningful in relation with the module's content, so as to support collaboration, reflection and evaluation of the experience (notebook, portfolio, qualitative and quantitative evaluation forms filled in by teacher, peers and the student him/herself, etc.);
- Materials to support the development of activities (outlines of activities, proposed exercises, theoretical material, methodological indications, examples, guide to the use of the laboratory, suggestions of tools to use, etc.);
- Reports on experiences made by peers, if the teacher considers it suitable to make them available, as well as possibly existing materials related with the tools used, such as journal papers, web site of industries producing the tools, glossaries and notes of use);
- Assessment and self-assessment material;
- A pre-test aiming to help the students understand if they are prepared to tackle the module under consideration.

Each module includes a description of the work to be done, motivates its introduction, guides the student to acquire specific skills, encourages the development of self-regulation abilities.

4.2 From Educational Modules to Structured LOs

Learning modules are realized by means of LOs, designed so to structure and guide an articulated educational activity. We designed these LOs, which embody the modules, so that they can, in turn, make use of, or refer to, other LOs, with a different structure, corresponding to materials necessary to carry out the proposed activities. This organization implies having at disposal LOs of different types, depending on the characteristics of the educational modules they embody: 1) *Structured LOs*, based on a precise educational objective, characterized by a type which determines their structure and didactical function. 2) *Functional LOs*, which do not include a specific pedagogical orientation but have a general-purpose or context-related function. These correspond to auxiliary modules.

These two types of LOs are, in turn, divided into different subtypes, according to their structure and function. The hierarchy resulting from this characterization of LOs is represented in Fig. 4.

Functional LOs can take different types, according to the kind and function of their content. We distinguish, in particular, two general types, that is: 1) context-dependent ones, containing material which is relevant only in connection with some particular module; these include presentations, assessment modules, etc.; 2) general-purpose ones, whose content may be relevant for any module of a whole, articulated course; such as glossaries, templates, etc.. These two types of Functional LOs, in turn, are subdivided into several subtypes, according to their specific function. Hence, we give to each of them names such as *Glossary LO, Presentation LO, Template LO, Assessment LO*, etc.

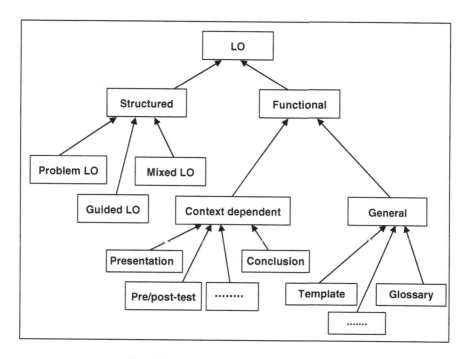

Fig. 4. Types of LOs devised in our proposal

Also *Structured LOs* can take different forms, depending on the objective of the correspondent modules. As a teacher can decide to apply a different educational approach in different phases of the overall learning path, based on the specific requirements of the situation (which depend on the students' competence and maturation level, and partially also on the nature of the topic addressed), we can devise different kinds of didactical modules. This possible diversification of modules led us to introduce a characterization of *Structured LOs* with different didactical aims, as shown in Fig. 5. We describe here briefly the three types we consider necessary for our purposes:

1. *Modules guided by the teacher.* In this case, the control of the activity, which initially relies mostly on the teacher, gradually passes to the students while they develop some abilities. Such modules aim to introduce content knowledge or some basic approach to problem solving. In this case, teaching and learning are very structured, though still based on the performing of activities. We call *Guided LOs* the correspondent of such modules.
2. *Modules oriented to autonomous exploration, where the control is strongly demanded to the student (or group of students).* In this case, a problem situation is proposed. The module includes groups of questions leading the students towards activities necessary to solve the given problem, as well as materials and tools relevant with respect to the task assigned. Here the evolution of learning can not be completely planned *a priori*, nor can it easily be evaluated with traditional methods. This approach is suitable for students who have already

acquired a basic preparation. It aims to develop high level cognitive abilities, as well as to support metacognition and autonomous learning. We call *Problem LOs* the correspondents of such modules.

3. *Modules based on a mixed approach, combining teacher guidance and autonomous exploration.* These can be formed by the combination of more than one LO of the previous two types. They correspond to *Mixed LOs.*

We wish to remark that both a *Problem LO* or a *Guided LO* may be suitably applied to support the learning of a same topic, but with different pedagogical aims, as illustrated by the examples in the next section.

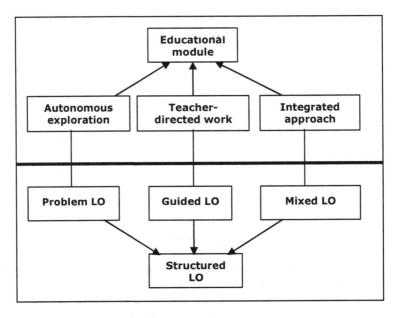

Fig. 5. Correspondence between different types of educational modules and LOs

4.3 Examples of Structured LOs

Guided LOs and *Problem LOs* can be used to tackle a same problem by applying different pedagogical approaches, which could be required by the characteristics of some educational situations. Let us see, for example, a meaningful problem among those considered within the TIGER environment, that is, how to analyse the unexpected behaviour of a robot.

To acquire this ability, it is necessary that students learn to analyse conceptually and understand several problem situations; they must learn to reflect on the variables of the problems and on the elements of the context that may influence their behaviour, on what tests should be carried out to verify such influence, on the order to follow when performing such tests. The complexity of this task depends on the characteristics

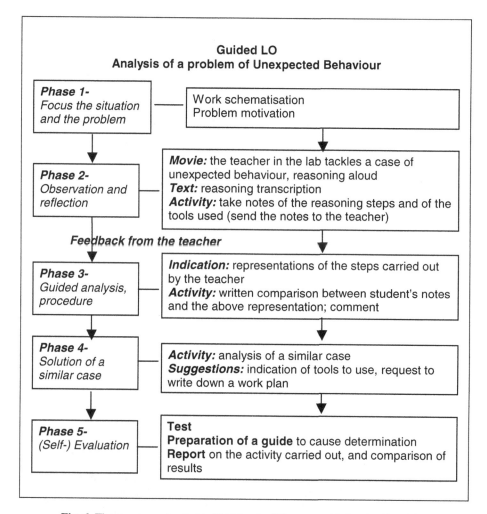

Fig. 6. The structure of a Guided LO for the "Unexpected behaviour" problem

of the problem at hand. This motivates the need to have LOs of different kinds on this topic, so to assist the students during the subsequent phases of their learning.

If the students are at the beginning of their work in this field, and have no practical experience, teacher's guidance is necessary, to help them learn *by examples* how experts reason on this kind of problems; hence, we will make use of a *Guided LO*, like the one sketched in Fig. 6. We note that in this case the activity is articulated into 5 phases. First the teacher (real or virtual) gives a general idea of the situation and motivates the problem [11]. The second phase is still characterized by a central presence of the teacher, who shows how to reason to find the cause of the problem so to tackle it effectively; the focus is on developing analytical abilities, not on the acquisition of some procedure, since it is obviously not possible to figure out a priori all the possible causes of unexpected behaviour. The students start to become active by recording the reasoning steps exemplified. A feedback from the teacher at this point aims to check if the students are approaching the task in the correct way. In the next step, the students are asked to analyse deeply the procedure applied, so to make sure they understand correctly all important steps, still supported by comments of the teacher. In the fourth phase, they are requested to solve (conceptually) by themselves a similar case and to sketch a work plan. Finally, they need to self evaluate their work, before being evaluated by the teacher. The self-evaluation phase, in particular, is very important for the students to improve their meta-cognitive abilities (which include awareness of what they know and don't know). This is an important pre-requisite for they to be in condition to proceed in their learning path.

In Fig. 7, on the other hand, we show the structure of a *Problem LO* on the same topic. Here the activity consists of only 3 phases, where the central and most important one must be carried out essentially autonomously.

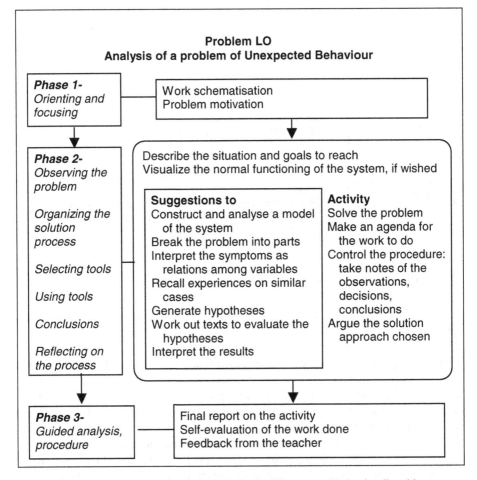

Fig. 7. The structure of a Problem LO for the "Unexpected behaviour" problem

The initial phase still consists in a focus on the situation considered, analogously to what happens in the previous example. The second phase points out the goals to be reached and offers the possibility to visualize the normal functioning of the observed robot. It gives also suggestions on what tools could be chosen and how they should be used to solve the problem, as well as recalls on how to organize the work from a conceptual point of view. Finally, a phase of self-evaluation and formal evaluation concludes the module.

5 Conclusion

LOs are currently considered a valuable tool to support web-based learning, since it allows to efficiently build courses at reasonable cost. However, there are a number of problems to solve in order to exploit this opportunity efficiently, mainly concerning the pedagogical aspects [4].

In order to overcome these problems, we propose a vision of LOs which models a teacher's behaviour while planning an educational activity. When we model this activity with a (structured) LO, we endow the LO with the same pedagogical approach of the correspondent didactical proposal.

Our approach, which is currently adopted within the TIGER project, has several advantages from the educational point of view:

- it gives an operative tool to help the teacher gain familiarity with the concept of LO;
- it enriches the expressive power of LOs by representing not only learning materials but also pedagogical approaches;
- it gives the possibility to shape templates based on different pedagogical approaches, hence providing materials which are easier to re-use in different educational situations rather than ready-to-use proposals;
- it gives indications on a possible approach to create LOs of constructive kind, hence capturing the essential nature of the didactical process, which is constantly in evolution.

Acknowledgement

This work has been partially supported by the Italian Ministry of Education, University and Research , Firb Research Project 'TIGER-Telepresence Instant Groupware for Higher Education in Robotics' and Project VICE- Virtual Communities for Education.

References

1. Ausubel, D. (1963). The Psychology of Meaningful Verbal Learning, New York: Grune & Stratton
2. Bruner, J. (1966). Toward a Theory of Instruction. Cambridge, MA: Harvard University Press

3. Busetti E., Dettori G., Forcheri P., Ierardi M.G. (2004a). Guideline towards effectively sharable LOs, ICWL 2004, Lecture Notes in Computer Science. 3143, Springer-Verlag, pp: 416-423.
4. Busetti, E., Forcheri, P., Ierardi, M.G., Molfino, M. T. (2004b). Repositories of Learning Objects as Learning Environments for Teachers. Proceedings of ICALT 2004, pp.450-454, IEEE Comp. Soc. Press.
5. Dillenbourgh, P. (ed.) (1999). Collaborative Learning - Cognitive and Computational Approaches, Oxford U.K.: Elsevier Science Ltd.
6. Fabri D., Falsetti C., Ramazzotti S., Leo T., (2004). Robot control designer education on the Web Robotics and Automation, 2004. Proceedings. ICRA '04. 2004 IEEE International Conference on, Robotics and automation, New Orleans,(USA), Apr. 2004, Volume: 2, Pages:1364 – 1369.
7. Hacker, D·J·, Dunlosky, J;, Graesser, A.C., eds. (1998). Metacognition in educational Theory and practice. Mahwah, New Jersey: L. Erlbaum Associates.
8. Jonassen, D.H & Land, S.M. ed. (2000). Theoretical Foundations of Learning Environments, Erlbaum Associates: New Jersey
9. Littlejohn, A. (ed.) (2003). Reusing on line resources: a sustainable approach to e-learning. Kogan Page, London
10. Piaget, J. (1976). The grasp of consciousness, Harvard University Press
11. Pintrich, P. R. (1999) The role of motivation in promoting and sustaining self-regulated learning, International Journal of Educational Research, :31 (6), 459-470
12. Vygotsky, L.S. (1978). Mind in Society. Cambridge, MA: Harvard University Press
13. Zimmerman, B. J.. & Schunk D.A (eds.) (2001). Self-regulated learning and academic achievement: theoretical perspectives (pp. 1-37). Lawrence Erlbaum Associates, Mahwah, NJ.

Using Web Based Answer Hunting System to Promote Collaborative Learning

Guanglin Huang and Wenyin Liu*

Department of Computer Science, City University of Hong Kong,
83 Tat Chee Avenue, Kowloon Tong, Kowloon, Hong Kong SAR, China
hwanggl@cs.cityu.edu.hk, csliuwy@cityu.edu.hk

Abstract. In this paper, we share our pedagogical experience to motivate and facilitate an interactive and collaborative learning atmosphere by using an answer hunting system. In the software engineering practice course we are teaching, a problem that may deteriorate the learning quality is that, the students lack the opportunities of communication and discussion with the instructor both in class and out of class since they do not have many common time slots. Therefore, a web based answer hunting system is carefully designed and built to facilitate the communications between the students and instructor, and among the students. This system is designed based on the Q&A competition metaphor. The students are encouraged to participate in the competition to learn more knowledge, share more knowledge, and earn more participation marks.

Keywords: Q&A, Q&A Competition, Answer Hunting System, Web Based Learning, Web Forum, Computer Education, Human Communication.

1 Introduction

Although there are great and rapid advances in the web and e-learning technology, due to many problems, such as lack of teacher immediacy [1], web based learning cannot fully take the place of the traditional, classroom-centered teaching method. However, web based learning is becoming a more and more important and popular method to acquire knowledge. Furthermore, web based learning can be regarded as a very good auxiliary method to traditional teaching methods to achieve higher learning quality.

We have been instructing an undergraduate course on software engineering practice at the City University of Hong Kong for several years. In this course, the students are taught in lectures with some well-known industrial approaches to software development, and they are required to practise them in the tutorial and lab sessions and in the after-class project work. The students in each tutorial/lab session form a large group and are asked to develop a software project to mock a real software development process. Real software development environments are simulated. All projects are proposed by the instructor for real usage. The instructor

---

* Corresponding author.

R.W.H. Lau et al. (Eds.): ICWL 2005, LNCS 3583, pp. 387–396, 2005.

and teaching assistants (TAs) play the roles of customers and the students play the roles of Program Managers, Dev Leads, SDEs, Test Leads, and Testers. Students can still consult the instructor and TAs for managerial, procedural, and technical issues. The course is conducted in the traditional mode, that is, the lectures and tutorials are delivered face to face in the classrooms. However, we have found the following disadvantages in the traditional teaching method for this course:

1. **Beside the lecture and tutorial time, there are few ways for student-instructor and student-student communications.** Most students in this course are local students who go home after daytime classes. Hence, except for the lecture and tutorial time, they have few chances to discuss the project work together with their fellow classmates (team members). Actually, they are not so familiar among each other. The ways are limited to phone, email and instant message communication, which are pretty informal such that the project manager cannot easily manage communication to facilitate the development process. As one student complained in an anonymous survey: "*The project arrangement in general is very good but not in communication. Give more chances for communication among the group members, then, I think they should work faster~*". The instructor is usually very busy with other duties and cannot devote much time for the students after class in the face to face mode.

2. **The students are reluctant to interact with the instructor in the class face to face.** We have also observed that it is hard to make the students to actively participate in the class discussion with the instructor. One important reason for this is that many students think it is not cool to interact with the instructor actively. Another reason is that the communication language in the class is English, which is not the native language for the students. The students may concern their oral English expression proficiency, so they probably choose to just listen to the instructor and keep silent. In this situation, the instructor cannot observe active response from the students; and without the feedback from the students, the instructor can hardly adjust his teaching methodology adaptively. This will be a negative factor to influence the teaching quality.

3. **Email communication between the students and instructor is an inefficient way.** Email is frequently used by the students to ask the instructor when they have questions or enquiries. However, email has many limitations and it is not a good way for the efficiency purpose. First, the instructor could not check email very frequently. Furthermore, the instructor usually receives many emails (up to 200 in our case) from various sources a day. Such question and enquiry requests may be easily ignored at first. In these situations, questioning by email cannot result in a fast response. Second, the questions and enquiries from different students are usually quite similar. In most cases, several questions are actually the same, but asked in different emails. It is not a smart way for the instructor to reply them one by one in very detail. The instructor needs to keep an answer log so as to make the Q&A process efficient. Therefore, a more formal and efficient way is needed.

4. **The instructor can hardly monitor the learning and developing process of the students.** Usually, the instructor wishes to be able to keep an eye on the students'

discussion, so that he could give some guidance if he thinks necessary. Sometimes, the instructor can also learn something from the students' discussion, such as web resources that the instructor did not know. However, in the traditional teaching mode, there are few ways that the instructor can accomplish that.

In this paper, we share our pedagogical experience to motivate and facilitate an interactive and collaborative learning atmosphere. A web based enquiry and learning system is carefully designed and implemented for use in the course we conduct. The main idea of this system is similar to the popular answer hunting system. That is, a special forum is constructed for asking and answering questions. The users of the forum can post questions and give some credits for solutions, and he could also try to answer others' questions to earn credits. To accelerate the answer hunting cycle, several basic document understanding techniques are employed. Furthermore, some promotion schemes are also designed to encourage the student users to participate in the forum's activities more actively.

In the rest of this paper, we first review related work and systems in Section 2, and then present how we instantiate our pedagogical idea and show our design detail in Section 3. The experiment is presented in Section 4, where the results are also provided and analyzed. Finally, we conclude this paper in Section 5.

2 Related Work and Systems

Many educational practitioners have reported their studies about the usage of web based forum on distant education. Most people agree that the web based courses lack an important quality: teacher immediacy, which fosters positive student attitudes. Therefore, many researchers have proposed the solution via the online media stream service, such as, the students could interact with the instructor via a "virtual classroom"[2], or "virtual universities" [3]. In these systems, the students could communicate with their course instructor via an online video. However, these systems are so highly equipment dependent that they are not a cheap and easy way to implement. Therefore, other text based communication methods are more commonly employed in practice. Typical text based methods include synchronous "chat room", and asynchronous "discussion forum" and "mail list". The "chat room" is a synchronous way of communication that the people must present online at the same time to share message, but usually, the message will no longer exist after the users quit the chat room. This way is very similar to the traditional class-centered method. However, it also suffers the disadvantage of the traditional method. That is, it requires a common time when the instructor and students are all free to discuss in this room. This is usually impractical. The "discussion forum" is an asynchronous, publicly accessible bulletin board where everyone could post and reply message at any time, and these posts are publicly viewable for all normal users. It is a good way for students to communicate with their fellow classmates and the instructor. However, the forum has no specific topic control. Usually the valuable information may be accompanied with many invaluable ones, making it hard for the users to find out what they want. The "mail list" is another commonly used method which is implemented via email.

The users can be connected to each other by sending and replying the information to a specific email address, an email daemon monitoring this email address can help to broadcast the received emails to all recipients in the email list. This method is easy to implement with little cost. However, the information is organized in a chaotic way. It is not a good way to share and search for valuable knowledge.

Compared with the methods mentioned above, answer hunting system is a better way to quickly obtain knowledge and manage knowledge for further use. Answer hunting system is a special web based forum. It is designed to benefit the asking and answering activities in the forum. Through this kind of system, a user is supposed to be able to obtain his answer quickly.

Among the existing answer hunting systems, Google Answers [4] is the most famous one. It is designed based on one commercial idea: for a common person, asking an expert is better than searching by himself only to obtain the answer of a question. Google Answers recruits a group of Researchers, which are stringently tested and trained to be experts at locating hard-to-find information resource on and off the web. A registered user can post his question to Google Answers; however, he should specify how much money he is willing to pay to get the answer. The questions posted will be answered by Researchers and the money offered for it will be given to the Researcher who answers it. Finally the asker can be informed of the answer by email. All the questions can be publicly viewable on the Google Answers website so that others can add their insights and experiences. However, a normal registered user can just write the comments to the question and cannot answer it and earn the money. Google Answers has gathered a rich collection of solutions to various questions on various fields. A user can search and view the database for the solved questions free of charge. This is indeed a very good way to share and retrieve knowledge.

Sina iAsk [5] is another good commercial answer hunting system, which mainly targets at the Chinese community. Unlike Google Answers, Sina iAsk is not directly money driven. Posting question in the forum does not cost any actual money. Everyone is voluntary to help others to get their answers. What he can gain is the credit in this cyber community. There is no Researcher or Expert in the Sina iAsk, every registered user could post his questions and answer others' questions if he knows. Therefore, the question asker should bear the risk that the quality of the answers may not be good. However, this issue may not be too serious, since usually the asker only needs to know the basic idea to solve the problem. Others' answer, even though with bad quality, can still bring in some valuable hints to the asker for him to solve the question. Therefore, in general, Sina iAsk achieves a pretty good user satisfaction. It also keeps a digest for the answered questions, which is a very good knowledge repository for all internet users.

Currently, existing answer hunting systems are only used commercially. None is reported for special use in the educational field. Motivated by the success of these commercial answer hunting systems, we have designed and implemented a similar answer hunting system for a course we instruct. We use it as an important auxiliary way to the traditional classroom centered teaching method to improve the learning quality and gain better students satisfaction. Unlike the open cyber communities, the users in our system are limited to the students who enroll in the course, and the topics are also much less diverse. In this special scenario, we could improve the system in many aspects. We hope with the help of such a system, a kind of collaborative learning atmosphere could be formed. In such a collaborative environment, the learning process can be advanced in a collaborative manner. That is, the students can share and discuss their ideas with others, and help others to solve their problems. In the following section, we will address the system design and construction issues in detail.

3   System Architecture Design and Considerations

Figure 1 illustrates the system architecture and information flow of our proposed answer hunting system. Basically, the system can be mainly divided into two parts: interactive question/answer delivery and automatic classification/search.

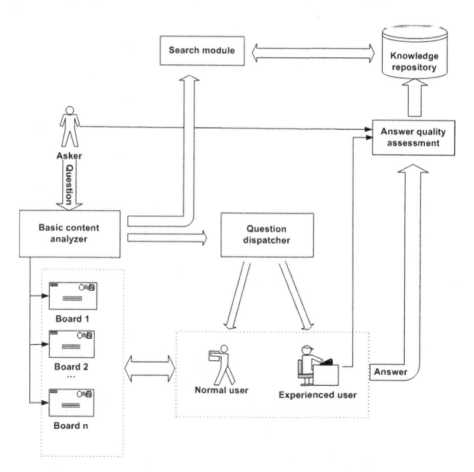

Fig. 1. Answer Hunting System Architecture

Once the user initiates/posts a question, he should also provide some additional narrative information, e.g., the question category. A content analyzer will be called to perform some basic lexical analysis to the question and the narrative information to identify the main concern of this question. Many well-studied content analysis techniques can be employed here, e.g., Chinese words segmentation, article abstract generation, document classification and clustering.

After content analysis, the question will be delivered to one or more boards, which fit the topic of the question the best, and posted there. Every user can browse in these boards, and answer the question if he wishes. At the same time, a question dispatcher will dispatch the same question to the message boxes of several normal registered users and one experienced user, based on the content analysis result. The rank of a user (e.g., experienced user) is determined based on the accumulated number and quality of his previous answers to other users' questions, and determined by the course instructor or TAs. Actually, the instructor and TA are also experienced users, which are critical in the initial stage when there are no other experienced users among the students. When receiving a question, a normal user is required to answer the question if he knows a solution; in case he does not have the answer, he is supposed to write some comments about the question. The main purpose of question dispatching is to inform and urge some students to answer the questions since some of them may not often to check the forum carefully. By doing so, we can keep the balance of the number of questions answered by each user and also make the question answered fast. Actually, if none of the notified users can answer this question, the experienced user will have to answer the question finally, at the end of a given period of time.

After the answers to the question are ready, the asker and the experienced user will be invited to evaluate the quality of the answers. The question asker's evaluation represents the user satisfaction to these answers. To guarantee the correctness of the answers, the experienced user should be included in the judgment committee. Furthermore, the experienced user can modify, edit and make a digest of the question and the model answer. Finally, good questions and answers are selected as distilled posts and stored into the knowledge repository (or FAQ), which can be searched automatically, as we will explained immediately.

Each time the asker submits his question, a search process in the knowledge repository (or FAQ) is automatically invoked, too, trying to give the asker an instant response with related information. Actually, the question can be regarded as a search query. The search process can be accomplished simply by keywords matching. Although this method is very simple in this module, it can instantly provide some links related to the question, and give the asker the clue to solve his problem.

All the users' participation activities are recorded, and credits are given to the users who actively join the discussion and answer questions. The authors whose posts are selected as the distilled or model posts are awarded with bonus credits. In our situation, to encourage the students to participate in discussions in the system, we operate the system using a "question answer competition" metaphor, and associate the final credits earned by a student from the system with the student participation mark, which will contribute to his final grade.

4 Practices and Analyses

We have set up a preliminary prototype system discussed above in the course CS3343 "Software Engineering Practice" at the City University of Hong Kong, by using and modifying the code of an open source PHP web forum project [6]. To better facilitate the student learning on the web, several other web based utilities are also provided and integrated into the original answer hunting system. Figure 2 shows the block diagram of the whole system constitution.

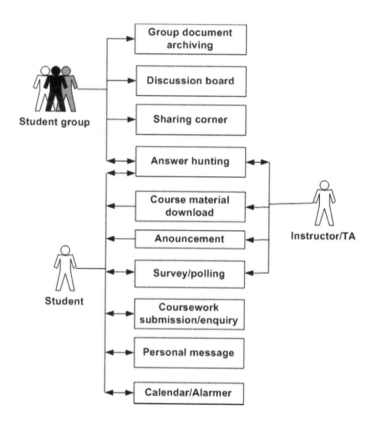

Fig. 2. The Component of Enhanced Answer Hunting System for CS3343

The whole system has successfully worked for 2 months by now. To examine the users' satisfaction to the answer hunting system, we conduct a survey to collect the students' feedback. Participants are limited to the registered students of CS3343. Each participant is required to seriously answer all of the following 9 questions.

For every question, the answer is in a five scale from 0 to 4: 0 for Strongly Disagree (SD), 1 for Disagree (DA), 2 for Neutral (NE), 3 for Agree (AG) and 4 for

Table 1. Questions used in the survey

No.	Question
#1	I think this system can provide the information that is good for my learning
#2	When I have question, I can get the answer through this system
#3	I would like to answer the question posted in the system if I know the answer
#4	This system is a better way to communicate with Instructor and TA, compared with email and phone
#5	This system is a better way to communicate with my fellow groupmates, compared with email and phone
#6	I am glad to share my knowledge and experience with my classmates through this system
#7	I would like to participate in the discussions in this system actively
#8	I think the functions of this system is good to our group's project development (such as, keeping the log, announcement, personal message service, etc)
#9	Overall, I think the system can benefit my learning in the course CS3343.

Table 2. Statistical results of satisfaction of the system

Question	Poor (SD&DA)	Neutral (NE)	Good (AG&SA)	Ave. Satisfaction (full mark is 4)
#1	0%	6%	94%	3.423
#2	1%	7%	92%	3.380
#3	0%	7%	93%	3.423
#4	1%	10%	89%	3.296
#5	1%	23%	76%	2.986
#6	0%	7%	93%	3.324
#7	0%	8%	92%	3.197
#8	1%	8%	90%	3.394
#9	1%	3%	96%	3.521
Overall	1%	9%	91%	3.334

Strongly Agree (SA). Therefore, for one question, 4 means the best satisfaction. Finally, we have collected 72 valid submissions to the survey. Table 2 shows the statistical results.

There are 4 boards in the system, and their corresponding statistical results of the numbers of posted questions, answers, and views (the number of times read by users) in the last two months are shown in Table 3.

As we can learn from the statistical data, in overall, the system has achieved a pretty good performance in the user's satisfaction. 91% students regard it as a good tool that can help their course studies. The statistics to the data of ask/answer/view in boards reveals that the students have regarded the system as a good place to discuss and solve problems. These evidences show that the proposed answer hunting system can be successfully applied in the web based learning domain.

Table 3. Statistic information of the boards in the system

Board	Ask	Answer	View
#1	22	98	1502
#2	7	28	553
#3	21	56	992
#4	15	25	617

5 Conclusion

In this paper, we share our experience of using a web based answer hunting system as an auxiliary way to supplement the traditional classroom-centered learning. We discuss some shortcomings of the traditional teaching method in our situation. Motivated by the success of several existing commercial answer hunting systems, we introduce this kind of system into the course we instruct. Since our case is relatively special in the aspects of both the nature of the users and the field of the topics, we carefully design its architecture for learning use. Our experiment shows our proposed system achieves a pretty good user satisfaction.

Acknowledgement

The work described in this paper was fully supported by a grant from City University of Hong Kong (Project No. 7001462). The authors also thank Miss Wan Zhang, for her contribution of assisting the survey preparation and analysis, and the students enrolled in the course at the City University of Hong Kong for their efforts in using and evaluating the system.

References

[1] H. Liu, X. Hu and X. Zhang, "Human Communication and Interaction in Web Based Learning: a Case Study of the Digital Media Web Course", Proc. of International Conference on Computers in Education, pp. 217-221, 2002.

[2] D. Helic, H. Maurer and N. Scerbakov, "Combining Individual Tutoring with Automatic Course Sequencing in WBT Systems", Proc. of WWW 2004, pp. 456-457, 2004.

[3] P. Xiang, Y. Shi, W. Qin and X. Xiang, "CUBES: Providing Flexible Learning Environment for Virtual Universities", Proc. of International Conference of Web based Learning 2004, pp.51-58, 2004.

[4] Google Answers, http://answer.google.com

[5] Sina iAsk, http://iask.sina.com.cn

[6] SmartIPB, http://www.smartipb.com.

The Impact of E-Learning on the Use of Campus Instructional Space

Tatiana Bourlova and Mark Bullen

The University of British Columbia, Distance Education & Technology,
Centre for Managing and Planning Learning Environments,
2329 Main Mall #1170, Vancouver, B.C. V6R 1Z4, Canada
tatiana.bourlova@ubc.ca
mark.bullen@ubc.ca
http://www.maple.ubc.ca/

Abstract. The use of e-leaning is growing in universities and colleges across North America but these institutions do not fully understand how and in what form it can contribute to their missions, what the indicators of the successful implementation of e-learning would be, and how to assess the changes caused by e-learning. The study approaches e-learning from the institutional perspective, outlining the effects of e-learning on the use of the instructional space on campus.

1 Introduction

The use of e-learning is growing in universities and colleges across North America but these institutions do not fully understand how and in what form it can contribute to their missions, what the indicators of the successful implementation of e-learning would be, and how to assess the changes caused by e-learning. The following study approaches e-learning from the institutional perspective, outlining the effects of e-learning on the use of the instructional space on campus. E-learning is defined as the use of the Internet and Internet-based communication technologies to deliver education and training.

Many Canadian universities are unable to meet the increasing demand for higher education because of a lack of adequate instructional facilities. Often, highly qualified applicants are denied access because of this space shortage (Johnston, 2002). Another factor contributing to the access problem is growing tuition fees. For instance, in the province of British Columbia university tuition fees increased by approximately 50% between 2001 and 2003 and more increases are expected (Dumaresq, et al., 2004). The growing cost of education leads many students to seek employment to meet financial needs (Survey of First-Year University Students, 2001, 2004; Graduating Students Survey, 2000, 2004). While the number of on-campus students who are employed grows, they are also spending more time on education than they did just a decade ago (PCEIP, 2003). At the same time student enrolment in higher education institutions is growing. It has been estimated that by 2011, universities in Canada will need collectively to respond to a projected 20-30% increase in demand (AUCC, 2003).

R.W.H. Lau et al. (Eds.): ICWL 2005, LNCS 3583, pp. 397–405, 2005.

Universities are employing a variety of strategies to deal with this increased demand. E-learning has been suggested as one strategy. E-learning has its roots in distance education which has been used by higher education institutions for over 60 years to provide flexible access to learners who are unable to come to campus. However, a number of studies suggest most students enrolled in distance education courses are now full-time students on campus (Zemsky, Massy, 2004; Hartman, Dzuiban, Moskal; 2004). In addition to e-learning as distance education, we see an increasing use of what is called mixed-mode (Bates, 2001, 2003) or blended forms (Hartman, et al. 1999, 2004) that involve reduced face-to-face contact supplemented with Internet-delivered instruction and interaction. For the next five years the University of British Columbia, for instance, plans to increase the use of e-learning to 12.5% of all undergraduate full time equivalent students (FTEs) (ACCULT, 2000). Other universities and colleges may have similar plans to make more use of mixed-mode e learning. But we do not fully understand how e-learning can be used to deal with the access problems beyond providing fully online distance education courses. For most students this is not a preferred option as the on-campus experience, at least at the undergraduate level, is still highly valued by both students and academics (Bates, 2001, 2003). Using e-learning in mixed-mode forms, in which some face-to-face instruction is replaced by Internet-based activity, is a preferred option (Massy, Zemsky, 2004). But what impact will this use of e-learning have on the use of campus classroom space? Can e-learning be used to meet the needs of working students in a flexible schedule, and to ease the pressure on the university campus facilities caused by the growing demand?

In 2002, the Centre for Managing and Planning E-Learning (MAPLE) at the University of British Columbia began to investigate the impact of e-learning on the campus. This research has resulted in the creation of a basic model for assessing the changes to the campus instructional space occupancy caused by the hypothetical implementation of e-learning in its fully online form for a certain number of courses on campus.

2 Modes of E-Learning and Implementation Scenarios

Our study examined several aspects of a university system: the size of the on-campus population, courses and programs (in terms of the modes of instruction, overall number of the courses and instruction time), and instructional space occupancy. The purpose of the study was to find a way of accurately predicting the effects of e-learning on campus space use so that university administrators might be better able to manage the pressure of increasing demand and stagnant or declining funding.

In order to estimate the cumulative effect of e-learning on campus instructional space, clear definitions for the different modes of e-learning are needed. Most researchers and practitioners distinguish three basic modes of e-learning (Hartman & Dziuban, 2004):

- In *web-enhanced mode* involves the enhancement of face-to-face courses through the pedagogically significant use of the Web using a course management system, but seat time is not reduced.
- *Mixed mode* (blended) instruction involves a fundamental redesign of instruction in which some face-to-face teaching is replaced with online instruction and

"the socialization opportunities of the classroom are combined with the techno-logically-enhanced learning possibilities of the online environment" (p.3).

- *Wholly online* instruction implies online instruction with no face-to-face in-structional contact. This mode of instruction, used for the students on campus, has a potential to reduce the demand for on-campus facilities, such as class-rooms and laboratories.

It has been suggested that mixed-mode implementations of e-learning hold the most promise for making more efficient use of classroom space while maintaining the qual-ity of instruction (Bates, 2001, 2003; Hartman, Dziuban, Moskal, 1999, 2004). How-ever, these definitions do not refer directly to any quantitative indicators, which could be used for the assessment of impact. How much e-learning must be implemented at a university for it to make a meaningful difference to instructional space occupancy? What formats of e-learning have the most impact?

There are several interconnected steps involved in estimating the impact of e-learning on campus: establishing the measurement units for certain elements of the campus system, defining the historical trends in their functioning, defining e-learning in terms of the chosen elements, and finally, discovering and describing the functional dependencies between the variables in question.

We constructed and tested several indicators. If the statistics on the nature of courses (modes of instruction) is available, it is easy to define the extent of e-learning in an institution. Unfortunately, these statistics often do not exist, and classroom use databases often do not indicate how many courses on campus use e-learning, and to what extent. Another uncertainty in measuring the amount of e-learning in an institu-tion is that it can vary for every mixed mode (blended) course. For example, if a tradi-tional classroom-based course requires student attendance in a class twice a week, then using a mixed-mode e-learning approach could require students to be on-campus just once a week, once every two weeks or once a month. Thus, the amount of time that students are required to spend on campus in mixed-mode implementations can vary considerably. Researchers at the Rochester Institute of Technology define blended courses through the course activities or the time-on-task. If approximately 25% to 50% of the face-to-face classroom activities are replaced by instructor-guided online learning activities, then the course is blended (Blended Learning Project, 2004). Indeed, the proportions of in-class and online course activities can vary con-siderably. In our research, to identify the proportion of e-learning in a mixed mode course we use *"class-hour equivalent"* as a unified measure. By class-hour equivalent we mean the number of hours that an online course, or online portions of a blended course, requires for instruction. Another unit of measure is *the number of students enrolled* in the courses. The amount of e-learning can be estimated through the pro-portion of registrations in the traditional face-to-face courses to the number of regis-trants in the courses with e-learning. One more unit of measure that can be used to estimate the overall extent of e-learning in a university is a *course*. We can define the amount of e-learning in a higher education institution via the proportion of traditional campus-based courses to the courses in e-learning formats. With these indicators the base level of e-learning on campus can be defined. The *overall impact* then can be estimated as the difference between the projection of the current trends in classroom space occupancy, and the changes, that are likely to result from the introduction of a certain amount of e-learning. We developed three e-learning implementation scenarios to find out in what conditions these types and amounts of e-learning make a difference for the instructional space occupancy.

Scenario #1: One classroom-based course is transformed into one online course. This example illustrates the case when a course was initially taught face-to-face, and later transformed to fully online mode (i.e., replacing classes on campus). For instance, if an additional section (or several sections) of the course are offered online, then the impact of this implementation (the difference) can be calculated using the following variables: the number of registrations in the course (which can grow exponentially after the implementation of e-learning), the number of classrooms (the course would not need additional classrooms), and the hours when the classrooms were occupied (the periods of time when the course required scheduling classrooms, which would also decrease).

Introducing additional online sections, or replacing existing classroom-based courses, could result in an increase in enrollments without a corresponding increase in the use of instructional space on campus. In a different case, if an online course was initially created for online delivery (as a distance course), it produces no effect on the campus space occupancy. However it is still possible to estimate the weight of this course in the overall amount of e-learning at the institution using the class-hour equivalent variable.

Scenario #2: One classroom-based course is transformed into two sections of mixed mode format. This scenario produces a different impact. If half of the instructional time is used for face-to-face teaching and another half goes online, the number of registrations in the course could double, without an increase in instructional space occupancy. Big lecture courses can be split in this way in order to reduce class size and to increase the amount of teacher-student interaction.

The impact of mixed mode e-learning also can be estimated via *the number of registrations*. So, we can define how many new registrants can take the course due to the scheduling of additional sections. The class-hour equivalent in this case would represent how many hours of instruction would not require scheduling the classrooms on-campus. However, the impact on the instructional space occupancy will be zero in this case, because the same classroom would be occupied for the same hours, as it was before the introduction of e-learning. But more students could use it due to e-learning.

Scenario #3: One classroom-based course is transformed into one mixed mode course. This scenario represents the implementation of a mixed mode course format that could result in students spending fewer hours on campus. If a classroom-based course has been transformed into the mixed mode course, with half of the course time intended for classroom activities and another half - for online instruction, then *the number of registrants* could probably stay the same, the same *classroom* would be required for the course, and only the *schedule time* would be different.

The effect in this case could be that - with the same number of registrants, the classrooms (or laboratories) are occupied less and can be scheduled for some other classes. In this scenario, the resulting impacts can be measured via the class-hour equivalent, indicating the proportion of online and in-classroom course activities and the corresponding changes in instruction space occupancy on campus.

These basic assumptions were used for creating the model for the evaluation of the impact of e-learning at the University of British Columbia. To determine how much of these types of e-learning UBC currently has, and its impact on campus facilities, a snapshot of the campus conditions was made. It included the historical change in student enrolment, the number and types of courses, and on-campus instructional space occupancy.

3 UBC Case Study

Over the last ten years student enrolment at UBC has outgrown the increase in instructional space and the increase in instructors. The number of students on campus grew by 3.2% per year while the amount of space increased by only 0.2% and the number of instructors increased by 2.3% (PAIR, 2002; 2003).This disproportion could be partly responsible for the lack of university seats available to students. Access is a pressing issue for the universities as demand continues to increase. E-learning is one way of addressing the lack of physical space, but universities still need to attract and retain high quality faculty, capable and willing to use e-learning.

Currently only about 1% of all UBC courses are offered in mixed mode format, and 2% are offered online as distance courses (OECD, 2003). It is quite evident, that these small amounts of e-learning do not have much impact on the UBC instructional space occupancy. However, it still useful to know if e-learning were implemented more widely, what impact it would have on instructional space. The purpose of this study was to develop a method for measuring that impact.

We used data from the period 1997-2003 provided by UBC Classroom Services. Work time and academic terms were defined as follows:

- Academic terms: the first term runs from the 4th to 16th weeks, and the second term runs from the 21st to 34th weeks of academic year.
- Work-time: this is the time interval during which the classrooms are available for teaching. Work-time intervals usually vary from 14 hours down to 6 peak hours per day.

The number of classes outside of these terms' periods and beyond the peak hours were insignificant. We determined time intervals and the number of classrooms, during which these were occupied for instruction in a specified year/term. An average amount of time, during which the classrooms are occupied (*Occupancy Time*) is measured in hours and in the percentage of work-time. The number of classrooms occupied during a term (*Average Number of Occupied Classrooms*) is measured as a number of classrooms in use, regardless to their size, and as a percentage of the occupied rooms to the whole classroom pool.

The analysis of the UBC course schedules, made for the five year period from 1998/99 to 2002/03, reveals that on average 79.6% of the, classrooms are occupied at peak hours (415 out of 497). Of the six peak hours, on average the classroom space is occupied for 58.1% of that time or for three hours and 29 minutes. In terms of the standards for the use of the university classroom space, these figures represent a very good rate of utilization (Fink, 2002; 2003). But we also know that there is an access problem. How can we make the use of instructional space more efficient to address the problem of access?

We supplemented the statistical analysis with mathematical modeling, creating a descriptive image of the chosen functions of the campus system in order to predict and estimate how the system would be affected by e-learning implemented on campus. We developed a computer tool for a "what if" scenario, to find out whether there could be any proof for the improved use of instructional space on campus. The UBC historical data on the number of occupied classrooms and course schedule time were used for modeling the classroom occupancy for an hypothetical case in which four big classroom-based lecture courses are transformed into an e-learning format (testing the first scenario). The prognostic evaluation of the impact was based on a linear extrapolation of the current trend in the classroom space occupancy and the extrapolation of the hypothetical trend with the changes that occur with the suggested amount of e-learning.

The pie chart (Figure 1) shows the resulting on-campus/online course ratio for all UBC courses. The graphs on this figure show the difference between the current trend in classroom occupancy (solid line) and the hypothetical trend with the established amount of e-learning (dotted line). If this particular scenario were implemented for the selected courses on campus, then the result would be 11.27% difference in the classroom occupancy *time*; and 14.9% difference – in the number of occupied *classrooms* comparing to the previous occupancy of learning spaces. This means that out of 415 classrooms (that are occupied during peak hours on campus) 74 of these can be made available for the course instruction within the time periods during which these classrooms previously were in use (Bourlova; 2004). The parameters of this e-learning scenario can be changed and adjusted to the needs of a particular institution. This provides university administrators with more flexibility in managing instructional space and student enrolment. This achieved flexibility can be used for class scheduling in many different ways: accommodating more students in the most popular courses (offering additional course sections at the available classrooms), splitting big lecture classes into a small group teaching format, and also offering more diverse schedule options for the students and instructors on campus. The net effect of this scenario is that fewer classrooms are occupied for less time.

It is important to note that the outlined functional dependences are closely related to other campus conditions. The implementation of e-learning on-campus also requires the university to have enough professors to teach and the IT support staff to provide assistance to instructors and learners in the online environment. If these conditions are not met, then the advantages in improved use of instructional space become dubious. The positive impacts on the use of classroom space caused by e-learning would not be realized, if the university instructors are not motivated to teach using e-learning, or if adequate course design and technical support is not provided. Faculty support is critical to the successful implementation of e-learning (Hanrahan, Ryan, Duncan; 2001).

We have only tested the scenario, in which classroom-based courses are transformed into fully online format. The model shows it is possible to calculate and predict the potential impact of e-learning on campus before any decision on its implementation is made. With this model we also tested the applicability of the constructed variables to this kind of analysis. The model will be further developed to handle the mixed-mode scenarios of e-learning for on-campus use.

It is also important to emphasize that using e-learning to alleviate classroom space shortages should not be the primary reason for universities to adopt it. Research and practice suggests that e-learning, particularly in its mixed mode and distance education modes, can have a positive impact on the learning experience (Dzuiban, Hartam & Moskal, 2004; Bates, 2000). This study helps inform one aspect of university decision-making related to e-learning; decisions about whether and how to implement e-learning should be driven by its broader educational and social impact. Further studies are needed to clarify how and in what form e-learning can contribute to the instruction practices and to students educational experiences.

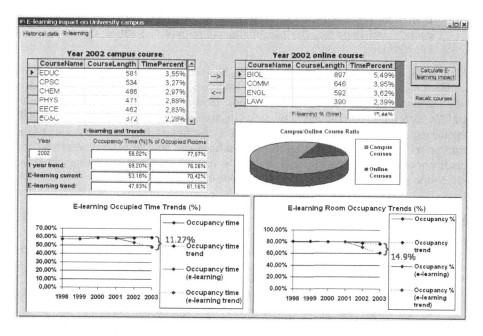

Fig. 1. Modeling the Impact of E-learning on the Campus Instructional Space Occupancy

4 Summary

The results of this study provide only a first step in the development of a full body of standard procedures for the evaluation of the diverse effects of e-learning when it is implemented in higher education.

Our analysis of the impact of e-learning on the university campus revealed that:

- The introduction of mixed-mode e-learning and fully online sections for non-distance courses leads to the reduction of classroom space occupancy on campus.
- E-learning will only have an impact on campus facilities if the course in question was initially taught face-to-face on campus and later transformed to fully online or mixed mode. The anticipated effect of the introduction of online sections for an existing classroom-based course is a potential increase in student enrolment without the increased use of instructional space on campus.

- If an online course was initially created for *distance education*, then its implementation has no effect on the campus space occupancy. In other words, even extensive use of e-learning at a higher education institution could have no effect on the campus instructional space occupancy if the e-learning courses are developed and delivered as distance courses and they do not replace existing face-to-face courses. The "weight" of the distance courses in the overall amount of e-learning at a university can be estimated using the "class-hours equivalent" variable.
- E-learning implemented for on-campus use provides flexibility in scheduling courses and improves the use of limited resources, such as classrooms and laboratories.

Many institutions do not collect the type of data needed for this type of study, as no standard indicators and procedures are yet established for the analysis of the impacts of e-learning on higher education institutions. However, this information can be crucial for successful planning based on the evaluation of the prior conditions and modeling the expected effects of the use of e-learning on-campus. Regular monitoring of the parameters of campus functioning that we outlined can help to better understand and predict how to manage the changes, realize the major benefits of e-learning and at the same time identify and prevent undesirable side effects.

References

1. ACCULT – Academic Committee for the Creative Use of Learning Technologies (2000). The Creative Use of Learning Technologies. UBC. Retrieved March, 2005, www.maple.ubc.ca/research/accult/index_accult.html
2. AUCC Publications (2003). Trends in Higher Education. Retrieved March, 2005, www.aucc.ca/publications/auccpubs/research/trends/summary_e.html
3. Bates, A. W. (2000). *Managing Technological Change: Strategies for College and University Leaders.* Jossey-Bass Publishers: San Francisco.
4. Bates, A. W. (2001). *National Strategies for E-learning in Post-Secondary Education and Training.* Paris: UNESCO: International Institute for Education and Planning.
5. Blended Learning Project Final Report for the Academic Year 2003-2004 (2004). Online Learning Department. Rochester Institute of Technology.
6. Bourlova, T. (2004). The Impact of E-learning on a University Campus. Final project report. Retrieved March, 2005, www.maple.ubc.ca/researc/impact_project.html
7. CAUT / ACPPU (2003). Almanac of Post-Secondary Education in Canada.
8. Dumaresq, Ch., Lambert-Maberly, A., Sudmant, W. (2004). University Accessibility and Affordability. PAIR. UBC. Retrieved July, 2004, www.pair.ubc.ca/studies/tuitafford0304.htm#_Toc64186002
9. Fink, I. (2002). Classroom Use and Utilization, Faculty Manager, FAIA, May/June 2002.
10. Fink, I. (2003). Benchmarking. A new approach to space planning. *Connecting the Dots... the Essence of Planning. The Best of Planning for Higher Education* 1997-2003. Ed. by Rod Rose. The Society for College and University Planning.
11. Graduating Students Survey. (2000). (2004). The Master Report for the Canadian Undergraduate Survey UBC. Retrieved May, 2004 www.pair.ubc.ca/studies/cusc2003.htm

12. Hanrahan, M., Ryan, M., Duncan, M. (2001). The professional engagement model of academic induction into on-line teaching. *International Journal for Academic Development.* Vol. 6, No. 2, pp. 130-142.

13. Hartman J., Dzuiban, Ch., Moskal, P. (2004). Blended Learning. *EDUCAUSE Centre for Applied Research.* Research Bulletin, vol. 2004, Issue 7, March 30, 2004

14. Hartman, J., Dziuban, Ch., Moskal, P. (1999). Faculty Satisfaction in ALNs: A Dependent of Independent Variable? Sloan Summer ALN Workshops. Illinois, August 16-18, 1999.

15. Johnston, A. D. (2002). The University Crunch. *MakLean's,* November 18. Retrieved May, 2003, http://www.macleans.ca/xta-doc2/2002/11/18/Universities2002/75463.shtml

16. OECD (Organization for economic co-operation and development). (2004). *E-learning case studies in post-secondary education & training.* UBC case study. Centre for educational Research and Innovation.

17. PAIR (2004). Planning and Institutional Research. The University of British Columbia Fact Book. Retrieved February, 2004, www.pair.ubc.ca/studies/factbook.htm

18. Report of the Pan-Canadian Education Indicators Program (PCEIP). Education Indicators in Canada, 2003, Retrieved December, 2004, www.cesc.ca ; www.statcan.ca

19. Survey of First-Year University Students (2001); (2004). Canadian Undergraduate Survey Consortium (CUSC) PAIR. UBC. Retrieved November, 2003; November, 2004, www.pair.ubc.ca

20. Zemsky, R., Massy, F. (2004). Thwarted Innovation. What Happened to e-learning and Why. A final report for the *Weatherstation Project* of the Learning Alliance at the University of Pennsylvania in cooperation with the Thomson Corporation. Retrieved May, 2004, www.thelearningalliance.info/Docs/Jun2004/ThwartedInnovation.pdf

The Research of Mining Association Rules Between Personality and Behavior of Learner Under Web-Based Learning Environment

Jin Du [1], Qinghua Zheng [1], Haifei Li [2], and Wenbin Yuan [1]

[1] Department of Computer Science, Xi'an Jiaotong University, Xi'an,
Shannxi, P. R. China, 710049
[2]Department of Mathematics and Computer Science at Union University,
Jackson, TN, U.S.A
Xian_dj@163.com

Abstract: Discovering the relationship between behavior and personality of learner in the web-based learning environment is a key to guide learners in the learning process. This paper proposes a new concept called personality mining to find the "deep" personality through the observed data about the behavior. First, a learner model which includes personality model and behavior model is proposed. Second, we have designed and implemented an improved algorithm, which is based on Apriori algorithm widely used in market basket analysis, to identify the relationship. Third, we have discussed various issues like constructing the learner model, unifying the value domain of heterogeneous model attributes, and improving Apriori algorithm with decision domain. Experiment result indicated that this algorithm for mining association rules between behavior and personality is feasible and efficient. The algorithm has been used in a web-based learning environment developed at Xi'an Jiaotong University.

1 Introduction

Web learning is a very promising area and it has the potential to revolutionize the education industry. Today, more than 420 universities have set up web-based virtual school in American□the number of student enrolled is about 1 800 000 and the kind of curriculums reaches 50 000, which overcover almost all of subjects of American university. Moreover, web-based learning has been applied in staff continued training among 60% of US enterprises.

Discovering the relationship between personalities and behaviors of leaner is an important issue in web-based learning environment. It's known that the personality of learner will affects his or her learning behavior mode to a certain extent. On the other hand, some kind of behaviors sequence must be the representation of some personality. However, although the psychologists and pedagogues had been studying the relations between personality and behaviors of learners for many decades, the web-based learning technology is a novel mode of modern education and it is new research field which combined with the psychology, cognitive science, information

R.W.H. Lau et al. (Eds.): ICWL 2005, LNCS 3583, pp. 406–417, 2005.

science, computer technology and so on. So, the problems to discovery the relationship between personality and behaviors focus on the two problems.

The first one is how to build the learner model, it is the key step to get the personality of learners in web based leaning system. Usually, the pedagogues study the learners model under the traditional learning environment, but research of learner model in web based learning system is still a blank field which have profound study foreground. Because the raw data have some specialty of their own, which are complex, dynamic, distributed, so the feature of the learners can not be represented by raw data directly. The complexity was demonstrated in that the dimension of attributes which describe the learner's personality is various, and the value type of the attributes is the quantitative, moreover, the learning behavior model is heterogeneous; The dynamic means that the data resource (e.g. web log on studying) was updated frequently; The distributed denotes that the resource of the data is broad, that include various questionnaire for personality and huge study logs in detail. So the learner model should be represented by mathematical model which is the combination of various science and technology such as information science, pedagogics and so on.

The second problem is which method should be selected to discovery the relationship between the personality and behavior and which is more adaptable and efficient? According to the features of learner model and the demand we expected, the technology of data mining is adopted. But the general algorithm to find the association rules between the 'behavior-personality' for learners have some shortage such as low efficiency, heavy calculation and redundancy results. In this paper, aiming to the particularity of the data to be mined, algorithm with decision attribute based on Apriori is proposed, the algorithm based on the personality model and behaviors model, and the advantage of algorithm was proved in application.

The following are the contributions of this paper. First, this paper proposes the personality mining as one of the key components in personalized web learning environment. Second, Apriori algorithm, which has been widely used for market basket analysis, has been extended with Decision Domains for personalized web learning environment. Third, an extensive experiment has been conducted to validate the feasibility of the new algorithm. As far as we know, our paper is the first to address the issue of relationship between personality and behavior for web-based learners. The rest of the paper is organized as follows. Section 2 discusses Learner Model, which include both personality model and behavior model. Section 3 describes the algorithm; Section 4 describes the performance evaluation. Section 5 describes the possible applications in personalized web-based learning. Section 6 describes the experiments. Section 7 concludes the paper with future work.

2 Learner Model

The learner model is the basis of personality network learning system. Today, the IEEE LTCS has proposed the IEEE 1484.2 PAPI (Public and Private Information), which describe the information about the learners such as age, background, region and so on, and include demographics, major, management, relation, security, preference, performance, works and so on information of learner at eight aspects[1].

Although the PAPI can content the demand of education well, under the personalized network learning environment, it is incapable to be taken as the basis to making out the strategy for personalized education yet. According to the demand on the personalized learning, we enlarge the learner model at non-intelligent aspects by introducing five factors such as personality, motive, concept, method. Furthermore, we import six kinds of study behavior in network education, such as courseware learning, web-based homework/examination, posting and browsing on BBS, answer question by web and interaction among teachers and students by multi-model. We constructed the learner model for the application of personality education. As the figure 1 shown, the grey blocks are the content what should be expanded.

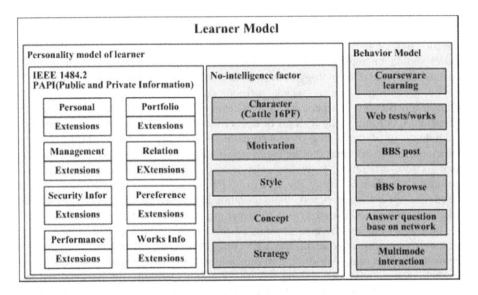

Fig. 1. The structure of LM (Leaner Model)

As the fig.1 shown, the Learner Model include both static model (described with personality model) and dynamic model (described with behavior model), it should be defined as the following tuple:

$$LM =< PM, BM >$$ (1)

2.1 Personality Model

PM was composed of some sub-model such as *character, motivation, style, concept* and *strategy,* which are stable elements in LM and represent the various profile of learner in personality respectively. The PM can be defined as:

$$PM =< L\_P, L\_M, L\_S, L\_C, L\_T >$$ (2)

Character was the summation of mentality tendency, which is relatively stable for some ones[3]. It was proved that character affected not only the style of interaction in common life, but also the style of behavior in learning[4]. In this paper, the personality was described by means of Cattell's 16PF (Personality Factor).

The **16PF(L_P)** was defined as following tuple:

$$L\_P :: \ =< UID, A, B, C, E, F, G, E, F, H, I, L, M, N, O, Q_1, Q_2, Q_3, Q_4 > \qquad (3)$$

The UID is the unique identity of the learner, the other components are the 16 personal factors, as the table 1 shown, each factor can be measured on a scale, determined by completing a questionnaire, and the word pairs below indicate the extremes of each scale. The letter codes were ascribed to each scale as a shorthand notation.

Table 1. Cattell's 16 Personality Factors

	Factor	Descriptors	
A	Warmth	Reserved	Outgoing
B	Reasoning	Less Intelligent	More Intelligent
C	Emotional Stability	Affected by feelings	Emotionally stable
E	Dominance	Humble	Assertive
F	Liveliness	Sober	Happy-go-lucky
G	Rule Consciousness	Expedient	Conscientious
H	Social Boldness	Shy	Venturesome
I	Sensitivity	Tough-minded	Tender-minded
L	Vigilance	Trusting	Suspicious
M	Abstractedness	Practical	Imaginative
N	Privateness	Straightforward	Shrewd
O	Apprehension	Self-Assured	Apprehensive
Q1	Openness to Change	Conservative	Experimenting
Q2	Self-Reliance	Group-dependent	Self-sufficient
Q3	Perfectionism	Self-conflict	Self-control
Q4	Tension	Relaxed	Tense

Similarly, the other elements of PM can be defined as following formal expression.

Study Motivation Information of Learner:

$$L\_M :: \ =< UID, M\_C, M\_I, M\_R, M\_D, M\_S, M\_E > \qquad (4)$$

Where M_C is information of challenge, M_I is interest, M_R is curiosity, M_D is independence, M_S is Success and M_E is extrinsic motivation.

Study Style Information:

$$L\_S :: =< UID, S_1, S_2, S_3, S_4, S_5, S_6, S_7, S_8 > \tag{5}$$

The 'Study Style' was defined as the composite of characteristic cognitive, affective, and physiological factors that serve as relatively stable indicators of how a learner perceives, interacts with, and responds to the learning environment (Keefe, 1979). The styles is multiple, Where S1: field independence ǀ field dependency; S2: impulsive ǀ reflectivity; S3: holist ǀ analytical; S4: serial ǀ random; S5: group-oriented ǀ individual-oriented: S6: visual ǀ auditory ǀ hand-on; S7: objective ǀ nonobjective; S8: open ǀ close.

Study Concept Information:

$$L\_C :: =< UID, C\_M, C\_E, C\_A > \tag{6}$$

Where C_M is Self-Management, C_E is Self-Efficiency, C_A is Self-Attribute.

Study strategy Information:

$$L\_T :: =< UID, T\_M, T\_C, T\_E, T\_R, T\_S, T\_O > \tag{7}$$

Where T_M is memory, T_C is cognize, T_E is self-management, T_R is retrieve, T_S is sense and T_O is intercommunicate.

In order to get the value of those attributes, we designed the various questionnaires respectively to collect the information of every element in PM. For example, concerning Cattell's 16PF, we us the classic questionnaire with 189 questions to get all values of 16 personality factors.

2.2 Behavior Model

The learning behaviors are action sequences of learner recorded by network learning log, and what should include all information of learner's activity under different learning mode which provided by learning system. Here, we describe the BM from 6 different aspects:

$$BM = \{B\_C, B\_T, B\_B1, B\_B2, B\_A, B\_I\} \tag{8}$$

B_C (Behavior on courseware learning): <User id, course id, unit id, entry, stay time>

B_T(Behavior on Test/homework):<User id, course id, test/homework id, finished, score, question sum, correct ratio>

B_B1(BBS posting): <User id, course id, article id, article type (post, reply), words, quality>

B_B2(BBS browsing): <User id, course id, article id, stay time>

B_A(Behavior of answer question): <user id, course id, speaks, speech words, online time>

B_I(Behavior of interaction): <User id, course id, class id, type(multimedia, e-board, text chat, application share), time>

Generally, the value of each attribute was gained statistically, and the BM represents the profile of the learner's behavior quantificationally. However, the different attribute has the different value field and type, in order to content the need of following mining, we should map the value of attributes of PM and BM into uniform integer range in dividing partition. For example, we can mapped the quantitative value into three interval: *high, middle, low* partition, and represent them with ascent integer *1,2,3*. After data converted, the every attributes of the LM (Learner Model) have the same value type and the same value range (e.g. 1,2,3). According to the type of attributes, the association rule mining among behavior and personality characters can be performed.

3   Algorithm to Mine Association Rules Between Behavior and Personality

3.1   Problem Explanation

After mapping the value of behavior model and personality model into uniform range, we can use the tradition algorithm Apriori to analyze the association rules among the attributes of behaviors and personalities. Firstly, let us define the problem more clearly use the following mathematical model[2]

Definition 1: Association Rule

- $I = \{i_1, i_2, \ldots\ldots, i_m\}$ the set of items
- Database D is a set of transactions.
- Transaction T is a set of items such that $T \subseteq L$. An unique identifier, *TID*, is associated with each transaction.
- T contains X, a set of some items in L, if $X \subseteq T$.
- Rule form: "Body $\Rightarrow$ Head [support, confidence]"
- Association rule, $X \Rightarrow Y$ $X \subset T$, $Y \subset T$, $X \cap Y = \varnothing$
- Confidence – % of transactions which contain X which also contain Y.
- Support - % of transactions in D which contain $X \cup Y$.

In our problem, the items are all attributes with values; the database D is the all records which include the results of questionnaires and of the log analysis on behavior sequence. The transaction T presents the description for one user, the user id is as same as the *TID*, which joint the character vectors of PM and BM together, so the all attributes can be seemed as undifferentiated each other. At last, we set the special threshold□min-support and min-confidence□ to get the association rules between the PM and BM.

However, the traditional algorithm, as Apriori or Aprioritid[6], deal with all attributes without distinguish. There are 3 types of rule mode as 1) PM-PM, 2) BM-BM, 3)Mixed. Especially, the last type is very complex, the body and head of rules maybe include the attributes of PM or BM or both. In order to get the rules as we expected, we have to scan all records to find all potential rules, and delete the rules uninterested. So some cost of time and calculation was wasted on analyzing and deleting phases.

In order to improve the efficiency of algorithm, and avoid the unnecessary cost, we should modify the traditional algorithm according to the demand of application. In our problem, we use the behavior sequence as the input parameters, and generate the rules as BM$\Rightarrow$PM. The elements of rule body belong to the attribute set in BM and elements of rule head belong to the PM's. In this way, we can deduce the personality from the learner's behavior sequence recorded by web logs.

Well, we can divide the all the items in Learner Model into different fields, and through the association analysis, to discover the relationships among the items (attributes with value) which belong to PM and BM. So, let's make definition at first.

Definition 2: Domain

The attributes set I in LM can been divided between 2 subsets: $I = I_P \cup I_B$, and $I_P \cap I_B = \phi$. We named I$_P$, I$_B$ as a domain, and the domain I$_P$, I$_B$ can been expressed as $I_P = \{p_1, p_2, \cdots, p_n\}$, $I_B = \{b_1, b_2, \cdots, b_m\}$.

In this paper, it proposes an 'Algorithm of Apriori with Decision Domains (named as DD for short)'. This algorithm can discover the rules of which the structure was foreknown (the items of head and body belong to different domains respectively, and the domain of head was expected).

3.2 Algorithm Analysis

Take a fact about association analysis into account.

If $a_1, ..., a_i \Rightarrow b_1, ..., b_j$ existed, $a_1, ..., a_i \Rightarrow b_1$, $a_1, ..., a_i \Rightarrow b_2$,...,

$a_1, ..., a_i \Rightarrow b_j$ must existed too, any subset of a frequent item set must be frequent.

So, we can translate the problem $I_A \Rightarrow I_B$ into the rule set as $\{ \wedge a_{i'} \Rightarrow b_{j'} \}$.

Definition 3: Decision Domain (DD)

Supposing the structure of the rules and the head of rules are foreknown, we want to find out the associate rules such as' $b_i, b_j, ..., b_m \Rightarrow p$ '.where, $\{b_i, b_j, ..., b_m, p\}$ is attributes set, $b_i, b_j, ..., b_m$, belong to domain I$_B$, p belong to I$_P$. Here, the head of rule p was known and name as *Decision Domain(DD for short)*.

Meanwhile, we notice such facts:

Theorem 1

During the association rules mining with DD, if k-items ($b_1, b_2, ..., b_{k-1}, p$) (the length of attribute tuple is k) is not a frequent items set, according to the Monotonicity Property of frequent items (A subset of a frequent itemset must also be a frequent itemset), the $b_1, b_2, ..., b_{k-1}$ must been invalid frequent items to generate the rule as $b_1, b_2, ..., b_{k-1}, ..., b_n \Rightarrow p$.

In this theorem, the 'invalid' means: even though ($b_1, b_2, ..., k-1, p$) can generate the frequent items such as ($b_1, b_2, ..., b_{K-1}, ..., b_n$), it can not generate frequent itemset as ($b_1, b_2, ..., b_{k-1}, ..., b_n, p$).

Therefore, while generating the association rules, we can delete the frequent items such as $b_a, b_b, ..., b_i, b_j, ..., b_n$, which only generate the rules as $b_a, b_b, ..., b_i \Rightarrow b_j, ..., b_n$, from all set of frequent itemset.

The process of 'Algorithm of Apriori with DD' is as following:

Step 1: *divide L_k (k-frequent items) between L_{ki} which includes decision domain and L_{k2} which excludes decision domain, both L_{k1} and L_{k2} are k-frequent items.*

Step 2: *generate the k-candidate set $C_{(k+1)1}$ which includes decision domain from $L_{k1} \square L_{k2}$*

Step 3: *counting the items in $C_{(k+1)1}$, generate (k+1) frequent items $L_{(k+1)1}$ which include decision domain.*

Step 4: *supposing the item which included in $C_{(k+1)1}$ and excluded in $L_{(k+1)1}$ is $b_i, b_j, ..., b_k, p$;*

Step 5: *delete all of items which include $b_i, b_j, ...b_k$ from L_{k2}*

Step 6: *generate k+1 candidate $C_{(k+1)2}$ which exclude decision domain from L_{k2}*

Step 7: *counting the items in $C_{(k+1)2}$, generate k+1 frequent items $L_{(k+1)2}$ which exclude decision domain;*

Step 8: *repeats step 1 ~ step 7 till the largest set of frequent items is generated.*

Example:

Table 2. Transaction data

UID	Items list
U_1	I_1, P
U_2	I_2, I_4, I_5
U_3	I_1, I_2, I_4, P
U_4	I_1, I_2, I_4, I_5
U_5	I_2, I_4, P
U_6	I_2, I_4, I_5
U_7	I_1, I_2, I_4, I_5, P
U_8	I_2, I_4, P
U_9	I_2, I_5, P
U_{10}	$I_2 \square I_3 \square I_4 \square P$

As the table 2 shown, I_1 , I_2 , I_3 , I_4 , I_5 are feature attributes of BM, P is the character of PM, totally 10 transactions in database D, |D|=10. We need to get the rules form as $I_i, I_j, ..., I_n \Rightarrow P$ through mining.

Set the min-support = 30%, the count of min-support is 3.

If we use the traditional algorithm such as Apriori, then we achieve the analyed result as table 3:

If we adopt the algorithm with DD, to delete the invalid frequent items set in course of mining, the result should be shown as table 4.

Table 3. The course of Traditional Apriori analysis

C_1		L_1	C_2		L_2	C_3		L_3
Itemset	Supp	Itemset	Itemset	Supp	Itemset	Itemset	Supp	Itemset
I_1	4	I_1	I_1, I_2	3	I_1, I_2	I_1, I_2, I_4	3	I_1, I_2, I_4
I_2	9	I_2	I_1, I_4	3	I_1, I_4	I_1, I_2, P	2	I_2, I_4, I_5
I_3	1	I_4	I_1, I_5	1	I_1, P	I_1, I_4, P	2	I_2, I_4, P
I_4	8	I_5	I_1, P	3	I_2, I_4	I_2, I_4, I_5	4	
I_5	5	P	I_2, I_4	8	I_2, I_5	I_2, I_4, P	5	
P	7		I_2, I_5	5	I_2, P			
			I_2, P	6	I_4, I_5			
			I_4, I_5	4	I_4, P			
			I_4, P	5				
			I_5, P	2				

Table 4. The course of association analysis with decision domain

C_{11}		L_{11}	C_{21}		L_{21}	C_{31}		L_{31}
Itemset	Supp	Itemset	Itemset	Supp	Itemset	Itemset	Supp	Itemset
P	7	P	I_1, P	3	I_1, P	I_1, I_2, P	2	I_2, I_4, P
C_{12}		L_{12}	I_2, P	6	I_2, P	I_1, I_4, P	2	
I_1	4	I_1	I_4, P	5	I_4, P	I_2, I_4, P	5	
I_2	9	I_2	I_5, P	2	L_2	C_{32}		
I_3	1	I_4	C_{22}		I_1, I_2			
I_4	8	I_5	I_1, I_2	3	I_1, I_4			
I_5	5		I_1, I_4	3	I_2, I_4			
			I_2, I_4	8				

In table4, when $L_{11} \square L_{12}$ generate $C_{21} \square C_{22}$, the following step needed to be executed.

Step 1: self-joining L_{11}, (as $L_{11} \bowtie L_{11}$). For the L_{11} have one 1-item only, so it can not generate 2-items.

Step 2: join L_{11} with L_{12}(as $L_{11} \bowtie L_{12}$), generate $(I_1,P)\square(I_2,P)\square(I_4,P)\square(I_5,P)$ *2-candidate items. After count supports of the 2-candidates, the support of (I_5,P) is under the min-support, so (I_5,P) is deleted. According to theorem 1, I_5 is invalid frequent item, so it should be deleted from L_{12}.*

Step 3: self-joining L_{12}(as $L_{12} \bowtie L_{12}$),in which the I_5 had been deleted, counting supports of the three 2-candidates (I_1,I_2), (I_1,I_4), (I_2,I_4) respectively;

Step 4: generate L_{21} and L_{22} from C_{21} and C_{22};

From the table4, it is known that, the association analysis algorithm with decision domain can descend the complexity of association analysis efficiently, through removing invalid frequent items and reducing the pass of database scanning,

4 Time Complexity Evaluation

In this section, we will compare time complexity of algorithm optimized with that of traditional Apriori algorithm, to evaluate the performance and show the advantage of the algorithm proposed.

Considering the complexity of algorithm is affected by the concrete transactions sequence, in order to illuminate more clearly, we make several suggestion first of all.

On the assumption that length of LM (the number of attributes of PM and of BM) in this database D is m, the sum of items belong to body domain(BM) is $m-1$, the item belong to head domain(PM) is 1. There are n transactions in database D. For the Apriori-generate C_2 from L_1 is the key step in all algorithm process, so, in this paper, we evaluate the advantage of this algorithm according to the sum of attributes which can be removed from L_1.

Supposing, when generate L_1 from C_1, the sum of items can be removed no-frequent items is M, the sum of invalid frequent items is N, so there are:

The time complexity of traditional algorithm Apriori would be illuminate as:

$$O(n * (C_m^1 + C_{m-M}^2 + \ldots\ldots + C_{m-M}^{m-M-1})) = O(n * 2^{m-M}) \tag{9}$$

The time complexity of Apriori Algorithm with Decision Domain is illuminated as:

$$O(n * (C_m^1 + C_{m-M-N}^2 + \ldots\ldots + C_{m-M-N}^{m-M-N-1})) = O(n * 2^{m-M-N}) \tag{10}$$

Obviously, when $N \geqslant 1$, then

$$O(n * 2^{m-M}) >> O(n * 2^{m-M-N}) \tag{11}$$

Hence, the algorithm with decision domain can reduce the number of k-candidates C_k efficiently, moreover, descend the time complexity in association rules analyzing.

5 Application

Under the web based learning environment, we describe the character of learners in two aspects, Behavior Model and Personality Model, the former was expressed by a set of vector such as $\vec{B} = (B_1, B_2, ..., B_m)$. The latter is static, gained through several questionnaires, such as Cattell's 16PF, can be expressed as:

$$\vec{p}_{L\_K} = (A, B, C, E, F, G, E, F, H, I, L, M, N, O, Q_1, Q_2, Q_3, Q_4) \tag{12}$$

We need to explain what does A, B, C, up to Q4 mean. Otherwise, people will have hard time to understand it.

We will get the rule such as: $\underset{b \in B', B' \in B}{\wedge} ((b, s'), s' \in S) \rightarrow (p, v')$ by our algorithm. B is the set of behavior attributes. B' is a subset of B and is not empty; S is the value range of some attribute b in B', s' is a possible value in S; $p \in P$, v' is a possible value in p.

For the limited of application condition, we analyzed only the behaviors of BBS, B_C and B_A to discover the relationship between character attributes and behavior. We set the min-support is 10%, and the min-confidence is 60%, the results of rules searching as the table shown.

6 Experiments

We developed 'Personalized English Learning System' and applied it in Xi'an Jiaotong University. After one month's using, we collected 324 students Cattell characters and about 146 000 web log records. The experiment show that, when the structure of rules is constrained, by dividing items into different domain, and filtering the items in the course of mining, the algorithm with decision domain will avoid the generation of redundancy rules, reduce the complexity of calculate and improve the analysis efficiency.

Table 5. The result compared between Apriori and Apriori with decision domain

Character	Apriori	Apriori with DD
amount of transaction examples	324	324
Amount of available rules	67	29
Running time	1420ms	843ms

According to the results of association analysis, the relationship between PM and BM as the table7 shown:□

Table 6. Part of relationship between BM and PM

BM \ Personality	B1	B2	B3	B4	B5	B6
A(Warmth)	PC			PC		PC
E(Dominance)		PC	PC	NC	PC	
G(Rule Consciousness)	PC					
L(Vigilance)	PC		NC		PC	
Q2(Self-Reliance)		PC	PC			
……						

Where, NC: negative correlation, PC: positive correlation, B1: Stay time in B_C, B2: The proportion of article type in BBS, B3: The words in B_BBS1, B4: The quality of article, B5: The proportion of question answered, B6: Total online time in B_A.

7 Conclusions and Future Work

The experiment show that, the Apriori algorithm with DD can discover the relationship between personality and behavior, improve the efficiency of mining. After get the personality features of learner by analyzing his/her behavior, how to adopt the proper study strategy and settle adaptive leaning material, will be our future work.

Reference

1. IEEE Learning Technology Standards Committee (LTSC), IEEE 1484.2 "PAPI Learner Model"
2. Agrawal R, Srikant R. Fast algorithm for mining association rules. Proceedings of 1994 International Conference on Very Large Databases. Santiago, Chile, 1994, 487-499
3. E. Vance Wilson, Student characteristics and computer-mediated communication, Computers & Education, 2000(34), 67-76
4. Eyong B. Kim, The role of personality in Web-based distance education courses Communications of the ACM, Volume 47, Issue 3 March 2004
5. Carey, J. M., Kacmar, C. The Impact of Communication Mode and Task Complexity on Small Group Performance and Member Satisfaction. Computers in Human Behavior, 13(1), 23-49
6. Jiawei Han, Micheline Kamber. Data Mining: Concepts and Techniques, Morgan kaufamnn Publishers. 2001
7. Liu Jun, Li Renhou, Zheng Qinghua, Study on the Personality Mining Method for Learners in Network Learning, Academic Journal of Xi'an Jiaotong University, 38(6) 2004. (EI indexed, AN: 04358329828)

Author Index

Bai, Huixian   236
Bourlova, Tatiana   397
Bullen, Mark   397
Busetti, Emanuela   375

Chan, S.F.   279
Chang, Ching-Pao   157
Chang, Yi-Chun   157
Chen, Jing   311
Chen, Juei-Nan   273, 320, 349
Chen, Yi-Chi   157
Chen, Yu   1
Cheng, Kai   56
Cheng, Shu-Chen   273
Cheng, Vivying   209
Cheung, William K.   244
Chiu, Chiung-Hui   157
Choy, M.   267
Choy, S.O.   279
Chu, Chih-Ping   157
Chu, William C.   320, 349
Coldwell, J.M.   355
Cui, Xie   78

Dang, Haifeng   236
Dettori, Giuliana   375
Du, Jin   406

Feng, Ling   311
Fernández-Manjón, Baltasar   144
Fong, Anthony   174
Fong, Joseph   174
Forcheri, Paola   375
Fung, Heidi   14

Gao, Zhao-Ming   197
Gu, Hongliang   1
Gupta, Suhit   86

Han, Peng   122, 221, 332, 340
Hao, Xiao-Wei   226
He, Qinming   49
He, Zhen   49

Hirota, Toyohiko   56
Hu, Weihua   364
Hu, Yunhua   236
Hu, Zuwei   122, 340
Huang, Guanglin   387
Huang, Shang-Ming   197
Huang, Yueh-Min   273, 320
Hui, Simon   38

Ierardi, Maria Grazia   375

Jeng, Yu-Lin   320
Jia, Weijia   291

Kaiser, Gail   66, 86
Kazuo, Ushijima   56
Klamma, Ralf   131
Komura, Taku   256
Kuo, Yen-Hung   320
Kwan, R.   279

Lam, Gibson   209
Lam, Mason H.   244
Lau, Rynson W.H.   256
Lee, Cynthia   244
Lee, Jickhary   174
Li, Frederick W.B.   256
Li, Haifei   406
Li, Lei   226
Li, Minglu   99
Li, Qing   311
Li, Yi   326
Lin, Hong-Xin   349
Lin, Xing-Yi   349
Lin, Yen-Ting   273
Liu, Chao-Lin   197
Liu, James   38
Liu, Jiming   244
Liu, Lijuan   291
Liu, Wenyin   387
López-Moratalla, Javier   144
Lu, Hongen   26
Lu, Weiming   186
Lubega, Jude   302

Martínez-Ortiz, Iván   144
Mørch, Anders I.   244
Moreno-Ger, Pablo   144

Nazir, U.   267
Newlands, D.A.   355
Ng, S.C.   279

Pan, Zhigeng   326, 364
Phung, Dan   66
Poon, C.K.   267
Pouyioutas, Philippos   111
Poveda, Maria   111
Pradhan, Sujan   26

Qiu, Ling   49

Rossiter, David   209

Shen, Liping   99
Shen, Ruimin   99, 122, 332
Shi, Yuanchun   1
Sierra, José Luis   144
Siu, Becky   256
Spaniol, Marc   131
Sun, Lily   302
Sun, Xia   236
Sun, Yu   221

Tang, Janti P.   244
Tong, Ren   332, 340

Urquiza-Fuentes, Jaime   163

Valetto, Giuseppe   66
Velázquez-Iturbide, J. Ángel   163

Waitz, Thomas   131
Wang, Jianxin   291
Wang, Minjuan   332
Williams, Shirley   302
Wong, Kelvin C.   244
Wu, Fei   186

Xiang, Limin   56
Xiuwen, Liu   78
Xu, Guangyou   1

Yang, Fan   122, 332, 340
Yicheng, Jin   78
Yu, Y.T.   267
Yuan, Wenbin   406
Yuen, Allan   14
Yun, Ruwei   326

Zhang, Mingming   364
Zhang, Tao   226
Zhang, Qian   221
Zhang, Xia   221
Zhang, Xiafen   186
Zheng, Qinghua   236
Zheng, Qinghua   406
Zhu, Jiejie   364
Zhuang, Yueting   186

Lecture Notes in Computer Science

For information about Vols. 1–3504

please contact your bookseller or Springer

Vol. 3632: R. Nieuwenhuis (Ed.), Automated Deduction – CADE-20. XIII, 459 pages. 2005. (Subseries LNAI).

Vol. 3626: B. Ganter, G. Stumme, R. Wille (Eds.), Formal Concept Analysis. X, 349 pages. 2005. (Subseries LNAI).

Vol. 3615: B. Ludäscher, L. Raschid (Eds.), Data Integration in the Life Sciences. XII, 344 pages. 2005. (Subseries LNBI).

Vol. 3607: J.-D. Zucker, L. Saitta (Eds.), Abstraction, Reformulation and Approximation. XII, 376 pages. 2005. (Subseries LNAI).

Vol. 3598: H. Murakami, H. Nakashima, H. Tokuda, M. Yasumura, Ubiquitous Computing Systems. XIII, 275 pages. 2005.

Vol. 3597: S. Shimojo, S. Ichii, T.W. Ling, K.-H. Song (Eds.), Web and Communication Technologies and Internet-Related Social Issues - HSI 2005. XIX, 368 pages. 2005.

Vol. 3596: F. Dau, M.-L. Mugnier, G. Stumme (Eds.), Conceptual Structures: Common Semantics for Sharing Knowledge. XI, 467 pages. 2005. (Subseries LNAI).

Vol. 3587: P. Perner, A. Imiya (Eds.), Machine Learning and Data Mining in Pattern Recognition. XVII, 695 pages. 2005. (Subseries LNAI).

Vol. 3586: A.P. Black (Ed.), ECOOP 2005 - Object-Oriented Programming. XVII, 631 pages. 2005.

Vol. 3584: X. Li, S. Wang, Z.Y. Dong (Eds.), Advanced Data Mining and Applications. XIX, 835 pages. 2005. (Subseries LNAI).

Vol. 3583: R.W. H. Lau, Q. Li, R. Cheung, W. Liu (Eds.), Advances in Web-Based Learning – ICWL 2005. XIV, 420 pages. 2005.

Vol. 3582: J. Fitzgerald, I.J. Hayes, A. Tarlecki (Eds.), FM 2005: Formal Methods. XIV, 558 pages. 2005.

Vol. 3580: L. Caires, G.F. Italiano, L. Monteiro, C. Palamidessi, M. Yung (Eds.), Automata, Languages and Programming. XXV, 1477 pages. 2005.

Vol. 3579: D. Lowe, M. Gaedke (Eds.), Web Engineering. XII, 633 pages. 2005.

Vol. 3578: M. Gallagher, J. Hogan, F. Maire (Eds.), Intelligent Data Engineering and Automated Learning - IDEAL 2005. XVI, 599 pages. 2005.

Vol. 3576: K. Etessami, S.K. Rajamani (Eds.), Computer Aided Verification. XV, 564 pages. 2005.

Vol. 3575: S. Wermter, G. Palm, M. Elshaw (Eds.), Biomimetic Neural Learning for Intelligent Robots. IX, 383 pages. 2005. (Subseries LNAI).

Vol. 3574: C. Boyd, J.M. González Nieto (Eds.), Information Security and Privacy. XIII, 586 pages. 2005.

Vol. 3573: S. Etalle (Ed.), Logic Based Program Synthesis and Transformation. VIII, 279 pages. 2005.

Vol. 3572: C. De Felice, A. Restivo (Eds.), Developments in Language Theory. XI, 409 pages. 2005.

Vol. 3571: L. Godo (Ed.), Symbolic and Quantitative Approaches to Reasoning with Uncertainty. XVI, 1028 pages. 2005. (Subseries LNAI).

Vol. 3570: A. S. Patrick, M. Yung (Eds.), Financial Cryptography and Data Security. XII, 376 pages. 2005.

Vol. 3569: F. Bacchus, T. Walsh (Eds.), Theory and Applications of Satisfiability Testing. XII, 492 pages. 2005.

Vol. 3568: W.-K. Leow, M.S. Lew, T.-S. Chua, W.-Y. Ma, L. Chaisorn, E.M. Bakker (Eds.), Image and Video Retrieval. XVII, 672 pages. 2005.

Vol. 3567: M. Jackson, D. Nelson, S. Stirk (Eds.), Database: Enterprise, Skills and Innovation. XII, 185 pages. 2005.

Vol. 3566: J.-P. Banâtre, P. Fradet, J.-L. Giavitto, O. Michel (Eds.), Unconventional Programming Paradigms. XI, 367 pages. 2005.

Vol. 3565: G.E. Christensen, M. Sonka (Eds.), Information Processing in Medical Imaging. XXI, 777 pages. 2005.

Vol. 3564: N. Eisinger, J. Małuszyński (Eds.), Reasoning Web. IX, 319 pages. 2005.

Vol. 3562: J. Mira, J.R. Álvarez (Eds.), Artificial Intelligence and Knowledge Engineering Applications: A Bioinspired Approach, Part II. XXIV, 636 pages. 2005.

Vol. 3561: J. Mira, J.R. Álvarez (Eds.), Mechanisms, Symbols, and Models Underlying Cognition, Part I. XXIV, 532 pages. 2005.

Vol. 3560: V.K. Prasanna, S. Iyengar, P.G. Spirakis, M. Welsh (Eds.), Distributed Computing in Sensor Systems. XV, 423 pages. 2005.

Vol. 3559: P. Auer, R. Meir (Eds.), Learning Theory. XI, 692 pages. 2005. (Subseries LNAI).

Vol. 3558: V. Torra, Y. Narukawa, S. Miyamoto (Eds.), Modeling Decisions for Artificial Intelligence. XII, 470 pages. 2005. (Subseries LNAI).

Vol. 3557: H. Gilbert, H. Handschuh (Eds.), Fast Software Encryption. XI, 443 pages. 2005.

Vol. 3556: H. Baumeister, M. Marchesi, M. Holcombe (Eds.), Extreme Programming and Agile Processes in Software Engineering. XIV, 332 pages. 2005.

Vol. 3555: T. Vardanega, A.J. Wellings (Eds.), Reliable Software Technology – Ada-Europe 2005. XV, 273 pages. 2005.

Vol. 3554: A. Dey, B. Kokinov, D. Leake, R. Turner (Eds.), Modeling and Using Context. XIV, 572 pages. 2005. (Subseries LNAI).

Vol. 3553: T.D. Hämäläinen, A.D. Pimentel, J. Takala, S. Vassiliadis (Eds.), Embedded Computer Systems: Architectures, Modeling, and Simulation. XV, 476 pages. 2005.

Vol. 3552: H. de Meer, N. Bhatti (Eds.), Quality of Service – IWQoS 2005. XVIII, 400 pages. 2005.

Vol. 3551: T. Härder, W. Lehner (Eds.), Data Management in a Connected World. XIX, 371 pages. 2005.

Vol. 3548: K. Julisch, C. Kruegel (Eds.), Intrusion and Malware Detection and Vulnerability Assessment. X, 241 pages. 2005.

Vol. 3547: F. Bomarius, S. Komi-Sirviö (Eds.), Product Focused Software Process Improvement. XIII, 588 pages. 2005.

Vol. 3546: T. Kanade, A. Jain, N.K. Ratha (Eds.), Audio- and Video-Based Biometric Person Authentication. XX, 1134 pages. 2005.

Vol. 3544: T. Higashino (Ed.), Principles of Distributed Systems. XII, 460 pages. 2005.

Vol. 3543: L. Kutvonen, N. Alonistioti (Eds.), Distributed Applications and Interoperable Systems. XI, 235 pages. 2005.

Vol. 3542: H.H. Hoos, D.G. Mitchell (Eds.), Theory and Applications of Satisfiability Testing. XIII, 393 pages. 2005.

Vol. 3541: N.C. Oza, R. Polikar, J. Kittler, F. Roli (Eds.), Multiple Classifier Systems. XII, 430 pages. 2005.

Vol. 3540: H. Kalviainen, J. Parkkinen, A. Kaarna (Eds.), Image Analysis. XXII, 1270 pages. 2005.

Vol. 3539: K. Morik, J.-F. Boulicaut, A. Siebes (Eds.), Local Pattern Detection. XI, 233 pages. 2005. (Subseries LNAI).

Vol. 3538: L. Ardissono, P. Brna, A. Mitrovic (Eds.), User Modeling 2005. XVI, 533 pages. 2005. (Subseries LNAI).

Vol. 3537: A. Apostolico, M. Crochemore, K. Park (Eds.), Combinatorial Pattern Matching. XI, 444 pages. 2005.

Vol. 3536: G. Ciardo, P. Darondeau (Eds.), Applications and Theory of Petri Nets 2005. XI, 470 pages. 2005.

Vol. 3535: M. Steffen, G. Zavattaro (Eds.), Formal Methods for Open Object-Based Distributed Systems. X, 323 pages. 2005.

Vol. 3534: S. Spaccapietra, E. Zimányi (Eds.), Journal on Data Semantics III. XI, 213 pages. 2005.

Vol. 3533: M. Ali, F. Esposito (Eds.), Innovations in Applied Artificial Intelligence. XX, 858 pages. 2005. (Subseries LNAI).

Vol. 3532: A. Gómez-Pérez, J. Euzenat (Eds.), The Semantic Web: Research and Applications. XV, 728 pages. 2005.

Vol. 3531: J. Ioannidis, A. Keromytis, M. Yung (Eds.), Applied Cryptography and Network Security. XI, 530 pages. 2005.

Vol. 3530: A. Prinz, R. Reed, J. Reed (Eds.), SDL 2005: Model Driven. XI, 361 pages. 2005.

Vol. 3528: P.S. Szczepaniak, J. Kacprzyk, A. Niewiadomski (Eds.), Advances in Web Intelligence. XVII, 513 pages. 2005. (Subseries LNAI).

Vol. 3527: R. Morrison, F. Oquendo (Eds.), Software Architecture. XII, 263 pages. 2005.

Vol. 3526: S. B. Cooper, B. Löwe, L. Torenvliet (Eds.), New Computational Paradigms. XVII, 574 pages. 2005.

Vol. 3525: A.E. Abdallah, C.B. Jones, J.W. Sanders (Eds.), Communicating Sequential Processes. XIV, 321 pages. 2005.

Vol. 3524: R. Barták, M. Milano (Eds.), Integration of AI and OR Techniques in Constraint Programming for Combinatorial Optimization Problems. XI, 320 pages. 2005.

Vol. 3523: J.S. Marques, N. Pérez de la Blanca, P. Pina (Eds.), Pattern Recognition and Image Analysis, Part II. XXVI, 733 pages. 2005.

Vol. 3522: J.S. Marques, N. Pérez de la Blanca, P. Pina (Eds.), Pattern Recognition and Image Analysis, Part I. XXVI, 703 pages. 2005.

Vol. 3521: N. Megiddo, Y. Xu, B. Zhu (Eds.), Algorithmic Applications in Management. XIII, 484 pages. 2005.

Vol. 3520: O. Pastor, J. Falcão e Cunha (Eds.), Advanced Information Systems Engineering. XVI, 584 pages. 2005.

Vol. 3519: H. Li, P. J. Olver, G. Sommer (Eds.), Computer Algebra and Geometric Algebra with Applications. IX, 449 pages. 2005.

Vol. 3518: T.B. Ho, D. Cheung, H. Liu (Eds.), Advances in Knowledge Discovery and Data Mining. XXI, 864 pages. 2005. (Subseries LNAI).

Vol. 3517: H.S. Baird, D.P. Lopresti (Eds.), Human Interactive Proofs. IX, 143 pages. 2005.

Vol. 3516: V.S. Sunderam, G.D.v. Albada, P.M.A. Sloot, J.J. Dongarra (Eds.), Computational Science – ICCS 2005, Part III. LXIII, 1143 pages. 2005.

Vol. 3515: V.S. Sunderam, G.D.v. Albada, P.M.A. Sloot, J.J. Dongarra (Eds.), Computational Science – ICCS 2005, Part II. LXIII, 1101 pages. 2005.

Vol. 3514: V.S. Sunderam, G.D.v. Albada, P.M.A. Sloot, J.J. Dongarra (Eds.), Computational Science – ICCS 2005, Part I. LXIII, 1089 pages. 2005.

Vol. 3513: A. Montoyo, R. Muñoz, E. Métais (Eds.), Natural Language Processing and Information Systems. XII, 408 pages. 2005.

Vol. 3512: J. Cabestany, A. Prieto, F. Sandoval (Eds.), Computational Intelligence and Bioinspired Systems. XXV, 1260 pages. 2005.

Vol. 3511: U.K. Wiil (Ed.), Metainformatics. VIII, 221 pages. 2005.

Vol. 3510: T. Braun, G. Carle, Y. Koucheryavy, V. Tsaousidis (Eds.), Wired/Wireless Internet Communications. XIV, 366 pages. 2005.

Vol. 3509: M. Jünger, V. Kaibel (Eds.), Integer Programming and Combinatorial Optimization. XI, 484 pages. 2005.

Vol. 3508: P. Bresciani, P. Giorgini, B. Henderson-Sellers, G. Low, M. Winikoff (Eds.), Agent-Oriented Information Systems II. X, 227 pages. 2005. (Subseries LNAI).

Vol. 3507: F. Crestani, I. Ruthven (Eds.), Information Context: Nature, Impact, and Role. XIII, 253 pages. 2005.

Vol. 3506: C. Park, S. Chee (Eds.), Information Security and Cryptology – ICISC 2004. XIV, 490 pages. 2005.

Vol. 3505: V. Gorodetsky, J. Liu, V. A. Skormin (Eds.), Autonomous Intelligent Systems: Agents and Data Mining. XIII, 303 pages. 2005. (Subseries LNAI).